MASTER DICTIONARY
of
FOOD AND WINE

MASTER DICTIONARY
of
FOOD AND WINE

Joyce Rubash, R.D., L.D.

VNR VAN NOSTRAND REINHOLD
—————————————— *New York*

Library of Congress Catalog Card Number 89-22496
ISBN 0-442-23465-1

Printed in the United States of America

Illustrations and jacket art by Marilyn Papas

Van Nostrand Reinhold
115 Fifth Avenue
New York, New York 10003

Chapman & Hall
2-6 Boundary Row
London SE1 8HN, England

Thomas Nelson Australia
102 Dodds Street
South Melbourne, Victoria 3205, Australia

Nelson Canada
1120 Birchmount Road
Scarborough, Ontario M1K 5G4, Canada

16   15   14   13   12   11   10   9   8   7   6   5   4

Library of Congress Cataloging-in-Publication Data
Rubash, Joyce.
    Master dictionary of food and wine   /   Joyce Rubash.
        p.   cm.
    Includes bibliographical references.
    ISBN 0-442-23465-1
    1. Food—Dictionaries.   2. Cookery—Dictionaries.   3. Wine and wine
making—Dictionaries. I. Title.
TX349.R83   1990
641.3'003—dc20   89-22496
                                                              CIP

Contents

Preface

The *Master Dictionary of Food and Wine* was conceived after I attempted to purchase for my secretary, Virginia Dare Moses, a food dictionary that had pronunciations as well as definitions. I searched for several years and could not find what she wanted, so I told Virginia that I would write one for her. This book is particularly for Virginia, but also for all those in foodservices who have difficulties spelling fettucine, pronouncing Leberklösse, and explaining what sambusik is.

There is a need for a food dictionary that is accurate, simply written, brief in definition, and self pronouncing. The *Master Dictionary of Food and Wine* will fill that need in the foodservice industry, not only for secretaries, but also for those who write menus, such as dietitians, foodservice directors, supervisors, and managers; those who place orders; and caterers, chefs, cooks, and bakers. In the educational field of food-related disciplines, the *Master Dictionary of Food and Wine* will be used as a supplement to textbooks, as a reference book, and as a personal dictionary for a professional library. It will also be used by household cooks, food journalists, and those who work in food-related media.

It is this writer's goal that *anyone* using this dictionary will find it simple to use, and can feel confident that the word is being spoken correctly.

ACKNOWLEDGMENTS

Many people, knowingly and unknowingly, had a hand in writing this book. Although one does the "writing," it takes a lot of people involved a little bit to complete such a task. Living in a large metropolitan area as I do, and having been employed with Rice University for twenty-two years, many human resources were readily available to me. Writing this book would have been difficult without these people.

Sincere, whole-hearted thanks to Herman Zaccarelli for his advice and encouragement and his confidence in me to write such a book from "day one" when I showed him a sample of the manuscript. Throughout the eighteen months of writing, he rejoiced with me in moments of triumph and bolstered me in moments of despair. I am truly grateful.

Thanks and gratitude are owed to a number of people who were so very gracious to give their time and linguistic talents, native or acquired, to assist me with correct pronunciations when I could not find references to help:

Dr. Joan Rea of Rice University, for help with Portugese, Italian, and Spanish words; Hannes Hofer, of Rice University, and a native of Denmark, for help with the Danish words; Gunter Lowe, Swiss-born and raised, for German pronunciations; Jacques Christoffel, native of France, for French word pronunciations; Dr. Maher Nasser, native of Lebanon, for assistance with those beautiful Arabic words; Ann Guy, of New York City, for her assistance with Hungarian words, and suggestions for terms to add to this volume; Mari Furuya, Tokyo-born and raised, for Japanese words; Ro-Ling Shih, native of China, for Chinese pronunciations; Henry Dykstra, native of Holland, for making Dutch pronunciations seem so easy; Dr. Lolita Ramos, native of India, for words of India; George Oliphant, retired chef, Rice University, for assistance with the Jewish words.

I want to thank my twin sister, Loyce Guy, for her help and support by reading various portions of the manuscript to be sure that the *Master Dictionary of Food and Wine* would be understood by lay persons as well as professionals.

Loving thanks to my granddaughter, Heather Rubash, for her untiring help when her Gran needed assistance sorting through list after list for specific words that needed to be completed, no matter how long the job took; and to my grandson, Michael Rubash, for being quiet while Gran worked on her book.

I mention last, and by no means least, my long-suffering family. Unending thanks to my husband Jim, who searched diligently for books I needed at the library: locating, checking out, carrying home, returning to library, rechecking; for the many hours he spent proofreading the text; and especially for his encouragement of my early retirement from Rice University in order to write this book. Loads of gratitude to my youngest son Brad, still living at home, who is the world's Number One "home-cooking, make-it-from-scratch" fan, for uncomplainingly putting up with microwave dinners and quickie meals necessitated by many long hours working on THE book.

All of these people helped make this book possible.

How to Use This Book

The *Master Dictionary of Food and Wine* is patterned after the standard dictionary format of word, pronunciation, word origin, and definition. For example,

> **ärter med fläsk** (EHR-ter med flesk). *Swe.* Yellow pea soup.
>
> **baccalà** (bahk-kah-LAH). *Ita.* Salt cod.

Entry words are listed alphabetically and set in **bold** type, followed by the pronunciation in parentheses, then the country of origin abbreviated and set in *italics,* and, lastly, the definition. Guide words are printed at the tops of facing pages, indicating the entries falling alphabetically between them.

PRONUNCIATIONS

The pronunciations are transliterations. These imitated pronunciations are to be read as if in English. Accented syllables are shown simply and clearly in capital letters. You will see that in some languages only part of a syllable is accented and that French words have no accented syllables.

No two languages are exactly the same. Some languages have sounds that do not appear in the English language. However, if the transliterated syllables are sounded out as if in English, and accents placed as indicated, the sounding of the word should be accurate, or in the case of a difficult language, close enough to be understood.

A few rules to remember when pronouncing these transliterations are

- When *ah, eh, ih,* and *oh* are presented together in a word or syllable, this forms the short sound of that vowel; that is, *a* as in *cat, e* as in *elephant, i* as in *fill,* and *o* as in *hot.*
- Any vowel presented alone before consonants is to be pronounced in its long sound; that is, *a* as in *cake, e* as in *emit, i* as in *item,* and *o* as in *Ohio.*

- Two transliterated sounds that appear in several languages, but not in English, and when presented in the following combinations, are to be pronounced as follows: *ahng* as in *hang*, but barely sounding the *g*, and *awng* as in *pong*, but barely sounding the *g*.
- Multiple *r*'s indicate trilling; that is, *rr* slightly trilled, *rrr* heavily trilled.
- Double o *(oo)* used in a word is pronounced as in *boo*.

WORD ORIGINS

The following is a list of the abbreviations used for the word origins:

Afr	African
Ara	Arabic
Bri	British
Chi	Chinese
Cze	Czechoslovakian
Dan	Danish
Dut	Dutch
Fin	Finnish
Fre	French
Ger	German
Gre	Greek
Hun	Hungarian
Ice	Icelandic
Ind	Indian
Ino	Indonesian
Iri	Irish
Ita	Italian
Jap	Japanese
Jew	Jewish
Kor	Korean
Lao	Laotian
Mal	Malayan
Mex	Mexican
NZe	New Zealand
Nor	Norwegian
Phi	Philippine
Pol	Polish
Por	Portugese
Rus	Russian
Sco	Scottish

Swe	Swedish
Thi	Thai
Tur	Turkish
USA	American (USA)

DEFINITIONS

The definitions given are concise and uncomplicated. Cross-references, synonyms, and alternative spellings have been included to clarify some definitions. For example, malfatti is defined as "Gnocchi of spinach and ricotta," and gnocchi is cross-referenced in its alphabetical place with its pronunciation, origin, and definition. Likewise, palsterzipfel is defined as "An Austrian jam-filled turnover" and turnover is listed and defined, or agnolotti is defined as "Squares of pasta stuffed with meat filling, such as ravioli, tortelli, tortellini," and ravioli, tortelli, and tortellini are listed and defined.

Commonly used synonyms are also listed for many entries. For example, the entry for baked custard indicates "Also called cup custard"; for field lettuce, "Also called lamb's lettuce"; for hazelnut, "Also known as filbert"; and for annatto, "Also known as bixin." And many languages have more than one spelling for numerous words. When known, these alternative spellings are listed as in the following examples: corvina, "Also spelled corbina"; kugelhopf, "Also spelled kugelhoph"; matzo, "Also spelled matzoh"; and panocha, "Also spelled penuche."

Aal (arl). *Ger, Dut.* Eel.

aal og rørawg (awl oa rUR-rehg). *Dan.* Eel with scrambled eggs.

aam (ahm). *Ind.* Ripe mango fruit.

aara (AH-dah). *Ind.* Flour, whole wheat flour.

aardappelen (AHR-dahp-puls). *Dut.* Potatoes; gebakken (khuh-BAHK-kuh) fried; gekookt (khuuh-KOHKT) boiled; puree (pew-RAY) mashed.

aardbeien (AHR-bay-uh). *Dut.* Strawberries.

abacate (ah-bah-KA-ta). *Por.* Avocado.

abacaxi (ah-bah-kah-SHEE). *Por.* Pineapple.

abaissage (ah-bay-sahzj). *Fre.* Rolling out pastry dough.

abaisse (ah-bess). *Fre.* A thin, rolled-out biscuit or pastry; a thin bottom crust.

abalone (ah-bah-LOHN-e). *USA.* A mollusk whose large adductor muscle is edible; used fresh, dried, canned; used especially in Japanese and Chinese cooking; called ormer in Europe.

abatis (ah-bah-tee). *Fre.* External poultry trimmings such as wing tips, necks, feet.

abats (ah-bahts). *Fre.* Giblets; edible internal organs such as liver, heart, sweetbreads.

abbacchio (ahb-bahk-KE-e-o). *Ita.* A very young suckling lamb.

abborre (AH-bor-rer). *Swe.* Perch.

abbrusttolito (ahb-broost-too-LEE-to). *Ita.* Toasted.

à blanc (ah blahnk). *Fre.* A method of cooking veal, pork, or poultry in stews and pot roasts, in which raw meat is placed directly in boiling stock, without first browning the meat.

ablette (ahb-leht). *Fre.* A type of carp.

abóbora (ah-BAW-boh-rah). *Por.* Pumpkin, squash, vegetable marrow.

aborinha (ah-bo-RI-nyah). *Por.* Zucchini.

abricot (ahb-ree-coh). *Fre.* Apricot.

abrikoos (ahb-ri-KO-zen). *Dut.* Apricot.

abrikos (ah-bree-KO-ssi). *Rus.* Apricot.

abruzze (ah-BROOZ-dzee). *Ita.* In the Abruzzi way; with hot red peppers and, sometimes, ham.

absinthe (AHB-senth) *Gre.* A green liqueur with wormwood leaves and anise; highly intoxicating.

abuñolado (ah-bhoo-noa-LAH-do). *Spa.* Fried in batter.

abura (ah-BOO-rah). *Jap.* Oil; sarada for salads, tempura for frying, goma (sesame oil) for seasoning.

aburage (ah-BOO-rah-geg). *Jap.* Deep-fried tofu.

açafrão (a-sa-frahng). *Por.* Saffron.

acciughe (aht-CHOO-gay). *Ita.* Anchovies.

aceite (ah-SAY-tay). *Spa.* Oil.

aceituna (ah-say-TOO-nah). *Spa.* Olive.

acelga (ah-THEHL-gah). *Spa.* Beet.

acepipes (a-se-PEE-peesh). *Por.* Hors d'oeuvres.

acerola (ah-see-ROLL-ah). *USA.* A small, soft, juicy, thin-skinned fruit that is crimson when mature, and has orange-yellow flesh; richest known source of vitamin C; a sweet flavor; used fresh, in preserves, purees and desserts. Also known as Barbados cherry, West Indian cherry.

acetary (ASS-ee-tah-ree). *USA.* Acidic fruit pulp.

acetic acid (a-SEE-tik ASS-ehd). *USA.* The acid in vinegar that is produced by a second fermentation.

aceto (ah-CHEH-toh). *Ita.* Vinegar.

aceto balsamico (ah-CHEH-toh bahl-sah-MEH-co). *Ita.* A very fine Italian vinegar with a dark, mellow, subtle flavor.

aceto-dolce (ah-CHEH-toh DOAL-chay). *Ita.* A sweet-sour mix of vegetables and fruits used as an antipasto.

acetosella (ah-CHEH-toh-sehl-lah). *Ita.* Sorrel.

achar (ah-CHAR). *Ind.* Pickle.

achiote (ah-shee-OA-teh). *Spa.* A red dye from fruit used to color cheese, butter, and confectionary.

acidophilus milk (ass-ceh-DOHF-eh-lus mehlk). *USA.* Slightly soured milk that is both easy to digest and healthful.

acidulated water (ah-SEHD-u-la-ted WAHT-er). *USA.* Water with lemon juice or vinegar added to prevent fruits and vegetables from discoloring; also used to blanch certain foods.

acini di pepe (ah-CHEE-nee dee PEE-pee). *Ita.* Tiny squares or rounds of pasta used in soup.

açorda (a-SOR-dah). *Por.* Garlic bread porridge.

acorn squash (A-corn). *USA.* Acorn-shaped dark green winter squash with a ridged surface and sweet yellow-orange flesh.

acqua (AHK-kwah). *Ita.* Water.

acquacotta (AHK-kwah-KOT-toh). *Ita.* A soup made with stale bread, into which an egg is added to each serving.

active dry yeast (AK-tehv dri yest). *USA.* Granular form of yeast; usually packaged in an air-tight, moisture-proof envelope containing 1 ounce yeast.

açúcar (a-SOO-kar). *Por.* Sugar.

açúcar granulado (a-SOO-kar gray-noo-LAH-doo). *Por.* Granulated sugar.

adas (AH-dahs). *Ara.* Lentils.

adega (ah-DE-ja). *Por.* Storage cellar, usually above ground.

aderezo (ah-deh-REH-soh). *Spa.* Salad dressing.

adobo (ah-DOH-boh). *Phi.* A stew with thick spicy sauce made piquant with vinegar; usually made with pork or game; sometimes with chicken or seafood.

adobo (ah-DOH-boh). *Phi.* Seasoning paste or sauce made of chilies, herbs, and vinegar.

adrak (ad-DAH-rahk). *Ind.* Fresh gingerroot.

advocaat (ahd-vo-KAHT). *Dut.* Eggnog, eaten with a spoon in The Netherlands.

aebleflaesk (EHB-blerr FLEHSK). *Dan.* Fried salt pork or bacon with fried apples.

aeblegrød (EHB-lerr-grurdh). *Dan.* Applesauce.

aeblekage (EHB-ler-kaaer). *Dan.* Apple cake.

aeblemost (EHB-ler-moast). *Dan.* Sweet cider.

aeblepidsvin (ehb-lerr-PIDS-vin). *Dan.* A dessert of apples, lemon juice, and toasted almonds.

aebleskiver (eh-bleh-SKEE-vor). *Dan.* Doughnuts.

aeg (ehg). *Dan.* Egg; blødkogt aeg (BLURDH-koat ehg), soft-boiled egg; hårdkogt (HAWR-koat), hard-boiled; kogt aeg (KOAT-ehg), boiled egg; omelet (oam-er-LEHT), omelet; pocheret (poa-SHAYR-et), poached; røraeg (RURR-ehg), scrambled eggs; spejlaeg (SPIGH-ehg), fried egg.

aemono (ah-moh-noh). *Jap.* Cold, dressed, saladlike foods.

aerter (AIR-terr). *Dan.* Peas.

affettato (ahf-feht-TAA-toh). *Ita.* Cold cuts.

affogato (ahf-foa-GAA-toh). *Ita.* Poached or steamed.

affumicato (ahf-foo-mee-KAA-toh). *Ita.* Smoked.

áfonya (AA-fawn-ya). *Hun.* Blueberries.

agar-agar (ah-gahr ah-gahr). *Chi.* A gelatin made of seaweed that does not melt at room temperature and has remarkable absorption capability.

agave (ah-GAH-veh). *Mex.* A cactus known as century plant.

age (ah-GOH-eh). *Jap.* Deep-fried.

agemono (AH-gee-mo-no). *Jap.* Fried.

agerhøne (AAERR-hurner). *Dan.* Partridge.

ägg (ehg). *Swe.* Egg; kokt (KOO-kah), boiled; stekt (STAY-kaht), fried; äggröra (ehg-RURR-ah), scrambled; förlorade (fur-LOO-rah-der), poached; löskokt (LURS-kookt), soft; lagom (LAA-gom), medium; håardkokt (HOArD-kokt), hard cooked.

agi (aji). *Spa.* Red-hot pepper used in spicy dishes.

aging (AJ-ing). *USA.* A method of maturing a food, such as wine, cheese, game, beef to improve its flavor.

agiter (azh-ee-tay). *Fre.* To stir.

agliota (AH-ly-o-toa). *Ita.* A sauce consisting of garlic slices, bread crumbs, and vinegar.

aglio (AH-ly-oa). *Ita.* Garlic.

agneau (ahn-yoh). *Fre.* Lamb.

agnello (ahn-NYEHL-loa). *Ita.* Lamb.

agnolotti (ahn-nyoa-LOT-tee). *Ita.* Squares of pasta stuffed with meat filling, such as ravioli, tortelli, tortellini.

agresto (ah-GREHZ-toa). *Ita.* The juice of unripe grapes, used occasionally in some sauces instead of vinegar.

agrimony (ah-GRIM-o-nee). *Bri.* An herb whose dark green, downy leaves used in tea blends and wines have a flavor reminiscent of apricot. The plant yields a golden yellow dye.

agrio (AH-greeh-oh). *Mex.* Sour.

agriões (a-gree-AWNGSH). *Por.* Watercress.

agrodolce (ah-roh-DOAL-chay). *Ita.* Sharp and sweet, pertains to the flavoring of a dish.

agua (AH-gwah). *Spa.* Water.

água (AH-gwa). *Por.* Water.

aguacate (ah-gwah-KAH-tay). *Spa.* Avocado.

água gelo (AH-gwa ZHAY-loo). *Por.* Ice water.

àgua mineral (AH-gwah mee-nay-RAHL). *Por.* Mineral water.

aguardiente (ah-wahr-DEHN-tay). *Spa.* A very strong Spanish liqueur.

aguglie (ah-GOO-ly-ay). *Ita.* Garfish.

agurk (ah-GOORK) *Dan, Nor.* Cucumber.

ahp sun (AHP sun). *Chi.* Dried duck gizzard.

ahtapot (okh-tu-BOOT). *Ara.* Octopus.

ahven (AHH-vayn). *Fin.* Perch; used in soup or served in lemon-butter.

aiglefin (ehg-ler-fang). *Fre.* Haddock.

aigre (ay-zhreh). *Fre.* Bitter, sour, possibly tart.

aïgroissade (ahee-grwah-sahd). *Fre.* Cooked vegetables mixed with a garlicky mayonnaise.

aiguillette (eh-gew-ee-ley). *Fre.* A very thin lengthwise-cut strip of meat or poultry.

ail (ahy). *Fre.* Garlic.

ailerons (ahy-rohn). *Fre.* Chicken wings.

aillade (ahy-lee-dah). *Fre.* Sauce of garlic, onion, chive, leek, herbs, spices, and oil.

aïoli (ahj o lee). *Fre.* A thick mayonnaise strongly flavored with garlic served with seafood.

aipo (IE-poh). *Por.* Celery.

airelle (ay-rehl). *Fre.* Bilberry, a variety of blueberry.

airelle rouge (ay-rehl roozh). *Fre.* Cranberry.

aisu kohi (ah-EES koh-hee). *Jap.* Iced coffee.

aisu ti (ah-EES tee). *Jap.* Iced tea.

ajam panggang (au AUM PAH-yahng). *Dut.* Grilled chicken flavored with ginger, saffron, garlic, chili peppers.

aji (AH-jee). *Jap.* Horse mackerel.

aji (AH-khee). *Spa.* Chili peppers.

ajin (ah-JEEN). *Ara.* Dough.

ajo (AH-khoa). *Spa.* Garlic.

ajonjoli (ah-hohn-hoh-LEE). *Mex.* Sesame.

ajouter (ah-zju-tay). *Fre.* To add an ingredient.

ajwain (AHJ-wahne). *Ind.* Celery-seed size spice with flavor of anise, oregano, and black pepper.

ajwi (AHJ-wee). *Ara.* Dates.

akee (AH-kee). *Afr.* A West African fruit that is one of the most strikingly beautiful and delicious of fruits; however, unless it has ripened to the point of voluntary opening, it is a deadly poison. All seeds must be removed as they are poison. When picked ripe, hulled and completely seeded, it may be eaten raw or cooked; parboiled it may be used hot or cold.

akni (ACK-nee). *Ind.* A delicate, aromatic broth used to poach or flavor certain foods.

akule (ah-KUHLE). *USA.* A Hawaiian food fish, usually salted and dried. Also known as bigeye scad.

akuri (ah-KUH-dree). *Ind.* Spiced scrambled eggs.

akvavit (ahk-vah-VEET). *Dan.* Aquavit.

ål (awl). *Nor.* Eel.

ål (oal). *Swe.* Eel.

à la (ah lah). *Fre.* In the style of.

à la broche (ah lah brosh). *Fre.* Roast in front of the fire on a spit or skewer.

à la carte (ah lah kahrt). *Fre.* According to a menu that prices items separately.

à la mode (ah lah mod). *USA.* "According to the fashion"; topped with ice cream. See beef à la mode, and tripe à la mode de Caen.

al burro (ahl BOOR-roa). *Ita.* A style of serving pasta; after the pasta has been cooked and drained, it is tossed in butter and served without a sauce.

al dente (ahl-DEN-tay). *Ita.* Pasta that is firm to the bite, chewy, slightly undercooked.

à l'étouffée (ah lay-too-fay). *Fre.* Smothered; food cooked very slowly in a lidded pot, condensing the food juices into a delicious residue, which when degreased if necessary, then deglazed, forms the sauce for the dish.

al forno (ahl FOR-noa). *Ita.* Baked; roasted.

al funghetto (ahl foon-GHEHT-toa). *Ita.* A method of cooking vegetables quickly over high heat and using an herb; so called after a method of cooking mushrooms. Vegetables usually cooked al funghetto are eggplant and zucchini.

al horno (ahl-HOR-noh). *Mex.* Baked or roasted in an oven.

al sangue (ahl SAHNG-goo-ay). *Ita.* Rare; describing the degree of cooking of meat.

alajú (ah-lah-KHOO). *Spa.* Pastry of sugar, nuts, and ginger.

alalunga (ahl-ah-LOON-gah). *Ita.* White tuna.

albedo (al-BED-o). *USA.* The white inner peel of oranges and other citrus fruit.

albicocca (ahl-bee-KOK-kah). *Ita.* Apricot.

albillos (AHL-bee-lious). *Spa.* White grapes.

albóndigas (ahl-BOHN-dee-gahs). *Spa.* Spicy meatballs of pork, beef; also a dumpling.

albuféra (ahl-bew-fay-rah). *Fre.* A suprême sauce with meat glaze and pimento butter.

albumen (ahl-BU-mehn). *USA.* The protein portion of egg white, also found in milk, some plants, and seeds.

alcachofa (ahl-cah-CHOH-fah). *Spa.* Artichoke.

alcaparras (ahl-kah-PAH-rrahs). *Spa.* Capers.

alcaravia (al-cah-RA-vjah). *Por.* Caraway.

alcohol (AL-co-hol). *USA.* A colorless, flammable liquid. Whiskey.

ale (ael). *USA.* Bittersweet malt beverage.

aletria (ah-le-TREE-ah). *Por.* Vermicelli, sometimes used as dessert in a pudding.

alewife (AAL-wif). *USA.* A food fish of the herring family, abundant on the Atlantic coast.

alewife caviar (AAL-wif CAH-vee-ahr). *USA.* An inexpensive caviar substitute made from the processed roe of herring.

alface (ahl-FAH-say). *Por.* Lettuce.

alfajores (ahl-fah-HOA-rehs). *Spa.* Sweet pastry made with corn and honey.

alfalfa (ahl-FAHL-fah). *USA.* A legume widely grown for hay and forage whose seeds are used as sprouts in salads.

alföldi marharostélyos (OL-furl-dee MOR-hor-rawsh-tay-yawsh). *Hun.* Steak Alföldi style, with a rich sauce and stewed vegetables.

alfostigo (al-fos-TEE-goo). *Por.* Pistachio nut.

algérienne (ahl-ger-een). *Fre.* Garnished with tomatoes braised in oil and sweet potato croquettes.

algin (AHL-gehn). *USA.* A thickening agent derived from seaweed, used mostly in processed foods.

alheira (al-EIH-rah). *Por.* Sausage of smoked ham, nuts, and garlic.

alho (AHL-yoh). *Por.* Garlic.

alho franceses (AL-yoosh fran-SES-esh). *Por.* Leeks.

alice (ahl-EE-chay). *Ita.* Anchovy.

alici (ahl-EE-chee). *Ita.* Anchovies in salt.

alicot (ah-lee-koht). *Fre.* Giblets.

aliñado (ah-lee-NAH-doh). *Spa.* Seasoned.

aliño (ahl-lee-NOH). *Spa.* Seasoning.

aliolo (ah-lee-OO-loa). *Spa.* A thick mayonnaise strongly flavored with garlic served with seafood.

alkannet (AHL-kahn-neht). *USA.* Natural food additive used to color fats and cheeses.

all' olio (ahl OL-yoa). *Ita.* In oil.

all-purpose flour (ahl-PUHR-puhs flowr). *USA.* A blend of soft and hard wheat flours, bleached or unbleached, that has many general uses including thickening.

alla griglia (AHL-lah GREE-lyah). *Ita.* Grilled.

alla parmigiana (AHL-lah pahr-mee-JAA-nah). *Ita.* A description used for vegetables that are boiled and served with melted butter and grated Parmesan cheese; also for veal scallops sautéed in butter and finished with Parmesan.

allemande sauce (ahl-mahnd saus). *Fre.* Smooth white sauce with butter, egg yolk, added; a basic classical sauce; an egg-thickened velouté.

alligator (AHL-lee-ga-tohr). *USA.* A large reptile of the Gulf Coast swamplands whose tail meat is particularly relished and used in stews.

alloro (ahl-LOH-roa). *Ita.* Bay leaves, laurel.

allspice (AHL-spis). *USA.* A mildly aromatic spice tasting like a combination of clove, nutmeg, and cinnamon.

allumette (ahl-lee-meht). *Fre.* A strip of puff pastry with a sweet or savory filling or garnish; also potatoes, peeled and cut into matchstick-size strips.

almamártás (OL-mom-maar-taash). *Hun.* Applesauce.

almás palacsinta (OL-maash PO-lo-cheen-to). *Hun.* Apple pancake.

almejas (ahl-MEH-hah). *Spa.* Clams.

almendrado (ahl-meh-DRAH-doz). *Spa.* Macaroon.

almendras (ahl-MEHN-drah). *Spa.* Almonds.

almond (AH-mund). *USA.* Edible kernel of the fruit of the almond tree, used as a nut.

almôndegas (ahl-MOHN-day-gahss). *Por.* Meat balls, croquettes.

almond oil (AH-mund oyl). *USA.* Yellow-white oil extracted from almonds that is odorless and has mild nutty flavor.

almond powder (AH-mund pouw-dehr). *USA.* Very finely ground almonds, used in Chinese desserts.

almuerzo (ahl-MWER-soh). *Mex.* Late breakfast or brunch.

aloo (AH-loo). *Ind.* Potato.

aloo bokhara (AH-lu bahk-HA-row). *Ind.* Sour, dried plums or prunes.

alose (ah-lo-seh). *Fre.* Shad.

alouettes (al-wet). *Fre.* Larks, a great delicacy.

aloyau (al-wa-jo). *Fre.* Sirloin, always beef.

alperche (al-PAIR-ssesh). *Por.* Apricot.

alsacienne (ahl-sah-cyeen). *Fre.* Garnished with sauerkraut and ham or sausages, or with other Alsatian specialties.

Altenburger (AL-ten-berg-er). *Ger.* A soft, uncooked cheese made from goat's milk that has a delicate white mold on the exterior and a creamy, smooth, flavorful interior.

alubiu (ah-LOO-bee-ah). *Spa.* Bean, same as shell beans.

alum (AH-lum). *USA.* Astringent compound used as a preservative, such as in pickles.

amadai (ah-MAH-dah-ee). *Jap.* Red tilefish.

amai (ah-mah-ee). *Jap.* Sweet.

amalgamer (ah-mahl-gah-meh). *Fre.* Blend or combine ingredients.

amande (ahm-end). *Fre.* Almond.

amandel (um-MUN-del). *Dut.* Almonds.

amandine (ahm-ah-deen). *Fre.* Made or garnished with almonds.

amaranth (AHM-ah-ranth). *USA.* A vegetable with edible dark green leaves and stems like asparagus; taste is a cross between spinach and mild-tasting cabbage.

amarelles (ahm-ah-RELLZ). *USA.* Cultivated, sour cherries with colorless juice.

amaretti (am-ah-RETT-tee). *Ita.* Crisp macaroons made with bitter almonds.

amaretto (am-ah-RETT-o) *Ita.* A sweet, almond-flavored liqueur.

amassada (ah-mah-SAH-dah). *Por.* Mashed, as in potatoes.

amatriciana (ah-mah-tree-CHAA-nah). *Ita.* With tomatoes, ham, and pecorino cheese.

amazu shoga (AH-mah-zoo SHO-gah). *Jap.* Pink, pickled ginger, usually eaten with sushi.

ambrosia (am-BRO-zha). *Ita.* A dessert made of oranges and shredded coconut.

ambrosia (am-BRO-zah). *Mex.* An herb with an extremely sweet scent, whose leaves are used in cold beverages in the same way that mint is used.

amchoor (AHM-choor). *Ind.* Dried slices and powder of sour unripe mangos, used for a sweet-sour taste.

amêijoas (ah-MAY-zhoahs). *Por.* Small, succulent clams.

ameixas (a-MAY-shash). *Por.* Plums.

amêndoas (ah-MEN-doh-ahss). *Por.* Almonds.

amendoim (ah-men-doh-EE). *Por.* Peanut.

américaine (ah-mer-e-cahn). *Fre.* Garnished with lobster tail and truffles.

amiral (am-eh-rehl). *Fre.* Garnish of mussels, oysters, crayfish, and mushrooms.

amontillado (ah-mon-tee-LAH-doa). *Spa.* A medium sherry.

amóras (ah-MAW-rahss). *Por.* Berries.

amoroso (AH-moa-ROA-soa). *Spa.* A dark, sweet sherry.

amorphous sugar (ah-MOR-fuss SCHU-gahr). *USA.* Sucrose melted, allowed to dry, then crystallized, making a very brittle, very hard, solid, transparent mass; rock candy.

Amsterdamse korstjes (AHM-stehr-dahm KOHR-sjuh). *Dut.* Spice cake.

an (ahn). *Jap.* Sweet red-bean paste; azuki beans boiled with sugar that comes in two textures: koshi-an, smooth puree, and tsubushi-an, chunky texture.

anadama (ah-nah-DAY-mah). *USA.* A yeast bread made from white flour with cornmeal and molasses.

anago (ah-NAH-goh). *Jap.* Conger eel.

Anaheim chili (AN-ah-heim CHILL-ee). *Mex.* A fairly hot greenish-yellow chili pepper that is generally used fresh, toasted, canned, but never dried. Also known as guero, California pepper, or sweet green pepper.

ananas (ah-nah-nahs). *Fre, Ger, Dut, Swe.* Pineapple.

ananas (ah-nah-NAHSS). *Rus.* Pineapple.

ananás (UN-ah-nus). *Por.* Pineapple.

ananasso (AH-nah-nahs-soa). *Ita.* Pineapple.

ananász (Oon-non-naas). *Hun.* Pineapple.

anardana (ahn-NAHR-dahn-nah). *Ind.* Dried seeds from sour pomegranates used in Indian cooking.

anatra (AA-nah-trah). *Ita.* Duck; also spelled anitra.

ancho (AHN-choh). *Mex.* A deep-red chili pepper, mild in flavor. Used dried, not fresh.

anchoaïde (anh-shwah). *Fre.* Mashed anchovy spread on toast.

anchoas (ahn-CHO-ahss). *Spa.* Anchovies.

anchois (ahn-swa). *Fre.* Anchovy.

anchova (ahn-SHOH-vahss). *Por.* Anchovy.

anchovy (an-CHO-ve). *USA.* Any of numerous small fishes resembling herring used for making sauces, salads, and relishes.

ancienne (ahn-syen). *Fre.* In the old way; with white rice, béchamel sauce, and mushrooms.

and (ung). *Dan.* Duck.

anda (AHN-dah). *Ind.* Egg.

andalouse (ahn-dah-loos). *Fre.* Garnished with tomatoes, sweet red peppers, eggplant.

andijvie (ahn-DAY-vee). *Dut.* Endive.

andouille (ahn-doo-ee). *Fre.* Smoked pure pork sausage, usually served cold as an hors d'oeuvre.

añejo (ah-NAY-khoa). *Spa.* Ripe, as referring to cheese.

aneth (ah-neht). *Fre.* Dill.

aneto (ah-NEH-toa). *Ita.* Dill.

angel cake (ANG-jel kahk). *USA.* A sponge cake made with stiffly beaten egg whites, producing a white, airy cake.

angel flake coconut (ANG-jel flahk CO-co-nuht). *USA.* Coconut flakes cut wider than the standard cut, making it moister, used in confections and baking.

angel food cake (ANG jel food kahk). *USA.* See angel cake.

angel hair (ANG-jel haer). *USA.* The thinnest pasta made.

angelica (an-JEL-eh-cah). *USA.* An herb of the parsley family, used to flavor liqueurs and confections; imparts a green color.

angélique (an-geh-leek). *Fre.* Angelica.

angels on horseback (AIIN-jels ohn HORS-bahk). *USA.* An hors d'oeuvre of oysters wrapped in bacon, skewered, broiled.

anglaise (ng-glayz). *Fre.* In English style, that is, plainly boiled, roasted, fried.

angler (AHN-glur). *USA.* Monkfish.

Angostura bitters (anj goh-STUHR-rah BEHT-tuhrs). *USA.* Reddish-brown aromatic bitters produced in Trinidad, used primarily in making cocktails.

anguila (ahn-GEE-lah). *Spa.* Eel.

anguilla (ahng-goo-EEL-lah). *Ita.* Eel.

anguille (ahng-geey). *Fre.* Eel.

anguilles à l'escaveche (ahng-geey ah les-kah-vehsh). *Fre.* Pickled eels, first fried in oil, then cooled in aspic.

anguria (ahng-GOO-ree-ah). *Ita.* One of the names for watermelon.

anho (ah-nyoo). *Por.* Lamb.

anhydrated (ahn-HIY-drah-ted). *USA.* Dehydrated, dried.

anice (AH-nes). *Ita.* Anise.

anijs (ah-NICE). *Dut.* Anise.

animelle (ah-nee-MEHL-lay). *Ita.* Sweetbreads.

animelle (ahng-ee-mehl). *Fre.* Testicles of animals, usually bull, pig, lamb.

anise (ahn-ess). *Fre.* An herb of the carrot family having carminative aromatic seeds, similar to the flavor of licorice.

aniseed oil (AN-eh-seed oyl). *USA.* Oil from the aniseed; gives the licorice flavor to anisette.

anisette (ann-ei-set). *Fre.* A colorless sweet liqueur flavored with aniseed.

anitra (AA-nah-trah). *Ita.* Duck; also spelled anatra.

Anjou (ahn-zju). *Fre.* A variety of pear, very sweet, used fresh as dessert, or with cheese.

anka (AHNG-kah). *Swe.* Duck.

ankerias (AHN-kay-ri-ahss). *Fin.* Eel.

anlann (AN-lann). *Iri.* Sauce.

annatto (ahn-NET-toh). *USA.* Food-coloring agent derived from the seeds of a Central American plant, used to color butter and cheese. Also known as bixin.

anraith (AN-reeh). *Iri.* Soup.

anraith glasraí (AN-reeh GLASS-ree). *Iri.* Vegetable soup.

Anschovis (ahn-SHO-fiz). *Ger.* Anchovies.

ansjos (ahn-SHOOSS). *Nor.* Anchovy.

ansjovis (ahn-SHOO-viss). *Swe.* Anchovies; marinated sprats.

antioxidant (AHN-tee OHX-ee-dehnt). *USA.* A substance that inhibits the browning process of fruits and vegetables when exposed to the air.

antipasto (ahn-tee-PAHS-toh). *Ita.* The appetizer or first course served that may consist of prosciutto or other hams, salami or other sausages, stuffed eggs, pickled and fresh vegetables, fish, and seafood.

antojito (ahn-toh-HEE-toh). *Mex.* "Little whim"; hors d'oeuvre; small snack food.

aonegi (hoh-SOH-neh-gee). *Jap.* Spring onion, green onion.

ao-togarashi (oh-TOH-gah-rah-shee). *Jap.* Small green peppers.

apaz onion (ah-PAHZ UN-yun). *USA.* Edible wild onion that looks and tastes similar to pearl onions.

apee (A-P). *USA.* A cookie made from butter, sugar, and sour cream created by Ann Page, who carved her initials AP on top of each cookie.

apelsin (ah-perl-SSEEN). *Swe.* Orange.

apel'sin (ah-pyeel'SEE-ni). *Rus.* Oranges.

apenoten (AH-puh-no-tuh). *Dut.* Peanuts.

apéritif (ahp-ree-teef). *Fre.* Wine or spirits served as an appetizer.

aperitivo (ah-pay-ree-TEE-voa). *Ita.* Wine or spirits served as an appetizer.

aperitívet (O-pah-ree-tee-veht). *Hun.* Aperitif.

aperitivo (ah-pehry-TEE-voh). *Mex.* Appetizer.

Apfel (AH-pferl). *Ger.* Apple.

Apfelbröisi (AH-pferl-brur-isee). *Ger.* Bread pudding with apples, sultana raisins.

Apfelmus (AH-pferl-mus). *Ger.* Applesauce.

Apfel pfannkuchen (AH-pferl PFAHN-eh-KU-chuhn). *Ger.* Apple pancakes

Apfelsaft (AH-pferl-zaft). *Ger.* Apple juice.

Apfelschnitzchen (AH-pferl-schneht-zhen). *Ger.* Apple fritters.

Apfelsine (ah-pferl-ZEE-ner). *Ger.* Orange.

Apfelstrudel (AH-pferl-shtroo-derl). *Ger.* Apple strudel.

Apfeltorte (AH-pferl-TOHR-tah). *Ger.* Apple cake.

Apfelwein (AH-pferl vain). *Ger.* Apple cider.

aphrodisiac (ahf-roh-DE-ze-ahk). *USA.* A food or drink, usually, believed to arouse the sexual appetite.

apio (AH-pyoh). *Spa.* Celery.

apio (AH-peeoo). *Por.* Celery.

appalam (AHP-blahm). *Ind.* Lentil wafers.

appareil (ah-par-c-zj). *Fre.* A ready-mix for use in a preparation.

appelbeignets (AHP-pul-bayn-yays). *Dut.* Apple fritter.

appelen (AHP-puln). *Dut.* Apples.

äppelfläsk (EHP-ple-flesk). *Swe, Dan.* A dish of apples, onions, and Canadian-style bacon.

äppelformar (EHP-pel-FOR-mar). *Swe.* Apple muffins.

äppelkaka med vaniljsås (EH-perl-kaa-kah mayd vah-NILY-soass). *Swe.* Apple cake with vanilla custard.

appelmoes (AHP-pul-moos). *Dut.* Applesauce.

äppelmos (ehp-lay-mooss). *Swe.* Applesauce.

appelsap (AHP-pul-sahp). *Dut.* Cider.

appelsiini (AHP-pay-lseeni). *Fin.* Orange.

appelsiinimehua (AHP-pay-lseeni-MAY-hoon). *Fin.* Orange juice.

appelsinsaft (ah-berl-SEEN-sahft). *Dan, Nor.* Orange juice.

appeltaart (AHP-pul-tahrt). *Dut.* Apple cake.

appelvin (EHP-lay-veen). *Swe.* Apple cider.

Appenzell (AHP-en-zell). *Ger.* A whole-milk firm, buttery, piquant cheese of cow's milk made in large wheels in Switzerland, it is straw-colored with holes and a brownish-yellow rind.

Appenzellerbitter (AHP-pen-zell-er-beht-ter). *Ger.* A Swiss flowery liqueur.

appetizer (ahp-eh-TI-zohr). *USA.* A food or drink that stimulates the appetite and is usually served before a meal.

apple (AHP-pul). *USA.* Fruit of the apple tree that may be eaten raw or cooked, made into sauce, preserves, or juice, and used in cooking and baking. Some common varieties include Baldwin, Cortland, Gravenstein, Jonathan, and McIntosh, which are all-purpose apples; Delicious, Golden Delicious, and Winesap, which are table apples; and Rome Beauty and York Imperial, which are cooking apples.

äpple (EHP-ler). *Swe.* Apple.

apple brown betty (AHP-pul brown BEHT-tee). *USA.* A dessert of layered apples and buttered crumbs.

apple butter (AHP-pul BUT-er). *USA.* A preserve of apples that has been slowly cooked for a long time until reduced to a spicy, thick, dark spread.

apple charlotte (AHP-pul chahr-laht). *USA.* A dessert of cooked apples and bread slices of French origins.

apple pandowdy (AHP-pul pahn-dow-dee). *USA.* A homely, humble dish of spiced, sliced apples covered with a crust.

apple schnitz (AHP-pul schnetz). *USA.* Dried apple slices used in Pennsylvania German cooking.

apple snow (AHP-pul sno). *USA.* A once-popular dessert of egg whites, sugar, applesauce, and served with whipped cream or custard sauce.

applejack (AHP-pul-jahk). *USA.* A brandy distilled from fermented cider.

applesauce (AHP-pul-saus). *USA.* A puree of apples, sugar, and usually spices.

apricot (AP-ri-cot). *USA.* Orange-colored fruit of the apricot tree, resembling the peach and plum in flavor.

aprikos (ah-pri-KKOOSS). *Swe.* Apricot.

Aprikosen (Ahp-ree-KOAZ-zern). *Ger.* Apricot.

a puntino (ah poon-TEE-no). *Ita.* Medium well done; describing the degree of cooking of meat.

aquavit (ah-kar-VEET). *Nor, Swe.* A strong, colorless liquor distilled from grain or potatoes, flavored with caraway, served very cold as an appetizer or with meals.

Arabica (ah-RAB-ie-kah). *USA.* Fine Colombian coffee first discovered in Arabia. Today, it is the finest coffee available.

arachide (ah-rah-szwid). *Fre.* Peanut.

arachide (ah-RAH-kee-day). *Ita.* Peanuts.

arachis huile (ah-rah-szwis weel). *Fre.* Peanut oil.

aragosta (ah-rah-GOS-stah). *Ita.* Spiny lobster.

arak (A-ra) *Ara.* A strong, anise-flavored liqueur.

arán (ar-ANN). *Iri.* Bread.

arán coirce (ar-ANN KUR-ka). *Iri.* Oat bread.

arán cruithneachta (ar-ANN krih-NAKH-ta). *Iri.* Wheat bread.

arán donn (ar-ANN dunn). *Iri.* Brown bread.

arán prátí (ar-ANN PRA-tee). *Iri.* Potato bread.

arán rósta (ar-ANN RAW-sta). *Iri.* Toast.

arància (ah-RAHN-chah). *Ita.* Orange.

aranygaluska (O-rron-gol-loosh-ko). *Hun.* Sweet dumpling.

araq (AH-rock). *Ara.* Anise-flavored wine.

arare (ah-lah-la). *Jap.* A small, crispy wheat cracker that can be sweet, or savory with soy sauce, sesame, seaweed.

arbi (AHR-bee). *Ind.* Indian starchy root vegetable.

Arborio rice (ar-boh-REE-oh rice). *Ita.* Short, fat-grained Italian rice, used for risotto.

Arbroath smokies (AR-brohth SMOH-kees). *Sco.* Small haddock that are gutted, salted, and smoked, but not split until broiling before serving.

Arbuckle's (AHR-buck-uhls). *USA.* A name synonymous with coffee in the Old West, much as Kleenex™ is for tissue today.

arbuz (ahr-BOOZ). *Rus.* Watermelon.

archiduc (ahr-schwe-dehk). *Fre.* Seasoned with paprika and blended with cream.

ardishawki (ah-dee-SHO-kee). *Ara.* Artichoke.

arenque (ah-REHN-kayss). *Spa, Por.* Herring.

Argenteuil (ar-zjen-teel). *Fre.* Garnished with asparagus.

arhar dal (ahr-HAHR dahl). *Ind.* Yellow lentils.

aringa (ah-REENG-gah). *Ita.* Herring.

arista (ah-REES-tah). *Ita.* Roast loin of pork, usually seasoned with a mixture of garlic, pepper, and rosemary.

arlésienne (ahrl-ehs-yehng). *Fre.* A garnish containing tomatoes.

armadillo (ahr-mah-DEHL-lo). *USA.* An armored-plated mammal, mostly of the Southwest, whose meat is rarely eaten in the United States today, except for some westerners who consider it an unusual delicacy to be stewed.

Armagnac (ahr-mahg-yahk). *Fre.* A dry, smooth, dark, aromatic brandy.

Arme Ritter (AHR-mee REET-tert). *Ger.* French toast.

Armenian Bole (ar-MEHN-e-un Bol). *USA.* Ferric oxide, an additive used to color food.

Armenian cucumber (ar-MEHN-e-un Q-kum-ber). *USA.* A coiled shape cucumber 10–18 inches long, with a mellow-sweet taste, ridges, and edible skin.

Armenian wax pepper chili (ar-MEHN-e-un wahx PEHP-per chill-e). *USA.* Elongated, shiny yellow chili pepper with a mild, sweet taste; use fresh or pickled.

armoricaine (ahr-mor-ree-kehn). *Fre.* In the Breton way; with brandy, white wine, onion, tomatoes, herbs.

aromatic (ahr-oh-MAH-tik). *USA.* A pleasantly scented plant or herb used to flavor food or drink.

aromatic rice (ahr-oh-MAH-tik rice). *USA.* Rice with a natural aroma and flavor similar to that of roasted popcorn or nuts; fragrant rice.

arnab (ARR-nahb). *Ara.* Rabbit.

arrack (A-ra). *Ara.* A strong anise-flavored liquour; same as arak.

arraia (ah-RAI-ah). *Por.* Skate, ray.

arrôs (ah-ROHSS). *Por.* Rice.

arroser (ah-roh-zer). *Fre.* To baste or moisten.

arrosto (ahr-ROA-stoa). *Ita.* Roast, roasted.

arrowroot (AIR-row-root). *USA.* An easily digested flour or starch used as a thickening agent in soups and gravies that remains clear when cooked; sometimes called Chinese potato.

arroz (ah-RROS). *Spa.* Rice.

arroz blanco (ah-RRROS BLAHN-koh). *Spa.* Plain boiled white rice.

arroz con leche (ah-RRROS kohn LEH-cheh). *Spa.* Rice pudding.

arroz con pollo (ah-RRROS kohn POH-yoh). *Mex.* A dish of chicken with rice, tomatoes, peas or asparagus, cooked together.

arroz refogado (ah-RRROS ree-foh-GAH-dohz). *Por.* Savory rice.

arsekka (ahr-SEHK-kah). *Ita.* Mussel.

arselle (ahr-SEHL-lay). *Ita.* Scallops, a mollusk.

ärter (AER-toor). *Swe.* Peas.

ärter med fläsk (AER-toor med flesk). *Swe.* Yellow pea soup.

artichaut (ahr-tee-shoa). *Fre.* Artichoke.

artichoke (AR-tee-chok). *USA.* Globe or French; bud of a thistle plant, served boiled with leaves pulled off, dipped into sauce, and the tender bottom portion eaten.

Artischocke (ar-ti-sho-KE). *Ger.* Artichoke.

artisjok (AHR-tee-schok). *Dut.* Artichoke.

ärtsoppa (AErT-sop-pah). *Swe.* Yellow pea soup with smoked salt pork, traditionally served on Thursday in winter.

arugula (ah-roo-GOO-lah). *Ita.* A peppery, piquant, aromatic salad lettuce-type herb loved by Italians; also called roquette, rugola and misticanza, but not to be confused with a poisonous weed called rocket.

arum root (ah-room root). *Jap.* A root used to make a translucent cake called konnyaku and translucent noodles called shirataki.

arwa chawal (AHR-wa CHAH-val). *Ind.* Long grain rice.

asado (ah-SAHR-doh). *Spa.* Roasted or broiled.

asadura (ah-ssah-DOO-rah). *Spa.* Offal; liver, lights, and chitterlings.

asafetida (ah-sah-feh-TEE-dah). *Ind.* A brown, smelly resin used in small quantities in cooking partly for flavor and mostly for its digestive properties.

asakusa nori (ah-SAH-koo-sah NOH-lei). *Jap.* Crisp, paper thin, edible seaweed; sea lettuce.

asar (ah-SAHR). *Mex.* To roast or broil.

asciutta (ahs-chee-OOT-toa). *Ita.* A dry pasta that can be served stuffed or in a sauce.

ascorbic acid (ah-SCOR-bek ASS-ehd). *USA.* Vitamin C; used as an antioxidant to retard spoilage and to preserve the red color of fresh or preserved meats.

Ashley bread (ASH-lee brehd). *USA.* A southern batter bread made with rice flour, similar to spoon bread.

Asiago d'Allevo (Ah-zee-AA-goa d'Ahl-LEH-voa). *Ita.* A cheese made of skim milk and aged up to two years, it is pale yellow and smooth with holes, and has a thin brownish rind.

Asian pear (A-zuhn pehr). *USA.* Apple like in shape; skin may be green yellow or russet; crisp like an apple; juicy flavor of a pear; eaten fresh or baked; the oldest cultivated pear known.

asier (ah-SEE-yor). *Dan.* Sweet-sour pickled cucumber garnish.

asparagi (as-SPAA-rah-jee). *Ita.* Asparagus.

asparagus (ah-SPAR-ah-gus) *USA* A perennial plant of the lily family, widely cultivated for its green young shoots that have minute scalelike leaves. White asparagus is regular asparagus that is heavily mulched before cutting to prevent it from ever getting the sunlight that causes it to turn green.

asparagus bean (ah-SPAR-ah-gus bean). *USA.* Oriental green bean that grows about 12-15 inches long with flavor somewhat stronger than ordinary green beans. Also called long beans, yard-long beans.

asparges (ah-SPAHRS). *Dan.* Asparagus.

asparges (as-SPAHR-ggerss). *Nor.* Asparagus.

aspargesbønner (ah-SPAHR-ggerss-BURN-nerr). *Nor.* String beans.

aspartame (AHS-pahr-tahme). *USA.* Artificial sweetener that is 200 times sweeter than sugar and tastes very much like sugar.

asperge (ahs-spehr-rez). *Fre.* Asparagus.

aspergesoep (ahs-PEHR-zhuh soop). *Dut.* Asparagus soup.

aspic (ass-pehk). *Fre.* A gelatinous substance used in molds of decorative shapes in which slices or pieces of food are placed.

aspide (AHS-pee-duh). *Por.* Aspic.

assado (ah-SAH-doh). *Por.* Roast.

assaisonnement (ahs-eh-zone-men). *Fre.* Seasoning, condiment, or dressing.

Assam (ahs-SAHN). *Ind.* A tea from India that is strong and pungent, used to blend with milder teas.

assiette anglaise (ahs-zjet ahn-glez). *Fre.* Plate of assorted cold meats.

assiette volantes (ahs-zjet vo-lahn-tehs). *Fre.* The small entrees and hors d'oeuvres that a plate will hold.

Asturias (ahs-TOU-reeahs). *Spa.* A strong, sharp-flavored cheese from Spain.

asupara (ah-SOO-pahprah). *Jap.* Asparagus.

ásványvizet (AASH-vaan-vee-zeht). *Hun.* Mineral water.

ata (AH-tah). *Ind.* Chappati flour; very finely ground whole wheat flour of low gluten, used in making Indian breads.

atemoya (ah-tee-MOU-ya). *USA.* A gray-green, thick-skinned, heart-shaped fruit with a puddinglike pulp with black seeds; very sweet taste, slightly juicy, melting texture.

athénienne (ah-tee-neen). *Fre.* Garnished with onion, eggplant, tomato, and sweet red pepper fried in olive oil.

atholl brose (AH-thohl broz). *Sco.* A famous drink of heather honey, whisky, and the creamy liquor of strained oatmeal paste; recipe is at least 500 years old.

atole (ah-TOH-leh). *Mex.* A thick beverage made with masa and flavored with sugar, fruit, chocolate, and sometimes chili.

attelet (aht-teh-leh). *Fre.* A small skewer with an ornamental top used to thread garnishments for decorating hot or cold dishes served in a grand style.

attereau (aht-teh-roa). *Fre.* Skewer; refers to alternating food pieces on a skewer, usually coated in batter and deep fat fried.

attorta (aht-TOAR-tah). *Ita.* Delectable pastry filled with toasted almonds, chocolate, and candied fruit.

atum (a-TOOM). *Por.* Tuna fish.

atún (ah-TOON). *Spa.* Tuna fish.

Auberginen (oa-berr-ZHEE-nern). *Ger.* Eggplant.

aubergine (oa-behr-zheen). *Fre, Ita, Bri.* Eggplant.

au beurre (oa burr). *Fre.* Cooked in or with butter sauce or browned butter.

au bleu (oa blu). *Fre.* Plain boiled; used with reference to freshwater fish.

Auflauf (AUF-lauf). *Ger.* Souffle.

au four (oa fur). *Fre.* Baked in the oven.

Aufschnitt (AUF-schneht). *Ger.* Cold cuts.

au gras (oa graws). *Fre.* Cooked in fat or a rich meat gravy.

au gratin (oa graw-ton). *Fre.* Made with crumbs, scalloped, often with a cheese sauce.

augurken (ow-KHOOR-kuh). *Dut.* Pickles.

au jus (oa zhus). *Fre.* Served with the meat's natural juices.

au lait (oa leh). *Fre.* Served with added milk.

au maigre (oa meg-re). *Fre.* Served without meat.

au naturel (oa nat-eh-rel). *Fre.* Plainly cooked or served raw.

aurore (oa-ror). *Fre.* Béchamel made pink with tomato puree.

au ruban (oa ry-bu). *Fre.* Describes sugar syrup during the crystallization process when the syrup reaches the stage of forming a ribbon when dropped from a spoon.

Ausbackteig (AUS-bahk-tahg). *Ger.* Dough; paste.

Auster (AUS-ter). *Ger.* Oyster.

autrichienne (oa-tree-shyen). *Fre.* Austrian style, flavored with caraway seeds and paprika.

aux croutons (oa kroo-toa). *Fre.* Food served with dried bread cubes, the croutons.

avêia (ah-VAY-yah). *Por.* Oatmeal.

aveline (ahv-eh-leen). *Fre.* Hazelnut, filbert.

avella (ah-VELL-lah). *Ital.* Hazelnut.

avellanas (ahb-hay-LYAH-nahss). *Spa.* Filberts, hazelnuts.

aves (AH-vehs). *Mex.* Birds.

aves de corral (AH-vehs da kah-RAHL). *Mex.* Chickens, poultry.

avgolemono (ahv-gho-LLEH-mon-no). *Gre.* A soup made with egg yolks and lemon juice. Also, can be a sauce.

avocado (av-oh-KAH-doh). *USA.* A dark green pear-shaped fruit with a large pit and pulpy yellow-green flesh, served peeled, sliced, cubed, pureed in salads and dips.

avond koffie (AH-vuns KAWF-fee). *Dut.* Evening coffee served with cookies, cake.

avond thee (AH-vuns tay). *Dut.* Evening tea served with cookies, cake.

awabi (AH-wah-bee). *Jap.* Abalone.

Awenda bread (AH-wen-dah brehd). *USA.* A bread of American Indian origin made of hominy grits.

ayu (AH-yoo). *Jap.* Freshwater trout.

azafrán (ah-thah-FRAHN) *Spa.* Saffron.

azeda (ah-ZAY-dah). *Por.* Sour.

azedinha (ah-zay-DEE-nyah). *Por.* Sorrel.

Azeitão (ah-zay-TAHNG). *Por.* Rich, flat cheese with creamy paste.

azeite (a-ZAYT). *Por.* Olive oil.

azeitonas (ah-ZAY-toh-nahss). *Por.* Olives.

azijn (ah-ZEYN). *Dut.* Vinegar.

azúcar (ah-THOO-kahr). *Spa.* Sugar.

azuki (ah-ZOO-kee). *Jap.* A dried bean prized for its sweet flavor; when powdered it is used in confections and puddings in China and Japan.

azyme (ah-zim). *Fre.* Unleavened bread.

baadhinjaana (bi-din-GEHN). *Ara.* Eggplant.

baak guo (bahk gwoah). *Chi.* Ginkgo nut.

baars (bahrs) *Dut.* Bass.

baba (bah-bah). *Fre.* Baba au rhum.

baba au rhum (bah-bah oh rum). *Fre.* A yeast cake with raisins baked in a cylindrical mold and soaked with a rum syrup.

babaco (BAH-bah-ko) *NZe.* A fruit with the appearance of a large star fruit and a flavor similar to strawberries with a hint of papaya and pineapple; when ripe its skin is a soft gold; eat raw or cooked.

baba ghanoush (BAH-bah gehn-OOSCH). *Kor.* Eggplant puree flavored with lemon, olive oil, garlic, and crushed sesame seeds called tahini.

babao fàn (ba-bao fan). *Chi.* Glutinous rice pudding.

baba rannouj (Ba-ba rahn-NOOG). *Ara.* Roast eggplant with tahini.

babbelaars (BAH-bah-lahrs). *Dut.* Buttercake.

babeurre (bah-buhr). *Fre.* Buttermilk.

babka (bahb-kah). *Fre.* Baba.

baby beef (BA-bee beef). *USA.* Meat from a calf younger than 12 months old.

bacalao (bah-kah-LAH-oh). *Spa.* Salt cod, codfish.

bacalhau (bacal-YAH-oo). *Por.* Salt codfish; prepared at least 1001 ways.

baccalà (bahk-kah-LAH). *Ita.* Salt cod.

bachelor's button (BAHCH-lohrz BUHT-ton). *USA.* A cookie with a cherry on top.

Bachforelle (bahk-fo-REH-lo). *Ger.* Brook trout.

backen (BAH-kern). *Ger.* To bake.

Bäckerei (beh-ker-RIGH). *Ger.* Pastries.

Backhuhn (BAHK-hoon). *Ger.* Chicken rolled in breadcrumbs, then fried.

backobst (BAHK-obst). *Ger.* Dried fruit.

backpflaume (BAHK-pflauma). *Ger.* Prune.

Backstein (BAHK-stain). *Ger.* Bavarian version of Limburger cheese.

Backwerk (BAHK-verk). *Ger.* Cakes, pastries.

baclava (bak-LEH-wah). *Ara.* Baklava.

bacon (BAY-kuhn). *USA.* A cut from the side of pork; can be fresh, cured, and/or smoked; generally used sliced.

bacon (bay-kon). *Fre.* Salt pork.

bacon og aeg (BA-kohn oa ehg). *Dan.* Bacon and egg.

badaam (bah-DAHM). *Ind.* Almond.

bade (ba-RRAY). *Ind.* Small doughnut-shape fried bean dumpling.

badi elaichi (ba-RREE eh-LIE-ee-jee). *Ind.* Black cardamom pods.

bagda jheengari (BAHG-da JEEN-ga-ree). *Ind.* Giant prawns.

bagel (BAY-guhl). *Jew.* A doughnut-shape roll that is boiled then baked giving it a hard crust and a soft interior.

bagesse (bahzh-jess). *Fre.* Sugar cane.

baghar (bag-HAAR). *Ind.* Spice-perfume butter used for flavoring yogurt, dals, vegetables, relishes, and some meats.

bagna (bah-nah). *Fre.* Beach bread; a crusty loaf of bread coated with olive oil, and filled with hard-boiled eggs, anchovies, tomatoes, onions, sweet peppers, radishes, ripe olives; prepared by hotels and restaurants along the Riviera to be eaten on the sands as a picnic lunch.

bagña cauda (BAA-nah KAH-oo-dah). *Ita.* A garlic and anchovy sauce served warm over raw vegetables.

Bagnes (bah-nyees). *Fre.* A hard, delicately flavored cheese of Switzerland.

baguette (bahg-eht). *Fre.* A long, thin loaf of French bread.

bagún (ba-GOON). *Iri.* Bacon.

baht ghok (baht goak). *Chi.* Star anise.

bái-án-di-jiu (bai-laan-dee-jyoe). *Chi.* Brandy.

bái cài (bai tsai). *Chi.* Chinese cabbage, bok choy.

bái cù (baak chou). *Chi.* White vinegar.

bai fan (baak fahn). *Chi.* Plain rice.

bai fun (baak fuhn). *Chi.* Translucent noodles.

baigan (BAYN-gun). *Ind.* Eggplant.

bain-marie (bane-mah-ree). *Fre.* A container to provide a hot-water bath for keeping cooked food hot.

bainne (ban-ya). *Iri.* Milk.

bainne gabhair (BAN-ya GO-wayr). *Iri.* Goat's milk.

bajai halászlé (BO-yo-ee HO-llaas-lay). *Hun.* Fish and potato soup.

ba jiao (bah jee-aw). *Chi.* Seed from the magnolia family with anise flavor; Chinese anise; star anise.

bake (bak). *USA.* To cook by dry heat, usually in an oven; when applied to meat, is referred to as roasting.

bake blind (bak blind). *USA.* To partially bake a pastry shell unfilled and weighted.

Baked Alaska (bakd Ah-LAHS-ka). *USA.* Dessert of ice cream set on sponge cake, covered with meringue, and quickly browned in a very hot oven.

baked custard (bakd KUS-tahrd). *USA.* Custard baked in an oven, usually in heavy ceramic cup. Also called cup custard.

bakelse (BAA-kerl-see). *Swe.* Pastry, fancy cake.

baker's cheese (BAY-kerz cheez). *USA.* A special sour cheese used by bakers, similar to cottage cheese, but smoother and softer.

baking chocolate (BA-kehng CHOK-o-leht). *USA.* The bitter, or unsweetened, chocolate used in pastries and confections.

baking powder (BA-kehng POW-der). *USA.* A leavening agent for pastry goods and quick breads.

baking soda (BAY-kehng SOH-dah). *USA.* Sodium bicarbonate; a leavening agent used with acid such as sour milk.

baklava (BAAK-lah-vah). *Ara.* A sweet pastry made with phyllo dough, chopped nuts, honey, and butter, usually cut into diamond shapes.

bakonyi betyárleves (BOK-kawn-yee BEHT-yaar-leh-vehsh). *Hun.* Soup Bakony style: a richly spiced mix of chicken, beef chunks, thin noodles, mushrooms, and vegetables. Also called outlaw soup.

bakonyi gombamártás (BOK-kawn-yee GAWM-bom-maar-taash). *Hun.* Mushroom soup.

balachan (BAH-lah-chahn). *Mal.* A salty, pungent Malaysian condiment of fermented shrimp or other seafood. Also spelled balchan.

ballottine (bahl-loat-teen). *Fre.* Stuffed boneless meat, poultry, fish, or game that is rolled into a bundle.

baloney (bah-LOH-nee). *USA.* A USA-made variation of bologna.

balsamella (bahl-sah-MAYL-lah). *Ita.* Béchamel sauce.

balsamic vinegar (bahl-SAHM-ick VEHN-eh-gar). *USA.* A very fine Italian vinegar with a dark, mellow, subtle flavor.

balsam pear (BAHL-sum pahr). *USA.* Bitter melon, a Chinese fruit.

balut (bah-oot). *Phi.* A fertilized duck egg nearly ready to hatch, a delicacy to Filipinos.

bamboo shoots (BAHM-boo shuht). *USA.* Sprouts of young bamboo plants, used in Chinese cooking.

bami (BAH-mee). *Dut.* Indonesian noodle dish made of pork, shrimp, eggs, onions, and vegetables such as green beans, peas, cabbage, cauliflower, leeks, celery; various combinations can be expected.

bamyi (BAM-ya). *Ara.* Okra.

banan (bah-NAHN). *Rus.* Banana.

banán (BO-nnaan). *Hun.* Banana.

banana (BAH-nah-nah). *Jap.* Banana.

banana (bah-NAH-nah). *USA.* Tropical fruit that is long, usually with yellow skin; grows in clusters; use raw or cooked.

banana fig (bah-NAH-nah fig). *USA.* Banana slices that are sun-dried without preservative, dark and sticky, resembling figs in appearance.

banana pepper (bah-NAH-nah PEHP-pehr). *USA.* A mild, yellow-green pepper, 3–4 inches long; good in salads or filled with a savory stuffing.

banana squash (bah-NAH-nah squash). *USA.* A winter squash shaped like a banana.

banane (bah-NAA-nah). *Ita, Ger.* Banana.

banane (bah-nan). *Fre.* Banana.

Banbury cake (BAHN-burry kak). *Bri.* An oval flaky pastry filled with currants, lemon peel, and spices.

bancha (bahn-CHAH). *Jap.* A coarse, cheap grade of green tea.

bàngbàng ji (bong-bong jee). *Chi.* Cold chicken spiced with sesame.

banger (BAHN-jehr). *Bri.* Slang for sausage made of ground pork and breadcrumbs.

banira (bah-NEE-rah). *Jap.* Vanilla (the flavor), as vanilla ice cream.

bankebiff (BAHN-keh-biff). *Nor.* Beefsteak browned in lots of butter, then simmered in stock.

bankekød (BON-kay-kerth). *Dan.* Stewed beef.

banket letter (bahn-KEHT LEH-tehr). *Dut.* French flake pastry with almond paste filling.

bannock (BAHN-uhk). *Sco.* A large, round cake of barley, wheat, or oatmeal.

bao (ba-aw). *Chi.* Abalone.

baobab (ba-OH-bahb). *Afr.* A fruit called monkey bread from a tree in central Africa.

bap (bahp). *Bri.* A small round loaf of soft, white bread eaten at breakfast in Scotland and England.

Baptist cake (BAHP-tiest kahk). *USA.* A New England deep-fried doughnut-like confection made of yeast dough. Also known as hustlers, holy pokes, and huff juffs.

baqdunis (bahk-DOO-nees). *Ara.* Parsley.

baqlawa (bahk-LAH-wah). *Ara.* Var. baklava.

baqli (BAHK-lee). *Ara.* Herbs.

bar (bahr) *Fre.* Sea bass.

bär (bah). *Swe.* Berry.

bara jheenga (BAH-ra JEEN-gah). *Ind.* Lobster.

bárányhúst (BAA-raan-yhoost). *Hun.* Lamb.

baraquille (bah-rah-kee-yuh) *Fre.* A triangular stuffed pastry hors d'oeuvre.

barashek (bah-RAH-shash). *Rus.* Lamb.

barbabietola (bar-bah-bee-EH-toa-lah). *Ita.* Beet root, beets.

barbacoa (bahr-bah-KOH-ah). *Mex.* Meat cooked in a barbecue pit.

Barbados cherry (bahr-BA-dohs CHEH-ree). *USA.* Acerola.

Barbados sugar (bahr-BA-dohs SCHOO-gahr). *USA.* Brown sugar.

barbecue, barbeque (BAR-bee-que). *USA.* To roast or broil on a rack over hot coals, usually in a highly seasoned vinegar sauce.

barberry (BAHR-bear-ree). *USA.* Red berries from the barberry tree that are pickled or ripened and made into preserves, syrup, and wine; acidic. Also called Oregon grapes.

barbo (bahr-boo). *Nor.* Barbel, a freshwater fish of the carp family.

barbue (bahr-bew). *Fre.* A European flatfish of the flounder family.

bardé (bar-day). *Fre.* Larded; covered with salt pork or slices of bacon.

barfi (BAHR-fee). *Ind.* Fudge.

barigoule (bah-ree-gouw). *Fre.* Artichokes blanched and stuffed, wrapped in bacon, braised in white wine, and served with the reduced broth.

barista (bahr-RIH-stah). *Ind.* Crisp fried onion shreds used in Moslem cooking.

bar-le-Düc (bahr-luh-duk). *Fre.* A preserve originally made of selected whole white currants seeded by hand with the aid of knitting needles; now gooseberries, strawberries, or other berries are used; often served with the cheese course of a meal.

barley (BAHR-lee). *USA.* A grain used in soups, as a cereal, and for making malt for beer, ale, and whiskey.

barley flour (BAHR-lee flowr). *USA.* A flour made by pulverizing barley grains.

barley, pearl (BAHR-lee perl). *USA.* Polished barley used in cooking.

barm (bahrm). *USA.* Yeast; formed on fermenting malt liquors.

barmbrack (bahrm-brahk). *Iri.* Bread speckled with dried fruits.

baron (BAHR-ohn). *Bri.* An extra-large cut of beef that includes part of the ribs and both sirloins.

Baron (bah-rowng). *Fre.* The saddle and two legs of lamb.

barquette (bahr-keht). *Fre.* A boat-shaped pastry shell filled and baked as an hors d'oeuvre or sweet; also vegetable cases for stuffing, such as squash.

basala (BA-sol). *Ara.* Onions.

basbousa (bas-BOO-sa). *Ara.* Semolina baked in the oven, often with nuts, and steeped in syrup.

bascoutou (bahs-KOO-tee). *Ara.* Sweet crackers.

baskoot (bahs-KOOT). *Ara.* Biscuit; cookie.

basil (BAAZ-uhl). *USA.* A sweet, pungent herb of the mint family much used in Mediterranean cooking; the basis of pesto. Varieties include African basil (camphorlike scent), cinnamon basil (medium leaves, cinnamon aroma), clove basil (clove pungency), holy basil (spicy clove scent, used in the cuisines of India), lemon basil (sharp citrus essence), lettuce leaf basil (fruity scent), opal basil (heavy perfume scent), purple basil (leaves add color as well as a sweet, lavender perfume essence to a salad), and sweet basil (fruity fragrance).

basilic (bah-see-leek). *Fre.* Food in a sauce seasoned with basil.

basilico (bah-ZEE-lee-koa). *Ita.* Basil.

basmati rice (baz-MAH-tick rice). *Ind.* A long-grain rice that is aromatic and delicate; flavor, texture, and aroma compliment western and European foods.

bass (bahs). *USA.* A name for many unrelated fish.

baste (bast). *USA.* To moisten with a liquid such as melted fat, meat drippings, or water at intervals during cooking.

baster (BAS-stur). *USA.* A ladle, cup, or syringe used to pour liquid or fat over cooking food.

básu oíngguo (ba-sse ping-guo). *Chi.* Hot candied apples.

batarde (bah-tahr-de). *Fre.* A sauce of white roux with water, egg yolks, butter, and lemon juice; means "bastard," for its indirect relationship to other classic sauces.

batata (ba-TAA-tis). *Ara.* Potato.

batatas (ba-TA-tash). *Por.* Potatoes.

Batavian endive (bah-TA-vee-un EN-dive). *USA.* Similar to curly endive with broader, paler, less highly crimped leaves, and less bitter. Also known as escarole or chicory escarole.

batinjan (bi-din-GEHN). *Ara.* Eggplants.

baton, batonnet (bah-toh, bah-toh-nah). *Fre.* Little sticks of vegetables or potatoes; larger than julienne.

bat out (baht awt). *USA.* To flatten slices of raw meat with a cutlet bat.

batter (BAHT-tuhr). *USA.* A mixture of liquid and flour that can be poured, spooned, or dipped.

batter bread (BAHT-tuhr brehd). *USA.* An unsweetened bread from southern United States made of white cornmeal and eggs. Also called spoon bread.

batter-dip (BAT-tur dip). *USA.* Pieces of food that are dipped in batter, then baked or fried.

battiykha (bat-TEEKH). *Ara.* Watermelon.

battuto (bah-TOO-toa). *Ita.* A base for stews and soups: onion, garlic, celery and herbs, cooked in oil.

baudroie (boa-drwah). *Fre.* Monkfish.

bauern (BOW-errn). *Ger.* Peasant- or country-style.

Bauernbrot (BOW-errn-broat). *Ger.* Peasant rye bread.

Bauernfrühstück (BOW-errn-fry-styk). *Ger.* A lunch dish of fried potatoes topped with scrambled eggs, ham, and cucumber.

Bauernomelett (BOW-errn-om-lett). *Ger.* Bacon and onion omelet.

Bauernschmaus (BOW-errn-schmowss). *Ger.* Austrian dish of sauerkraut, pork, sausages, and dumplings.

Bauernsuppe (BOW-errn-zupp-e). *Ger.* A peasant soup of bacon, vegetables, and legumes.

bauletti (baa-oo-LEHT-tee). *Ita.* Veal roll-ups; saltimbocca.

Baumkuchen (baum-KU-zon). *Ger.* A Christmas cake traditionally baked tall in many layers to resemble the rings of a tree trunk and iced with chocolate to resemble bark.

Bavarian cream (ba-VAR-ri-an kreem). *USA.* A French dessert of cold custard and gelatin with whipped cream folded in as it begins to stiffen.

Bavarois (bav-ar-waz). *Fre.* Bavarian.

bavaroise (bah-vah-rwaz). *Fre.* A sweetened tea drink enriched with egg yolks, milk, and citrus.

bavette (bah-veht). *Fre.* Flank steak; sirloin tip.

bavosa (bah-VOA-sah). *Ita.* Liquid in the center, in reference to a frittata or omelet.

bawd (bawd). *Sco.* Hare, rabbit.

bayd (beyD). *Ara.* Eggs.

Bayer (BAH-yerr). *Nor.* A dark colored, light-tasting beer.

bay leaf (bay lef). *USA.* The dried leaf of the European laurel.

bazilla (bi-SIL-la). *Ara.* Peas.

bean (ben). *USA.* Numerous varieties available world wide. See specific types, e.g., lima, green, fava.

bean curd (ben kuhrd). *USA.* Tofu.

bean flour (ben flawr). *USA.* Soybean flour.

bean sprouts (ben sprouts). *USA.* Tiny tender green young shoots of the mung bean, alfalfa seeds, radish seeds.

bean threads (ben threds). *USA.* Translucent noodles made from mung beans used in Chinese cooking.

beard (berd). *USA.* To remove the beard from oysters or mussels.

béarnaise (bay-ahr-nayz). *Fre.* A classic French sauce of reduced wine vinegar, shallots and tarragon, egg yolks and butter served on grilled meat and fowl.

beat (bet). *USA.* To mix by stirring vigorously resulting in a smooth light and fluffy texture.

Beaufort (boa-foa). *Fre.* A whole-milk cheese similar to Gruyère.

bécasse (bay-kahss). *Fre.* Woodcock.

beccaccia (bayk-KAHT-chah). *Ita.* Woodcock.

beccafico (bech-kah-FEE-koa). *Ita.* Game birds.

béchamel sauce (bay-scha-mell saus). *Fre.* Cream sauce made with chicken broth instead of milk; one of the basic sauces.

bêche de mer (behsh dah meh). *Fre.* A sea slug relished for its gelatinous texture. Also called sea cucumber.

beckasin (bah-kah-SIN). *Swe.* Snipe.

bécsi heringsaláta (BAY-chee HEHR-eeng-shol-laa-to). *Hun.* Herring salad with vinegar.

beechnut (BEECH-nuht). *USA.* The fruit of the beech tree; flavor is midway between that of the hazelnut and the chestnut; slightly astringent taste that is dispelled with roasting.

beechnut oil (BEECH-nuht oul). *USA.* Oil extracted from the beechnut; has a distinctive, but not unpleasant flavor.

beef à la mode (bef ah lah mod). *Fre.* A well-larded large cut of beef cooked slowly in water with vegetables, similar to braised beef.

beef cotto (bef KOHT-o). *USA.* Low calorie cooked salami that is coarse-cut; contains whole peppercorns as seasoning.

beef-ham (BEF-hahm). *Bri.* Rump of beef salted and cured like hams.

beef pudding (bef PUHD-eng). *Bri.* A meat pie that has been boiled or steamed.

beef Stroganoff (bef STROH-gah-noff). *USA.* Beef strips sauteed with chopped mushrooms and onions, then thickened with sour cream.

beef tea (bef tee). *USA.* An extract made by stewing beef in water for several hours.

beef Wellington (bef WELL-ehng-tuhn). *USA.* Beef filet covered with chicken liver pâté topped with sauce perigueux.

beer (behr). *USA.* Alcoholic beverage amber in color made from various grains, water, and yeast.

beet (bet). *USA.* A garden plant with thick, long-stalked edible leaves and a swollen round root; also called beetroot; a close relative is the gold beet.

Beetensuppe (BET-en-zuppe). *Ger.* Borsch.

beetroot (BET-ruht). *Bri.* Beets.

beet sugar (bet SCHU-gahr). *USA.* Sucrose from the sugar beet.

beignets (ben-yea). *Fre.* Fritters.

beignets (ben-YEAZ). *Bri.* A kind of pancake, fried in deep fat.

beignets de bénichon (ben-yeaz dah bee-nee-shon). *Fre.* Very thin Swiss fritters, rich with eggs, cream, and kirsch.

Beijing kao ya (bay-jing kao ya). *Chi.* Peking roast duck; an elaborate and famous dish eaten with the fingers.

Beilagen (beil-AG-en). *Ger.* Accompanying dishes.

Beinwurst (BEEN-voorst). *Ger.* Popular Swiss sausage.

békacomb gombával és rákkal (BAY-kots-awmb GAWM-baa-vol aysh RAAK-kol). *Hun.* Frog's legs with freshwater crabmeat and mushrooms.

bekon (BEH-kohn). *Jap.* Bacon.

bekon to tamago (BEH-kohn oh tah-MAH-goh). *Jap.* Bacon and eggs.

Bel Paese (behl pah-AY-zay). *Ita.* A semisoft, rich, creamy, mild-flavored cows' milk cheese.

belegtes Brot (be-LAYK-tes broat). *Ger.* Open-face sandwich.

Belgian endive (BEHL-gjun EN-dive). *USA.* A specially cultivated chicory whose leaves are cut off and shielded from the light so that new pale yellow leaves grow back in their characteristic cigar shape; used fresh in salads or braised in various preparations. Also called wiltoff chicory and French endive.

bellevue (behl-vu). *Fre.* Food enclosed in aspic through which it can be plainly seen.

bell pepper (behl PEP-ur). *USA.* Large, sweet apple-shape green pepper used fresh or cooked; also available in red and gold.

Belon oysters (beh-loh OY-sturs). *USA.* Choice oysters from the river Belon.

beluga caviar (bee-LU-ga KAH-vee-ahr). *USA.* Choicest Russian caviar from the white sturgeon; has largest egg, gray in color. Also beluge (Iranian).

ben cotto (bain KOT-toa). *Ita.* Well done, as for steak.

Bénédictine (bay-nay-dehk-tang). *Fre.* A liqueur made principally at the Abbey of Fécamp in Normandy, France.

beni shoga (beh-nee shoh-gah). *Jap.* Pickled or vinegared ginger; natural color is white, may be bought tinted pink or red.

benitade (beh-nee-TAH-deh). *Jap.* Red benitade sprouts having a slightly tangy aftertaste; used in salads.

benløse fugle (BERN-lur-say FOO-lee). *Nor, Dan.* Beef "birds" rolled around pork and onions, with a spicy gravy.

Bercy (burr-cay). *Fre.* A sauce of white wine and fish fumet, or meat glaze and beef marrow, reduced with shallots, butter, and parsley.

berenjena (behr-ehn-HEH-nah). *Spa.* Eggplant.

bergamot orange (BEHR-zhah-mo OHR-ahnj). *USA.* Bitter, pear-shaped, very acid French orange that has a very pleasant taste; oil extracted from the rind is used in confectionery, as well as perfumery, and pharmaceuticals.

bergamot pear (BEHR-zhah-mo paher). *USA.* A particular variety of pear.

Bergkäse (berg-KAY-zer). *Ger.* A hard, yellow cheese from the Bavarian Alps.

Berliner Pfannkuchen (behr-LEE-ner PFAN-koo-khern). *Ger.* Fancy jelly doughnuts.

Berliner Weisse (behr-LEE-ner veissr). *Ger.* A pale, tart, low alcohol ale, usually drunk with a dash of raspberry syrup.

berlingela (bay-reen-ZHEN-lah). *Por.* Eggplant.

Berlingozzo (bay-leen-GOAZ-zah). *Ita.* Cream cake.

Bermuda onion (behr-MOOD-dah UHN-yuhn). *USA.* Large, brown skinned and mild flavored onion. Also known as Spanish onion.

Berner Platte (BEHR-nerr PLAH-ter). *Ger.* A Swiss speciality; a copious mound of sauerkraut or green beans topped with a variety of meats, such as bacon, ham, pork chops, pigs' feet, sausages, or ribs.

berry (BEAR-ree). *USA.* General term for all fruits that contain seeds in the pulp, such as blackberries, strawberries. Technically, a tomato is a berry.

berry sugar (BEAR-ree SCHU-gahr). *USA.* A finer grind of granulated sugar, still coarse enough to discern individual crystals; best used in meringues and for sweetening drinks and fruits.

besan (BAY-sahn). *Ind.* Chick-pea flour.

beschuit (buh-SKHIRT). *Dut.* Holland rusk, double toasted.

beschuittaart (buh-SKHIRT-tahrt). *Dut.* Rusk cake.

besciamella (bay-chee-MAYL-lah). *Ita.* Béchamel sauce.

bessenvla (BES-sen-vlah). *Dut.* Currant pudding.

betasuppe (bay-ter-SSEW-pper). *Nor.* Mutton broth.

betterave (beh-ter-rahv). *Fre.* Beetroot; beets.

beurre (berr). *Fre.* Butter; au beurre nois, "with butter sauce browned in a pan."

beurré. (berr-ay). *Fre.* Buttered.

beurre blanc (berr blahnk). *Fre.* A white sauce for seafood, poultry, or vegetables made of white wine, shallots, and butter.

beurre Chivry (berr sheev-reh). *Fre.* Butter flavored with parsley, tarragon, chives, and shallots.

beurre fondue (berr fawng-dew). *Fre.* Melted butter.

beurre manie (berr mah-neeh). *Fre.* Equal parts of butter and flour, kneaded into a paste to thicken sauces and gravies; kneaded butter.

beurre noir (berr nohr). *Fre.* A fish sauce of browned butter, capers, parsley, and vinegar.

Beuschls (BOY-sherlz). *Ger.* Stewed calves' lungs with a sweet-sour tang; usually served with Knödel.

bhara (BAH-rah). *Ind.* Stuffed.

bharat (BHAH-raht). *Ara.* A blend of seasonings.

bharta (BHAR-rah). *Ind.* Smoked eggplant fried with onions, tomatoes, and herbs.

bhatoora (bheh-TOO-rah). *Ind.* Leavened dough made of yogurt, potatoes, and white flour, rolled into circles then deep fried.

bhindi (BHIN-dee). *Ind.* Okra.

bhojia (BHOO-jee-ah). *Ind.* Highly spiced stir-fried vegetables.

bhona (BOU-nah). *Ind.* Fried.

bhorji (BHOOR-jee). *Ind.* Scrambled; generally applied to scrambled eggs.

bianco d'uovo (bee-AHNG-koa d-WAW-vah). *Ita.* Egg white.

bianchetti (bee-ahn-KAYT-tee). *Ita.* Whitebait; fish.

bian dòu (bien doh). *Chi.* Beans.

bias (BI-uhs). *USA.* In a slanting manner; as cutting celery stalks on the bias.

biatas (bee-a-tass). *Iri.* Beetroot.

bibb lettuce (behb LETT-us). *USA.* A salad green of the butterhead family, considered the finest grown anywhere; the prime variety of butterhead lettuce.

bicarbonate of soda (bi-CAHR-boh-nate of SO-dah). *USA.* A leavening agent used with sour milk.

bicchiere (bee-kee-AY-rea). *Ita.* A measuring cup.

biefstuk (BEEF-sterk). *Dut.* Sirloin tip or bottom round of beef.

biefstuk van de haas (BEEF-sterk vahn deh hahs). *Dut.* Filet mignon.

bien cuit (byang kwee). *Fre.* Well done, as referring to steak.

bier (beer). *Dut.* Beer.

Bierkaltschale (BEER-kahlt-scarler). *Ger.* Cold beer soup; favorite in summer.

Bierplinsen (BEER-plen-zen). *Ger.* Cooked meats or sausages dipped in a beer batter and deep-fried.

Bierwurst (BEER-voorst). *Ger.* A fat, reddish brown sausage of pork, pork fat, and beef.

bieten (BEE-ten). *Dut.* Beets.

bietola (bee-ay-TOA-lah). *Ita.* Swiss chard.

bietoline (bee-ay-toa-LEE-nay). *Ita.* Erbette; a vegetable similar to spinach or beet greens; having an elongated smallish leaf and a slim, tender green stalk.

bife (BEE-fay). *Por.* Beefsteak.

biff (bif). *Nor.* Beefsteak.

biff à la lindstrom (bif ah lah lend-STRUM). *Swe.* Chopped beef, similar to hamburger patties, but with chopped potatoes, beets, and onions mixed in.

biffstek (BEHF-stayk). *Swe.* Beefsteak.

biftec (beef-TAYK). *Spa.* Beefsteak. Sometimes spelled bistec.

bifteck (beef-tehk). *Fre.* Beefsteak.

bifuteki (bee-FOO-teh-kee). *Jap.* Beefsteak.

bigarade (bee-gah-rahd). *Fre.* A brown sauce for roast duck made of cara-melized sugar, lemon and orange juice, demi-glace and stock.

bigoli (bee-GOA-lee). *Ita.* A large form of spaghetti, homemade, using only water, flour and a small amount of egg.

bijane (bee-zhahn). *Fre.* A cold soup prepared by putting crumbled bread into sweetened red wine.

bikesmad (BEHK-sey-meth). *Dan.* Beef hash served with a fried egg.

bilberry (BILL-ber-ree). *USA.* Blueberry.

Billy Bi (beh-lee bee). *Fre.* A mussel soup with cream and white wine.

bind (bind). *USA.* Add a liquid, egg, or melted fat to a dry mixture to cause to stick together; to form a cohesive mass.

Bing cherry (behng CHEHR-ree). *USA.* A variety of cherry that is round and plump with a dark red, almost black color. Flesh is purple-red with dark purple juice.

bing-gan (bing-gaan). *Chi.* Crackers.

bing-jí-líng (bing-gee-ling). *Chi.* Ice cream.

bing zhèn píjiu (bing dzen pee-jiu). *Chi.* Iced beer.

birch beer (burch beer). *USA.* Carbonated soft drink made from the sap of the black birch tree.

bird's nest (burdz nehst). *USA.* Yan cai; the nests of cliff-dwelling birds, soaked in water to restore their gelatinous texture and used to garnish soups at banquets and special occasions; very expensive.

bird's nest (burdz nehst). *USA.* Straw potatoes deep-fried in a special holder to form a nest and filled with other food, such as peas.

birne (BEER-ner). *Ger.* Pear.

birnenbrot (BEER-nen-broat). *Ger.* Sweet bread, rather like a fruitcake, full of dried fruits.

biryani (beh-ree-YON-nee). *Ind.* A pilaf-type rice dish; the national dish of India.

Bischofsbrot (BISH-ofs-broat). *Ger.* A cake of dried fruit and chocolate drops; bishop's bread.

biscoitos (bees-KOY-tohss). *Por.* Cookies.

biscotte (bees-kott). *Fre.* Rusk; biscuit.

biscotti (bee-SKOAT-tee). *Ita.* Cookies; biscuits.

biscotti di prato (bee-SKOAT-tee dee PRAH-toa). *Ita.* Hard-textured sweet cookies with almond pieces; often eaten dipped in vin santo.

biscuit (BEHS-kitt). *USA.* A small quick bread made from dough that has been rolled out and cut, or dropped from a spoon, and baked.

biscuit (BEHS-kitt). *Bri.* A wide variety of small flat cakes, cookies, breads.

biscuit (bees-kwee). *Fre.* A wide variety of small flat cakes, cookies, breads.

biscuit à la cuillere (bees-kwee ah lah cwee-yehr). *Fre.* Ladyfingers.

biscuit tortoni (BEHS-kiht tohr-TOHN-ee). *USA.* A frozen dessert made with cream, eggs, and crushed macaroons.

Bishop's cake (BEHS-shup's cake). *USA.* A light cake with almonds and raisins.

biskopskake (BEH-skop-kar-keh). *Nor.* Bishop's cake.

Biskote (bee-SKOT-teh). *Ger.* Ladyfinger.

biskvit (bees-KVEET). *Rus.* Sponge cake.

Bismark herring (BEHZ-mawrk HEH-renj). *Ger.* Herring marinated in vinegar, filleted and split, seasoned with onion, and eaten with sour cream.

bisque (behsk). *Fre.* A thick soup usually made with cream, egg yolks, and fish or shellfish; made with a fairly dark roux, if it's Cajun.

bissar (BEHS-sahr). *Afr.* Dried beans cooked in water and oil until a jelly is formed; eaten cold or hot.

bistec (beef-TAYK). *Spa.* Beefsteak. Sometimes spelled biftec.

bistecca (bee-STAYK-kah). *Ita.* Beefsteak.

biswa tulsi (BEHS-wah TUHL-see). *Ind.* Sweet basil.

bitter almond oil (BEHT-ter AH-mond oul). *USA.* The oil extracted from bitter almonds; has a high concentration of prussic acid; is considered poisonous by some authorities; others advise using a very minute amount to flavor; not available in the American markets.

bitter almonds (BEHT-ter AH-mondz). *USA.* Used only as flavoring, and called for in some classic European recipes; bitterness is caused by the considerable amount of prussic acid contained in these nuts.

bitterballen (bee-teht-BAHL-lehn). *Dut.* Tiny croquettelike meatballs eaten as a canapé with drinks; not at all bitter.

bitterkoekjes (BEE-tur-kook-yus). *Dut.* Macaroons.

bitterkoekjespudding (BEE-tur-kook-yus-POOD-ing). *Dut.* Pudding with raisins, fruit, rum or wine, and macaroons.

bitter melon (BEHT-ter MEL-un). *USA.* The Chinese melon, foo gwah; zucchini-shape, green, crocodile-skinned; bitter; silvery-green flesh, pale brown seeds; used cooked only.

bitter orange (BEHT-ter ornj). *USA.* Seville orange; a bitter orange with a thin skin used to make marmalade and to lend piquancy to meat, fish dishes, and various drinks.

bitters (BEHT-ters). *Bri.* An alcoholic solution of bitter, aromatic plant products used as flavoring in mixed drinks; also, a very dry heavily hopped ale.

bittersweet (BEHT-ter-sweet). *USA.* Being at once pleasantly bitter and sweet; as chocolate prepared with very little sugar.

bivalve (BI-valv). *USA.* Animal with hinged two-valve shell, such as clam, scallop, oyster.

biwa (BEE-wah). *Jap.* Loquats.

bixin (BEHX-un). *USA.* Another name for annatto, a coloring agent for butter and cheese.

bizcocho (beeth-KOA-choa). *Spa.* Biscuit, cake, ladyfinger.

bizcochos borrachos (beeth-KOA-choa boh-RRAH-choh). *Spa.* Sugared sponge cake, splashed with wine and sprinkled with cinnamon.

björnbär (BURRN-baar). *Swe.* Blackberry.

bjørnebaer (BYUR-ner-baer). *Nor.* Blackberry.

blåbar (BLAW-baer). *Nor.* Blueberries; huckleberries; popular in pancakes and in cold soup.

blåbär (BLOA-baer). *Swe.* Blueberry.

black bass (blahk bahss). *USA.* A small freshwater fish with firm, lean, delicate white flesh; skin must be removed before cooking to eliminate objectionable mossy, weedy flavor.

black beans (blahk behns). *USA*. Frijoles Negros; dried beans from Mexico that resembles the red kidney bean, sweet in taste, ebony in color; used in rice dishes, stews, and soups.

blackberry (BLAHK-bear-re). *USA*. A purplish-black berry that is juicy, sweet, but seedy; used in cobblers, pies, tart, and turnover fillings.

black-bottom pie (blahk-BOHT-um pi). *USA*. A custard pie with a layer of heavy chocolate custard on the bottom.

black cabbage (blahk KAHB-bahj). *USA*. An Italian vegetable with very dark-colored elongated leaves.

black chanterelle (blahk chan-ter-RELL). *USA*. A European wild mushroom with an earthy flavor; grayish-black, fluted in shape; should be eaten cooked.

blackened (BLAHK-und). *USA*. A Cajun method of cooking fish and meats, using an intensely hot cast iron skillet to capture the taste of cooking directly over an open fire.

black-eyed peas (BLAHK-iyd peez). *USA*. Tiny, off-white African beans with a black "eye"; used fresh or dried; an essential ingredient in Hopping John.

black Mike (blahk mike). *USA*. A term used by loggers for stew of meat and vegetables.

black mission fig (blahk MEHSH-shun fehg). *USA*. A variety of fig with sweet flavor, purple-black skin, crimson flesh; eat fresh or cooked.

black pepper (blahk PEP-purr). *USA*. A pungent, East Indian condiment that is the dried, unripened fruit of a semiwoody vine, ground with the outer black coating still on.

black pudding (blahk PUHD-eng). *USA*. Blood sausage.

black sea bass (blahk CEE-bahss). *USA*. A small saltwater fish with lean, delicate white flesh; used widely in Chinese cuisine. Also known as sea bass.

blackstrap molasses (BLAHK-strahp mo-LASS-esz). *USA*. Unrefined, dark, thick syrup produced in sugar refining.

black turnips (blahk TUHR-nuhp). *USA*. A large, black Italian vegetable resembling a turnip; has white interior, sharp, pungent flavor, crisp texture; must be peeled before eating.

black walnut (blahk WALL-nuht). *USA*. The oily edible nut of the black walnut tree.

blakhan (BLA-kahn). *Ind*. A salty, pungent shrimp paste, related to other Oriental fermented fish condiments.

blanc (blahng). *Fre*. A cooking stock of flour and water, in which certain foods, such as mushrooms and artichokes, are cooked to retain their color.

blanch (blahnch). *USA.* To plunge into boiling water (or fat) for very short time usually in preparation for further cooking by another method, or to loosen skins of fruits and vegetables.

blancmange (BLAHNG-mahnzh). *Fre.* A pudding or custard.

blandad frukt (BLAHN-dahd frewkt). *Swe.* Mixed fruit.

blandad grönsaker (BLAHN-dahdb GRURN-saak). *Swe.* Mixed vegetables.

blanquette (blang-ket). *Fre.* A white stew of veal, lamb or chicken in an egg-yolk-thickened cream sauce.

bláthach (bla-akh). *Iri.* Buttermilk.

Blau (blaus). *Ger.* Same as the French au bleu. See bleu, au.

blawn fish (blown fish). *Bri.* Fish that has been hung in a breezy place to get a fresh outdoorsy flavor.

blaze (blaz). *USA.* To pour liquor over food and ignite.

blé (blee). *Fre.* Wheat.

bleek (blake). *Dut.* Pascal-type celery.

blend (blehnd). *USA.* To mix two or more ingredients thoroughly until uniform.

blended flour (BLEHND-ehd flaur). *USA.* Two or more classes of flours blended for specific purposes, such as for making pretzels.

bleu (bluh). *Fre.* Blue; or very rare, as for steak.

bleu, au (ah blur). *Fre.* A method of preparing fish especially trout, by plunging the fish, absolutely fresh if not actually alive, into a boiling water and vinegar mixture, seasoned with salt, and spiced with thyme and bay leaf, which causes the skin of the fish to take on a bluish color; served with melted butter or hollandaise sauce.

Bleu d'Auvergne (blur d'oa-veh-awng-yeh). *Fre.* A cows' whole-milk soft, blue cheese with a distinctive flavor.

blinde vinken (BLIN-duh VING-kuh). *Dut.* Stuffed veal or beef.

blind Huhn (blint hoon). *Ger.* A casserole of beans, bacon, dried apples, and various vegetables.

blinis (blyee-NI). *Rus.* Pancakes, of a light batter, served with caviar and sour cream.

blintzes (blehnz-ez). *USA.* A thin pancake, rolled or folded, with a filling, usually cheese.

bloater (BLO-ter). *Bri.* A large, fat, salted herring, usually whole and ungutted, then cold-smoked to a pale gold color; gutted just prior to serving.

blockwurst (BLOK-vurst). *Ger.* A salamilike sausage of pork and beef.

blodfersk (BLEWD-fehrshk). *Nor.* Blood-fresh, an expression used to denote freshness of fish.

blodkorv (BLOOD-korv). *Swe.* Black (blood) pudding, a type of sausage.

bloedworst (BLOOT-worst). *Dut.* Sausage made with blood, oatbran, raisins, pork fat; served boiled, broiled, or fried.

bloemkool (BLOOM-kohl). *Dut.* Cauliflower.

blomkål (BLOOM-koal). *Nor, Swe.* Cauliflower.

blomkaal (BLOAM-kawl). *Dan.* Cauliflower.

blommer (BLOAM-err). *Dan.* Plums.

blond de veau (blon de vo). *Fre.* White veal stock.

blond de volaille (blon de voh-laj). *Fre.* Clear chicken stock.

blondir (blon-deer). *Fre.* To cook lightly in fat.

blood (bluhd). *USA.* Used as a thickening agent for a sauce when made to accompany a meat dish, usually game or fowl.

blood orange (bluhd orahnj). *USA.* A member of the orange family, with pulp that is rust, scarlet, garnet or purple, and a dramatically sanguine juice with overtones of raspberries; skin is orange or red-flecked; resembles a valencia orange.

blood sausage (bluhd SAW-sahj). *USA.* A sausage of diced pork fat and blood from freshly killed pigs, black in color. Also known as black pudding.

bløtkake (blurdh-kaa-ker). *Nor.* A layer cake with a rich filling of whipped cream, egg yolks, nuts.

blueberry (BLU-bear-ree). *USA.* The blue or black, small, round fruit of the blueberry bush; eaten fresh or cooked in jellies, syrups, and baked products.

blue cheese (blu cheez). *USA.* Cheese injected with mold to form the blue veining that gives the cheese its characteristic flavor. Blue-veined cheeses include French Roquefort, American Maytag Blue, and Italian Gorgonzola.

blue crabs (blu krahbz). *USA.* A variety of crab best known in its soft-shell stage.

bluefish (BLU-fisch). *USA.* An important food fish related to the pompanos found off the Atlantic coast; bluish above and silvery below; has a delicate flavor when gutted, scaled, and iced immediately after being taken from the water; pan-fry small blues, fillet then bake or broil the larger ones.

blue meat (blu meet). *USA.* A term used to designate the meat of an unweaned calf.

Blue Point (Blu Pohnt). *USA.* An outstanding species of oyster found off the coast of Long Island; served raw.

Blumenkohl (BLOO-mern-kohl). *Ger.* Cauliflower.

Blutwurst (BLOOT-voorst). *Ger.* Blood sausage.

bobi (bah-BI). *Rus.* Broad beans.

bobotee (BOH-boh-tee). *USA.* A puddinglike dish of milk, bread crumbs, almonds, onions and hot sauce.

bócài (baw tsai). *Chi.* Spinach.

Bock (bok). *Ger.* A dark, strong Bavarian beer.

böckling (BURK-ling). *Swe.* Small smoked herring.

Bockwurst (BOK-voorst). *Ger.* Sausage of pork, veal, lemon juice, eggs, milk; eaten in the spring.

bodega (bo-DEE-go). *Spa.* Wine cellar.

boerenkool (BOOR-uh-kohl). *Dut.* Kale.

boerenkool met roke worst (BOOR-uh-kohl met rohk worst). *Dut.* A hotchpotch of crispy kale and potatoes served with smoked sausage.

boeuf (buhf). *Fre.* Beef; boeuf à la jardinière, braised beef with vegetables; boeuf roti, roast beef.

boeuf à la mode (buhf a la mod). *Fre.* Pot roast de luxe; meat sliced very thin and even, covered with sauce, and platter garnished with beautifully arranged vegetables.

boeuf bouilli (buhf bu-ji). *Fre.* Boiled beef.

boeuf salé (buhf sah-lee). *Fre.* Corned beef.

bøf (burf). *Dan.* Beef.

bogavente (boa-ghah-BEN-tay). *Spa.* Large-clawed lobster.

bohne (BOA-nern). *Ger.* Bean.

boil (boyl). *USA.* To bring a liquid to the boiling point, which is 212°F for water at sea level.

boiled custard (boyld KUS-tahrd). *USA.* Custard cooked on top of the stove, as opposed to custard baked in an oven.

boiled icing (boyld I-ceng). *USA.* The product of whipping hot sugar syrup into beaten egg whites; Italian meringue.

boiler onions (BOY-luhr UN-yun). *USA.* Small, round, tender white onion with mild flavor, used in casseroles, soups, stews, or creamed.

bok choy (bahk chee). *Chi.* A clump of snow-white stalks ending in wide, dark-green leaves, related to Chinese cabbage; used alone or in stir-fry. Also known as baak choy, pak choi, celery mustard, and Chinese mustard.

bok goh (baak gqoak). *Chi.* Ginkgo nut.

bokking (BAWK-king). *Dut.* Red herring; a bloater.

bola (BOH-lah). *Mex.* Ball; shape such as meatball.

bola (BOH-lah). *Jew.* A cut of Kosher forequarter meat.

bolacha (boh-LAH-shah). *Por.* Crackers.

boletus (boh-le-tus). *Fre.* A genus of wild mushroom, whose most prized edible varieties are bolete, cepe and porcini; have fleshy caps and stems and range from white to very dark brown; eaten fresh or dried.

bolillo (boh-LEE-yoh). *Mex.* Small hard roll.

bolita (boh-LEE-tah). *Mex.* Little ball; such as shape of little ball.

bölledünne (BURL-leh-dewn-neh). *Ger.* A Swiss onion custard pie.

boller (BOAL-er). *Dan.* Meatballs or fishballs.

bollito (bo-LEE-toa). *Ita.* A meat dish made up of various kinds of boiled meats, served with a green parsley sauce.

bollo (BOH-yoh). *Spa.* Small loaf or roll.

bolo (BOH-loh). *Por.* Cake.

bologna (bo-LONE-yah). *Ita.* A large sausage of ground pork with cubes of white fat, and seasoned with coriander, pistachio nuts, and wine; not akin to U.S. baloney.

boluó (baw-luo). *Chi.* Pineapple.

bomba di riso (BOAM-bah dee REE-zoa). *Ita.* A molded bombe of rice with a rich filling of ground meat, herbs, mushrooms, diced cheese or ham.

Bombay duck (Bom-BAY duk). *USA.* Bombil.

bombe (baumb). *Fre.* A frozen dessert made of a combination of two or more frozen mixtures packed in a round or melon-shaped mold; Bombe glacée.

bombil (BOHM-behll). *Ind.* A fish that is split, boned, filleted, and dried; used to flavor curry dishes. Also known as Bombay duck.

bombons (bohm-BOHSS). *Por.* Candy.

böna (BUR-nah). *Swe.* Bean.

bonbon (bahn bahn). *Fre.* Candy, confections.

bone (bohn). *USA.* To remove the bones from meat or fish.

bone broth (bohn brohth). *USA.* Soup made from boiling cracked bones.

boned and rolled (bohnd and rolld). *USA.* Meat cuts that are boned by the butcher, rolled up, and tied for roasting.

bonen (bo-nen). *Dut.* Beans.

boniatos (bou-neeAH-tous). *Spa.* Sweet potatoes.

boniatos confitadas (boa-nee-AH-toass kon-fee-TAY-doas). *Spa.* Candied sweet potatoes.

bonite (boh-nee-teh). *Fre.* Bonito.

bonito (boh-NEE-toa). *Jap.* A small member of the tuna family, used primarily in Japanese cooking, dried, salted, or flaked.

bonne femme (bong fam). *Fre.* In simple home style, for example, soups, stews, and casseroles.

bønner (BURN-err). *Dan.* Beans.

bönor (BUR-noor). *Swe.* Beans.

boova shenkel (BOO-vah SHEHN-kehl). *USA.* A stew and dumpling dish from the Pennsylvania Dutch.

boquerones (boa-kay-ROAN-nayss). *Spa.* Fresh anchovies; whitebait.

borage (BOU-raj). *USA.* An herb whose young leaves are used to flavor vegetables and in salads. The tiny flowers can be used in beverages, or when dipped in egg white, sugared, and dried, can be used as cake and confection decorations.

borda (BAW-rdo). *Hun.* Chop.

bordelaise (bore-da-lays). *Fre.* A brown sauce in which Bordeaux or Burgundy constitutes one of the ingredients.

bordure (boar-dewr). *Fre.* Mashed rice or potato used to border or decorate hot foods.

Borjú (BAWR-yoo). *Hun.* Veal.

borjúpaprikás (BAW-ryoopo-pree-kaash). *Hun.* Veal fricassee with onions, pepper rings, tomatoes, and a seasoning of paprika and garlic.

borlotto bean (boar-LOT-toa behn). *Ita.* A common dried bean, splotched brown, and used in soups or cooked to a smooth paste.

Bornholmeraeggekage (born-HAHL-meyr-egg-gee-kay-yee). *Dan.* Omelet with Bornhol smoked herring, radishes and chives.

borracho (boh-RRAH-choh). *Mex.* Cooked with wine, liquor.

borsch (bohrsh). *Rus.* A soup made with beets, meat broth, and vegetables and always served with sour cream.

borscht (bohrsh). *Pol.* Borsch.

borsot (BAWR-shawt). *Hun.* Black pepper.

borstplaat (BAWRST-plaht). *Dut.* Sugar candy; hard-baked fondant.

borststuk (BAWRST-stook). *Dut.* Brisket.

bosbessen (BOS-bessen). *Dut.* Blueberries.

Boston baked beans (BOSS-ton bakd benz). *USA.* Navy beans flavored with molasses and salt pork, baked in an earthenware pot.

Boston brown bread (BOSS-ton brahn bred). *USA.* A sweet, rye bread flavored with molasses.

Boston cracker (BOSS-ton kraker). *USA.* A large, thin slightly sweet cracker, similar to the common cracker.

Boston cream pie (BOSS-ton creme pi). *USA.* A round cake, split and filled with a custard or cream filling, topped with chocolate icing.

Boston lettuce (BAHS-ton LETT-us). *USA.* A salad lettuce with a small, slightly loose head; dark green outer leaves, pale green inner leaves; a variety of butterhead lettuce.

bot (bawt). *Dut.* Flounder.

boter (BO-tur). *Dut.* Butter.

boterham (BO-tur-ahm). *Dut.* Cold cuts.

botifarra (boo-ti-FAR-ra). *Spa.* Spiced sausage.

bottagio (boa-tah-JEE-o). *Ita.* Pork stew.

bottarga (boa-TAHR-jah). *Ita.* Mullet roe, used in antipasto.

bottom round (BAHT-tum round). *USA.* The cut of beef from the hind-quarter that is adjacent to the tip, being the lower portion of the round.

bouchées (boo-shay) *Fre.* A mouthful; small puff-paste patties.

boucher (bu-cher). *Fre.* Butcher.

bouchon (bu-shon). *Fre.* Cork.

boudin (BOO-den). *USA.* A Cajun sausage with rice mixed with the stuffing; white boudin is made with pork; red boudin has pork blood added; other meats as well as seafood can also be used.

boudin noir (boo-den nwar). *Fre.* Blood sausage.

bouillabaisse (boo-yah-behss). *Fre.* The national soup of France; a highly seasoned fish soup made especially at Marseilles; served in plates with dry toast.

bouilli (BOO-yee). *USA.* A classic Cajun soup made with the internal organs of beef.

bouilli (bu-jee). *Fre.* Fresh boiled beef or other meat.

bouillir (bu-jir). *Fre.* To boil.

bouillon (boo-yawn). *Fre.* Broth or unclarified stock made from beef, veal, or chicken; concentrated brown stock.

boula (BOO-lah). *USA.* A green pea and green turtle soup, flavored with sherry, usually topped with cheese and sometimes whipped cream.

boulage (bu-lajz). *Fre.* To shape dough for baking.

boulangère, à la (bu-lahn-zehr). *Fre.* A garnish of braised potatoes and onions.

boule-de-neige (bul-de-nejg). *Fre.* A round, dessert pastry covered in whipped cream to resemble snowballs.

boulette (boo-leht). *Fre.* Meatballs or anything formed in a sphere, then cooked, usually fried.

bouquet (boo-keh). *Fre.* Volatile oils from herbs and plants that give aroma.

bouquet garni (boo-keh gahr-nee). *Fre.* Herbs and seasonings, usually including parsley, thyme, and bayleaf, among others, tied in cheesecloth and used to flavor sauces and soups; removed before serving. Also known as fagot.

bouquetière, à la (bu-keh-tyehr). *Fre.* Garnishes of vegetables arranged on the meat platter.

bouquettes (boo-kehtt). *Fre.* Buckwheat pancakes with raisins in the batter, served in Belgium.

bourgeoise (bohr-zhwaz). *Fre.* Usually means served with vegetables.

bourguignon (bohr-ghee-n'yang). *Fre.* A classic stew of beef braised in red wine with onions and mushrooms.

bourride (boo-reed). *Fre.* A garlicky fish stew; served on crusty bread.

boysenberry (BOYZ-un-ber-ree). *USA.* A berry that looks like a large blackberry and tastes like a raspberry.

braciola (brah-cee-OHL-lah). *Ita.* A chop or cutlet.

braciola di maiale (brah-CHOA-lah dee maa-ee-AA-lay). *Ita.* Pork chop.

braciolette ripiene (brah-choa-LAH-tay ree-pee-EH-nay). *Ita.* Stuffed veal rolls; veal birds.

braciolini (brah-chee-oa-LEE-nee). *Ita.* Beef rolls stuffed with bits of pork or sausage.

bräckkorv (BREHK-korv). *Swe.* Smoked pork sausage.

bradán (brad-dan). *Iri.* Salmon.

brændende kærlighed (BRAY-ne-ne KAYHR-li-heth). *Dan.* Literally, "burning love"; mashed potato with bacon.

Bragenwurst (BRAH-gun-voorst). *Ger.* A long, thin, smoked sausage made of pig's brains, onions, flour, and oats.

brains (branes). *USA.* Usually from a calf or lamb. To prepare, blanch in acidulated water, then poach in court boullion or fry in butter, serve with brown butter; also cooked in scrambled eggs.

braise (braz). *USA.* To cook by browning or searing in fat, then cooking tightly covered in small amount of liquid at low temperature, either in the oven or over direct heat.

brak geal (brak gyal). *Iri.* Sea trout.

bramble jelly (BRAHM-bul JEHL-lee). *USA.* A jelly made from crab apples and blackberries.

bramble pie (BRAHM-bul pi). *Bri.* A deep-dish pie made from wild blackberries.

bran (brahn). *USA.* The outer covering of a cereal grain; one of the beneficial fiber foods.

brandade (brahng-dahd). *Fre.* Salted codfish pureed with oil and seasoned with garlic.

brandon puff (BRAN-dohn puhf). *USA.* A muffin made with cornmeal and flour.

brandy (BRAN-di). *Dut.* An alcoholic liquor distilled from wine.

bran flour (brahn flowr). *USA.* Flour made from finely ground wheat bran.

brasato (brah-SAA-toa). *Ita.* Braised.

Braskartofler (brahs-kahr-TOAF-lerr). *Dan.* Fried potatoes.

Braten (BRART-ern). *Ger.* Braised or roasted meat.

Brathandl (BRART-hehndl). *Ger.* Roast chicken.

Brathering (brart-HAY-ring). *Ger.* Grilled or fried herring, that is pickled; served cold.

Brathuhn (BRART-thoon). *Ger.* Roast chicken.

Bratwurst (BRART-voorst). *Ger.* A sausage of spiced pork.

Bräune Tunke (BROY-neh TOON-kay). *Ger.* Brown sauce.

Braunschweiger (BROWN-schvahg-er). *Ger.* Liver sausage; rich flavor, smooth consistency; made from pork, pork liver, smoked bacon; delicately seasoned with coriander, ginger, mustard, onion, pepper, other seasonings.

Braunsweiger Kuchen (BROWN-schvahg-er KOOK-hern). *Ger.* Brunswick cake, rich in butter, eggs, raisins, currants, and almonds.

brawn (brahvn). *Ger.* Head cheese, a jellied loaf made from the edible meat of a pig or calf head.

Brazil nut (BRAH-zeel nuht). *USA.* The three-sided nut of a wild Brazilian tree; the nutmeat is white, creamy, and high in fat.

brazo de gitano (BRAH-soh del gee-TAH-noh). *Spa.* "Gypsy's arm"; a jelly roll.

breac (brak). *Iri* Trout.

bread (brehd). *USA.* To dip a food into an egg-milk mixture, then coat with fine breadcrumbs prior to cooking.

bread flour (brehd flowr). *USA.* Made from hard wheat with high gluten content that gives structural support to products; gives elasticity to the dough, allows it to expand and hold the gas liberated by the yeast; feels gritty to touch; one of the world's basic foods.

bread fruit (brehd froot). *USA.* Sweet, starchy, green, tropical, round fruit with pulp similar to bread when baked.

bread sauce. (brehd saus). *Bri.* A sauce for poultry and game, made with milk thickened with bread crumbs.

bread stick. (brehd stehk). *USA.* A yeast-bread product that is 8–10 inches long, and about 1 inch in diameter when baked; crispy texture.

breakfast cream (BREHK-fahst krem). *USA.* Light cream.

bream (brehm). *USA.* Various species of fish throughout the world; best known are the American porgy and the Mediterranean gilthead; a small bony freshwater fish used mostly in stews.

bree (broo). *Sco.* Soup.

brème (braym). *Fre.* Bream.

Bremer Kükenragout (Breh-mer KOOK-hern-rah-goo). *Ger.* Stewed chicken and vegetables in cream sauce.

brennevin (BROWN-veen). *Nor.* Brandy.

Brennsuppe (brehn-zuppe). *Ger.* Brown soup; made of flour browned in the oven or dry skillet, flavored with onions and wine.

bretone (bray-TOU-nay). *Spa.* Brussel sprouts.

bretonne (breh-ton). *Fre.* A garnish of fresh white haricot beans.

brew (broo). *USA.* To cook or heat in liquid to extract flavor, as in preparing tea.

brewer's rice (broo-ehrz rice). *USA.* Broken grains of rice used as an ingredient in beer brewing.

brewer's yeast (broo-ehrz yeest). *USA.* High protein yeast used in brewing beer that is used as nutritional supplement.

Brezel (BRET-sehl). *Ger.* Pretzel.

brick (brehk). *USA.* A cow's whole-milk cheese whose taste and texture is similar to cheddar; brick-shape.

brider (bree-dayr). *Fre.* To truss.

Brie (bree). *Fre.* A cheese with a smooth buttery interior; a fine aroma and taste; white surface, ripened rind; made in flat disc.

brigidini (bree-gee-DEE-nee). *Ita.* Anise-flavored cookies.

brik (breek). *Ara.* Phyllo; leaf-thin pastry sheets, made from flour and water; used for sweet and savory dishes by layering with fillings. Also known as filo, yukka, malsouka.

brill (brehl). *USA.* A European flatfish of the flounder family.

brine (brin). *USA.* Solution of salt and water used to draw natural sugars and moisture from food to preserve it.

bringa (BRING-ah). *Swe.* Brisket, breast.

bringebaer (BRING-er-bahr). *Nor.* Raspberry.

brinjal (BREEN-jahl). *Ind.* Eggplant.

brioche (bree-ohsh). *Fre.* A slightly sweetened, rich bread of French origin; baked in a fluted mold with a button on top.

brisket (BREHS-kett). *USA.* An economical cut of meat from the breast, including part of the ribs and shoulder.

brisler (BREESS-lerr). *Dan.* Sweetbreads.

brisling (BREHZ-leng). *USA.* A small fish similar to the herring; sprat.

brisquet (brehs-keeht). *Fre.* Brisket.

Bristol cream (Brehs-tohl krem). *Bri.* A dessert sherry; one of the most elegant.

broa (broah). *Spa.* Cornbread.

broad beans (brohd behns). *USA.* Fava beans; large, meaty bean that is light-green when fresh; eaten raw, cooked fresh, dried, or canned; important nutritionally; used worldwide.

broccoli (BROI I-klee). *USA.* A green vegetable of Italian origin that is a type of cauliflower. Used cooked or raw in salads and with dips.

broccoli rabe (BROK-ko-lee RAH-beh). *Ita.* Broccoli.

brochan (BROX-ehn). *Sco.* Porridge, gruel.

broche (brosh). *Fre.* Skewer; cooked on a skewer.

brochet (bro shch). *Fre.* Pike.

brochette (bro-shet). *Fre.* A skewer for grilling chunks of meat and vegetables; kabobs.

brocoli (broc-coa-lay). *Fre.* Broccoli.

bróculo (BROK-ko-lo). *Nor.* Broccoli.

bröd (brurd). *Swe.* Bread.

brød (brur). *Dan, Nor.* Bread.

brodettato (braw-dayt-TAH-toa). *Ita.* Stewed.

brodetto (braw-DAYT-toa). *Ita.* Fish stew or soup.

brodo (BRAW-doa). *Ita.* Broth.

brodo ristretto (BRAW-doa reez-TRAYT-toa). *Ita.* Consommé.

broil (braughl). *USA.* To cook under a direct flame or over a charcoal fire.

broiler (braughl-ehr). *USA.* As a food, refers to a young chicken of either sex that weighs about 2½ pounds. See also capon, cock, fryer, roaster, stag chicken, and stewing chicken.

bromelain (BRO-meh-lynn). *USA.* Enzyme from the pineapple used to tenderize meat.

bronzino (brahn-DZEE-noa). *Ita.* Sea bass.

brood (broht). *Dut.* Bread; bruin (brirn), brown; krenten (KREN-tuh), raisin; rogge (RAWKH-uh), rye; roosteren (ROHS-turtn), toast; wit (vit), white.

broodbeleggingen (brot-BEH-lahg-ghen-en). *Dut.* Toppings for sandwiches; anything to be put on a slice of bread.

broodje (BROHT-yus). *Dut.* Sandwich roll.

broodmaaltyd (brot-MAHL-tayd). *Dut.* A bread meal, or rather a meal of sandwiches.

broodpap (BROHT-pahp). *Dut.* Bread pudding.

broonie (BROO-nee). *Bri.* Oatmeal gingerbread cookies.

broqueta (broh-KAY-tah). *Mex.* Skewer; brochette.

Broschen (BRO-shehn). *Ger.* Sweetbreads.

Brot (broat). *Ger.* Bread.

Brotchen (BROAT-khern). *Ger.* Rolls.

broth (brauth). *USA.* The clear liquor in which meats or vegetables have been cooked.

Brotkoch (BROAT-kokh). *Ger.* Molded bread pudding.

Brotsuppe (BROAT-zuppe). *Ger.* Bread soup; a way to use stale bread tastily by combining with meat stock and flavoring with nutmeg.

Brottorte (BROAT-tor-ter). *Ger.* A torte of breadcrumbs, eggs, almonds, with hot wine bath poured slowly over entire cake while hot.

brou (broo). *Fre.* A liquor made from green walnuts, flavored with cinnamon and coriander.

brouille (broo-yay). *Fre.* Scrambled.

brown (brown). *USA.* To cause the surface of food to turn dark brown by using high heat, leaving the inside moist; accomplished by frying, broiling, grilling.

brown and serve (braughn ahnd suhrv). *USA.* A term used to indicate that a product has been baked to the point of doneness, but not browned; browning is done just prior to serving; usually refers to bread products.

brown betty (brown BEHT-tee). *USA.* A pudding of apples, bread crumbs, spices, and sugar.

browned flour (brownd flawr). *USA.* Used as a sauce enhancer and thickener; has a nutty and baked aroma.

brownie (BROWN-nee). *USA.* A rich chocolate confection, usually frosted with chocolate, and cut in squares.

brown onion sauce (brown-UN-yun saus). *USA.* Lyonnaise sauce.

brown rice (brown ris). *USA.* Unpolished rice having only the hull removed; usually long-grain; the least processed form of rice.

brown sauce (brown saus). *USA.* Sauce Espagnole; the French basic brown sauce, used in many other sauces; made of brown roux, brown stock, brown mirepoix, tomatoes, and herbs slowly cooked together, and strained.

brown stock (brown stohk). *USA.* Thin liquid from simmering roasted meat in water with seasonings for several hours.

brown sugar (brown SCHU-gahr). *USA.* A soft sugar whose crystals are covered with a coating of molasses.

brugnon (brew-nawng). *Fre.* Nectarine; a smooth-skinned peach.

Brühne (BREW-er). *Ger.* Consommé.

bruin brood (BRIRN broht). *Dut.* Whole wheat bread.

bruiss (bruce). *USA.* A dish of boiled milk and bread.

brûlant (brew-lahngt). *Fre.* Flaming; flambé; drenched in brandy, set aflame.

brule (brew-leh). *Fre.* Caramelized as in Crème Brûlée, or flamed as in burnt brandy.

brun (brang). *Fre.* Method of braising in which meat is seared first.

bruna bönor (brewna BUR-noor). *Swe.* Brown beans.

brunekager (BROON-kaaer). *Dan.* Brown spice cookies.

brun fisksuppe (brewn FISK-ssewp-per). *Nor.* Fish soup, darkened with browned flour and butter.

brunie bonen (brirn BOH-nuh). *Dut.* Kidney or brown beans.

brunkaalssupe (broon-KAHL-soo-bber). *Dan.* Brown cabbage soup.

Brunnenkresse (broo-nen-KRE-seh). *Ger.* Watercress.

brunoise (broo-noyz). *Fre.* Very small diced or shredded vegetables such as celery, carrots, leeks, and turnips cooked for soups, sauces.

Brunstück (BROON-stewk). *Ger.* Brisket.

brunsviger kager (BROONZ-veeg-err kaaer). *Dan.* Brunswick cookies; rich in butter and sugar, topped with almonds and cinnamon.

Brunswick stew (BRUHNZ wchk steu). *USA.* A stew of chicken and various vegetables.

bruschetta (broo-SKEHT-toa). *Ita.* Coarse-textured bread, toasted over coals and liberally dressed with extra virgin olive oil. Also known as fett'unta or fregolotta.

brush (bruhsh). *USA.* To coat food with melted fat or liquid.

brush roast (bruhsh rohst). *USA.* A dish of oysters cooked over a wood fire on wire and served with chowchow, butter, and corn bread.

Brussels lof (BROOS-suls lawf). *Dut.* Endive.

Brussels sprouts (BRUSS-ul sprouts). *USA.* Small green vegetable resembing a tiny cabbage.

brut (broot). *Fre.* Unsweetened; having a natural flavor.

brylépudding (bru-LEPU-ding). *Swe.* Caramel cream.

brysselkål (BREW-serl-koal). *Swe.* Brussels sprouts.

bubble and squeak (BUB-uhl and squek). *Bri.* Boiled beef fried with cabbage and potatoes.

bubbly jock (BUB-bly jahk). *Sco.* Turkey.

buccellato (book-chahl-LAH-toa). *Ita.* Cake with currants and flavored with anise seed.

bûche de Noël (bush-dah-Noel). *Fre.* Yule log; traditional Christmas dessert; genoise decorated with buttercream to resemble a log.

buck and breck (buhk and brehk). *USA.* A pickled condiment, similar to chowchow; served cold.

Bückling (BEWK-ling). *Ger.* Smoked herring.

buckwheat flour (BUHK-wheht flowr). *USA.* Flour made from the seed of the buckwheat cereal grain.

budding (BOOTH-eng). *Dan.* Pudding.

budin (boo-DEEN). *Spa.* Pudding.

bùding (boo-DING). *Chi.* Pudding.

budino (boo-DEE-noa). *Ita.* Pudding.

budino di pasta (boo-DEE-noa dee PAHS-toa). *Ita.* Noodle pudding.

budino di ricotta (boo-DEE-noa dee ree-KOT-toa). *Ita.* Cheese pudding.

budino torinese (boo-DEE-noa taw-ree-NAY-zeh). *Ita.* Chestnut pudding.

budo (boo-DOH). *Jap.* Grapes.

bue (BOO-eh). *Ita.* Beef.

buey (bway). *Spa.* Beef.

buffalo wings (BUHF-fah-lo wengs). *USA.* Deep-fried chicken wings brushed with hot sauce; a fiery dish.

buffet (boo-fah). *Fre.* A table displaying a variety of foods.

buisson (bwee-sawng). *Fre.* A garnish of small groups of shrimp, crayfish; also a method of twisting pastry to a pointed end.

bulger (BULL-jger). *Ara.* Cracked wheat; precooked and prepared wheat; oldest known processed food.

buljong (BUL-jong). *Swe, Nor.* Beef broth.

bulka (BOOL-koo). *Rus.* Roll.

bullabesa (BOOL-yah-beh-sah). *Spa.* Fish stew.

bul'on (bool'YON). *Rus.* Broth.

bun (buhn). *USA.* Any of various sweet or plain small flatish, round roll.

Bundkuchen (bunt-KOO-khern). *Ger.* Gugelhupf; a sweet yellow cake.

Bundnerfleisch (BEWND-nerr-flighsh). *Ger.* Very thinly sliced cured, air-dried beef.

Bunter Hans (BEWNT-nerr hahnz). *Ger.* A large bread dumpling cooked in a napkin to hold its shape, then served with cooked vegetables or stewed fruits.

buñuelo (boo-NYUE-loh). *Spa.* Fritter; crisp, puffy round coated with sugar and cinnamon.

burdock (BURR-dahk). *Jap.* A long, slender, neutral tasting ròot used for its crunchy texture; gobo.

burghul (BURR-ghul). *Ara.* Crushed wheat; usually comes in fine ($^\#$1), medium ($^\#$2), and coarse ($^\#$3); not to be confused with cracked wheat, or bulgur.

burgonyakrémleves (BOOR-gawn-yok-ray-leh-vehsh). *Hun.* Cream of potato soup.

burgonyát (BOOR-gawn-yaat). *Hun.* Potatoes.

burgoo (BURR-goo). *USA.* Meat and vegetable stew thickened with okra.

Burgos (BOOR-gous). *Spa.* A ewes' milk cheese; rindless, mild, soft, pleasant; often served for dessert.

buri (boo-ree). *Jap.* Yellowtail, a food fish.

burnet (BURR-net). *USA*. An herb whose leaves impart a delicate cucumber flavor to winter salads; the leaves become tough in hot weather and taste of watermelon; use in salad, vinegars, soups, and with asparagus, celery, beans, and mushrooms.

burrida (boor-REE-dah). *Ita*. Fish stew with garlic, oil, tomatoes, dried mushrooms, onions, celery, saffron.

burrito (boo-RREE-toh). *Spa*. Warm, soft flour tortilla filled with savory ingredients such as hot and spicy meats, beans, cheese, tomatoes, and green onions, topped with guacamole and sour cream.

burro (BOOR-roa). *Ita*. Butter.

burro banana (BOUR-roh bah-NAH-nah). *Mex*. A variety of banana with a tangy lemon-banana flavor, a flat, square appearance; eat fresh or use in fruit salads and in desserts. Also known as chunky banana.

burtukaal (bor-too-KOHD). *Ara*. Orange.

busecca (boo-ZAYK-kah). *Ita, Swe*. A thick tripe soup usually made with beans and always with onions.

bushmills (BUSH-mehlz). *Iri*. A smoky-flavored whisky.

Busserl (BOOS-sehrl). *Ger*. "Kiss"; small pastries.

bustard (BUH-stahrd). *Afr*. A game bird; a food bird.

buster (BUHS-tuhr). *USA*. A shedding crab whose shell has "busted" loose.

buta (boo-TAH). *Jap*. Pork.

butaniku (boo-TAH-nee-koo). *Jap*. Pork.

buterbrod (boo-teer-BROD). *Rus*. Sandwich.

butifarra (boo-teh-FAH-rah). *Spa*. Catalonian sausage.

butirro (boo-TEER-roa). *Ita*. Small ball of cheese formed around a lump of butter; served sliced.

butter. (BUTT-tur). *USA*. A solid emulsion made by churning cream; used as a food spread, as a seasoning, for sautéeing, in baking.

Butter (BOOT-er). *Ger*. Butter.

butter bean (BUHT-ehr bean). *USA*. Lima bean.

buttercream (BUHT-ehr-kreem). *USA*. Mixture of butter, sugar, and egg yolk, variously flavored; used to ice cakes and confections, and to decorate or garnish.

buttercrunch lettuce (BUHT-ter-krunch LEHT-us). *USA*. A salad lettuce with a small, slightly loose head; dark green outer leaves, pale green inner leaves; a variety of butterhead lettuce.

buttercup squash (BUHT-ter-kup squash). *USA*. A turban-shaped winter squash with a distinctive pale "beanie"; heavy rind, deep ivy-green, marked with uneven, narrow stripes the color of the cap; medium-sweet orange flesh is fine-textured, creamy, and mild.

butterfly (BUHT-ter-fli). *USA.* To cut open, but not completely through, spread apart or flat; usually meat or fish.

butterhead lettuce (BUHT-ter-hehd LEHT-us). *USA.* A salad green lettuce with a small, slightly loose, soft head having delicate leaves that are dark green on the outside and pale yellowish green on the inside; has a buttery taste. Varieties include Boston, buttercrunch, bibb, White Boston, May King, and Manoa.

Buttermilch (BOO-tur-milc). *Ger.* Buttermilk.

buttermilk (BUHT-ehr-melk). *USA.* Liquid remaining after butter has been churned; contains no butterfat.

butternut (BUHT-ehr-nuht). *USA.* Large edible nut or kernel from the white walnut tree; a walnut.

butternut squash (BUHT-tehr-nuht squwash). *USA.* A hard rind, winter squash with a buttery taste; must peel before using.

butter swirls (BUHT-ehr swehrls). *USA.* The result of a technique to slightly thicken a sauce by swirling unsalted butter in the sauce, bit by bit, making a visible spiral in the hot sauce as it melts.

Butterreis (BOO-tur-rais). *Ger.* Rice.

Butterteig (BOO-tur-taik). *Ger.* Puff pastry.

button mushroom (BUHT-uhn MUSH-rohm). *USA.* A variety of cultivated mushroom with pure white flesh and a round, half-ball shaped smooth cap.

cabbage (KAH-bahj). *USA.* A leafy garden plant with a short stem and a dense globular head; eaten raw or cooked. Varieties include green, Chinese, celery, red, savoy, bok choy, Swiss chard, pe tsai.

cabello de ángel (kah-BHAY-loh day AHN-khayl). *Spa.* "Angel's Head"; a squash pudding.

cabidela (kah-bee-DAY-lah). *Por.* Sauce made with chicken blood.

cabillaud (kah-bee-yoa). *Fre.* Fresh cod.

cabra (KAH-brah). *Spa, Por.* Goat.

Cabrales (kah-BRAH-layss). *Spa.* A goats' milk cheese, blue-veined, earthy, pungent, mellow.

cabrito (kah-BREE-toh). *Spa, Por.* Kid, young goat.

caça (CAH-ssa). *Por.* Wild game.

cacao (kah-kah-oa). *Fre, Ita, Dut.* Cocoa.

cacao (kah-KA-oh). *USA.* The dried, partially fermented fatty seeds of the cacao tree, used for making chocolate, cocoa, and cocoa butter.

cacau (ka-KAoo). *Por.* Cocoa, usually made very sweet.

cacciagione (kaht-chah-JOA-nay). *Ita.* Game.

cacciatora (koch-a-TORE-re). *Ita.* Prepared in a spicy tomato sauce with a minimum number of ingredients such as a hunter would have on hand.

cacerola (kah-seh-ROH-lah). *Mex.* Casserole.

Caciocavallo (kah-choa-kah-VAHL-loa). *Ita.* A cows' whole-milk cheese, straw-colored, delicate and sweet to pungent depending on age; good as table cheese or for cooking; sometimes smoked.

caciucco (kah-cee-OOK-choa). *Ita.* Highly seasoned fish soup served with rounds of garlic-flavored toast.

cadas (ahds). *Ara.* Lentils.

Caesar salad (CEE-zuhr SAHL-lahd). *USA.* A tossed salad of romaine, garlic, anchovies, croutons; served with a dressing of olive oil, coddled egg, lemon juice, and grated Parmesan cheese.

café (kah-fay). *Fre, Por.* Coffee.

café (kah-FEH). *Spa.* Coffee.

café au lait (kaf-fay-ah-leh). *Fre.* Coffee with hot milk.

café cargado (kaf-FEH kar-GAH-doh). *Spa.* Strong coffee.

café Carioca (kah-FEH ca-ree-O-ca). *Por.* Coffee diluted with hot water.

café com crême e açúcar (kah-FEH com krem eh a-SOO-kar). *Por.* Coffee with cream and sugar.

café com leite (kah-FEH com late). *Por.* Coffee with hot milk.

café complet (kah-fay kom-pleh). *Fre.* The traditional continental breakfast of coffee and rolls.

café con panna e zucchero (kahf-FAI kon PAHN-nah un TSOOK-kay-roa). *Ita.* Coffee with cream and sugar.

café dé bil (kaf-FEH day behl). *Spa.* Weak coffee.

café double (kah-fay dewbl). *Fre.* Double-strength coffee.

café frappé (kah-fay frah-pay). *Fre.* Iced coffee.

café noir (kah-fay nwahr). *Fre.* Black coffee; after dinner coffee.

café simples (kah-FE H SEE-plesh). *Por.* Black coffee.

cafézinho (kah-feh-ZEE-nyoh). *Por.* Small cup of black coffee.

caffè (kahf-FAI). *Ita.* Coffee.

caffè espresso (kahf-FAI ex-SPRES-so). *Ita.* An especially strong coffee prepared by forcing steam under pressure through the powdered coffee causing the moisture to fall into the cup, then condense to form the beverage; requires a special espresso maker.

caffelatte (kahf-fai-LAHT-tay). *Ita.* Coffee with hot milk.

caffè nero (kahf-FAI NAY-roa). *Ita.* Black coffee.

caife (KA-fee). *Iri.* Coffee

cai juan (caeh juan). *Chi.* A pancakelike wrapper around a filling of finely chopped pork, shrimp, vegetables, bean sprouts, water chestnuts, grated fresh ginger, seasoned with soy sauce, then fried. Also known as egg roll.

caille (kahy). *Fre.* Quail.

caillé (kah-yea). *Fre.* Curd.

cáis (kaash). *Iri.* Cheese. Also spelled cáise.

caju (kah-ZHU). *Por.* Cashew nut.

Cajun (KAY-gjuhn). *USA.* A hot, spicy cuisine famous in southern Louisiana.

cake (kahk). *USA.* A leavened sweet batter or dough put into small flat pans, then baked; usually stacked in layers, and covered with icing or frosting.

cake (kayk). *Dut.* Cake.

cake flour (kak flowr). *USA.* Milled from soft wheat; very fine granulation; low protein content; low gluten content; bakes to a crumbly texture.

calabacita (kah-lah-bah-SEE-tah). *Spa.* Zucchini.

calabash (KAH-lah-bahsh). *Spa.* Passion fruit.

calabaza (kah-lah-BAH-tha). *Spa.* Pumpkin; any large squash.

calamaretti (kah-lah-mah-RAYT-tee). *Ita.* Small squid.

calamari (kah-lah-MAA-ree). *Ita.* Squid.

calamondin (kahl-eh-MAHN-dehn). *USA.* A Philippine variety of tangerine, the size of a kumquat.

calas (KAH-lahs). *USA.* A breakfast confection of rice mixed with flour, spices, and sugar, dropped from a spoon and deep-fried; a New Orleans specialty.

calcium chloride (KAHL-ce-um CHLO-ride). *USA.* A firming compound used by commercial canners, especially in tomatoes.

caldeirada (kahl-day-RAH-dah). *Por.* Fish soup with different kinds of fish, onions, potatoes, and olive oil; the Portugese bouillabaisse.

calderata (kahl-deh-RAH-tah). *Spa.* A thick fish stew.

caldo (KAHL-doa). *Ita.* Hot.

caldo (KAHL-doh). *Spa.* Broth.

caldo de carne (KAHL-doo duh KAHR-nee). *Por.* Meat bouillon.

caldo de gallina (kahl-doh day gahl-LEE-nah). *Spa.* Chicken broth.

caldo verde (KAHL-doo vAIrd). *Por.* Green soup; made with mashed potatoes and finely chopped green vegetables.

calibougas (kah-lee-BOO-gahs). *USA.* A beverage of rum, spruce beer, and molasses.

caliente (kahl-LEEN-tah). *Spa.* Hot.

California dry chili (Cahl-eh-FORN-yah dri CHILL-e). *USA.* A long chili that has been left on the vine to dry; turns red.

Californian chili (Cahl-eh-FORN-eh-un CHILL-le). *USA.* A fairly hot, greenish-yellow Mexican chili pepper; used fresh or canned, but never dried. Also known as guero, sweet green pepper.

calimyrna fig (kahl-eh-MURN-a fehg). *USA.* A small, amber-skinned fig with a sweet, nut-like flavor; eaten fresh, in fruit salads, or in preserves and chutney; goes well with poultry, lamb and rice dishes.

callaloo (cahl-LAH-loh). *Spa.* A Carribean stew of the leafy green tops of taro, cooked with okra, eggplant, tomatoes, onions, garlic, chilies, spices, herbs, meat, crab, and coconut milk.

callos (KAH-lyoass). *Spa.* Tripe.

calmar (kahl-mahr). *Fre.* Squid.

Calvados (kahl-vah-doa). *Fre.* Apple brandy.

calzone (KAHL-zone). *Ita.* A savory stuffed turnover made of pizza dough.

camarão (kah-mah-ROW). *Por.* Shrimp.

camarón (kah-mah-ROH-neh). *Spa.* Shrimp.

cambric tea (KAHM-brehk tee). *USA.* A drink of hot water, milk, sugar, and maybe a dash of tea; a thin, white beverage, as cambric is a thin, white fabric; usually given to children to make them feel part of the social gathering.

Cambridge sauce (KAM-brehg sahus). *Bri.* A mayonnaise-based sauce of sieved hard-boiled egg yolks, anchovies, capers, chives, chervil, mustard, and spices; served with cold meat.

Camembert (kahm-ehm-behr). *Fre.* A cows' milk cheese, pale yellow, soft, creamy, rich; crusty exterior; has white mold rind.

camote (kah-MOH-teh). *Spa.* Sweet potato.

campagnola (kahm-pahg-NOA-lah). *Ita.* Country style.

Canadian bacon (kah-NAH-dee-un BAY-kon). *USA.* Cut from the boned pork loin, which is cured then smoked, fully-cooked, and sliced. Also known as Canadian-style bacon.

canapé (kahn-nah-pay). *Fre.* Appetizer served either hot or cold as an hors d'oeuvre and eaten with fingers.

canapé (kah-nah-PEH). *Mex.* Appetizer, hors d'oeuvre.

canard (kahn-nahrd). *Fre.* Duck.

canard sauvage (kahn-nahrd soa-vahjg). *Fre.* Wild duck.

candito (kahn-DEE-toa). *Ita.* Candied.

candy (KAN-dee). *USA.* To preserve or cook with heavy syrup. To cook with sugar and fat to achieve a glaze, as with carrots and sweet potatoes. A confection.

canela (kah-NEH-lah). *Spa.* Cinnamon.

Canestrato (kah-neh-STRAH-toa). *Ita.* A strong flavored popular Sicilian cheese.

cane syrup (kane SEHR-up). *USA.* Syrup made from the concentrated sap of sugar cane; can be substituted for molasses.

caneton (kahn-er-tawng). *Fre.* Duckling.

cangrejo (kahn-GREH-khoa). *Spa.* Crab.

canistel (kah-NEHS-stuhl). *USA.* An egg-shaped fruit with a thin, glossy skin covering pumpkin-colored flesh that is somewhat flaky; flavor similar to sweet potato mixed with heavy cream; mixes well fresh with orange slices, almonds and coconut.

canja de galinha (KAHN-zah duh gah-LEE-nah). *Por.* A rich chicken soup.

canned ham (kahnd hahm). *USA.* Various ham cuts that have been processed and completely cooked before canning.

cannèlla (kahn-NEHL-lah). *Ita.* Cinnamon.

cannelle (kahn-nehl). *Fre.* Cinnamon.

cannellini (kahn-eh-LEE-nee). *Ita.* White kidney beans.

cannelloni (kahn-eh LONE-ee). *Ita.* Pasta tubes with a savory stuffing, baked in a sauce.

cannoli (ka-NO-le). *Ita.* Deep-fried horn-shaped pastry stuffed with cheese, chocolate, pudding, or whipped cream.

Cantal (cahn-tah). *Fre.* A cows' milk cheese with a nutty, full flavor, cylindrical in shape; similar to Cheddar.

cantaloupe (KAN-tah-lope). *USA.* Muskmelon.

canterellen (kahn-tuh-REL-luh). *Dut.* Chanterelles.

cantucci (kahn-TOO-cee). *Ita.* Hard-textured sweet cookies with almond pieces. Also known as cantuccini, biscotti di prato.

cao-mí (tsao may). *Chi.* Strawberries.

caoireoil (KEE-ry-awil). *Iri.* Mutton.

capão (kah-PAHNG). *Por.* Capon.

capeado (kah-pay-AH-doh). *Spa.* Dipped in batter and fried.

capelan (kah-peh-lah). *Fre.* Fish resembling smelts but of the cod family.

capelli d'angelo (kahp-PAYL-lee dahn-GEHL-o). *Ita.* Angel hair pasta.

capellini (kah-payl-LEE-nee). *Ita.* Thin noodles.

capers (KA-purr). *USA.* The flower buds of the caper plant, pickled for use as a garnish or flavoring.

capilotade (kahp-ee-loa-tahd). *Fre.* A kind of hashed game or chicken.

capirotada (kah-pee-roh-TAH-dah). *Mex.* Bread pudding.

capitone (kah-pay-TOA-nee). *Ita.* Large conger eel.

capocollo (kah-poa-KOAL-loa). *Ita.* Cooked, boneless pork butt that has been rolled in spices and pepper and is served in thin slices.

capon (KA-pahn). *USA.* A castrated male chicken; well fattened; distinctive taste. Also see broiler, cock, fryer, roaster, stag chicken and stewing chicken.

caponata (kah-poa-NAH-tah). *Ita.* A vegetable salad of fried eggplant, onions, tomatoes, anchovies, capers, and olives.

capozella (kah-poa-ZEHL-lah). *Ita.* Lamb's head.

cappelletti (cahp-ah-LET-tee). *Ita.* A moist, stuffed pasta usually served in soup; said to resemble "little hats"; similar to tortellini.

capperi (kahp-PAY-ree). *Ita.* Capers.

cappone (kahp-POA-nay). *Ita.* Capon.

cappon magro (KAHP-pon MAHG-roa). *Ita.* An elaborate salad of cooked vegetables, anchovies, fish, lobster, and garlic-rubbed biscuits.

cappuccino (kahp-pook-CHEE-noa). *Ita.* Espresso coffee with hot frothy milk, sprinkled with cinnamon and cocoa.

câpres (kah-preh). *Fre.* Capers.

capretto (kah-PREH-toa). *Ita.* Kid, young goat.

Caprino Formaggio (kah-PREE-noa Foar-MAHD-joa). *Ita.* Goat cheese.

capriolo (kah-pree-O-loa). *Ita.* Roebuck, deer.

capsicum (KAP-ci-kom). *USA.* A genus of chili peppers.

caracoles (kahr-rah-LOHL-ehs). *Spa.* Snails.

carambola (kah-rahm-BOH-la). *USA.* A tropical fruit with glossy, yellow, waxy skin; very juicy, crisp, almost translucent flesh; has five longitudinal ribs, when sliced across is star shaped. Also called starfruit.

caramel (kahr-a-mehl). *Fre.* A coloring substance made by boiling sugar in water until a rich dark brown color; used in candy, desserts, sauces, stocks.

caramelize (KAR-mah-liz). *USA.* To heat sugar until a brown color and a characteristic flavor develops.

caramelized sugar (KAR-mah-lizd SCHU-gahr). *USA.* The seventh stage of sugar crystallization: begins at 310°F to 338°F, between these temperatures syrup turns dark golden, but it will turn black at 350°F.

caramella (kah-rah-MEHL-lah). *Ita.* Caramel, or any hard candy.

caramelo (kah-rah-MAY-loo). *Por.* Caramel.

caranguejo (kah-rehn-GAY-zhoh). *Por.* Crab.

caraway (KAHR-ah-way). *USA.* An herb that produces a black, ribbed seed used for brewing tea, baking, flavoring meats and vegetables, and flavoring the liqueur kummel; leaves used in salads and soups.

carbonado (kahr-boh-NAH-doh). *Spa.* An Argentine stew made of beef, apples, pears, potatoes, tomatoes, and onions.

carbonara (kahr-boa-NAHR-ah). *Ita.* A spaghetti sauce made of cream, bacon, eggs, and Parmesan.

carbonnade (kahr-bon-nahd). *Fre.* Stewed or braised meat.

carbonnade flamande (kahr-bon-nahd flah-mahngd). *Fre.* A beef stew made of bacon, onions, and brown sugar and simmered in beer.

carciòfi (kah-CHO-fee). *Ita.* Artichokes.

cardamom (KARD-ah-mahm). *USA.* A Middle Eastern herb of the ginger family with an aromatic fruit whose seeds are used as a condiment and a flavoring.

cardinal (kahr-dee-nahl). *Fre.* A red-colored sauce used for fish garnish; made of mushrooms, truffle slices; usually hen lobsters are used to get the naturally red tint.

cardinal fish (KAR-dee-null feesch). *USA.* A red mullet found in the Mediterranean, called king of the mullets; very similar to the redfish found on the East and Gulf coasts of the United States.

cardinal suppe (kahr-dee-NAHL ssewpper). *Nor.* Creamy soup with bits of ham and noodles.

cardon (kahr-dawng). *Fre.* Cardoon.

cardoni (kar-DOHN-nee). *USA.* A member of the thistle family; looks somewhat like celery; has artichoke-like flavor; use cooked, diced in salads, deep-fried or marinated.

cardoon (kahr-dawng). *Fre.* A vegetable grown for its fleshy, silver-gray stalks that grow in bunches, like celery; stalks are flat, long, wide, with notched sides, suedelike finish; a relative of the artichoke; also spelled cardon.

cari (kah-ree), *Fre.* Curry; many times spelled "curry".

carmine (kahr-meen). *Fre.* Red coloring used in confectionery.

carnab (AR-nab). *Ara.* Rabbit.

carne (KAHR-neh). *Ita, Spa, Por.* Meat.

carne asada en horno (KAHR-neh ah-SAH-dah en OHR-noh). *Spa.* Baked meat.

carne asada en parrilla (KAHR-neh ah-SAH-dah en pahr-REE-yah). *Spa.* Boiled meat.

carne de cerdo (KAR-neh dah SEHR-doh). *Mex.* A dish of pork and corn.

carne de porco à Algarvia (KAHR-nuh duh POR-koo ah al-GAHR-veeah). *Por.* Fried pork and clams.

carne de vinha de Alhos (KAHR-nuh duh VEE-nyah duh AH-lious). *Por.* Pickled pork dish.

carne in umido (KAHR-nay un OO-mee-doa). *Ita.* Stewed beef.

carneiro (kahr-NAY-roh). *Por.* Mutton.

carne lessa (KAHR-nay LAYS-sah). *Ita.* Boiled beef.

carne picada (KAHR-nuh peek-AH-da). *Por.* Chopped or minced meat.

carne tritata (KAHR-nay tray-TAH-toa). *Ita.* Minced meat.

carob (KAHR-uhb). *USA.* Pods of the Mediterranean evergreen locust tree, high in protein and sugar, eaten fresh and dried; used as a chocolate substitute; locust bean.

carob flour (KAHR-uhb flowr). *USA.* A chocolate flavored flour or powder milled from the carob tree pod; a nutritious, low fat substitute for chocolate.

Carolina rice (kahr-oh-li-nah ris). *USA.* A variety of rice, long-grained, angular, white, bright, and shiny.

caroline (kah-o-leen). *Fre.* Small eclair, served as an hors d'oeuvre.

carota (kah-RAW-tah). *Ita.* Carrots.

carottes (kah-rot). *Fre.* Carrots.

carottes Flamandes (kah-rot flah-mohnd). *Fre.* Creamed carrots, in the Flemish style.

carp (karp). *USA.* A freshwater fish found in Asia, Europe, and the United States; unless farmed has a muddy taste.

carpa (KAHR-pah). *Ita.* Carp. Also called carpione.

carpaccio (kahr-paak-CHEE-o). *Ita.* Raw beef filet sliced very, very thin; served with mustard sauce, or oil and lemon juice.

carp caviar (kahrp kah-vee-AHR). *USA.* A caviar substitute; the roe or eggs of the carp.

carpe (kahrp). *Fre.* Carp.

carpeau (kahrp-oa). *Fre.* Small carp.

carpione (kahr-pee-O-neh). *Ita.* Carp. Also called carpe.

carrageenan (KAHR-ah-ghee-nahn). *USA.* A seaweed of North America and northern Europe; reddish-purple, white when dried; eaten fresh or dried; excellent source of gelatin; used in sweet and savory dishes; Irish moss.

carré d'agneau (kah-ray dah-noa). *Fre.* Rack of lamb.

carrelet (kah-rer-leh). *Fre.* Flounder, plaice.

carrettes (KAHR-rhettz). *USA.* Small very sweet carrots about 1 to 2 inches long. Also known as French carrots.

carrot (KAHR-roht). *USA.* A root vegetable that is orange; has mild, sweet taste; use cooked or raw in salads.

carrots Vichy (KAHR-rohtz VEE-chee). *USA.* Pared and sliced carrots prepared in Vichy water and glazed.

carte du jour (kahrt dew zuhr). *Fre.* The bill of fare for the day.

casaba (kah-SAH-bah). *Ara.* A Turkish, globular-shaped winter melon with chartruse-yellow rind that wrinkles at the pointed end; flesh is thick, soft, creamy-white, sweet, and juicy.

casal (AH-sal). *Ara.* Honey.

casalinga (kah-sah-LEEN-gah). *Ita.* Homemade.

cascabel (KAHS-sah-behl). *Mex.* A small, round, dried chili pepper with reddish-brown skin; fairly hot; the seeds rattle in the dried pod.

cashew (KASH-u). *USA.* A kidney-shaped nut favored in Indian, Asian and South American cooking; used to make wine, vinegar and liqueur.

casing (KA-sing). *USA.* A natural or synthetic membranous case used for sausage forcemeat.

casiyr (a-SEER). *Ara.* Juice.

cassata (kas-SAA-tah). *Ita.* A rich chocolate dessert of sponge cake, cut in layers, filled with a mixture of ricotta cheese, candied fruits, chopped chocolate, and a liqueur.

cassava (kah-SAH-vah). *Spa.* A tropical tree whose root is used to make flour for bread and tapioca pearls for thickening soups and puddings; a pure starch.

casserole (cahss-rohl). *Fre.* A dish served in a bowl or pan, made with rice, pastry crust, or pasta, and filled with minced meat, vegetables, seafood, or cheese, that is usually baked then served.

casseruola (kas-say-RWO-lah). *Ita.* Casserole.

cassia (KASH-e). *USA.* A reddish-brown spice often confused with cinnamon.

cassis (kahs-seess). *Fre.* Black currant liqueur.

cassoulet (kass-oo-lcht). *Fre.* Garlic flavored bean stew usually containing sausages, poultry, and meat.

castagna (kah-STAA-nah). *Ita.* Chestnut.

castagnaccio (kah-staa-nahk-CHEE-o). *Ita.* A sweet cake made with chestnut flour, pine kernels, and currants.

castagnaci (kah-staa-NAH-chee). *Ita.* Fritters or waffles made of chestnut flour.

castagnoles (kahs-tahg-nyohl). *Fre.* Batter fritters.

castanhas (kahss-TAH nyahss). *Por.* Chestnuts.

castigane alla fiamma (kah-stee-GAH-nay AHL-lah fee-AHM-mah). *Ita.* Brandied chestnuts.

castor sugar (KAHSS-tohr SCHU-gawr). *Bri.* Superfine sugar.

castradina (cah-strah-DEE-nah). *Ita.* Mutton. Also called castrato.

castrato (kah-STRAH-toa). *Ita.* Mutton. Also called castradina.

catalane, à la (kah-tahl-ahn). *Fre.* A garnish of sauteed eggplants and rice pilaf served on large cuts of meats.

catfish (KAT-fehsh). *USA.* A fresh- and saltwater fish with no scales, whiskers, delicate flesh, and very few bones.

caudle (KAHU-dull). *Bri.* A hot spice drink of wine or ale with bread or gruel, eggs, and sugar added.

caul (kahl). *Fre.* The thin, fatty, lacy membrane from a pig's or lamb's intestines, used to contain and cover pâtés or roasts; melts away during cooking.

cauliflower (KAUL-ee-flawr). *USA.* A garden plant grown for its compact edible head of white undeveloped flowers.

cavallucci di siena (kah-vahl-LOO-chee dee cee-N-ah). *Ita.* Small cakes made of honey, candied fruit, and nuts.

caveau (kah-voh). *Fre.* A little cellar for keeping fine wines.

caviale (kah-vee-AH-lay). *Ita.* Dried fish roe; a local caviar substitute.

caviar (kav-ee-AHR). *Fre.* The salted roe or eggs of the sturgeon or other large fish, pressed, and used as relish. See also specific varieties: beluga, malosol, oscietr, pausnaya, sevruga, ship, and sterlet; caviar substitutes: carp, herring, hon tarako, karasumi, and lumpfish are listed in this volume.

cavolfiore (kah-voal-fee-OA-ray). *Ita.* Cauliflower.

cavolfiore alla romana (kah-voal-fee-OA-ray AHL-loa roa-MAH-nah). *Ita.* Cauliflower in oil.

cavolfiore alla villeroy (kah-voal-fee-OA-ray AHL-loa veel-lay-ROA-ee). *Ita.* Cauliflower with lemon sauce.

cavolfiore indorato e fritto (kah-voal-fee-OA-ray een-doa-RAH-toa ay FREET-toa). *Ita.* Breaded, fried cauliflower.

cavolini di bruxelles. (kah-voa-LEE-nee dee broos-SAYL). *Ita.* Brussels sprouts.

cavolo (KAA-voa-loa). *Ita.* Cabbage.

cavolrapa (kah-voal-RAH-pah). *Ita.* Kohlrabi.

cavroman (kahv-ROA-mahn). *Ita.* Mutton or lamb stew, with potatoes, pepper, and onions.

cayenne pepper (ki-ANN PEP-per). *Mex.* Dried red chili pepper, finely ground; also used fresh.

cazuela (kah-SWEH-lah). *Spa.* Earthenware casserole.

cebiche (theh-BEE-cheh). *Spa.* Raw fish or shellfish marinated in lime juice; not cooked by heat, but by chemical reaction of lime juice.

cebolas (say-BOH-lah). *Por.* Onions.

cebolla (theh-BOH-lah). *Spa.* Onion.

Cebreto (theh-BREH-tou). *Spa.* A blue-veined cheese; yellow rind; creamy paste.

ceche (CHEE-chay). *Ita.* Very tiny, young eels, fried with garlic and sage, or mixed with eggs and flour and served as little pancakes.

ceci (CHAY-chee). *Ita, Spa.* Chick-peas; garbanzo beans.

cefalo (kay-FAH-lee). *Ita.* Gray mullet.

celeriac (seh-LEHR-e-ahk). *USA.* Celery root; a variety of celery having a large edible root.

céleri-rave (seh-ler-ree-rahv). *Fre.* Celery root.

celery (SELL-ree). *USA.* An herb of the carrot family with leafstalks eaten raw or cooked.

celery root (SELL-ree root). *USA.* A large, bulb-type root with light brown skin and white flesh; eaten raw or cooked; also known as celeric.

celery seed (SELL-ree seed). *USA.* The seed of the celery plant; used in the pickling process as a seasoning.

celestine (see-les-teen). *Fre.* A garnish for clear soup, consisting of fine strips of fried pancakes.

cellophane noodles (cehl-lo-FAHNE NOO-duhls). *USA.* Oriental translucent noodles made from mung beans.

celtuce (cehl-TUSS). *USA.* A stem lettuce; use only the stem or seedstalk; use raw or braised, as waterchestnuts; very high vitamin C content.

cenci (CHEH-chee). *Ita.* Fried sweets.

cenders (sohn-druh). *Fre.* Baked in hot ashes.

cenouras (seh-NOH-rahss). *Por.* Carrots.

centollos (theen-TOHL-loas). *Spa.* Crabs.

cèpe (sehp). *Fre.* Boletus mushroom.

cerdo (THEHR-doa). *Spa.* Pork; used interchangably with puerco.

cerdo (SAYR-doo). *Por.* Wild boar.

cereal (CEH-ree-uhl). *USA.* Grain suitable for food; also, prepared foodstuff made from grain, such as oatmeal, grits, cornflakes, or branflakes; eaten hot or cold.

cereal cream (CEH-ree-uhl kreem). *USA.* Cream containing 10.5-18% milk-fat; same as half-and-half.

cerejas (say-RAY-zhahss). *Por.* Cherries.

cerezas (thay-RAY-thahss). *Spa.* Cherries.

cerfeuil (sehr-fuhy). *Fre.* Chervil.

ceriman (CEH-ree-muhm). *USA.* The fruit of the subtropical plant commonly known as the split-leaf philodendron; has a cucumber-shaped fruit, covered with tiny hexagonal platelets that fall off when ripe, soft, juicy flesh tastes like fresh pineapple and ripe banana; eat fresh or use as a chutney base. Also known as monstera.

cerise (suh-reez). *Fre.* Cherry.

cernaux confits (sehr-noh kon-fees). *Fre.* Pickled green walnuts.

cervelas (sehr-veh-la). *Fre.* A garlic-flavored pork sausage.

Cervelatwurst (SEHR-veh-layt-voorst). *Ger.* Spiced beef and pork sausage.

cervelle (sehr-vehl). *Fre.* Brains, usually from calf or lamb.

cerveza (thayr-BHAY-thah). *Mex.* Beer.

cèrvo (CHEH-voa). *Ita.* Venison.

cestino da viaggio (cheh-STEE-noa dah vee-ahg-JEE-o). *Ita.* Picnic lunch to take on a trip.

cetriòlo (chay-tree-O-loa). *Ita.* Cucumber.

cha (chah). *Jap.* Tea.

chá (shah). *Por.* Tea.

chá (tsah). *Chi.* Tea.

Chabichou (shah-bee-shoo). *Fre.* A soft, mild goat's milk cheese, conical or cylindrical in shape.

chah (chah). *Ind.* Tea.

chahr ziu (chaah dsda-ow). *Chi.* Barbecued pork.

chai (CHYAH-yoo). *Rus.* Tea.

chair blanc (sher blan). *Fre.* White meat.

chair noire (sherr nawr). *Fre.* Dark meat.

challah (HKAH-lah). *Jew.* A braided egg bread, traditional on the Sabbath.

chalota (shah-LOU-tah). *Por.* Green onion.

chalupa (chah-LOO-pah). *Mex.* Oval- or boat-shaped tortilla dough, pinched up around edge and filled.

chamomile (KAHM-oh-mehl). *USA.* A small fragrant plant with daisylike flowers that produce a delightful apple-scented tea.

champ (chahmp). *Iri.* Mashed potatoes beaten to a light foam, combined with some cooked vegetables (usually cabbage or onions), and served with a huge dollop of melting butter in the center.

champagne grapes (sham-PAIN grahpz). *USA.* A variety of grapes that are tiny, like currants, with a very sweet flavor; used as garnish on plates, on beverage glasses, or on cheese boards; not the wine grape.

champanhe (sham-PAH-nyay). *Por.* Champagne.

champignons (shahng-peen-yawn). *Fre, Ger, Dut.* Mushrooms.

champiñon (sham-pee-NYOHN). *Mex.* Mushroom.

channa. (CHAH-nah). *Ind.* Chick-peas.

chanquettes. (chahn-KAH-tays). *Spa.* Tiny fried fish.

chanterelle (shang-tee-rell). *Fre.* A golden-orange, apricot scented, trumpet-shaped, wild mushroom with a ruffled edge.

chantilly (shang-tee-yeh). *Fre.* Served with whipped cream.

chantilly cream (shang-tee-yeh). *Fre.* Sweetened and flavored whipped cream.

chao (tsao). *Chi.* To stir-fry; sauté.

chao fan (tsao fan). *Chi.* Fried rice.

chao gwoo (tsao gwu). *Chi.* Straw mushrooms; is a bud containing a miniature mushroom; fresh, canned, dried.

chao jidàn (tsao gee-dan). *Chi.* Scrambled eggs.

chao miàn (chow mein). *Chi.* Fried noodles.

Chaource (shah-oorceh). *Fre.* A soft, creamy cheese produced in the Champagne district.

chao yùlánpiàn donggu (tsao yoo lan pien doong gu). *Chi.* Black mushrooms sautéed with bamboo shoots.

chap (shah). *Fre.* The lower jaw, or half of cheek of a pig.

chapati (cha-PAH-tee). *Ind.* Thin griddle-baked whole wheat bread.

chapelure (sha-pehl-lewr). *Fre.* Breadcrumbs made by crushing oven-dried bread with a rolling pin and passing through a sieve.

chapon (shah-pawng). *Fre.* The heel of bread rubbed with garlic, seasoned with oil and vinegar, added to salad.

char (shr). *USA.* A fat fish with very firm, delicate, white to deep red flesh; found in various deep lakes and rivers in the Northern Hemisphere; superior to salmon in taste.

charcoal-grilled (CHAR-koal-grield). *USA.* To cook over glowing charcoal embers, to impart that special flavor, usually done out-of-doors.

charcuterie (shahr-kew-ter-ree). *Fre.* Meat specialities of French butcher shops, such as sausages, ham, galantines, patés, rillettes.

charcutière (shahr-kew-tehr). *Fre.* A sauce of sauteed onions, white wine, vinegar, demi-glace, mustard with julienne gherkins added before serving; served with meats.

chard cabbage (chard CAHB-bahg). *USA.* Chinese cabbage.

charentais (shahr-ahng-tehs). *Fre.* A melon of yellow-green ribbed skin, orange flesh; sweet, succulent.

charlotte (shahr-loht). *Fre.* A dish of custard.

charlotte russe (shahr-loht rews). *Fre.* A dessert made in a mold lined with cake slices or lady fingers, filled with a custard, whipped cream, and strawberries on top.

charni (CHAR-nee). *Ind.* Chutney.

Chartreuse (shahr-truz). *Fre.* Liqueur made of angelica leaves, hyssop, cinnamon bark, balm, mace, and saffron.

chartreuse ragoût (shahr-truz raa-GOO). *Dan.* A casserole of prettily arranged carrots, cabbage and meat or chicken.

chá shao bao (cha shaoo baoo). *Chi.* Steamed bun stuffed with roast pork.

chasseur (shahs-sur). *Fre.* A garnish of mushrooms, sliced and sauteed, flavored with shallots and moistened with white wine.

chat (chaht). *Ind.* A cold dish made with vegetables, fruits, and spices; eaten as a snack or appetizer.

châtaignes (shah-tayg-nehs). *Fre.* Chestnuts.

chateaubriand (shah-toa-bree-ahng). *Fre.* A superb thick filet steak, served with a brown sauce of fat, lemon, parsley, seasonings, and Spanish sauce.

château potatoes (SHAH-toe po-TA-toes). *USA.* Potatoes cut in long strips and cooked in butter.

charni (CHAR-nee). *Ind.* Chutney.

chaud (sho). *Fre.* Hot.

chaud-froid (sho-fro). *Fre.* Chicken fricassee served cold, covered with its gravy, glazed with aspic.

chaunk gobhi (chawnk GOHB-hee). *Ind.* Brussels sprouts.

chausson aux pommes (sho-so oa pom). *Fre.* Apple turnover.

Chavignol (shah-vee-nah). *Fre.* A small, soft goat's milk cheese; semihard to hard; aging brings out goaty flavor.

chawal (CHAH-val). *Ind.* Rice.

chayote (chah-YOH-teh). *Mex.* Pear-shaped vegetable.

Cheddar (CHEDD-ehr). *Bri.* A cows' whole milk, hard cheese with a smooth texture, orange color, and a flavor ranging from mild to sharp, depending on age.

cheese (chez). *USA.* A generic term for the products made from milk curd separated from whey, sometimes fermented, usually molded under pressure, and ripened for use as food; countless varieties worldwide.

cheesecake (CHEZ-kak). *USA.* A cake made with a mixture of beaten eggs, cream cheese or cottage cheese, sugar, flavorings; baked in a mold lined with sweet crumbs.

chef's salad (chehfs SAH-lahd). *USA.* Mixed green salad with hard-boiled egg and julienne meats added.

chemise (sher-meez). *Fre.* With skins on; generally applies to potatoes; ice cream covered with a thin coating.

chemiser (shuh-mee-zyay). *Fre.* To coat a mold; with aspic, breadcrumbs, ice cream, and so forth.

chenna (CHAY-nah). *Ind.* Chhena.

cherba-bel-frik (SHUR-ba-beel-freek). *Afr.* Green corn soup.

chereshnya (VEESH-nyee). *Rus.* Cherry.

cherimoya (che-ree-MOY-a). *Spa.* A sweet, low-acid tasting fruit with silky smooth, juicy, and cream-colored flesh that is slightly granular like a custard of fine pears. Also known as custard apple, white sapote.

Cherries Jubilee (CHEH-reez JUB-eh-lee). *USA.* An elegant dessert of vanilla ice cream topped with a flaming sweet-cherry sauce.

cherry (CHEH-ree). *USA.* The fruit of a cherry tree; sour or pie cherries are of the Morello and Montmorency varieties; sweet cherries the Black Tartarian and Napoleon.

Cherry Heering (CHEHR-ree HEER-eng). *Dan.* Cherry brandy.

cherry tomatoes (CHEH-ree toh-MAH-tohs). *USA.* A variety of tomatoes that is tasty, globular, about one inch in diameter; available in red, pink, or yellow.

chervil (CHUR-vul). *USA.* An herb of the parsley family; delicate flavor; slightly aniselike; use fresh for fullest flavor.

Cheshire (CHESS-shur). *Bri.* A hard cows' milk cheese, made in colors: red, white, blue; called Chester on the continent.

Chester (chess-ter). *Fre.* Cheshire.

chestnut. (CHESS-nuht). *USA.* The edible nut of the chestnut tree; used for various culinary preparations, and in the confection of sweets and pastries.

cheston crappin (TSHEHS-tuhn KRAHP-pen). *Sco.* Chestnut stuffing.

cheveaux d'ange (sheh voh danj). *Fre.* Angel hair pasta, the thinnest vermicelli.

chèvre (shevr). *Fre.* Goats' milk cheese that is soft and fresh.

chevreuil (sherv-rery). *Fre.* Venison.

Chevrotin (sheh-vroh-teen). *Fre.* A dried goats' milk cheese, eaten year round.

chhena (CHAY-nah) *Ind.* A very fine grained, fresh cheese made from curdled milk; used for making Indian milk sweets. Also spelled chenna.

chícharo (CHEE-chah-roh). *Mex.* Pea.

chicharroón (chee-char-RROHN). *Mex.* Crisp-fried pork rind.

chicken (CHEH-kehn). *USA.* The common domestic fowl whose flesh is used for food. Also see broiler, capon, cock, fryer, pullet, roaster, stag chicken, and stewing chicken.

chicken cacciatore (CHEH-kehn kotch-ah-TORR-ree). *USA.* A dish in which the chicken is cooked with tomatoes and mushrooms.

chicken-fried steak (CHEH-kehn-frid-stahk). *USA.* Steak rolled in flour, dipped in egg batter, rolled in flour again, and fried crisp.

chicken Kiev (CHEH-kehn KEE-ev). *USA.* Chicken breast spread with herb butter, rolled, dipped in egg batter, rolled in breadcrumbs, and deep-fried.

chicken of the woods (CHEH-kehn of the woods). *USA.* A mushroom that is rather large and fan shaped; flesh is white or salmon-orange, with deep orange to yellow skin; must be cooked.

chicken paprika (CHEH-ken pahp-REE-kah). *USA.* The Hungarian dish, paprikas csirke, of chicken braised with onions and garlic, with plenty of paprika and sour cream.

chicken steak (CHEH-kehn stahk). *USA.* A cut of beef from the chuck, in small individual portions with a characteristic white streak down the center.

chicken tetrazzini (CHEH-kehn tet-tra-ZEE-neh). *USA.* Strips of cooked chicken and spaghetti in a sherry-flavored cream sauce with grated Parmesan.

chick-pea (CHEHK-pee). *USA.* A round legume, dried or fresh; used extensively in Mediterranean, Middle Eastern, Indian, and Mexican cooking; an important ingredient in couscous, hummus, and many soups and stews.

chicorée frisée (sheek-or-ray fri-zay). *Fre.* Curly-leaf chicory.

chicória (shee-KOU-reeah). *Por.* Chicory.

chicory (CHICK-oh-ree). *USA.* A plant whose long, tight fitting, bleached white leaves are used as a salad green; roots are commonly roasted, ground, mixed with coffee, or used alone as a coffee substitute. Also called curly endive.

Chicory escarole (CHICK-oh-ree ESS-cah-role). *USA.* Batavian endive; a bitterish salad green with closely packed greenish-white outer leaves which may look like celery ribs.

chiffon (schef-FAHN). *Fre.* Having a light delicate texture achieved by adding whipped egg whites or whipped gelatin.

chiffonade (sher-fon-NAHD). *Fre.* Minced or shredded vegetables or meat sprinkled over soups or salads.

chih mah (zhi ma). *Chi.* Sesame seeds, white or black.

chikin sarada (chee-KEEN sah-rah-dah). *Jap.* Chicken salad.

chikin supu (chee-KEEN soo-poo). *Jap.* Chicken soup.

chikuwa (che-KUH-wah). *Jap.* Fish paste.

chilaquiles (CHEE-lah-KEE-lehs). *Mex.* Dish made with stale tortillas.

chili (CHILL-lee). *USA.* The fruit of the Capsicum family, pepper plants; many varieties from mild to fiery hot; used in many cuisines throughout the world.

chili con carne (CHILL-lee kohn KAR-neh). *USA.* A spicy stew of ground beef, minced chilies, chili powder, with or without beans.

chili con queso (CHILL-ee kohn kaa-so). *USA.* Melted cheeses seasoned with finely chopped chilies; served very hot with tortilla chips.

chili powder (CHILL-e POW-der). *Mex.* A mixture of various dried herbs and spices and chili peppers used for seasoning; always includes cumin, oregano, coriander.

chilindrón (chee-leen-DROHN). *Spa.* A garnish of sweet red peppers, onions, tomatoes, garlic, and ham.

chill (chehl). *USA.* To reduce the temperature of a food by refrigerating until thoroughly cold.

chimichanga (chee-mee-CHAHN-gah). *Mex.* Like a burrito, but deep-fried.

chine (chineh). *USA.* The bony part, or backbone, adhering to the filet; usually cut away leaving only the muscle.

Chinese anise (chi-NEEZ ANN-ehs). *USA.* An herb whose star-shaped seeds are used for flavoring many oriental foods, meats, curries, confections, pickles; the oil is used for flavoring baked goods and ice cream. Also called star anise.

Chinese artichoke (chi-NEEZ AR-tee-chok). *USA.* A tuber that produces a mintlike plant; tuber is white, thin and crisp-fleshed; can be eaten raw or cooked.

Chinese beans (chi-NEEZ benz). *USA.* Long beans; bright green beans, about a foot long, flavor stronger than ordinary green beans. Also called asparagus beans.

Chinese cabbage (chi-NEEZ CAHB-bahg). *USA.* A Chinese vegetable that is slightly elongated, but chunky, with fairly white and wide ribs and frilly, dark green leaves; use alone or stir-fry. Also known as bái cài, bok choy, chard cabbage, Chinese mustard, dà báicài, shirona.

Chinese cinnabar melon (chi-NEEZ CEN-nee-bahr MEH-lun). *USA.* A melon with a deep red color, smooth texture; sweet, subtle flavor; ideal breakfast fruit or use in fresh fruit salads.

Chinese gooseberry (chi-NEEZ GOUS-bear-ri). *USA.* Kiwifruit.

Chinese mustard (chi-NEEZ MUHST-urd). *USA.* Chinese cabbage.

Chinese naval orange (chi-NEEZ NA-vuhl orange). *USA.* A sweet-flavored orange with a low-acid content; eaten fresh.

Chinese okra (chi-NEEZ OH-krah). *USA.* A dark green, heavily ridged okra, about 10-12 inches long, 1-inch diameter.

Chinese parsley (chi-NEEZ PARS-lee). *USA.* Coriander.

Chinese pea pods (chi-NEEZ pea pohds). *USA.* Snow peas.

Chinese red stew (chin-NEEZ rehd stu). *USA.* Meats cooked without browning in liquid that is half soy sauce and half water, seasoned with ginger, scallions and sherry; meat is colored during cooking; of Chinese origin.

Chinese sausages (chi-NEEZ sau-SAHGE). *USA.* Spicy pork sausages, about five inches long, reddish in color; sometimes dried.

Chinese spinach (chi-NEEZ SPEHN-itch). *USA.* A dark green leafy vegetable. Also called tampala.

chingchao mingzia (ching tsao ming sia). *Chi.* Sauteed prawns.

chinook (sheh-NOOK). *USA.* Member of the salmon family; most prized of North American species; tasty flesh, large flakes, high oil content, soft texture; best eaten au natural.

chinquapin (CHEHNK-ah-pehn). *USA.* Pine nut. Also known as crenata, Indian nut, pignola, and piñon.

chiodi di garofano (kee-O-dee dee gah-RO-fah-noh). *Ita.* Cloves.

chipolata (kee-poa-LAH-tah). *Ita.* Small Italian sausages.

chipolatas (shee-po-lah-tahs). *Fre.* Small pork sausages.

chipotle (chee-POT-tleh). *Mex.* Name of a smoked chili.

chipped beef (chehpt bef). *USA.* Flakes of dried beef; used to flavor foods and in cream sauce.

chips (chehpz). *Bri.* Deep-fried potato pieces.

chiqueter (shee-kwee-teh). *Fre.* To flute the rim or edge of pastry with a special knife or the fingertips.

chirashi zushi (chee-RAH-shee SOO-shee). *Jap.* A type of sushi that consists of rice filled or topped with bits or slices of various vegetables and seafood, arranged in a lacquer box.

chitterling (CHEHT-ehr-lehng). *USA.* The small intestines of pigs when prepared as food. Commonly called chitlings or chitlins.

chives (chivz). *USA.* An herb of the onion family; has tiny tubular leaves, delicate onionlike flavor; use finely chopped and raw.

chi zhi (cheh dzi). *Chi.* Black bean sauce.

chlodnik (CLOHD-nehk). *Pol.* A warm weather borsch made with beets, onions, cucumbers, seasonings; served cold with dollop of sour cream.

chocola (sho-ko-LAH). *Dut.* Chocolate.

chocolat (shok-kol-lah). *Fre.* Chocolate; used as a beverage.

chocolate (CHOHK-o-late). *USA.* Ground roasted cacao beans prepared for use as beverage, confection, coloring agent; available in several forms: candy coating, chips, squares, flakes, powder, blocks, sweet, semisweet, unsweetened. See also white chocolate.

chocos (SHOU-koos). *Por.* Squid.

chokladglass (shook-LAAD-glahss). *Swe.* Chocolate ice cream.

chokoreto (choh-KOH-reh-toh). *Jap.* Chocolate; (the flavor), as chocolate cake.

cholent (HKOHL-lent). *Jew.* A slowly cooked dish of brisket, potatoes, barley, and lima beans.

chongos (CHOAN-gos). *Spa.* A custard seasoned with lemon and cinnamon.

chop (chohp). *USA.* Cutting food into pieces less than ¼ inch with a knife or sharp tool. See cube, dice, and mince. Also, a small cut of meat usually including part of a rib.

chorizo (choh-REE-soh). *Mex.* Spicy sausage.

choron (shoa-rawng). *Fre.* A bearnaise sauce colored pink with tomato puree.

chota piaz (CHO-tah pih-YAZ). *Ind.* Shallot.

choti elaichi (CHO-tee ee-LIE-a-chee). *Ind.* Green cardamom; also white bleached cardamom.

chou (shoo). *Fre.* Cabbage.

choucroute (shoo-kroot). *Fre.* Sauerkraut.

chou farci (shoo fahr-see). *Fre.* Stuffed cabbage.

choufleur (shoo-flurr). *Fre.* Cauliflower.

chou rouge (shoo roozh). *Fre.* Red cabbage.

chouriço (shoh-REE-soh). *Por.* Pork sausage; one of numerous varieties.

choux de Bruxelles (shoo der brews-sehl). *Fre.* Brussels sprouts.

choux paste (shoo paste). *USA.* Cream puff pastry; a simple paste of flour, boiling water, beaten eggs, butter; pâté à choux.

chowchow (CHOW-chow). *USA.* A mustard-flavored vegetable pickle.

chowder (CHOW-der). *USA.* A thick soup of fish, meat or vegetables, to which salt pork, milk, diced vegetables, even bread and crackers may be added.

chow fun (chow fuhn). *Chi.* Wide, flat rice noodles.

chow mein (chow meen). *USA.* A dish made of stewed vegetables and meat with fried noodles.

choysum (choy-sum). *Chi.* Chinese chard; bok choy heart, more tender than bok choy.

chub (chuhb). *USA.* A member of the whitefish family; correctly known in the United States as the cisco.

chuck (chuk). *USA.* A cut of beef from between the neck and shoulder.

chuka bifun (CHOO-koo BEE-fuhn). *Jap.* Thin translucent Chinese-style rice noodles.

chukandar (choo-KAHN-dahr). *Ind.* Red beets.

chuleta (choo-LEH-tah). *Spa.* A chop.

chun juan (chwon jwahn). *Chi.* Spring roll; a thin pastry wrapper stuffed variously, rolled up, deep fried.

churrasco (shoo-RRAHSS-koh). *Por.* Barbecue.

churros (choo-roaz). *Spa.* Deep-fried dough, flavored with cinnamon, rolled in sugar while hot.

chutney (CHUT-ne). *Ind.* A condiment, with a pureed texture; made of raisins, garlic, shallots, pimentos, apples, mustard, brown sugar pounded together in a mortar, then cooked in boiling vinegar.

cialde (chee-AHL-dey). *Ita.* Wafers.

ciboulette (cee-boo-layt). *Fre.* Chives.

cibreo (chee-RAY-oa). *Ita.* An ancient dish of cocks' combs and sweetbreads, served with a molded vegetable timbale.

cicely (SIS-eh-le). *USA.* An herb of the parsley family; anise-flavored leaves, stems, and seeds used in salads and bouquet garnis. Also called sweet cicely.

cichorei (see-cho-RYE). *Dut.* Chicory.

cicoria (chee-ko-REE-ah). *Ita.* Chicory; endive.

cider (SI-der). *USA.* Usually slightly fermented apple juice. Sweet cider is unfermented apple juice.

cider vinegar (SI-der ven-eh-gur). *USA.* Fermented apple juice with varying alcoholic content and often sparkling; 5–6% acetic acid; full-bodied.

cigala (thee-GAH-lahss). *Spa.* Saltwater crayfish.

cilantro (cee-LAHN-troh). *USA.* Fresh coriander.

cilantro (thee-LAHN-troh). *Spa.* Fresh coriander (leaves and stems).

ciliègia (chee-lee-AY-jay). *Ita.* Cherry.

cima ripiena (chee-mah ree-PEE-nah). *Ita.* Veal breast with a pocket cut and stuffed with various fillings.

Cincho (THEEN-cho). *Spa.* A hard and pungent ewes' milk cheese.

cinghiale (chee-ng-gee-AA-lay). *Ita.* Boar, usually braised, served with a sweet and sour sauce of vinegar and chocolate.

cinnamon (SIN-ah-mon). *USA.* The highly aromatic bark of a tree of the laurel family used as a spice.

cioccolata (choak-koa-LAA-tah). *Ita.* Chocolate.

cioppino (cheh-PEE-noh). *USA.* A fisherman's stew made with fish, lobster, shrimp, crab, mussels, clams, mushrooms, and seasonings; California fish stew.

cipollines (chee-pol-LEE-neez). *Ita.* Pearl onions, round in shape, belong to shallot and garlic family.

ciruelas (thee-RWAY-lahss). *Spa.* Plums.

ciruelas pasa (thee-RWAY-lahss PAH-ssahss). *Spa.* Prunes. Also called ciruelas secas.

cisco (SIS-co). *USA.* A member of the whitefish family, usually smoked. Commonly called chub.

ciseler (cee-zur-lay). *Fre.* To make incisions on the back of a fish to hasten its cooking; to cut in julienne strips, or to shred.

citroen (see-TROO-nuh). *Dut.* Lemon.

citrom (TSEE-trawm). *Hun.* Lemon.

citron (CEH-tron). *USA.* A type of lemon cultivated for its very thick skin, usually preserved and used in cake making and confectionery.

citron (cee-troa). *Fre, Dan, Swe.* Lemon.

citron fromage (see-TROAN froam-aa-sher). *Dan.* Lemon-flavored dessert.

citron kram (see-TROON kraam). *Swe.* Lemon dessert.

citronne (cee-tro-nay). *Fre.* Anything with the taste or flavor of lemon.

citron vert (cee-tro vehr). *Fre.* Lime.

citrus (CEH-trus). *USA.* Any of a genus of often thorny trees and shrubs of the rue family grown in warm regions for their edible fruit with firm, thick rind and pulpy flesh. Includes citron, grapefruit, lemon, lime, mandarin, orange, tangerine, ugli fruit, as well as any of these crossbred, such as tangelo, or temple orange.

ciuppin (thee-OO-peen). *Ita.* Variety of fish stew.

civet (cee-veh). *Fre.* A stew using furred game, cooked in red wine.

civet de lièvre (cee-veh der ljehvr). *Fre.* Hare or rabbit stewed in wine and herbs; commonly referred to as "jugged and stewed."

civette (cee-veht). *Fre.* Chives.

clabber (KLAH-ber). *USA.* Sour milk that has thickened and curdled but not separated from the whey.

clafouti (clah-foo tee). *Fre.* A fruit pastry made of cherries baked in custard.

clam (klahm). *USA.* Bivalve mollusk of many varieties; includes hard-shell (e.g., quahog and cherrystones) and soft-shell.

Clamart (clah-mahr). *Fre.* A garnish of peas.

clambake (KLAIIM-bak). *USA.* Process of steaming an assortment of foods, such as clams, lobsters, chicken, unhusked corn, and whole potatoes in a pit dug in the beach, layered with hot rocks, and covered with seaweed; cooks by steam of seaweed and hot rocks; originated in New England.

clapshot (KLAHP shoat). *Bri.* Mashed potatoes and mashed turnips with chopped chives and butter or bacon drippings.

clarified butter (klar-ah-FIED BUT-ter). *USA.* Butter that has been heated gently until the milky solids separate, then the clear liquid poured off, discarding the milky solids. Also called drawn butter.

clarify (KLAR-i-fi). *USA.* To make clear or pure by skimming or adding egg white and straining.

clavo (KLAH-voh). *Mex.* Clove.

clementine (KLEM-en-tine). *USA.* A virtually seedless North African orange of the Mandarin family; very flavorful, juicy, a refreshing bittersweet zip.

cloche (klosh). *Fre.* Under cover.

clooty dumpling (KLUT-tee DUHM-pleng). *Sco.* A type of plum pudding.

clos de girofle (cloa day zhee-roafl). *Fre.* Clove.

clotted cream (KLOT-ted krem). *Bri.* Thick cream made by slowly heating whole milk on which the cream has been allowed to rise, then skimming the cooled cream from the top.

cloudberry (KLOWD-bear-ree). *USA.* An Artic berry that resembles a yellow raspberry with a sweet, mossy taste.

cloud ear (klowd ear). *USA.* A crinkly fungus, black when dried, has a crisper texture than dried mushrooms after soaking in water; swells to an "ear" when soaked.

cloute (clew-teh). *Fre.* Studded, as with cloves.

clove (klov). *USA.* The dried flower bud of a tropical tree of the myrtle family; used as a spice and a source of an oil.

cloverleaf roll (KLO-ver-lef roll). *USA.* Yeast roll made by putting three small balls of dough in a muffin tin, letting them rise, then baking; shape of baked roll looks like a cloverleaf.

club steak (klub stak). *USA.* A tender and flavorful cut of beef from the loin between the T-bone and the rib section.

cluck and grunt (kluhk ahnd gruhnt). *USA.* An Old West term for eggs and bacon.

coarsely chop (KORS-lee chohp). *USA.* Cutting food into small pieces, about $3/16$ inch.

coarse salt (kors sawlt). *USA.* A squarish-grained salt; sprinkled on meats, pretzels, rolls, and breads before baking; not to be confused with rock salt, which is inedible. Also known as kosher salt or sea salt.

coat (koht). *USA.* To cover entire surface with flour, fine bread crumbs, sauce, batter, or other food as required.

cobbler (KOBB-ler). *USA.* A deep dish fruit pie with a biscuit dough top.

cocada (koa-KAH-dah). *Spa.* Coconut custard.

cochineal. (kosh-ee-nehl). *Fre.* A liquid red coloring agent used for coloring such as icing, sauces.

cochinillo (koa-chee-NEE-lyoa). *Spa.* Suckling pig.

cochino (koa-CHEE-noa). *Spa.* Pig.

cochon (ko-shawng). *Fre.* Pig. Also porc.

cochon de lait (ko-shawng der leh). *Fre.* Suckling pig.

cocido (koa-THEE-dhoa). *Spa.* Stew. Also means cooked, as opposed to fresh.

cock (kock). *USA.* A male chicken that is too old to roast, but makes a well-flavored adjunct for the stock pot; also see broiler, capon, fryer, roaster, stag chicken, and stewing chicken.

cock-a-leekie (kock-ah-LEE-ke). *Sco.* A soup made of chicken boiled with leeks.

cockles (KOCK-uls). *Bri.* European bivalve mollusk similar to oysters.

cocktail (KOCK-tale). *USA.* An appetizer, either a beverage or a light, highly seasoned food, served before a meal.

cocktail avocado (KOCK-taul ah-vah-KAH-doh). *USA.* A small, buttery flavored, seedless fruit of the Fuerte avocado; often treated as a vegetable; use fresh in salads, dips, sandwiches, soups, or eat out of hand.

coco (KOH-koh). *Mex, Por.* Coconut.

cocoa (KO-ko). *Spa.* Chocolate with part of the fat removed then pulverized to powder form.

cocoa (KO-ko). *USA.* A hot beverage made with cocoa powder, milk, and sugar.

cocomero (koa-KOA-may-roa). *Ita.* Watermelon.

cocomoka (KOH-koh-moh-kah). *USA.* A beverage, served hot or cold, combining coffee and cocoa as the base.

coconut (KOH-koh-nuht). *USA.* Edible seed-nut of the palm tree with brown, shaggy, hard, barklike shell; meat is white and flavorful, and can be used raw or cooked in dishes; cavity is filled with a milky liquid.

coconut oil (KOH-koh-nuht oyl). *USA.* An almost colorless oil extracted from fresh coconuts; liquid and semisolid forms.

cocotte (koh-koht). *Fre.* Casserole; food prepared and served in the same dish.

cocozelle (kok-ah-ZEL-le). *USA.* A summer squash resembling the zucchini.

coctel (KOK-tehl). *Mex.* Cocktail.

cod (kahd). *USA.* A food fish family of the North Atlantic with numerous members; flesh is lean, firm, white, mild, large flakes. Haddock, pollock, and hake are of the cod family.

coda di bue (koa-dah dee BOO-ee). *Ita.* Oxtail.

coddes. (KAH-dees). *USA.* Codfish cakes, breaded and deep-fried; especially in Maryland.

coddle (KAH-dle). *USA.* To simmer gently, below the boiling point, in liquid for a short time.

codorniz (koa-doarn-NEETH). *Spa, Por.* Quail.

coelho (koh-AYL-yoh). *Por.* Rabbit.

coeur (kurr). *Fre.* Heart.

coeur à la crème (kurr ah lah krehm). *Fre.* A very simple, classic dessert made by combining cream cheese and heavy cream, then molded in a heart-shaped form that allows the whey to drain off, unmolded, and garnished with strawberries, or other berries.

coffee (KAUF-fee). *USA.* A beverage made from roasted and ground coffee beans.

coffee cream (KAUF-fee kreem). *USA.* Cream containing 18–30% milkfat; widely used in coffee; also called light or table cream.

Cognac (kon-yahk). *Fre.* Brandy from the French town of the same name.

cogumelo (koh-goo-MEH-lohss). *Por.* Mushrooms.

coing (kwahn). *Fre.* Quince.

Cointreau (kwahn-tro). *Fre.* A colorless, sweet, orange-flavored liqueur.

col (kohl). *Spa.* Cabbage.

Colbert, à la (koh-behr). *Fre.* A preparation for fish in which the fish is dipped in egg, breadcrumbed, fried, and served with a butter mixed with chopped parsley and tarragon.

Colby (KOL-be). *USA.* Cheese similar to Cheddar, but softer body and more open texture; mild to mellow flavor; light cream to orange color.

colcannon (kohl-CAHN-un). *Iri.* A dish of cabbage, leeks, potatoes and milk, served with a hidden "treasure" within.

Colchesters (KOAL-chuh-strs). *Bri.* Oysters from the famous beds of Colchester.

colère, en (ahng ko-lehr). *Fre.* Fish, usually whiting, cooked with its tail in its mouth, giving it a so-called angry look; often dipped in egg batter, rolled in breadcrumbs, and deep-fried.

coleslaw (KOHL-slahw). *USA.* A vegetable dish used as a salad made basically of shredded cabbage; other vegetables and fruits such as grated carrots, finely chopped apples, chopped celery, nuts, may be mixed with a slaw dressing.

coliflor (ko-lee-FLOR). *Spa.* Cauliflower.

colin (ko-lahnk). *Fre.* Hake.

colinabo (ko-lee-NAH-boa). *Spa.* Turnip.

collards (KAH-lards). *USA.* Collard greens; a vegetable with dark green, paddlelike leaves resembling cabbage, on long, heavy, tough stalks; taste between cabbage and kale.

collé (koal-lay). *Fre.* Gelatin added.

collop. (KOHL-luhp). *Bri.* A thin slice of meat; same as the French scallop.

colza (KOL-za). *Ita.* An herb of the mustard family whose seeds yield oil for salads and frying and blending with butter; the leaves and young shoots can be braised as a vegetable. Generally known as rapeseed.

comfrey (KOHM-free). *USA.* A medicinal herb used to make a tea; fresh young leaves have been eaten for centuries, sparingly, in salads, or cooked as greens. It is now known that the leaves contain small amounts of an alkaloid that can cause liver damage; use sparingly.

comino (koh-MEE-noh). *Mex.* Cumin.

common cracker (KOHM-mohn KRAHK-kehr). *USA.* Very crisp, hard, thick wheat flour crackers; used split in half.

composé (kom-po-say). *Fre.* A salad that is arranged in the bowl or plate, rather than tossed.

compota (kohm-POA-tah). *Spa.* Stewed fruits; preserves.

compote (kom-poo-tay). *Fre.* Stew of fruits or vegetables, often flavored with spices and liqueur, served cold.

compound butter (KOHM-pound BUT-er). *USA.* Butter seasoned with herbs, shallots, and wine.

compressed yeast (KOHM-prehsd yeest). *USA.* A small cake of yeast weighing ³⁄₅ oz; light greyish-tan in color; used in baking.

concasse. (kon-kaas). *Fre.* Coarsely chopped, such as tomatoes or parsley.

concasser (kon-kaas-say). *Fre.* Rough chopping with a knife, or breaking up in a mortar.

conch (kohnk). *USA.* A mollusk whose muscle is made into chowder, fritters, used in salads, or breaded and fried.

conchiglia (koa-keej-LEE-ah). *Ita.* Shellfish; also pasta shells.

concombre (kawng-kawng-br). *Fre.* Cucumber.

Condé (kawng-day). *Fre.* A pâtisserie of leftover flaky pastry rolled out in strips and used variously for sweet or savory dishes; traditionally strips are covered with royal almond icing, sprinkled with powdered sugar, and baked.

condensed milk (kon-DENSD mehlk). *USA.* Milk with its water content reduced by one-half. With sugar added in the ratio of 18 lbs to 100 lbs of milk, it is called sweetened condensed milk; not to be confused with evaporated milk.

condimento (koan-dee-MAYN-toh). *Ita.* Seasonings.

condiments (KON-de-munts). *USA.* Seasonings that enhance the flavor of foods: spices, herbs, sauces, pickles, relishes.

conejo (koa-NAY-khoh). *Spa.* Rabbit.

coney (KOHN-nee). *USA.* A hot dog.

confectioners' sugar (kon-FEC-shun-ers' SCHUH-gahr). *USA.* Very finely ground sugar with cornstarch added; quick dissolving. Also known as powdered sugar, and, in France, icing sugar.

confectionery (kon-FEC-shun-ary). *USA.* The transformation of sugar into sweets.

confeitado (kon-fay-TAH-doo). *Por.* Candied. Sometimes called conservado.

confeito (kon-FAY-too). *Por.* Candy.

confiserie (kawng-fee-ser-ree). *Fre.* Confectionery.

confit (kawng-fee). *Fre.* Meat or poultry cooked and preserved in its own fat; fruits or vegetables cooked and preserved in brandy or liquor syrup.

confit d'oie (kawng-fee dwah). *Fre.* Slices of goose preserved in goose fat, a rare delicacy.

confiture (kawng-fee-tewr). *Fre.* Preserves or jam made from fruit.

cong (tsoong). *Chi.* Scallions.

congbào yángròu (tsoong bao yang row). *Chi.* A dish of lamb quick-fried with scallions.

congeal (kon-GEEL). *USA.* To change a liquid into a solid by lowering the temperature of the food sufficiently to bring about gelation.

congo eel (KONG-go eeul). *Bri.* One of the names for the ocean pout, a fish of the eelpout family whose flesh is sweet, white and has few bones.

congre (kong-reh). *Fre.* Large sea eel.

coniglio (koa-NEE-lyo). *Ita.* Rabbit.

conserva de fruta (kon-SER-vah duh FRU-tah). *Por.* Jam.

conservado (kon-ser-VAH-doo). *Por.* Candied. Sometimes called confeitado.

conserves (KON-servs). *USA.* Glorified jams made from a mixture of fruits, usually including citrus; raisins and nuts are frequently added.

consommé (kawngs-som-may). *Fre.* Clarified double-strength brown stock made from two or three kinds of meats; a clear brown broth to which various savories may be added. See specific types listed below.

consommé Alexandra (ah-lehx-ahn-drah). Chicken broth with chicken balls and lettuce.

consommé allemande (ahl-manged). Strong beef broth with slices of frankfurter.

consommé Alsacienne (ahl-sah-ceene). Beef broth with noodles.

consommé Bellevue (bel-ve). Combination of chicken consommé and clam broth.

consommé cardinal (kahr-dee-nahl). Fish broth with pink lobster balls.

consommé colbert (coa-bahr). Broth with a soft-poached egg in it.

consommé soubrette (soo-breht). Chicken broth garnished with green peas and chopped shrimp.

consommé vaudoise (vahn-dwah). Beef broth with julienne vegetables.

contre-filet (kawngtr-fee-leh). *Fre.* Loin strip steak of beef.

converted rice (kon-VER-ted ris). *USA.* Rice that has been steamed and dried before milling for higher nutritional content and easier processing.

cookie (KUHK-kee). *USA.* Any of various small sweet flat or slightly raised cakes in a multitude of shapes and flavors; called biscuits throughout most of the world.

cooking salt (KUHK-eng sawlt). *USA.* A finely-ground, free-flowing salt used in food preparation; table salt.

cool (koul). *USA.* Allow to come to room temperature.

copeaux (koo-po). *Fre.* Pastry twists.

copeaux en chocolat (koo-po ahng shok-kol-lah) *Fre.* Chocolate shavings.

coppa (KOAP-pah). *Ita.* Cured pork shoulder.

coppa gelata (KOA-pah jay-LAA-to). *Ita.* Mixed ice cream dessert.

coq au bruyère (kok oa brwee-yehr). *Fre.* Wood grouse; prepared in the same manner as pheasant.

coq au vin (kok-oa-vang). *Fre.* Cut-up chicken braised in red wine with onions and mushrooms.

coquillage (kok-kee-lazg) *Fre.* Shellfish.

coquille (kok-kee). *Fre.* Served in a scallop shell.

coquille Saint Jacques (kok-kee sang zhahk). *Fre.* Scallops in cream sauce on half shell.

coquina (koh-KEEN-ah). *USA.* A periwinkle clam.

coral (KAH-rahl). *USA.* Lobster roe; turns a bright reddish color when cooked; used for sauces and butters.

coratèlla (koa-rah-TAYL-lah). *Ita.* Organ meats such as liver, heart, sweetbreads.

corbina (korh-BEE-nah). *USA.* Corvina; a fish of the drum family.

cordeiro (coor-DAY-roo). *Por.* Lamb.

cordero (kohr-DEH-roh). *Spa.* Lamb.

cordero lechazo (kohr-DEH-roh lay-CHAH-thoh). *Spa.* Suckling lamb.

cordial (KOHR-duhl). *USA.* A sweet, syrupy liqueur.

core (kohr). *USA.* To remove the core from a fruit.

coriander (KOH-ree-ahn dehr). *USA.* An herb used for its leaves and seeds; dried seeds have a warm, nutty flavor and aroma; leaves have strong, musty flavor. Also known as cilantro.

corn (korn). *USA.* A sweet, yellow food grain eaten as a vegetable while still in its soft stage of growth either with the loose kernels removed from the cob or cooked on the cob; maize.

corn bread (KORN-brehd). *USA.* A quick bread of cornmeal and flour.

corn dog (korn dawg). *USA.* A frankfurter-on-a-stick, dipped in cornmeal batter, fried till crisp on outside.

corned beef (kornd beef). *USA.* Cuts of beef including the plate, chuck, brisket, and round that are boned, trimmed, seasoned with bay leaves and whole peppers, then cured or "corned."

corned bief (KOHR-nehd beef). *Dut.* Corned beef.

Cornell bread (kohrn-NEHL brehd). *USA.* A high-protein bread developed by Cornell University made by substituting part of the unbleached white flour with one tablespoon each of soya flour and wheat germ, and one teaspoon of nonfat dry milk.

cornet (kohr-nah). *Fre.* Horn or cornucopia shaped; as a pastry stuffed with a creme filling; slices of meat rolled into a cone and stuffed.

corn flour (korn flowr). *Bri.* Cornstarch; a very fine flour milled from corn; a thickening agent.

corn flour (korn flowr). *USA.* Milled of white or yellow corn; fine granulation; if used in baking, must be mixed with other flours.

cornichons (korn-ee-shawng). *Fre.* Pickles.

Cornish hen (KORN-esh hen). *Bri.* A crossbreed chicken with delicate flesh; Rock Cornish game hen.

Cornish pastry (KORN-esh PAS-tre). *Bri.* A pastry turnover stuffed with meat or vegetable filling.

cornmeal (KORN-mehl). *USA.* Coarsely ground white or yellow corn; if used in quick or yeast cornbreads, must be mixed with other flour.

corn oil (korn oyl). *USA.* A pale yellow fatty oil obtained from the corn kernel; liquid and semisolid forms.

corn pone (korn poneh). *USA.* A flat bread made of cornmeal dough, fried or baked.

corn salad (korn SAHL-ad). *USA.* A salad green, use raw in salad, or cook like spinach. Also known as lamb's lettuce, mache.

cornstarch (KORN-starch). *USA.* Very finely milled white corn flour, used as thickening agent and in baking.

corn sugar (korn SCHU-gar). *USA.* A crystallized dextrose-glucose obtained by hydrolizing cornstarch with acid; less sweet than sucrose sugars.

corn syrup (korn SEHR-up). *USA.* A syrup of dextrose and glucose; generally used in canning and jelly-making; available in a mild-tasting light, and a stronger-tasting dark.

corvina (kohr-VEE-nah). *USA.* A catchall name for fish of the drum family. Also spelled corbina.

cos (kos). *Bri.* Romaine lettuce.

còscia (KOAS-chee-ah). *Ita.* Thigh; as thigh of chicken.

coscia de montone (KOAS-chee-ah da moan-TOA-nay). *Ita.* Leg of lamb. Also called cosciotto.

cosciotto (koa-SHAWT-to). *Ita.* Leg of lamb. Also called coscia de montone.

costata (kos-TOA-to). *Ita.* Rib chop.

costela (coosh-too-LAY). *Por.* Rib.

costeleta (coosh-too-LET-ash). *Por.* Cutlet; chop.

costeletas de carneiro (coosh-too-LET-ash der car-NAY-roo). *Por.* Mutton chops.

costcletas de porço (coosh-too-LET-ash der POR-coo). *Por.* Pork chops.

costillas (kohs-TEE-yahs). *Spa.* Ribs, chops.

costmary (KOHS-mah-ree). *USA.* An herb with a minty taste and bitter overtones; use sparingly in sauces, soups, stuffings.

costole (KOS-toa-lay). *Ita.* Ribs.

costoletta (koas-toa-LAYT-tah). *Ita.* Cutlet.

côte (koat). *Fre.* Rib.

cotechino (koa-teh-KEE-no). *Ita.* A large pork sausage seasoned with nutmeg and cloves; delicate to spicy.

cotelette (koh-toh-LET). *Dut.* Cutlet.

côtelette (kot-ter-leht). *Fre.* Chops.

cotogno (koa-TOA-nyah). *Ita.* Quince.

cotoletta (koa-toa-LAH-tah). *Ita.* Braised chop or cutlet.

cotriade. (cot-ree-ahd). *Fre.* Fish soup.

cottage cheese (KAHT-tehgj chez) *USA.* A soft, bland, creamy white, uncurded cheese made from soured skim milk. Also known as Dutch cheese, pot cheese.

cottage potatoes (KAHT-tehgj poh-TAY-toes). *USA.* Potatoes, cooked and cold, then sliced or diced, sautéed in butter without stirring to get a golden-brown crust, then turned to brown on other side. Also called country-fried.

cottage pudding (KAHT-tehgj PUD-deng). *USA.* Plain cake covered with a hot, sweet, puddinglike sauce.

cotto (KOA-to). *Ita.* Cooked.

cottonseed flour (KAHT-tun-seed flowr). *USA.* With at least four times the protein value of wheat, this flour is often used to enrich breads.

cottonseed oil (KAHT-tun seed oyl). *USA.* A pale yellow fatty oil obtained from the cottonseed; liquid and semisolid form.

couche-couche (COUS-cous). *USA.* A Cajun fried corn dough, served with milk and preserves or cane syrup.

coulibiac (cool-ee-bee-ak). *Fre.* A hot fish pie filled with layers of salmon or fish, rice, mushrooms, herbs, onions.

coulis (koo-lees). *Fre.* A thick liquid sauce made by pureeing vegetables, fruit, fish, chicken, crustaceans, and game; used over meat, chicken or fish entree as a low calorie garnish.

coulis (koo-lees). *Fre.* The juices that run out of meat during the cooking process.

Coulommiers (coo-loa-meea). *Fre.* A cows' whole milk soft cheese with white rind flora, creamy white and flavorful interior.

country captain (KOUN-tree KAHP-tain). *USA.* A curried chicken dish with bacon strips, onions, garlic, celery, tomatoes, and seasoned with orange juice, curry powder and thyme.

country-fried potatoes (KOUN-tre-frid poh-TAY-toes). *USA.* Cottage potatoes.

country ham (KOUN-tre hahm). *USA.* A ham that has been dry-cured and heavily salted; requires soaking followed by long simmering. Smithfield is one type of country ham.

country style spareribs (KOUN-tre stil SPAR-rebs). *USA.* The backbones of pork from the shoulder end of the loin.

coupe (koop). *Fre.* Ice cream dessert.

coupe Jacques (koop zhahk). *Fre.* Lemon and strawberry ices with fruit steeped in cherry brandy.

courgette (koor-zheht). *Fre.* Zucchini.

couronne, en (ahng ky-rohn). *Fre.* In the shape of a ring.

court-bouillon (kort boo-yon). *Fre.* A highly-seasoned broth in which fish has been boiled.

couscous (KOOS-koo-see). *Ara.* An ancient North African dish made with millet flour or crushed rice steamed in the top of a two-part pot with meat such as mutton or chicken, stewed in the bottom part; served together with hot sauce.

couve (koh-vay). *Por.* Cabbage.

couve de Bruxelas (koh-vay duh broo-SAY-lahsh). *Por.* Brussels sprouts.

couve flor (koh-vay FLOR). *Por.* Cauliflower.

couve Lombarda (koh-vay lom-BAHR-dah). *Por.* Collard greens.

cowpeas (KOW-peez). *USA.* Black-eyed peas.

cozida (kou-ZEE-dah). *Por.* Boiled.

cozida de Portuguesa (kou-ZEE-da duh por-too-GAY-zah). *Por.* Traditional mixture of boiled beef, vegetables, potatoes, rice, sausages.

cozza (KOAT-say). *Ita.* Mussel.

crab (krahb). *USA.* Clawed crustacean with many edible varieties; delicate, white flesh; very versatile to use.

crab apple (krahb AHP-puhl). *USA.* A tiny, round very tart apple with yellow skin with red to maroon blush; must be cooked as apple jelly, tarts, apple butter, or use as garnish.

crab butter (krahb BUHT-tuhr). *USA.* The white-yellow fat inside the back shell of crabs, used in dressings or sauces.

crab claws (krahb claus). *USA.* The large pinchers at the end of the two legs on either side of the mouth; a delicacy.

crabe (krahb). *Fre.* Crab.

crab legs (krahb lehgs) *USA.* The first three or four legs on either side of the body of the Alaskan king crab; boiled or steamed and served with melted butter.

crabmeat (KRAHB-meht). *USA.* The meat of crabs; best from the claws.

cracked wheat flour (krahkd wheet flowr). *USA.* In this flour, the wheat has been cut rather than ground. It gives up little of its starch as a binder and must be used with all-purpose or whole wheat flour.

cracker (KRAHK-ker). *USA.* A dry, thin, crisp bakery product that may be leavened or unleavened, made in various shapes and variously flavored.

cracker flour (KRAHK-ker flowr). *USA.* Flour milled from soft wheat; has low water-absorbing capacity.

crackling (KRAHK-lens). *USA.* Crispy, fried pieces of fresh pork fatback. Also called cracklins.

cracknels (KRAHK-nehls). *USA.* Hard, crisp biscuits; cracklings.

crackseed (KRAHK-seed). *USA.* A Hawaiian speciality; various seeds of fruit that have been smashed and preserved with salt; salty-sweet taste that hints of licorice.

cranberry (KRAHN-bear-ee). *USA.* A red, acidic berry used in sauce, baked goods, meat garnishes.

crapaudine (krah-poo-deen). *Fre.* Method of preparing fowl, usually pigeon, giving the appearance of a toad.

crapaudine sauce (krah-poo-dee-nay saus). *Fre.* Tangy sauce with onions, pickles, mushrooms, mustard, and wine.

crappin (KRAHP-pen). *Sco.* Stuffing.

crauti (krah-OO-tee). *Ita.* Sauerkraut.

cravo (KRAH-voo). *Por.* Clove.

crawfish (CRAHW-fisch). *USA.* Cajun pronunciation for crayfish.

crayfish (KRA-fisch). *USA.* A freshwater crustacean of many species, resembling a small lobster with firm flesh and subtly, but delicately flavored.

cream (krem). *USA.* That part of the milk that rises to the top; butterfat, milk fat. Terms used to describe cream include half-and-half, cereal, light, coffee, table, whipping, whipped.

cream (krem). *USA.* To mix fat and sugar, or fat and eggs, until soft, smooth, and creamy.

cream cheese (krem cheez). *USA.* A soft cows' whole milk cheese; delicate, slightly acid flavor; creamy, bland in taste.

cream of tartar (kreem uv TAHR-tahr). *USA.* A white crystalline salt used in baking powder.

cream puff (krem puhf). *USA.* A round shell of pastry that creates an internal hollow space when baked, that is filled with various flavored custards or creme.

cream puff pastry (krem puff PA-stry). *USA.* A simple paste of flour, boiling water, eggs, butter that puffs up on baking, leaving a cavity that is generally filled with a flavored creme filling.

cream soup (krem soop). *USA.* A thick soup to which cream, butter has been added, and usually vegetables.

Crécy, à la (kray-cee). *Fre.* With carrots.

crema (KRAI-mah). *Ita, Spa.* Cream.

crema batida (KRAI-mah bah-TEE-dhah). *Spa.* Whipped cream.

crema di pollo (KRAI-mah day POAL-lo). *Ita.* Cream of chicken soup.

crema di verdura (KRAI-mah day veh-DOO-rah). *Ita.* Puree of vegetables, often with milk or cream, and sometimes thickened with pureed potatoes or sieved cooked rice.

crema española (KRAI-mah ays-pah-NOH-lah). *Spa.* A dessert made of milk, gelatin, and eggs.

crema rovesciata (KRAI-mah roa-vays-chee-AH-to). *Ita.* Baked custard.

crême (KREH-may). *Por.* Cream.

crème (krehm). *Fre.* Cream.

crème a l'anglaise (krehm lahng-las). *Fre.* Custard.

crème bachique (krehm bac-ee-shah). *Fre.* Custard flavored with cinnamon and Sauternes.

crème beurre (krehm burr). *Fre.* Hard sauce.

crème brûlée (krehm brew-lah). *Fre.* A rich custard with a caramelized brown sugar crust.

crème chantilly (krehm shang-tee-ye). *Fre.* Sweetened whipped cream, flavored with vanilla or liqueur.

crème chiboust (krehm chee-boos). *Fre.* Creme pastry with sweetened egg whites added.

crème choisy (krehm shwah-see). *Fre.* Lettuce soup.

crème de cassis (krehm deh kahs-seess). *Fre.* A liqueur made from black currants, used to make aperitifs.

crème de menthe (krehm deh menthe). *Fre.* A liqueur made from peppermint; flavoring for food and drink; aperitifs.

crème d'orge (krehm doarj). *Fre.* Soup made with fine barley.

crème fouetté (krehm fooeh-tay). *Fre.* Whipped cream.

crème fraîche (krehm fraysh). *Fre.* A cultured heavy cream with a tangy taste.

crème frite (krehm freet). *Fre.* Fried cream; a creme filling chilled until it can be cut in squares, dipped in finely crushed cake crumbs, deep-fried, and sprinkled with powdered sugar and rum.

crème glacée (krehm glahs-say). *Fre.* Ice cream; sometimes means a sundae.

crème pâtissière (krehm pah-tees-syehr). *Fre.* Variously flavored pastry cream used to fill tarts, cream puffs, eclairs, pastries.

crème pralinée (krehm prah-lee-neh). *Fre.* Creme pâtissière flavored with powdered praline, used to fill pastries.

crème renversée (krehm rehn-vehr-seh). *Fre.* Custard baked in caramel-lined mold, chilled, and served by inverting on plate.

crenata (koo-leh-NAH-tah). *Jap.* Pine nut.

crenshaw melon (KREN-shaw MEHL-uhn). *USA.* A melon with a golden, netless rind at its peak of ripeness, has a slightly wrinkled stem end, gold-pink flesh, and a rich aroma.

creole (KRE-ol). *USA.* Made with tomatoes, peppers, onions, seasonings; any soups, garnishes, sauces so prepared.

creole mustard (KRE-ol MUHS-tahrd). *USA.* A hot, spicy mustard made from mustard seeds marinated in vinegar.

crêpe (krayp). *Fre.* A small, very thin and crisp pancake served for tea or dessert.

crepes (KRAH-payz). *Ita.* Pancakes.

crepes do ceu (KRAY-puhsh do SAY-oo). *Por.* Pancakes richly filled with whipped cream and candied fruit.

crêpes parmentier (krayp pahr-mehn-teh). *Fre.* Potato pancakes.

crêpes suzette (krayp sue-zeht). *Fre.* Crepes with an orange sauce, orange-flavored liqueur, heated and flambéed.

crépine (kreh-pee-neh). *Fre.* Pig's caul; a fatty, lacy membrane enclosing the paunch, that melts away when cooked.

crépinette (kreh-pee-neht). *Fre.* Small pork sausage wrapped in caul instead of a casing.

crescent (krehss-SCEHNT). *USA.* A curve-shaped roll of butterflake pastry.

Crescenza (krehz-CHAY-tsah). *Ita.* An uncooked, cows' milk cheese that is rindless, buttery, smooth, delicate. Also called Stracchino.

crescione (krays-chee-OA-nay). *Ita.* Watercress.

crespella (krehz-PAYL-lah). *Ita.* A stuffed, thin pancake; a crepe.

cresson (krehs-sawng). *Fre.* Watercress.

crêtes de coq (creh-tehs der kok). *Fre.* Cockscombs, a great delicacy.

crevette (krer-veht). *Fre.* Shrimp.

criadillas (kree-ah-DHEE-lyahss). *Spa.* Sweetbreads.

crisp (krisp). *USA.* To make foods brittle and firm, as in chilling vegetables or heating cereals or crackers in the oven to remove excessive moisture.

crisphead lettuce (KRISP-hehd LEHTT-us). *USA.* Iceberg lettuce.

crispito (KRIS-pee-toh). *Mex.* A corn tortilla tightly rolled and fried; used with dipping sauces.

croaker (KRO-ker). *USA.* One of the many members of the drum family; having delicate, finely flavored flesh.

crocchette (kroa-KAYT-tay). *Ita.* Croquettes. Also croche.

croche (KROA-kay). *Ita.* Croquettes. Also crocchette.

croche di riso alla torinese (KROA-kay dee REE-zoa ahl-lay toa-ree-NAY-zay). *Ita.* Rice fritters.

croissant (krwa-sahng). *Fre.* Crescent; applies to rolls and confectionery of crescent shape.

cromesquis (kroam-es-kee). *Fre.* Finely ground poultry or shellfish rolled in thin bacon slices, dipped in batter, fried in deep fat.

croquants (kroa-kough). *Fre.* Confections that crunch between the teeth.

croque madame (kroak mah-dahm). *Fre.* Chicken and cheese sandwich.

croquembouche (kroa-kough-boosh). *Fre.* A pyramid of bite-size cream puffs, held together with sugar glaze, and covered with caramel.

croque monsieur (kroak mer-syur). *Fre.* Grilled ham and cheese sandwich.

croquesignole (crook-SIN-yawl). *USA.* A Cajun doughnut, without a hole, sometimes square.

croquetes (krou-KAY-tuhsh). *Por.* Croquettes.

croquetes de Camarão (krou-KAY-tuhsh duh kah-mah-RAHNG). *Por.* Croquettes made of shrimp, usually part of the appetizer course.

croquetjes (croh-ket-YER). *Dut.* Croquettes.

croquette (kroa-keht). *Fre.* A savory or pattie prepared with minced meat, fowl, or fish with sauce to bind, shaped variously, then egged, crumbed, and fried.

cròsta (KROAZ-tah). *Ita.* Crust.

crostacei (kroa-sta-KAY-ee). *Ita.* Shellfish.

crostata (kroa-STAH-tah). *Ita.* Pie.

crostata di fragole (kroa-STAH-tah dee FRAA-goa-lay). *Ita.* Strawberry pie.

crostatina (kroa-stah-TEE-nah). *Ita.* Tart.

crostini (kroa-STEE-nee). *Ita.* Crouton; toasted bread cubes.

crostini alla fiorentina (kroa-STEE-nee AHL-lah fee-oa-ray-TEE-nah). *Ita.* Toasted bread spread with a chicken liver mixture.

crostini alla napoletana (kroa-STEE-nee AHL-lah nah-poa-lay-TAH-nah). *Ita.* Fried or toasted bread spread with tomatoes and anchovies.

crostini alla Parmigiana (kroa-STEE-nee AHL-lah Pahr-mee-jaa-AHN-ah). *Ita.* Toasted bread with cheese and anchovies.

crostini di mare (kroa-STEE-nee dee MAH-ray). *Ita.* Fried or toasted bread spread with minced shellfish.

croustade (kroos-tahd). *Fre.* A toasted shape or shell of bread in which various mixtures are served.

croûte (kroot). *Fre.* Bread or pastry in which a meat is baked, then served.

croûte au pot (kroot oa po). *Fre.* Beef-vegetable soup, topped with a thick slice of bread and grated cheese.

croute aux morilles. (kroot oa mor-ree). *Fre.* Morels on toast.

croûton (kroo-to). *Fre.* Small cube of fried or toasted bread used for garnishing dishes or salads.

crowdie (KREW-dee). *Sco.* A breakfast dish made of finely ground oatmeal with buttermilk.

crown roast (krown rost). *USA.* Loin from the rib section of beef, pork, lamb, tied into a crown shape, and roasted; paper frills placed on end of bones before serving; center cavity filled with stuffing or vegetables.

cru (krew). *Fre, Por.* Raw.

crudités (krew-dee-tay). *Fre.* Raw vegetables used as appetizers.

crudo (KROO-do). *Ita, Spa.* Fresh; raw.

cruller (KRUEL-lehr). *Dut.* A rich doughnut in the form of a twisted strip fried in deep fat.

crumb (kruhmb). *USA.* To cover with crumbs; to break bread, crackers, cookies into small particles.

crumpet (KRUM-pet). *Bri.* A muffin similar to English muffins, except the batter is more liquid, and muffin rings must be used when preparing in order to define the shape.

crush (kruhsh). *USA.* Press to extract juice or oils, usually in a mortar, or with side of knife.

crustacean (krus-STA-shun). *USA.* Water dwelling anthropods with a hard shell: lobster, shrimp, crab, crayfish.

crystallize (KRYS-tahl-lize). *USA.* To cause to form crystals, as in making fudge.

császárkörte (CHEH-ssaar-kurr-tae). *Hun.* Type of pear.

cseresznye (CHeh-rehsn-yeh). *Hun.* Cherries.

csirkét (CHEE-rkayt). *Hun.* Chicken.

csuka (CHOO-ko). *Hun.* Pike.

cú (chu). *Chi.* Vinegar.

cuaresmeño (thoo-ahays-MEEN-yo). *Mex.* A dark green, round, hot chili pepper.

cube (qub). *USA.* Cutting food into shapes the same width, depth, and thickness; usually ⅜ inch or larger, depending on the dish in which it is to be used. See dice, chop, and mince.

cucumber (QUE-kum-ber). *USA.* A vine-vegetable related to the gourd family; a basic salad ingredient; dark-green skin, white flesh with a pale greenish cast, crisp texture; also used for pickles and relishes.

cuìpí ji (tswei pee jee). *Chi.* Chicken cooked to have a crispy skin.

cuisine minceur (kwee-zeen mahns-uhr). *Fre.* Low-calorie cuisine.

cuisse (kwees). *Fre.* Drumstick.

cuisseau (kwee-so). *Fre.* Leg of veal.

cuisses de grenouille (kweess dar grer-nooy). *Fre.* Frog legs.

cuissot (kwee-so). *Fre.* Haunch of venison.

cukrot (TSOO-krawt). *Hun.* Sugar.

cullen skink (KUHL-lehn skehnk). *Sco.* Creamed haddock.

culotte (koo-loht). *Fre.* Rump of beef.

Cumberland sauce (KUHM-ber-lund saus). *USA.* Red currant jelly thinned with port, flavored with shallots, orange zest, mustard, and served with game.

cumin (QUE-men). *USA.* An herb grown for its seeds, which give chili its characteristic flavor; used whole, roasted, and ground; important in the cuisines of India, the Middle East, and Mexico; major ingredient in curry powders.

cuore (koo-OA-ray). *Ita.* Heart.

cupcake (KUHP-kahk). *USA.* An individual portion of cake baked in a muffin tin, usually frosted with icing, or dusted with powdered sugar.

cup custard (kuhp KUHSS-tahrd). *USA.* Baked custard.

Curaçao (KYUR-dah-so). *Dut.* A liqueur made from the dried peel of the green sour orange. Sold as Cointreau, triple sec, and Grand Marnier.

curd (kuhrd). *USA.* The thick, casin-rich part of coagulated milk.

curdling (KUHR-dle). *USA.* The separation of a sauce or pudding containing eggs into a watery liquid with thick, almost solid, particles in it. The sauce is still edible, but the appearance is unpleasant.

cure (keur). *USA.* A process of preserving by aging, drying, salting, or smoking.

curly endive (KUHR-lee EHN-dive). *USA.* A bitter, green, plant with sticky leaves; used in salads; cooked as a vegetable. Also known as chicory.

currant (KUHR-runt). *USA.* Small black, seedless raisin used in cakes, jellies, syrups, liqueurs; used fresh in ice cream, yogurt, sorbets. See also red currants.

curry (KUHR-ree). *USA.* Highly spiced condiment from India; a stew seasoned with curry.

cuscinetti (kooz-chee-NAYT-tee). *Ita.* Fried cheese sandwiches.

cush (koosh). *USA.* A cornmeal pancake.

cushaw (koo-SHAH). *USA.* A variety of large crookneck squash.

Cussy (key-see). *Fre.* An elaborate garnish of mushrooms stuffed with pureed chestnuts, giblets, and truffles.

custard (KUHS-tahrd). *USA.* A sweet puddinglike mixture made of eggs and milk that can be baked or cooked. Also called baked custard, cup custard, boiled custard.

custard apple (KUHS-tahrd AHP-puhl). *USA.* A tropical fruit with jade green peel, sweet, low-acid flesh that is silky smooth and juicy, cream-colored, with a slight granular finish, like a custard of fine pears. Also known as cherimoya, white sapote.

custard marrow (KUST-urd MAR-row). *USA.* A pear-shaped vegetable of the melon family, with green, prickly, ribbed skin. Also called chayote and mirliton.

cut in (kuht en). *USA.* To cut a solid fat into flour with knives or pastry blender until fat particles are the desired size.

cutlet (KUHT-leht). *USA.* Thin slice of meat, a scallop.

cygne (sig-nah). *Fre.* A swan shaped pastry filled with crème Chantilly.

cymling (SEHM-len). *USA.* A yellow or white round summer squash with a scalloped edge. Also known as pattypan.

D

dà báicài (da bai tsai). *Chi.* Chinese cabbage.

dab (dahb). *Fre.* A flatfish of the sole family; flesh is white, rather soft, easily digested.

dacquoise (dah-kwahs). *Fre.* A pastry made of meringue with ground nuts, baked in flat discs, filled with flavored whipped cream or buttercream, and berries.

dadar-isi (DAH-dahr-EE-see). *Dut.* Indonesian stuffed omelet.

dadels. (DAH-dehls). *Dut.* Dates.

dadlar (DAH-dlahr). *Swe.* Dates.

dà-dòu (dah-doe). *Chi.* Soy beans.

daging smor (DAHKH-ingh smor). *Dut.* Indonesian stewed meat in a rich black sauce.

dagmarsuppe (DAHG-mahr-ssuppe). *Nor.* A soup made with cream, sherry, and tiny green peas.

Dagwood sandwich (DAHG-wood SAHND-wich). *USA.* A sandwich made of many slices of bread filled with a variety of meats, lettuce, tomatoes, pickles, and such.

dahchini (CAH-chee-nee). *Ind.* Cinnamon or cassia.

dahi bhalle (da-HEE BHAH-lay). *Ind.* Fried bean dumplings in spice-and herb-laced yogurt.

dai choy goh (dah-ee choy gwa). *Chi.* A gelatin made from seaweed; does not melt at room temperature.

daikon (DAH-ee-kohn). *Jap.* A giant, white radish; very crisp, tender, mild, sweet; eaten raw, or cooked like turnips; at least a foot in length.

daizu (DAH-ee-zoo). *Jap.* Dried soybeans.

dajaaj (da-JEHJ). *Ara.* Chicken.

dal (dahl). *Ind.* Legumes: lentils, dried peas, and beans.

dalchini (dahl-CHEE-nee). *Ind.* Cinnamon.

damascos (dah-MAHSS-kohss). *Por.* Apricots.

Dampfbraten (Dampf-BRAHT-un). *Ger.* Beef stew.

Dampfnudeln (Dampf-NOOD-eln). *Ger.* Sweetened yeast dumplings, served with stewed fruit or jam.

dan (dahn). *Chi.* Egg.

Danablu (DAAN-aabloo). *Dan.* A cow's whole milk blue cheese.

dàn-gao (caan-gau). *Chi.* Cake.

Danish pastry (DAAN-ish PA-stre). *USA.* A yeast pastry filled variously, fruit, cheese, custard, and served at breakfast.

dariole (dah-ree-ool). *Fre.* A small cylindrical mold; also, the little cakes baked in this mold.

Darjeeling (dahr-jee-lehng). *Ind.* A variety of tea, used as a beverage.

darne (dahrn). *Fre.* A thick slice of a large fish; fish steak.

d'Artois (dahr-twah). *Fre.* A pastry of puff-paste and jam.

dasheen (dah-sheen). *Chi.* Taro.

dashi (dah-SHEE). *Jap.* Fish stock made of dried bonito and seaweed.

dates (datz). *USA.* Edible fruit of the palm tree, by composition, about half sugar. Of Arabian origins, three varieties are now grown in the United States: Medjool, Deglet Noor and Khadrawy.

dátiles (DAH-tee-layss). *Spa.* Dates.

Datteln (DAH-terln). *Ger.* Dates.

datteri (DAHT-tay-ree). *Ita.* Dates.

dattero di mare (DAH-tay-roa dee MAH-ray). *Ita.* Date mussel, a type of shellfish.

dattero farciti (DAH-tay-roa fahr-CHEE-tee). *Ita.* Stuffed dates.

dattes (daht). *Fre.* Dates.

daube (doab). *Fre.* Stew

dauphine, à la (doa-fawng). *Fre.* Puff paste with potato puree, shaped into balls or piped in shapes, and deep fried.

dauphinois (doa-fee-nwah). *Fre.* A dish of potatoes prepared using Gruyère.

daurade (doa-rahd). *Fre.* Gilthead; a food fish of the bream family.

dà xia (da siah). *Chi.* Prawn; large shrimp.

dayolya (DOT-taw-yo). *Hun.* Dates.

De Arbol chile (De ARR-bol CHILL-ee). *USA.* A small, long, and thin dried chili with brilliant red, thin, shiny skin; very hot; should be used with caution.

debrecziner. (DAEB-rae-sseen-eer). *Hun.* A spicy, coarse textured sausage resembling the frankfurter.

decouper (deh-koo-peh). *Fre.* To carve; to cut in pieces.

deem sum (dihm suhm). *Chi.* A snack or appetizer. See dim sum.

deep fry (dep fri). *USA.* A method of immersing food in deep boiling fat to seal the exterior while keeping the interior moist. Also known as deep fat frying and French frying.

deer (dehr). *USA* A highly desirable game animal.

deghi mirch (DAY-ghee meerch). *Ind.* Indian paprika made from mild Kashmiri pepper pods.

déglaçage (deh-glah-ssahj). *Fre.* The operation of pouring any liquid into the pan in which food has been cooked in butter or other fat; deglaze.

deglaze (dee-glaz). *USA.* To dilute with liquid such as wine, stock, or cream, the concentrated juices left in the pan when meat, fish or poultry has been roasted, braised, or fried.

degorger (deh-gor-jeh). *Fre.* To soak food for a variable time to cleanse it of any impurities.

degraisser (deh-grese). *Fre.* To remove excess fat from the surface of a liquid or a joint of meat.

degrease (dee-GREEZ). *USA.* To remove accumulated fat from surface of hot liquid.

degustation (deh-gys-tah-ssyoh). *Fre.* Tasting.

dehydrate (dee-HI-drate). *USA.* To render dry by removing water content.

déjeuner (day-zhuh-nay). *Fre.* Lunch; the meal in the middle of the day.

de la maison. (der lah meh-sawng). *Fre.* Specialty of the house.

del giorno (dayl jee-OAR no). *Ita.* Of the day; same as the French *du jour.*

Delikatessaufschnitt (deh-li-kah-tess-OWF-schnitt). *Ger.* Assorted cold cuts.

Delmonico (del-MOHN-ee-koh). *USA.* A boneless steak cut from the rib section of beef. Also a Spencer steak.

Delmonico potatoes (del-MOHN-ee-koh poh-TAHT-toes). *USA.* Potato balls boiled, tossed in butter, lemon juice, parsley, pepper, and salt.

Demeltorte (deh-mehl-tohrt). *Fre.* An Austrian pastry filled with candied fruit.

demerara sugar (deh-MEHR-ah-rah SCHOO-gar). *Bri.* Raw cane sugar, partially refined, naturally light brown; very similar to turbinado.

demi (deh-me). *Fre.* Half.

demi-deuil (deh-me douj). *Fre.* Half-mourning.

demi-glace (deh-me glacs). *Fre.* Brown sauce mixed in veal stock, reduced in half, flavored with madeira or sherry.

demi-loaf (DEHM-ee lohf). *USA.* A term to describe a small, individual-size loaf of bread.

demi-sel (deh-me-sehl). *Fre.* A square, soft, fresh, slightly salted cows' whole milk cheese.

demitasse (deh-mee-tahss). *Fre.* After-dinner coffee served in small cups; usually black and strong.

denerver (deh-nehr-veh). *Fre.* The removal of tendons, gristle, membranes from meat, game, and poultry.

dent-de-lion. (dehnt-deh-leeo). *Fre.* Dandelion.

dentice (DEHN-tee-chay). *Ita.* Any of several white-fleshed fish found mostly along the Riviera.

depecer (deh-peh-seh). *Fre.* To carve.

depouiller (deh-puj-eh). *Fre.* To skim fat or scum off the surface of a sauce or stock.

Derby (DAHR-bee). *Bri.* A large, flat cows' milk cheese, uncooked, pale, mild, hard.

desayuno (deh-sah-YOO-noh). *Mex.* Light breakfast.

deshebrar (dehs-ay-BRAHR). *Spa.* To shred.

déshydrate (day-zi-drate). *Fre.* Dehydrate.

désossé (day-zose). *Fre.* Boneless.

dessert (deh-SZERT). *USA, Fre.* The last course of a meal; usually sweet-meats or fruit are served.

dessert (des-SAlrt). *Dut.* Dessert.

detrempe (day-trup-eh). *Fre.* A mixture of flour and water used in the preparation of flaky pastry.

Deventer koek (DAY-vun-tur kook). *Dut.* Spice cake (from Deventer).

devil (DEH-vehl). *USA.* To prepare food with hot seasonings such as cayenne or mustard, or serve with hot sauce.

devil's food cake (DEH-vehlz food kak). *USA.* A rich, light, moist, very chocolate cake.

Devonshire cream (Deh-vun-sheer krem). *Bri.* A thick cream made by slowly heating whole milk on which the cream has been allowed to rise, then skimming the cooled cream from the top.

dewberry (DU-behri). *USA.* A sweet, edible berry related to the blackberry.

dextrose (DEHX-stroos). *USA.* Grape sugar; used to thicken and sweeten baked goods, candy, caramels.

dhania (DHAH-nee-yah). *Ind.* Coriander.

dhan-sak masala (DHAHN-sahk ma-SAH-la). *Ind.* Spice blend used for making Dhan-sek, a chicken, lentil, and vegetable stew.

diablé (dee-ahb-lay). *Fre.* "Devil"; any dish with sharp and hot seasonings.

diable (dj-ahbl). *Fre.* A strongly flavored sauce containing herbs, vinegar, white wine and shallots.

diablo (dee-AHB-loh). *Mex, Spa.* "Devil"; with sharp and hot seasonings.

diablotins (dj-ahb-ble-ten). *Fre.* Cheese-flavored croutons, for garnishing soup.

dibs (dehbs). *Ara.* Carob syrup.

dice (dics). *USA.* To cut in one-fourth inch cubes. See cube, chop, and mince.

dick (dik). *Ger.* Thick.

dieppoise (deh-pwah-say). *Fre.* Saltwater fish garnished with mussels and crayfish in white wine reduction sauce.

Dijon (deh-zjohn). *Fre.* A white-wine based mustard.

dijonnaise (deh-zjoh-naze). *Fre.* Mustard-flavored sauce.

dilan (dehl-LAHN). *Ara.* Ribs, as for meat or leafy vegetables.

dill (dehl). *USA.* An ancient herb whose seeds are baked in breads; whose leaves are used fresh, dried, frozen in salads, soups, sauces; and whose flowers flavor pickles and vinegars.

dillilammas (dil-li-LAHM-mah-stah). *Fin.* Boiled mutton in dill sauce.

dillkött (DIL-chot). *Swe.* Boiled veal with dill sauce.

dillsås (DILL-soass). *Swe.* Dill sauce.

dilute (deh-LUTE). *USA.* To diminish the strength or flavor of a mixture, usually with water.

dim sum (dehm suhm). *Chi.* Small dishes eaten as snacks, or hors d'oeuvres, such as, fried shrimp balls, hargow, spring rolls, won ton.

dinde (dahnd). *Fre.* Turkey hen.

dindon (dahn-dun). *Fre.* Tom turkey .

dindonneau (dahn-dun-no). *Fre.* Young turkey.

dîner (deh-na). *Fre.* Dinner; to dine.

dió (DEE-aw). *Hun.* Walnuts.

dip (dehp). *USA.* A sauce or soft mixture, savory or sweet, into which food may be dipped.

diplomat pudding (DEH-plo-maht PUHD-eng). *Bri.* A dessert of ladyfingers and candied fruit soaked in brandy or liqueur, alternately layered in a mold with custard.

diplomat sauce (DEH-plo-maht saus). *Bri.* Sauce normande with lobster butter, garnished with truffles, diced lobster.

dirty rice (DEHR-tee rics). *USA.* A Cajun dish of rice cooked with chicken gizzards and livers.

disjoint (dis-JOINT). *USA.* To cut chicken, turkey or other poultry into pieces at the joints.

disossato (dee-soas-ZAH-to). *Ita.* Boned.

dissolve (dih-SOHLV). *USA.* To cause a dry substance to pass into solution in a liquid.

disznóhúst (DEES-naw-hoosht). *Hun.* Pork.

ditali (dee-TAH-lee). *Ita.* Short tubular form of pasta.

ditalini (dee-tah-LEE-nee). *Ita.* A tubular-shaped pasta about one-quarter inch both in diameter and length, and usually used in soups.

divinity (deh-VIN-eh-tee). *USA.* A white fudge candy made of whipped egg whites, sugar, and usually nuts.

djaj (da-JEHJ). *Ara.* Chicken.

Dobbeltøl (doubled-erl). *Dan.* Nonalcoholic dark beer.

Dobosch torte (doa-BAHSH tor-tah). *Ger.* Rich towering 10-layer cake with mocha cream filling.

Dobostorta (DAW-bawsh-tawr-to). *Hun.* A caramel glazed dessert of stacked layers of sponge cake spread with chocolate cream.

dobrada (dou-BRAH-dah). *Por.* Tripe.

dobrada com feijão branco (dou-BRAH-da kom fay-ZHAHNG BRAHN-koo). *Por.* Tripe, sausages, and white beans in a savory stew.

dolce (DOAL-chay). *Ita.* Sweet, as in sweet taste.

dolceforte (doal-chay-FOAR-ta). *Ita.* Sweet and strong; pertains to a method of flavoring a dish.

Dolcelatte (Doal-chay-LAHT-ta). *Ita.* A young, sweet, mild blue-veined cheese.

dolci (DOAL-chee). *Ita.* Sweet or dessert.

dolma (dol-MAH). *Gre.* Stuffed grape leaf using ground meat, rice, onions, mint, lemon.

Donaukarpfen (do-now-KAHR-pfern). *Ger.* Danube river carp.

donburi (don-BUR-e). *Jap.* A bowl of hot, boiled rice topped meat, fish, egg, or vegetables, colorful garnishes, and spicy condiments.

dòng de (doong de). *Chi.* Frozen.

dong gu (doong goo). *Chi.* Smoky flavored, dried, black mushrooms.

dong gua (doong gwa). *Chi.* Winter melon.

donut (DO-nuht). *USA.* Doughnut.

doodh (doohdt). *Ind.* Milk.

doperwtjes (doap-efr-vwtys). *Dut.* Green peas.

Doppelbock (Dohp-pul-bok). *Ger.* Extra strong Bock beer.

dorata (doa-RAH-tah). *Ita.* Gilthead; a food fish of the sea bream family.

dorato (doa-RAH-to). *Ita.* Dipped in egg batter and fried light golden brown.

doreshingu (doh-REHSH-sheen-goo). *Jap.* Salad dressing.

Doreye au riz (doa reh-yeh oa ree). *Fre.* Belgium rice tarts, come in many different versions.

Doria (dohr-ree-ah). *Fre.* A classical garnish for fish of cucumbers simmered in butter.

Dorsch (dorsch). *Ger.* Cod.

dorure (dohr-ewr). *Fre.* A beaten egg mixture for gilding pastry.

dosai (DOH-sah). *Ind.* Yeast pancakes.

dot (daht). *USA.* To scatter small bits of butter or margarine over the surface of food.

dou (doh). *Chi.* Bean.

double cream (DUH-buhl kreem). *USA.* Soft cream cheese in which the milk is enriched with added cream.

Double Gloucester (DUH-buhl GLOH-ster). *Bri.* A deep yellow cows' whole milk cheese with a rich, mellow flavor, dense texture, made in large flat rounds.

douce (doos). *Fre.* Sweet. Also called doux.

dou fu (doh foo). *Chi.* Bean curd; similar to tofu, but drier and firmer.

dòufù (doh-foo). *Chi.* Bean curd.

dough (doh). *USA.* A mixture of flour, liquid, and other ingredients, thick enough to roll or knead.

doughnut (DO-nuht). *USA.* A small ring-shaped cake made of yeast dough, usually fried.

dòu sha bao (doh sha bao). *Chi.* Sweet bean buns.

doux (doo). *Fre.* Sweet. Also called douce.

dòuyá (doh ya). *Chi.* Bean sprouts.

dou zhi (doh dz). *Chi.* Black beans.

Dover sole (Do-ver sohl). *Bri.* A member of the flatfish family; considered by many the best fish ever to eat.

dow ghok (doh gohk). *Chi.* Very thin beans, sometimes 18 inches long; taste is stronger than ordinary green beans. Also called long beans, asparagus beans, yard-long beans.

dow see (doh see). *Chi.* Salty fermented black beans used for sauces.

dragée (drah-zhee). *Fre.* A silver-coated nut or sugar bead used for decorating cakes.

dragoncello (drah-goan-CHAYL-lo). *Ita.* Tarragon.

drain (dran). *USA.* To place food in colander or strainer.

dram (drahm). *Nor.* Aquavit.

Drambuie (drahm-BOO-e). *Sco.* A heather honey flavored liqueur made from Scotch malt whiskey.

dranken (DRAHN-kehn). *Dut.* Drinks; beverages.

drawn (drahn). *USA.* A method of dressing fish by scaling and gutting, but leaving head, tail and fins intact.

drawn butter (drahn BUT-ter). *USA.* Clear, melted butter from which the milky solids have been removed.

dredge (drehg). *USA.* To thoroughly cover a food by coating or sprinkling with flour or other fine substance.

Dresden dressing (DREHZ-dehn DREHS-seng). *USA.* A cold sauce, made of hard-boiled eggs, onions, mustard, and other seasonings, that accompanies meats.

dress (drehs). *USA.* To mix with some sauce or flavoring just before serving, as to dress cooked vegetables with melted butter or to dress fresh greens with salad dressing.

dried (drid). *USA.* To remove moisture by means of heat.

dried beef (drid beef). *USA.* Beef rounds cured with salt and sugar, sliced paper thin, then dried, smoked and pressed; often referred to as smoked or sliced beef.

dried fruit (drid froot). *USA.* Fruit that has had part of the water content removed to preserve it, such as figs, prunes, apricots, peaches, pears, and additional speciality fruits.

drikker (DRIK-kehr). *Nor.* Drinks.

drippings (DREHP-engs). *USA.* Fat and liquid residue from frying or roasting meat or poultry.

dronningsuppe (DRON-neng-ssew-pper). *Nor.* Chicken broth fortified with sherry, egg yolks, cream, and forcemeat balls.

druiven (DRIR-vuh). *Dut.* Grapes.

drum (druhm). *USA.* A large family of fish, sometimes called croaker, of the Atlantic.

drupe (droop). *USA.* A general term for a fruit with a single stone.

dry milk solids (dri melk SAH-lehds). *USA.* Pasteurized milk particles, air-dried to remove most of the moisture.

drypasilla chili (dri-pah-SEE-ah CHILL-ee). *Mex.* A round, flatish chili pepper with a rich, sweet taste; mild to medium hot.

Dubarry (Doo-bah-ree). *Fre.* Small flowerettes of cauliflower, covered with mornay sauce, sprinkled with grated cheese, breadcrumbs, and browned.

dubbele boterham (dub-AY-lee BO-ter-rum). *Dut.* A sandwich made with two pieces of bread, such as is made in the United States.

dubbelsmörgås (dew-behl-SMURR-goass). *Swe.* Sandwich.

Dublin Bay prawn (DUB-len Bay prahn). *Bri.* Saltwater crayfish.

duchesse, à la (duh-shees). *Fre.* Boiled potatoes, pureed with eggs and butter, then piped through a pastry tube as a garnish.

duck (duhk). *USA.* Any of various edible swimming game birds, with short legs and neck, and webbed feet. For domesticated duck, see Long Island duck.

duck sauce (duhk saus). *USA.* Suan mei jiang, a Chinese sauce.

du corps (doo kowr). *Fre.* Good body, as applies to sauces or soups.

due (doo-ey). *Dan.* Pigeon (squab).

duff (duhff). *USA.* A steamed pudding with fruit, such as plum duff or cranberry duff.

dugléré (doog-lahr). *Fre.* Indicates the use of tomatoes.

du jour (doo-zhoor). *Fre.* "Of the day"; soup du jour is soup of the day.

dulce (DOOL-seh). *Mex.* Sweet.

dulces (DOOL-sehs). *Spa.* Sweets; desserts.

dulse (dehls). *Bri.* A coarse, edible seaweed used for gelatin.

dumpling (DUM-pleng). *USA.* A lump of dough steamed on top of a liquid, such as soup or stew.

Dundee cake (DEHN-dee kek). *Sco.* A fruit cake with a topping of almonds.

Dungeness crab (DUN-gen-ess krab). *USA.* The most popular of the Pacific crabs; pinkish-green and yellow before cooking, it becomes a brilliant red when cooked.

dunkeles Bier (DUNG-klerss beer). *Ger.* Dark, heavy beer.

Dunlop (DUHN-loap). *Sco.* A cows' milk cheese, moderately soft, moist, bland.

dünsten (DEWN-shtehn). *Ger.* To steam or stew, either fruit or meat.

dur (dyr). *Fre.* Hard; as hard boiled, of eggs.

duranzo (doo-RAHS-zoh). *Mex.* Peach.

durchgebraten (DURKH-geh-braat-en). *Ger.* Well done, as of steak.

durian (DUHR-ree-un). *Mal.* A large, oval, tasty, but foul-smelling fruit with a prickly rind; the large seeds are roasted and eaten like nuts.

duro (DOO-ro). *Ita.* Hard, as hard crust.

Dürre Runde (DEW-reh roont). *Ger.* A dried sausage.

durum wheat (DUHR-um wheet). *USA.* A very hard wheat whose grain is made into semolina flour.

dust (duhst). *USA.* To sprinkle lightly with flour, cornmeal, or sugar.

duva (du-va). *Swe.* Pigeon.

duxelles (dews-sehl). *Fre.* A kind of mushroom hash, used for seasoning sauces and as a spread.

dynya (DI-nyah). *Rus.* Melon.

dyreryg (DEWR-rewg). *Nor.* Venison that has been marinated, then cooked in sour cream.

dyrestek (DEWR-stehkt). *Nor.* Roast venison.

Dyrlaegens natmad (dewr-leh-yahns nat-meth). *Dan.* "Veterinarian's Midnight Snack"; a smørrebrød of dark rye bread, spread with spiced lard, liver paste, jellied consommé, veal.

E

eau de vie (oh duh vee). *Fre.* Fruit brandy; many varieties of which Kirschwasser is probably best known.

eau sucrée (oh su-crae). *USA.* A Creole word for "sugar water"; supposedly aids digestion and promotes sleep.

ebi (eh-BEE). *Jap.* Shrimp.

ebi suimono (eh-BEE soo-EE-moh-noh). *Jap.* Clear soup with shrimp.

ebis wantan men (eh-BEES wahn-tahn mehn). *Jap.* Curled white noodles plus dried Chinese-style won ton.

ecarlate (ay-kahr-laht). *Fre.* Scarlet; a red sauce containing lobster roe, red tongue, and so forth.

Eccles cake (EK-kuhls kahk). *Bri.* A small cake of puff pastry filled with currants and sprinkled with sugar.

ecetes torma (eht-seh-tehsh TAW-rmo). *Hun.* Horseradish sauce.

ecetet (eht-seh-teht). *Hun.* Vinegar.

échalote (ee-shah-lot). *Fre.* Shallot.

echaude (eh-shoad). *Fre.* Pastry made of dough then poached in water and baked in the oven.

éclair (ay-klahr). *Fre.* A finger-shaped pastry filled with cream or custard.

éclanche (ay-klahn-sheh). *Fre.* Shoulder of mutton.

écrevisse (ay-krey-vehs). *Fre.* Crayfish.

Edam (EE-duhm). *USA.* A round Dutch cheese of partly skimmed cows' milk with a mellow, nutlike flavor. It has the texture of firm yellow paste with red wax cover.

eda mame (eh-DAH mah-meh). *Jap.* Green soybean pods, used as a snack or appetizer.

Edammer (ay-DAHM-mur). *Dut.* Edam cheese.

eddik (EHD-dik). *Nor.* Vinegar.

eddike (EHDH-eegger). *Dan.* Vinegar.

édeskömény (AY-dehsh-kur-mayny). *Hun.* Caraway seeds.

édespaprika (AY-dehsh-pop-ree-ko). *Hun.* Milk paprika.

édességet (AY-dehsh-shy-geht). *Hun.* Dessert.

Edinburgh fog (EHD-en-berg fawg). *Bri.* Whipped cream flavored with sugar and vanilla and mixed with ratafia biscuits and chopped almonds.

Edinburgh rock (EHD-en-berg rahk). *Bri.* Sugar candy with a mellow texture.

eel (ehl). *USA.* A snakelike fish, with delicate flesh when caught in fast flowing water.

een broodje ei (AYn brood-yeh ay). *Dut.* Egg sandwich.

eend (aynt). *Dut.* Duck.

eendje (AYnd-yeh). *Dut.* Duckling.

efterrätt (AYF-terr-reht). *Swe.* Dessert, sweet.

egg (ehg). *USA.* The hard-shelled reproductive body produced by a domestic fowl. Chicken eggs are most commonly used in cooking.

egg (ehg). *Nor.* Egg; Eggerøre (EHGG-errurrer), scrambled egg; Hårdkokt (HAWR-kookt), hard-boiled; Kokt (kookt), boiled; and Litekokt (LITE-kookt), soft-boiled.

egg and crumb (ehg ahnd krum). *USA.* To dip food into diluted, slightly beaten egg, then dredge or sprinkle with crumbs.

egg foo yung (ehg foo yuhng). *USA.* A rich omelet made with the addition of Chinese vegetables, fish and meat.

eggnog (EHG-naug). *USA.* A drink consisting of beaten eggs, milk or cream, sugar, spices, and usually rum or brandy.

egg og bacon (ehg o BAY-kern). *Nor.* Bacon and eggs.

egg pie (ehg pi). *Bri.* A baked savory that is an ordinary pie crust filled with beaten or whole eggs and crumbled bits of crisp bacon.

eggplant (EHG-plahnt). *USA.* A perennial plant that yields a blackish-purple ovoid fruit, used as a vegetable. Also known as aubergine.

egg roll (ehg rohl). *USA.* Cai juan; pancakelike "skin" wrapped around a filling in the shape of a roll, then fried.

eggs Benedict (ehgs BEHN-ee-dehkt). *USA.* One-half of an English muffin topped with a slice of Canadian bacon, poached egg, and hollandaise sauce.

eggs Sardou (ehgs SAHR-doh). *USA.* Poached eggs with artichoke hearts, anchovies, chopped ham, truffle, and hollandaise sauce.

egg wash. (ehg wahsh). *USA.* Beaten egg diluted with a liquid, used to dip food in preparation for crumbing.

egg yolks (ehg-uohlk). *USA.* The yellow of the egg, used to thicken sauces, enrich foods, add color to foods; high fat content.

églefin (ehg-ler-fang). *Fre.* Haddock. Also spelled égrefin, aiglefin.

egres (eh-grahsh). *Hun.* Gooseberries.

Égyptienne (ay-zgeep-sjen). *Fre.* Egyptian style: with lentils.

ei (eye). *Dut.* Egg.

Eier (IGH-err). *Ger.* Eggs; Hartgekocht Eier (HAHRT-ger-KOKHT), hard-cooked; Rühreier (REWR-igherr), scrambled; Verlorene Eier (fehr-LO-rehm IGH-err), eggs poached in vinegar; Weich Gekochte Eier (vighkh ger-KOKH-ter IGH-err), soft boiled.

Eiercrème (IGH-err-krem). *Ger.* Custard.

eieren (AY-uh-ruh). *Dut.* Eggs; gekookte eieren (khuh-KOHKT AY-uh-ruh), boiled; harde eieren (hart AY-uh-ruh), hard-cooked; harde gekookte eieren (hart khuh KOKH-tuh AY-uh-ruh), hard boiled; Spiegeleiren (SPEE-khul-ay-uh-ruh), fried.

eieren met ham (AY-uh-ruh met HAHM). *Dut.* Ham and eggs.

eieren met spek (AY-uh-ruh met SPEK). *Dut.* Bacon and eggs.

eierenpannekoeken (AY-uh-ruh-PAHN-nuh-koo-kuh). *Dut.* Pancakes.

eiergehak (AY-uh-khuh-haak). *Dut.* Eggs with ground meat added.

Eierkuchen (IGH-err-ku-xon). *Ger.* Omelet.

Eier mit Speck (IGH-err meht shpehk). *Ger.* Bacon and eggs.

Eieröhrli (IGH-err-oh-rurht-lee). *Ger.* Zürich carnival cakes, fried in butter; very, very thin, but rich.

Eierpflanzen (IGH-err-phlant-zen). *Ger.* Eggplant.

Eierspeisen (IGH-err-shpai-zen). *Ger.* Egg dishes.

Eierteigwaren (IGH-err-taik-vaar-en). *Ger.* Egg noodles, spaghetti, macaroni.

einbern (AIN-bern). *Jew.* A brown roux.

Eingemacht (AIN-ga-mahk-ta). *Ger.* Preserved, such as preserved fruits.

Eintopf (AIN topf). *Ger.* One-dish meal.

Eis (eyess). *Ger.* Ice cream.

Eisbein (IGHS-bighn). *Ger.* Pickled pork knuckles.

éisc (ayshk). *Iri.* Fish, plural; one fish is isac.

Eisschokolade (eyess-shok-o-LAAD-eh). *Ger.* Iced chocolate.

ejotes (e-HOH-tehs). *Mex.* Green beans.

elaichi (ee-LIE-a-chee). *Ind.* Cardamom.

elderberry (EL-dur-bear-ri). *USA.* A blackish-purple berry of the elder tree, used in fruit soups, jellies, homemade wines; must be cooked.

eleesh (EH-lesh). *Ind.* Fatty fish found in Hooghly River.

elephant garlic (ELL-eh-fant GAHR-lick). *USA.* A very large, mild-flavored vegetable with a mild garlic flavor; does not have a strong garlic odor; looks similar to common garlic; whole cloves can be prepared like potatoes and onions; also use raw in salads.

elft (elft). *Dut.* Shad.

elg (ehlg). *Nor.* Elk.

elixir (ee-LICK-sur). *USA.* A liquid made by dissolving various edible substances in alcohol or wine with high alcoholic content.

elöetelt (eh-lur-aytehlt). *Hun.* Appetizer.

elote (eh-LOH-teh). *Mex.* Fresh corn.

embutidos (ehm-boo-TEE-dous). *Spa.* Pork sausages.

émincé (eh-manss). *Fre.* Thinly sliced leftover meat, covered with a seasoned sauce and heated through.

Emmental (EH-mehn-tah). *Ger.* A cows' whole-milk cheese made in Switzerland, with a hard brown rind, golden interior with large holes; mellow, rich nutty taste; large wheels. Also known as Swiss cheese.

empada (em-PAH-dah). *Por.* Pie.

empadinhas de camarão (em-pah-DEEN-yash deh cam-a-ROWNSH). *Por.* Little shrimp pies.

empanada (ehm-pah-NAH-dah). *Spa.* A tart with various fillings; a turnover.

empandita (ehm-pahn-DEE-tah). *Spa.* A pastry turnover with various savory fillings.

empanizado (ehm-pah-NEE-zah-doh). *Spa.* Breaded.

em sangue (ehm SAN-guh). *Por.* Rare, as in preparing steak.

emulsion (e-MULL-shun). *USA.* The dispersion of small droplets of one liquid into a second liquid with which it is incapable of mixing or attaining homogeneity without the use of an emulsifier, for example, the use of eggs in making mayonnaise.

en brochette (ahng broh-sheh). *Fre.* Broiled on a skewer.

enchiladas (en-chee-LAH-dah). *Mex.* Tortillas filled variously with meat, cheese, chilies, then rolled and served with sauce.

en cocotte (ahng-koh-koht). *Fre.* In individual casserole.

en croute (ahng-kroot). *Fre.* Wrapped and baked in pastry.

enoki (ee-NOH-kee). *Jap.* An abbreviated word for enokitake.

enokitake (ee-NOH-kee-tah-kee). *Jap.* Wild mushroom with tiny caps and thin stems; mild-flavored, pleasant crispness and aroma; used in soups and one-pot dishes. Also called enoki.

en jalea (ayn KHAY-leh). *Spa.* Jellied.

encurtidos (ehn-koor-TEE-doh). *Spa.* Pickles.

endive (EN-div). *USA.* A salad green with a bunchy head and narrow, curly, sticky leaves; center is yellow-white; taste is mildly astringent in center, outer green leaves tend to be slightly bitter.

endomame (en-DOH-mah-meh). *Jap.* Peas.

Engadiner Nusstorte (ehn-gun-DEE-ner NEUSS-tortr). *Ger.* Rich, flat Swiss cake filled with nuts and honey.

Engelsk bøf (EHNG-erlsk burf). *Dan.* English beefsteak; filet of beef.

English muffin (EHNG-glesh muhf-fehn). *USA.* A round, slightly coarse-textured, flat muffin, usually split and grilled or toasted.

enguias (ehn-GHEEAHSH). *Por.* Eels.

en papillote (ahng pah-pee-yoa). *Fre.* Meat, fish, poultry, and/or vegetables cooked in a parchment bag.

enriched rice (ehn-RICHD rice). *USA.* Rice having some of the nutrients replaced that were lost during milling.

enrollado (ehn-roh-LAH-doh). *Mex.* Rolled.

ensalada (een-sah-LAH-tah). *Spa.* Salad.

ensalada de pepino (een-sah-LAH-tah daa pah-PEE-noh). *Spa.* Cucumber salad.

ensalada de San Isidro (een-sah-LAH-tah daa Sahn Ehs ee-droh). *Spa.* Lettuce and tuna fish salad.

ensalada variada. (een-sah-LAH-tah BEHR-deh). *Spa.* Mixed green salad.

ensopado (ehn-sou-PAH-doo). *Por.* Thick, hearty soup of bread and meat.

Ente (EHN-ter). *Ger.* Duck.

Entenbrüstchen (ehnt-en-BRUST-khen). *Ger.* Breast of duckling.

Entenweissauer (ehnt-en-VIHSS-owehr). *Ger.* Duckling in aspic.

entrecôte (ahngtr-koat). *Fre, Ita.* A steak cut from between the ribs.

entrecôte château (ahngtr-kot sha-toah). *Fre.* A large steak.

entrecôte minute (ahngtr-kot meen cwt). *Fre.* Small steak.

entrecuisse (ahngtr-khis). *Fre.* The fleshy thigh joint of poultry or game birds.

entree (ahng-tray). *Fre.* The first course of a meal.

entree (AHN-tray). *USA.* The main course of the meal.

entremeses (ehn-treh-MEH-sehs). *Spa.* Hors d'oeuvres.

entremets (ehm-tray-mais). *Fre.* Dainty dishes of vegetables served as a second course. Hot or cold sweets and after-dinner savories served as a second course.

epaule (ay-pohl). *Fre.* Shoulder.

epazote (eh-pah-SOH-teh). *Mex.* An herb used in cooking.

eper (eh-oehr). *Hun.* Strawberries.

éperlan (ay-pehr-lahng). *Fre.* Smelt.

épice (ay-pis). *Fre.* Spice.

épices composes (ay-pees kom-poz). *Fre.* A classic combination of herbs and spices for seasoning; dried thyme, bay leaves, basil, sage, coriander, mace, and black pepper. Also called spice Parisienne.

epigramme (eh-pee-grahm). *Fre.* Slices of breast of lamb, dipped in egg, rolled in breadcrumbs, and fried in butter or grilled.

épinard (ay-pee-nahr). *Fre.* Spinach.

eple (EHP-ler). *Nor.* Apple.

eplesnø (EHP-le-snur). *Nor.* Apple snow pudding.

eplucher (eh-plew-sheh). *Fre.* To peel.

eponger (eh-poan-zhah). *Fre.* To drain vegetables on a towel.

Erba (EHR-bah). *Ita.* Herb.

erbette (ehr-BEHR-tah). *Ita.* A vegetable similar to spinach or beet greens; has an elongated smallish leaf and a slim, tender green stalk. Also called bietoline.

Erbsen (EHRP-sern). *Ger.* Peas.

Erdapfel (EHRT-ah-pferl). *Ger.* Potato.

Erdapfelnudeln (EHRT-ah-pferl-NOOD-len). *Ger.* Very small oblong Austrian potato dumplings rolled in fat-fried breadcrumbs.

Erdberren (EHRT-bay-ren). *Ger.* Strawberries.

erter (AE-terr). *Nor.* Peas.

ertesuppe (ae-terr-SEWP-per). *Nor.* A hearty pea soup.

ervanço (ehr-VAHN-soo). *Por.* Chick-peas; garbanzo bean.

ervilhas (ehr-VEEL-yahss). *Por.* Peas.

erwtensoep (EHR-tuh-soop). *Dut.* Famous split pea soup.

erwtjes (EHR-tyus). *Dut.* Peas.

escabeche (ehs-kah-BEH-cheh). *Spa.* Pickling marinade.

escalfado (ehsh-kahl-FAH-doo). *Por.* Poached.

escalibada (ays-kah-LAY-bah-dah). *Spa.* A mixture of vegetables grilled over charcoal.

escalopado (ehs-kah-loh-PAH-doh). *Mex.* Escalloped.

escalope (eh-skah-lop). *Fre.* Thin slices of meat or fish.

escalloped (eh-SKAHL-lahped). *USA.* Baked in a sweet or savory sauce, usually covered with breadcrumbs.

escargot (ays-skahr-go). *Fre.* Snail.

escarole (ES-kar-roll). *Ita.* A broad-leaf type of endive; slightly bitter; the leaves do not curl at the ends; foliage is deep green, slightly crumpled and closely bunched; use in salads.

espadon (eh-spohd-oa). *Fre.* Swordfish.

espagnole (ay-spah-nyol). *Fre.* Brown sauce.

espargos (ess-PAHR-gohss). *Por.* Asparagus.

espárrago (ehs-PAHRR-ah-goh). *Spa.* Asparagus.

espinaca (ehs-prr-NAH-kahs). *Spa.* Spinach.

espinafres (ess-pee-NAH-fray). *Por.* Spinach.

espresso (e-SPRESS-o). *Ita.* Coffee made by forcing steam through finely ground, darkly roasted coffee beans.

esqueixada (es-quah-ZAH-dah). *Spa.* Fish salad.

essence (ESS-scunc). *USA.* A concentrated substance that resembles an extract in possessing a quality in concentrated form; that is, fish essence, banana essence.

Essig (EHS-sikh). *Ger.* Vinegar.

essigfleisch (ICS-seg-flesh). *Jew.* Sweet and sour meat.

Essigkren (EHS-sikh-ren). *Ger.* Horseradish in vinegar, sugar, and spices.

Esterhazy Rostbraten (ehs-tehr-HAHt-cee hurst-BRAR-tern). *Ger.* Filet of beef with a rich stuffing, roasted with a chopped-vegetable sauce and basted with Madeira; an Austrian dish.

estofado (ehs-toh-FAH-doh). *Spa.* Stew.

estouffade (ehs-toh-fahd). *Fre.* Food cooked by slowly stewing; also, a clear brown stock used to dilute sauces and moisten braised dishes.

estragon (eh-strah-gohn). *Fre.* Tarragon.

etamine (eh-tah-meen). *Fre.* A cloth for straining sauces, or stocks.

etikkasilli (ay-tahk-kah-SIL-li). *Fin.* Pickled herring.

étolajat (AY-taw-loyot). *Hun.* Dessert.

etuvee (eh-too-veh). *Fre.* A method of cooking food with little or no liquid.

evaporated milk (e-VAHP-oh-rate-ed mehlk). *USA.* Milk with half of its water content removed, then sterilized; has a caramelized taste.

Exeter stew (EX-eh-tehr steu). *Bri.* A stew of beef, onions, and dumplings.

exhausting (ex-ZAUST-eng). *USA.* A term used in canning food meaning to drive out enough air to make the desired vacuum.

export (EKS-poht). *Nor.* Potent lager-type beer.

expresso (ex-SPREHS-so). *Ita.* Espresso.

extract (EX-strack). *USA.* A product obtained by evaporating animal or vegetable juice.

extruded (ex-STRU-dehd). *USA.* To shape by forcing, pressing or pushing through a die, or sieve.

eye of the round (eye ovf the rahund). *USA.* The round muscle in the center of the round section of the hindquarter of beef.

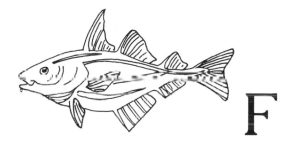

F

faakiha (FAK-ha). *Ara.* Fruit.

faaswulyaa (fa-SUL-yah). *Ara.* Beans.

fabada asturiana (fah-BAH-dah ahs-too-ree-AH-nah). *Spa.* A hearty stew of fava beans, meats, onions.

fadøl (fah-durl). *Dan.* Draught beer.

fagiano (fah-JAA-noa). *Ita.* Pheasant.

fagioli (fah-JOA-lee). *Ita.* Beans, usually kidney beans.

fagioli assolutti (fah-JOA-lee ahs-zoa-LOOT-tee). *Ita.* Kidney beans fried with garlic in oil.

fagiolini (fah-joa-LEE-nee). *Ita.* Green beans.

fagot (FAHG-gaht). *USA.* Herbs and seasoning vegetables tied together in a small cheesecloth bundle. Usually called bouquet garni.

fagylaltot (FOD-ylol-tawt). *Hun.* Ice cream.

fah chiu (fah chiu). *Chi.* A hot pepper for seasoning.

faht choy (faht choy). *Chi.* A hairlike seaweed.

faisan (feh-zahng). *Fre.* Pheasant.

faisan (figh-SSAHN). *Spa.* Game birds.

faisão (fay-ZAHNG). *Por.* Pheasant.

fajita (fah-HEE-tah). *Mex.* Warm, soft tortilla rolled with grilled spicy meats, chopped lettuce, tomatoes, green onions, grated cheeses, and topped with sour cream.

falafel (fah-LAH-fahl). *Ara.* Chick-pea patties made of ground peas mixed with herbs and spices, then fried.

fàn (fahn). *Chi.* Rice.

fannings (FAHN-engz). *USA.* Broken leaves from which a quick, strong tea is brewed.

får (fohr). *Swe.* Mutton.

faraona (fah-rah-OA-nah). *Ita.* Guinea hen roasted in clay to seal in juices and flavor.

farce (fahr-ceh). *Fre.* Forcemeats or stuffings.

farci (fahr-cee). *Fre.* Cabbage stuffed with sausage meat or other forcemeat, wrapped in muslin, and cooked in stock.

farcito (fah-CHEE-toa). *Ita.* Stuffed.

farefrikassée (FAWR-freek-ahssee). *Nor.* Fricasseed lamb.

fårestek (FAWR-sstayk). *Nor.* Roast leg of lamb.

farfahin (fahr-fah-HEHN). *Ara.* The herb purslane.

farfalle (fah-FAHL-lay). *Ita.* Butterfly-shaped pasta.

farfel (FAHR-fehl). *Jew.* Dried, grated egg dough; used as garnish in soup.

fårikål (FAY-nah-lawr). *Nor.* Lamb stewed with cabbage.

farina (fah-REE-nah). *Ita.* Flour.

farina (fah-REE-nah). *USA.* A creamy-colored, granular, protein-rich meal made from hard wheat other than durum, with the bran and most of the germ removed.

farinha de avêa (fah-REE-nyah duh ah-VAY-ah). *Por.* Oatmeal.

farmer cheese (FAHR-mehr cheez). *USA.* A cows' partly skimmed milk cheese similar to cottage cheese.

farsh (fahrsh). *Rus.* Stuffing.

fårsj oxbringa (fahrsk OOKS-BRING-a). *Swe.* Boiled beef.

färsk sill (faersk sil). *Swe.* Fresh herring.

fårstek (fooaar stayk). *Swe.* Leg of mutton.

fasan (fa-SAHN). *Swe.* Pheasant.

fasan (fah-SAAN). *Dan.* Pheasant.

Fasan (fah-ZARN). *Ger.* Pheasant.

Faschierter Braten (fah-SHEER-terss BRAR-tern). *Ger.* Meat loaf.

Fasnacht (FAAS-nakht). *USA.* Pennsylvania Dutch diamond-shaped potato dough yeast pastry that is fried, traditionally eaten on Shrove Tuesday.

fasol (fah-SSOL). *Rus.* Haricot bean, green bean, French bean.

fasulya (fa-SUL-ya). *Ara.* Lima beans.

fatia (fah-TEE-ah). *Por.* Slice.

fatias frias (fah-TEE-ahss FREE-ahss). *Por.* Cold cuts.

fatir (fi-TEER). *Ara.* Pancakes, often served with jam or honey.

fatta (FAHT-tah). *Ara.* Mutton stewed in broth with bread and rice.

fåttiga riddare (FOAR-ti RID-ahrer). *Swe.* French toast.

fatto in casa (FAHT-toa een KAH-sah). *Ita.* Homemade.

fausse tortue (fos tohr-ty). *Fre.* Mock turtle.

fava bean (FAV-ah been). *USA.* A broad bean of Mediterranean origin; large, meaty, pale green beans with large green pods; used fresh, dried, and canned; important worldwide for its nutritional value.

favas (FAH-vahsh). *Por.* Fava beans; broad beans.

fave (FAH-vay). *Ita.* Broad beans.

fazan (FAH-zhan). *Rus.* Pheasant.

fazant (fah-ZAHNT). *Dut.* Pheasant.

febras de porco (FAY-bahsh duh POUR-koo). *Por.* Leg of pork, cooked in red wine and brandy, seasoned with cloves, garlic, cumin.

fécule (fehk-eul). *Fre.* Refined potato starch used as thickener.

fegatelli (fay-gah-TAYL lee). *Ita.* Pork liver.

fegatini (fay-gah-TEE-nee). *Ita.* Chicken livers

fegato (fay-GAH-toa). *Ita.* Liver.

fegato d'oca (fay-GAH-toa dOA-kah). *Ita.* Goose liver.

fehérhagyma mártás (feh-HAYR-rod-ymo MAAR-taash). *Hun.* Onion sauce.

Feigen (FAIG-ahn). *Ger.* Figs.

feijão (fay-ZHOW). *Por.* Beans.

feijão de vagens (fay-ZHOW dat VAH-zhayz). *Por.* Green beans.

feijoa (fay-HO-a). *Spa.* A slightly bumpy, thin skinned, green fruit of South America, with a cream-colored granular, slightly soft flesh, like a pear; tart and perfumy; use fresh in salads or make into preserves. Also known as pineapple guava.

feijoada (fay-zhoh-AH-dah). *Por.* A hearty, soupy stew made of pork, beef, black beans, rice, seasoned with peppers, garnished with oranges.

Feingeback (FYENT-bak). *Ger.* Pastry.

fejes-salátát (feh-yaysh SHOL-laa-taat). *Hun.* Lettuce.

Felchen (FEHL-chehn). *Ger.* A kind of freshwater trout.

fenalår (FAY-nah-lawr). *Nor.* Smoked leg of mutton.

fennel (FEN-null). *USA.* An anise-flavored celerylike herb whose seeds and leaves are used for seasoning and whose stems, and in some varieties a bulbous base, are edible.

fenouil (fah-nujz). *Fre.* Fennel.

fen si (fen see). *Chi.* Translucent noodles made from mung beans.

fenugreek (FEN-uh-greek). *Ind.* An ancient herb whose maple-flavored leaves are used as a vegetable, in curry powder, as an artificial maple flavoring in candies and syrup; its celery-flavored seeds are used whole and ground.

feoil (fy-AWIL). *Iri.* Meat.

feoil mhairt (fy-AWIL wartch). *Iri.* Beef.

féra (fah-rah). *Fre.* A variety of salmon.

fermentation (fur-men-TA-shun). *USA.* A chemical change brought about by the action of bacteria, yeast, or mold.

fermière (fayr-myayr). *Fre.* In plain country style.

ferri (FEHR-ree). *Ita.* Grilled over an open fire.

fersken (FAYRSK-nerr). *Dan.* Peach.

fersk røget laks (fayrsk ROI-ert lahks). *Dan.* Fresh smoked Nova Scotia salmon.

Feta (FEH-tah). *Gre.* A crumbly, salty, white, rindless ewes' milk cheese.

fett'unta (feht-t'OON-tah). *Ita.* A favorite Tuscany dish of coarse-textured bread, toasted over coals and liberally dressed with extra virgin olive oil. Also called fregolotta or bruschetta.

fetta (fAYt-tah). *Ita.* A slice.

fettuccine (fayt-toot-CHEE-nay). *Ita.* Egg pasta in long, thin, flat strips. Also known as tagliatelle, pappardelle.

feuilles de betteraves (furee-lehs der beh-ter-rahv). *Fre.* Beet greens.

feuilletage (fuhy-leh-tah-zhay). *Fre.* Puff pastry; flaky, leafy.

feuilletée (fuhy-leh-tay). *Fre.* In leaves; said of very thin sheets of pastry, similar to phyllo.

fèves (fehv). *Fre.* Broad beans.

fiambres (FYAHM-brayss). *Spa.* Cooked meats served cold; boiled ham.

fichi (FEE-kee). *Ita.* Figs.

fichi secchi (FEE-kee sAY-chee). *Ita.* Dried figs.

fiddlehead (FEEHD-uhl-hehd). *USA.* The young sprouts of certain ferns, harvested while young and tender, used as a vegetable and for garnishes.

fideos (fee-DHAY-oass). *Spa.* Spaghetti; noodles.

field lettuce (feeld LETT-us). *USA.* A loose-leaf lettuce found in the wild in the United States; clusters are small with smooth green leaves; sometimes cooked as vegetable. Also called lamb's lettuce.

field peas (feeld pehs). *USA.* A small, edible pea grown for food and forage.

figado (FEE-gah-doh). *Por.* Liver.

figos (FEE-gohss). *Por.* Figs.

figs (fehgz). *USA*. The pear-shaped, edible fruit of the fig tree; eaten fresh and dried.

figue (fig). *Fre*. Fig.

fijn brood (fine broht). *Dut*. Fine bread.

fikon (FEE-kon). *Swe*. Figs.

filbert (FILL-bert) *USA*. The nut of a hazel shrub; round or slightly oval and flat on one end, amber colored; flavor is sweet; texture firm; rich in oil; pleasant to taste; used in confectionery. Also known as hazelnut.

filbunke (FIL-bewnk). *Swe*. Clabbered milk, junket. Not to be mistaken for yogurt.

filé (FEE-lay). *Hun*. Filet.

filé (fee-LEH). *Por*. Filet; tenderloin steak.

filé powder (fee-LAY). *USA*. Ground young dried sassafras leaves, used to flavor and thicken gumbos in Creole cooking. Also called gumbo filé.

filet (fee-leh). *Fre*. Boneless piece of red meat or beef; not to be confused with fillet which refers to fish or poultry.

filete (fi-LEH-teh). *Spa*. Filet.

filete de vaca (fi-LEH day vau kah). *Spa*. Beef tenderloin.

filet mignon (fee leh mee nyon). *Fre*. A small slice from the thick end of the tenderloin.

filetto (fee-LEHT-toa). *Ita*. Fillet.

filfil. (FIL-fil). *Ara*. Pepper.

filhó (fee-lee-OO). *Por*. Fritter, pancake.

fillet (FILL-eht). *USA*. Boneless piece of fish or poultry; not to be confused with filet, which refers to beef or red meat.

filling (FIL-eng). *USA*. A food mixture to fill pastries or sandwiches.

filmjölk (FIL-myohlk). *Swe*. Sour milk, similar to yogurt.

filo (PHE-lo). *Gre*. Phyllo.

filosoop (FEE-loh-sooph). *Dut*. "Philosopher's Dish"; made of minced meat, mashed potato, and onions, similar to shepherd's pie.

financière (fee-nahng-syehr). *Fre*. A meat or poultry garnish of cocks' combs and kidneys, truffles, sweetbreads, mushrooms, and olives.

finanziere (fee-nahn-ZEE-rah). *Ita*. Cibreo; a dish of cocks' combs and sweetbreads, served with vegetable timbales.

finely chop (fine-lee chahp). *USA*. Cutting food into very small pieces, less than ⅛ inch.

fine marineret sild (fin maaree-NAYT-ert seel). *Dan*. Fine pickled herring.

fines herbes (feen-zehrb). *Fre.* A combination of finely chopped fresh herbs.

finik (FEE-nyee-kee). *Rus.* Dates.

finocchio (feen-NOK-kee-oa). *Ita.* Fennel.

finocchiona (feen-nok-kee-OAN-ah). *Ita.* Fennel-flavored salami; never allow to age.

fiocchi d'avena (fee-OAK-kee dAHV-ay-nah). *Ita.* Oatmeal.

fiocchi di granturco (fee-OAK-kee day grahn-TOOR-koa). *Ita.* Cornflakes.

Fior di Latte (FEE-oar day LAHT-tay). *Ita.* A cows' milk cheese similar to Mozzarella.

fiore de zucchine ripiene (fee-OA-ray day tsook-CHEE-nay kree-pee-AY-nay). *Ita.* Stuffed zucchini flowers.

fiore mollo (fee-OA-ray MOAL-loa). *Ita.* Saffron-tinted cheese, soft and well flavored.

fiorentina (fee-oa-rayn-TEE-nah). *Ita.* Florentine style, usually with spinach.

fiorentina, bistecca (fee-oa-rayn-TEE-nah bee-stayk-kah). *Ita.* T-bone steak grilled over charcoal, in the Florentine style—rare and plain—but moistened after grilling with a few drops of olive oil.

fiori di zucca (fee-OA-ray day ZOO-kah). *Ita.* Batter dipped and fried squash blossoms.

Fior Sardo (FEE-oar Sahr-doa). *Ita.* Ewes' milk cheese, eaten fresh as table cheese or when aged, use for grating.

firm-ball stage (FURM-bahl staj). *USA.* The third stage of sugar crystallization: begins at 244°F. The syrup when dropped in a glass of water, will form a ball that will not flatten unless squeezed between the fingers.

firni (FIHR-nee). *Ind.* Pudding made with rice flour, almonds, and creamy milk.

Fisch (fish). *Ger.* Fish.

Fischbeuschlsuppe (fish-BOY-sherl-zup-per). *Ger.* A thick Austrian soup with lively flavoring; made from the lungs of freshwater fish.

Fischcrouton (fish-kroo-TONG). *Ger.* Fishballs.

Fischhackbraten (fish-HAHK-brar-tern). *Ger.* Baked fish loaf.

Fisch mit Kümmelkraut (fish met KEW-mehl-kroet). *Ger.* Fish with caraway-seasoned cabbage.

Fisch mit Feinen Kräuten (fish met FIGH-nern KROET-ehn). *Ger.* Austrian dish of fish seasoned with chopped herbs.

Fischrogen (FISH-roa-gehn). *Ger.* Roe.

Fischschüssel (fish-SHEWSS-el). *Ger.* Bacon and fish pie.

fish muddle (fesch MUHD-duhl). *USA.* Fish stew.

fisk (feesk). *Dan.* Fish.

fisk (fisk). *Nor, Swe.* Fish.

fiskbuller (FISK-bew-lahr). *Swe.* Codfish balls.

fiskeboller (FISK-bool-lehr). *Nor.* Fish balls.

fiskefars (FEESK-fars). *Dan.* Minced fish.

fiskefrikadellar (feesk-free-kah-DAY-ler). *Dan.* Fish balls.

fiskegrateng (FISK-graa-tteng). *Nor.* Fish soufflé.

fiskepudding (FISK-pewd-ding). *Nor.* Fish pudding.

fiskfärs (FISK-faer). *Swe.* Minced fish.

fiskkroketter (fiak-kroat-KEET-terr). *Swe.* Fish cakes; croquettes.

fisk med fyllning (fisk mayd FEWL-ning). *Swe.* With filling; stuffing.

fish og skalldyr (fisk o SKAHL-dewr). *Nor.* Seafood.

fisk på fat (fisk paw faht). *Nor.* "Fish on a platter"; fried, then baked in a sauce.

fisksnäcka (fisk-SNAHK-kah). *Swe.* Fish served in the shell.

fisksoppa (FISK-SO-pa). *Swe.* Fish soup.

five-spice powder (fiv-spic POW-dur). *USA.* A spicy Chinese seasoning consisting of ground cloves, fennel seeds, star anise, cinnamon, and Sichuan peppercorns or licorice root.

fjaerkre (FYEHR-krch). *Nor.* Poultry.

fläderbär (FLA-dehr-BAHR). *Swe.* Elderberries.

flaesk (flehsk). *Dan.* Pork, bacon.

flaeskesteg (FLEHSK-stayg). *Dan.* Roast pork.

flaeskesteg med Svaer (FLEHS-ker-stayg maydh svaer). *Dan.* Roast pork with red cabbage.

flageolet (FLA-zoe-lay). *Fre.* A very small green bean suitable as a garnish for meats, or as a delicately flavored puree.

flake (flak). *USA.* To break into small pieces, usually with a fork.

flake salt (flak sawlt). *USA.* A flake form of pickling salt.

flamande (fla-mahnd). *Fre.* A garnish of braised cabbage, diced pork belly, carrots, and potatoes. A hot-pot.

flambé (flahm-BAY). *Fre.* Served flaming; to douse with brandy, rum, or cognac, or other liquors, then ignite.

flameado. (flah-meh-AH-doh). *Spa.* Served flaming.

flan (flahn). *Fre, Bri.* An open fruit tart in sponge cake or pastry crust.

flan (flahn). *Spa.* A caramel cream custard that is baked.

flanchet (flahn-sheht). *Fre.* Flank steak.

flank (flahnk). *USA.* A cut of meat from between the ribs and the hip, the cut for London Broil.

flapjack (FLAHP-jahc). *USA.* Pancake.

fläsk (flahsk). *Swe.* Pork.

flatfish (flaht fisch). *USA.* Any saltwater fish, that, as an adult, has both eyes on one side: flounder, sole, turbot, halibut, and the European flounder, plaice.

flattbrød (FLAHT-brur). *Nor.* Very thin, crisp flat bread made of wheat, rye, barley flours.

flauta (FLAH-OO-tah). *Mex.* A large tortilla, or two overlapping, filled and rolled in a narrow long shape.

Fleisch (fleyesh). *Ger.* Meat.

Fleischbrühe (fleyesh-BRY-eh). *Ger.* Meat consommé.

Fleischgerichte (fleyesh-GEH-richt). *Ger.* Meat dishes.

Fleischkase (fleyesh-KEH-zeh). *Ger.* Meat loaf.

Fleischklösse (fleyesh-KLOHS). *Ger.* Meatballs.

Fleischkuchen (fleyesh-KU-zehn). *Ger.* Meat pies.

flensje (FLEN-shus). *Dut.* Thin pancakes; crèpes suzettes.

fleskepannekake (flehs-PAHN-ner-kkaaker). *Nor.* Pancakes with pork.

fleskepølse (flehs-PURLSS-err). *Nor.* Pork sausages.

flet (fleh). *Fre.* Flounder.

fleurette (flew-reht). *Fre.* Sweet cream.

fleurons (flew-rawng). *Fre.* Small half-moon shapes of puff paste, baked, used for garnishing entrees.

flitch (flich). *USA.* A side of bacon, smoked.

floating island (FLOT-eng I-luhn). *USA.* A dessert of clumps of meringue in custard.

flødekage (FLURDH-er-kaaer). *Dan.* Layer cream cake.

flødeskum (FLURDH-er-skoom). *Dan.* Whipped cream.

flødeost (FLURDH-oast). *Dan.* Cream cheese.

fløode (FLURDH-er). *Dan.* Cream.

florentine (FLOOR-en-teen). *Fre.* Prepared with spinach.

Fløte (FLUR-ter). *Nor.* Cream.

Fløtekaker (FLUR-ter-kaaker). *Nor.* Cream cakes.

Fløtesuppe (FLUR-ter-sewpper). *Nor.* Cream soup.

Fløtevafler (FLUR-ter-vaaf-lerr). *Nor.* Cream waffles.

flounder (FLAHN-dur). *USA.* One of the flatfish; has delicate, soft flesh.

flundra (FLEWN-drah). *Swe.* Flounder.

flour (flowr). *USA.* Finely ground meal of various grains. See specific name.

flour, to (flowr). *USA.* To coat with flour.

flour paste (flowr pahst). *USA.* A thickener of two parts liquid to one part flour, used for thickening sauces.

flummery (FLUM-mree). *Bri.* Cold sweet dish, mainly of oatmeal set in a mold, chilled, and turned out on a plate to be eaten with wine, cider, milk, or a sauce.

flummery (FLUM-ree). *USA.* A fruit pudding thickened with cornstarch.

Flunder (FLUHN-der). *Ger.* Flounder.

flute (fluht). *USA.* To make a grooved pattern on vegetables, fruit, or the edge of pie crust.

focaccia (foa-chah-CHEE-ah). *Ita.* Flat, round bread seasoned with sage and bacon.

focaccia di vitello (foa-chah-CHEE-ah day vee-TAYL-lo). *Ita.* Veal patties.

foderare (foa-day-RAH-ray). *Ita.* To line a mold or pan with dough or sponge cake slices or biscuits.

fodros fehér kalács (FAW-drawsh FEH-hayr KOl-laach). *Hun.* Spongy white milk-bread, available as rolls or in slices.

fofas de bacalhau (FOU-fahsh duh bah-kah-lee-YAU). *Por.* Codfish balls.

fogas (FAW-gosh). *Hun.* A local fish of the pike-perch family.

fogasszeletek Gundel módra (FAW-gosh-sehlehtehk GOON-dehl MAW-dro). *Hun.* Slices of fogas prepared Gundel style: breaded fillet of pike. Gundel was a famous Hungarian restauranteur.

fogosch (FOA-goash). *Ger.* Austrian freshwater troutlike fish.

foie (fwa). *Fre.* Liver.

foie de veau (fwa du vu). *Fre.* Calf's liver.

foie gras (fwa-grah). *Fre.* The liver of fat geese for making pâté de foie gras, which is cooked livers seasoned with truffles, wine, and aromatics.

fokhagymás mártás (FAWK-hody-maash MAAR-tash). *Hun.* Garlic sauce.

folares (fou-LAH-ruhsh). *Por.* Eggs baked in nests of bread.

fold in (fold ehn). *USA.* To incorporate into a mixture by repeated gentle overturnings without beating or stirring. Also called folding.

foncer (fohs-jer). *Fre.* To line the bottom of a pan with slices of ham or bacon.

fond (fahn). *Fre.* Strong gravy or meat stock.

fondant (FAHN-dant). *Fre.* Icing mixture used as coating for pastries and confections.

fond d'artichaut (fon d'ahr-tee-choh). *Fre.* Artichoke heart.

fondre, faire (fehr fon-druh). *Fre.* To "melt;" to cook vegetables very gently until softened, especially onions, leeks, and garlic.

fondue (FONG-du). *Fre.* Melted or blended cheese.

fonduta (foan-DOO-tah). *Ita.* A dish of melted Fontina cheese with eggs and sliced truffles.

fontana (foan-TAH-nah). *Ita.* The method of mixing pasta; putting the flour in the shape of a fountain on the table, into which eggs or liquid required to make the pasta or dough are placed.

Fontel (FOAN-tayl). *Ita.* A cows' whole milk cheese similar to Fontina.

Fontina (Foan-TEE-nah). *Ita.* A cows' whole milk pale yellow cheese with brown crust, creamy, mild, nutty.

foo gwah (foo gwah). *Chi.* Bitter melon; the size of a cucumber, brilliant green, has a bitter flavor; stuffed or stir-fried with meat.

fool (fuool). *Bri.* Pureed fruit mixed with cream and sugar.

foon tiu meen (foon tiu meen). *Chi.* Wide, flat noodles.

foo yung (foo yung). *Chi.* An omelet made with meat, poultry, seafood, vegetables or just eggs.

forcemeat (FORS-meet). *Fre.* Finely chopped, highly seasoned meat or fish; served alone or as a stuffing. Also called farce.

forel (fah-REHL). *Rus.* Trout.

forel (fo-REL). *Dut.* Trout.

forell (fo-RAYL). *Swe.* Trout.

Forelle (foh-REL-ea). *Ger.* Trout.

forestière (for-ees-tee-aire). *Fre.* A garnish of sauteed morels, diced bacon and potatoes; served with small cuts of meat and poultry.

forloren skildpadde (far-LAUREN skil-PAHD-deh). *Dan.* "Mock Turtle"; a very complicated dish made from calf's head, tongue, brains, meat balls, fish balls, and hard-boiled eggs.

forlorent (fo-LOOR-ernt). *Nor.* Poached.

formaggio (fohr-MAH-jee-oh). *Ita.* Cheese.

forno (FOHR-noh). *Ita.* Roasted, baked.

forrett (FOR-reht). *Nor.* Appetizer.

fortune cookie (FOHR-chun KOHK-kee). *USA.* Of Chinese origin, a thin cookie that is folded around a slip of paper on which is printed a proverb or humorous saying.

fouet (fweh). *Fre.* Whisk.

foul (fool). *Ara.* Fava beans, broad beans.

four, au (foor). *Fre.* Baked in the oven.

Fourme d'Ambert (furm d'am-bear). *Fre.* A cows' skimmed milk cheese; creamy with blue veins, dry rind; tall, cylindrical shape.

fourrage (foo-RAJ). *Fre.* Stuffing; filling.

fourré (foo-RA). *Fre.* Coated with sugar, cream.

four spices (for SPI-cez). *USA.* A French formula for seasoning sweets and meats, consisting of one teaspoon each cloves, nutmeg, ginger, and one tablespoon cinnamon when used with sweet, or white pepper when used with savory dishes. Also called quatre épices.

fózeléket (FURZ-ehlay-keht). *Hun.* Vegetables.

fragole (FRAA-goa-lay). *Ita.* Strawberries.

fragole di bosco (FRAA-goa-lay day boaz-koh). *Ita.* Wild strawberries.

fraiche (frehsh). *Fre.* Fresh. Also spelled frais.

frais (freh). *Fre.* Fresh. Also spelled fraiche.

fraisage (fray-sawgh). *Fre.* A technique for kneading dough by smearing it across the breadboard with the heel of the hand, then forming the mass into a ball.

fraise (frehz). *Fre.* Strawberry.

fraise des bois (frehz day bwah). *Fre.* Wild strawberry.

framboezas (frum-BOZ-en). *Por.* Raspberries.

framboise (frahn-bwahz). *Fre.* Raspberry.

frambozen (frahm-BO-zuh). *Dut.* Raspberries.

frambuesa (frahm-BWAY-ssahss). *Spa.* Raspberry.

franconia (fran-CON-i-a). *Ger.* Browned, as Franconia potatoes: whole potatoes browned with the roast.

frangipane (fronz-pahn). *Fre.* A type of puff pastry.

frangipane creme (fronz-pahn krehm). *Fre.* A substitute for custards that is made of eggs, milk, some flour, with lemon-peel, rum, brandy, vanilla to flavor.

frango (FRAN-goo). *Por.* Young chicken, broiler.

frango com ervilhas (FRAN-goo com ehr-VEEL-yahss). *Por.* Chicken prepared with olive oil and butter, port wine, tiny peas, and onions.

frango guisado (FRAN-goo ghee-ZAH-doh). *Por.* Chicken stewed with onions and tomatoes.

Frankfurter (FRAHNK-fuhr-tehr). *Ger.* Small sausage.

franks (frankz). *USA.* The abbreviated term for frankfurters.

franskbröd (FRAHNSK-brurd). *Swe.* French bread, roll.

franskbrød (FRANSK-brurdh). *Dan.* French bread.

frappé (fra-PAY). *Fre.* Beaten and iced; applies to water ice frozen to mush while stirring; usually drunk rather than eaten with a spoon or fork.

fraughan (fraun). *Bri.* Irish blueberries.

freddo (FRAYD-do). *Ita.* Cold.

freezer burn (FREE-zur buhrn). *USA.* The dry, fibrous and discolored food product resulting from inadequate packaging and protection against moisture loss that occurs in the freezing process.

fregolotta (fray-goa-LOT-tah). *Ita.* A popular Tuscan dish of coarse-textured bread, toasted over coals and liberally dressed with extra virgin olive oil. Also called fett'unta and bruschetta.

French fry (frehnch fri). *USA.* To deep-fat fry.

French icing (frehnch I-ceng). *USA.* A cooked icing using confectioners' sugar instead of granulated, with butter, egg, and flavoring.

French toast (frehnch tost). *USA.* Slices of day-old bread, dipped in sweetened egg batter, then pan-fried in shallow oil.

fresa (FRAY-ssahss). *Spa.* Strawberry.

fresca (FREHS-kah). *Mex.* Fresh.

fresco (FRAYZ-ko). *Ita, Spa, Por.* Fresh.

fresh ham (fresch hahm). *USA.* The hind leg of a pig which has not been cured or smoked.

Fresno chili (FREHZ-noh CHEHL-leh). *Mex.* A fairly hot, small, conical, light green to greenish-yellow chili pepper.

fressure (fray-suhr). *Fre.* Edible offal; liver, heart, brains, tripe.

friandise (free-uhn-deez). *Fre.* Small confections.

fricadelles (frick-ah-dell). *Fre.* Croquettes.

fricassee (frick-a-see). *Fre.* A white stew of chicken or veal.

fricassee (FRICK-a-see). *USA.* A light brown stew made by browning in a small amount of fat, pieces of fowl or veal, then stewing or steaming in a small amount of liquid.

Fridatten (frid-DAH-tern). *Ger.* Small Austrian pancakes cut in thin strips, used as garnish on soups.

fried cream (fryd krem). *USA.* A thick custard, thoroughly chilled, cut in squares, dipped in beaten eggs, rolled in finely crushed cake crumbs, deep-fried, sprinkled with powdered sugar and rum.

Friese (FREE-sah). *Dut.* A cows' milk cheese; very hard; spiced with cloves and cumin; strong flavor.

friesian Kaas (free-ZEE-ayn Kahz). *Ita.* A cheese flavored with cumin and cloves.

friggere (free-JAY-reh). *Ita.* Deep-fat frying.

frijoles (free-HOH-lehs). *Spa.* Beans.

frijoles blancos (free-HOH-lehs blahn-kohs). *Spa.* Navy beans.

frijoles negros (free-HOH-lehs KNEE-grros). *Spa.* Black beans.

frijoles refritos (free-HOH-lehs re-FREE-tohs). *Spa.* Refried beans.

frijoles rojos (free-HOH-lehs roa-hohs). *Spa.* Kidney beans.

Frikadellen (frik-kah-DEH-lern). *Ger.* Meatballs served cold.

frikadeller (free-kah-DAYL-err). *Dan.* A famous Danish dish of finely ground pork, veal, bread crumbs and onions, shaped into cakes and sautéed in butter.

frikadeller (FRIK-kah-del-lah) *Swe.* Meat balls

frio (FREE-ah). *Spa.* Cold.

frire (freer). *Fre.* To fry.

frisee (freh-zay). *Fre.* Endive; a salad green with curly, short, white inner leaves and greener outer leaves; taste is light and tart.

frit (free). *Fre.* Fried.

frito (FREE-toh). *Spa.* Fried.

frittata (free-TAT-tah). *Ita.* Flat, open-faced omelet.

frittella (free-TELL-lah). *Ita.* Fritter.

fritter (FREHT-ter). *USA.* Meat, vegetable, or fruit dipped in batter and fried.

fritto (FREET-toh). *Ita.* Fried.

fritto misto (FREET-toa meez-toh). *Ita.* Meat and vegetable dipped in batter and fried, then served together.

fritura (FREE-tu-rah). *Spa.* Fried food.

friture (free-tewr). *Fre.* Fried food.

frituurvet. (FREET-tuhr-faht). *Dut.* Oil.

frivolitées (free-vol-ee-tees). *Fre.* Testicles of a bull, pig, or lamb, breaded and fried. Also called animelles, lamb fries, mountain oysters, Rocky Mountain oysters.

frizzle (frehz-ul). *USA.* To pan fry until edges curl.

frog legs (frawg lehgs). *USA.* The hind legs of a frog, prepared by cutting off the feet and skinning the leg from the large end to the small end.

froid (frwah). *Fre.* Cold.

fromage (froh-mahzh). *Fre.* Cheese.

fromage de tete de porc (fro-majz day tet day pohr). *Fre.* Hog's head cheese.

fromage glace (fro-mazj glas). *Fre.* A dish of ice cream in a cheeselike shape, or anything glazed with cheese.

fromager (fro-mah-zjer). *Fre.* To add grated cheese.

Froschschenkel (FROSH-shehnkerl). *Ger.* Frog legs.

frossen fløde (FROA-sseen flurdh). *Dan.* Frozen whipped cream, served molded on fresh fruit.

frosted (FROHS-tehd). *USA.* A refreshing beverage made by whirling frozen citrus juices in a blender.

frosting (FROHS-teng). *USA.* Covering for cakes, pastries, made of sugar, butter, flavorings; cooked or uncooked; used in confectionery of all kinds; interchanges with icing.

Frucht (frukht). *Ger.* Fruit.

Fruchteis (FRUKHT-eyess). *Ger.* Fruit ice.

Fruchtpastete (frookht-pahs-TAY-teh). *Ger.* Fruit pie.

Fruchtsalat (frukht-sah-LAHT). *Ger.* Fruit salad.

fructose (FRUCK-tosc). *USA.* The natural sugar in fruit; sweeter than sucrose sugars by 1.7 to 1.

frugt (froogt). *Dan.* Fruit.

frugtcreme (FROOGT-krehm). *Dan.* Fruit pudding; a type of porridge.

frugtsuppe (FROOGT-soo-bber). *Dan.* Fruit soup of various dried fruits, often prunes and apricots, served hot or cold.

Frühlingskäse (fre-LINJ-kaiz). *Ger.* "Spring cheese"; Austrian cottage cheese mixed with cream, chives, parsley, caraway seeds; served on black bread garnished with stuffed olives and cucumber slices.

Fruhlingsuppe (fry-LINJ-zupe). *Ger.* A soup of meat stock with spring vegetables.

fruit (froot). *USA.* The edible reproductive body of a seed plant, having a sweet pulp associated with the seed, used chiefly in desserts or a sweet course.

fruit (frirt). *Dut.* Fruit.

fruitcake (FROOT-kak). *USA.* Basically a butter cake, with just enough batter to bind the candied fruits, dried fruits, nuts together; caked in tube pan or loaf pan; generally flavored with a brandy.

fruit cocktail (froot KOCK-tale). *USA.* A mixture of slightly cooked diced or cubed fruits in a thick or thin sweet syrup; a commercially canned product, usually used in gelatin salads and desserts, and in baked goods.

fruit cuit (frwee-cuhi). *Fre.* Stewed fruit.

fruits de mer (frwee der mehr). *Fre.* Seafood.

frukt (FROOK-ti). *Rus.* Fruit.

frukt (frewkt). *Nor, Swe.* Fruit.

frukt-kräm (FREWKT-kraim). *Swe.* Pureed fruit pudding.

fruktsoppa (FREWKT-sop-ah). *Swe.* Soup made from dried fruits.

fruktvin (FREWKT-veen). *Nor.* Fruit wine.

frumenty (FROU-men-tee). *Bri.* A porridge of wheat or oatmeal, boiled in milk, and served with raisins, spices, sugar.

frushie (FRUSH-ee). *Sco.* Crumbly fruit tart eaten with rich cream.

fruta (FROO-tah). *Spa.* Fruit.

fruta azucarada (FROO-tah ah-THOO-kah-rah-dah). *Spa.* Candied fruit.

frutta (fROO-tah). *Ita.* Fruit.

frutta di mare (FROOT-tee dee MAA-ray). *Ita.* Seafood.

fry (fri). *Bri.* A savory mixture of heart, lights, liver, and sweetbreads.

fry (fri). *USA.* To cook by plunging in hot fat until done.

fryer (FRI-ehr). *USA.* A young chicken of either sex that weighs 2½ to 3½ pounds; usually cut into serving size pieces, egg-and-crumbed or floured, then deep-fried.

fu (foo). *Jap.* Wheat gluten, used in soups, noodle broths, and one-pot dishes; high in protein, low in starch.

fudge (fuhdg). *USA.* A semisoft, chocolate candy, usually with nutmeats added.

fugu (foo-goo). *Jap.* Blowfish; has poisonous organs that must be removed by a licensed chef before being prepared.

fugu ryori (foo-goo ryoh-ree). *Jap.* Meals featuring blowfish, from which the poisonous organs have been removed by licensed chefs.

fuki (foo-kee). *Jap.* Coltsfoot; plant with large rounded leaves resembling the foot of a colt; light celery taste.

ful (fool). *Ara.* Fava beans.

Fullung (FOO-loong). *Ger.* Stuffing.

ful medames (fool MAY-da-mez). *Ara.* Egypt's national dish; cooked brown beans with a wide variety of seasonings.

fumé (foo-may). *Fre.* Smoked.

fumet (foo-maht). *Fre.* The flavor or essence of game, fish, or any highly-flavored concentrated substance used to impart a rich flavor.

funghi (FOONG-gee). *Ita.* Mushrooms.

funnel cake (FUHN-nell kahk). *USA.* A Pennsylvania Dutch deep-fried pastry made from batter dripped through a funnel, and swirled in spiral form in the hot fat; served with sugar or maple syrup.

furn (furn). *Ara.* Commercially made bread.

furutsu jusu (foo-ROO-tsoo joo-soo). *Jap.* Fruit juice.

fusilli (foo-SEEL-lee). *Ita.* Very thin, twisted strips of pasta.

fyldt (fewlt). *Dan.* Filled, stuffed.

fyll (fewl). *Nor.* Stuffing.

fyllda mandelkakor (fewld MAHN-dayl-KAA-roor). *Swe.* Filled almond buns.

fyll kålhode (fewl kawl-hooder). *Nor.* Stuffed head of cabbage.

G

gaasesteg (GAWSS-stayg). *Dan.* Roast goose.

Gabelfrühstück (gaa-berl-FREW-shtewk). *Ger.* "Fork breakfast," meaning that hot foods such as eggs and ham will be served.

gädda (yeh-dah). *Swe.* Pike.

gaffelbitar (GA-fehl-BI-tar). *Swe.* Herring tidbits.

gahwa (AH-wa). *Ara.* Coffee.

gai choy (gee-ah chee). *Chi.* Mustard cabbage.

gaika (GRYEHT-skee). *Rus.* Nut.

gairleog (garl-yog). *Iri.* Garlic.

gajar (GAH-jar). *Ind.* Carrot.

gajjak (GUH-JUK). *Ind.* Sesame brittle.

galamb (GOL-lomb). *Hun.* Pigeon.

galanga root (gah-LAHN-gah root). *USA.* A root of the ginger family, used fresh, dried or powdered to flavor foods in Southeast Asia.

galantina (gah-lahn-TEE-nah). *Ita.* Jellied meat, fowl, or fish.

galantine (gal-ahn-teen). *Fre.* Fowl or breast of veal, boned, stuffed with forcemeat, tongue, truffle, rolled, covered in aspic, and served cold.

galette (gah-leht). *Fre.* A light, French breakfast roll.

galinha (gah-LEE-nyah). *Por.* Chicken.

galinha recheada (gah-LEE-nyah ray-SHAY-dao). *Por.* Chicken stuffed with eggs and olives.

galinha salteada (gah-LEE-nyah sahl-TEE-ah-dah). *Por.* Sautéed chicken.

galinhola (gah-lee-NYOU-lah). *Por.* Woodcock.

gambas (GAHM-bahs). *Spa.* Shrimps, prawns.

gamberetti (gahm-bay-RAYT-tee). *Ita.* Small shrimp.

gamberi (gahm-BAH-ree). *Spa.* Crayfish.

gambero (gahm-BAY-roh). *Ita.* Shrimp.

game (gahm). *USA.* Wild fish, fowl, animals hunted for sport, and whose flesh is edible.

Gammelost (GAHM-mer-loost). *Nor.* A cows' skimmed milk blue cheese; is light yellow-brown; strong aroma.

gammon (GAHM-muhn). *Bri.* A very lean bacon; ham.

ganache (gah-nasch). *Fre.* A rich chocolate filling for pastry.

ganbian sijidou (gan-bien shi-jee-doh). *Chi.* Sauteed string beans.

Gans (gahns). *Ger.* Goose.

gans (khahns). *Dut.* Goose.

Gänsebraten (GEHN-zerbraa-tern). *Ger.* Roasted goose.

Gänsebrust (GEHN-zerbrust). *Ger.* Breast of goose.

Gänseleberpastete (GEHN-zert-lay-berr-pah-stayter). *Ger.* Goose liver pâté.

ganth gobhi (gahnt GOHB-hee). *Ind.* Kohlrabi.

ganzi (gan dze). *Chi.* Orange.

gao-yáng-ròu (gau-yaang-roe). *Chi.* Lamb.

garam masala (gahr-RAHM mahs-SAH-lah). *Ind.* An aromatic mixture of spices that supposedly "heat" the body, sprinkled over a dish before serving.

garbanzo (gar-BAHN-zo). *Spa.* A pea that is round, beige-yellow with a soft texture; a nutty flavor reminiscent of chestnuts. Also known as chick-pea.

garbure (gahr-bewr). *Fre.* A thick soup of meat, potatoes, and vegetables served with toasted bread.

garden cress (GAR-den Kress). *USA.* A green plant used in salads and savory fillings; has very tiny leaves, and frequently is used combined with baby mustard greens.

gardon (gahr-doh). *Fre.* A variety of carp.

garganelli (gahr-gahn-NEHL-lee). *Ita.* Homemade macaroni.

gari (GAH-ree). *Jap.* Sushi-shop jargon for vinegared ginger. Also known as beni-shoga.

garlic (GAHR-lehk). *USA.* An herb of the onion family with an odor that remains when used raw but disappears when cooked slowly; late garlic has firm bulbs and strong flavor; early garlic has large, flattened bulbs; covered with an off-white paperlike sheathing.

garlic chives (GAHR-lehk chivez). *USA.* An herb of the onion family; coarser, flatter, broader leaves than regular chives; garlic flavor.

garmugia (gahr-moo-GEE-ah). *Ita.* Beef stew with artichokes.

garnacha (gar-NAH-chah). *Mex.* A small round of tortilla dough filled with a savory stuffing and cooked; an appetizer or entree. Also known as picada.

garnalen (khahr-NAH-luh). *Dut.* Tiny shrimps.

Garnelen (gahr-NAY-lern). *Ger.* Shrimps, prawns.

garni (gahr-nee). *Fre.* Garnished.

garnish (GAHR-nesh). *USA.* An embellishment or trimming; to decorate, usually with other foods.

gås (goass). *Swe.* Goose.

gåsestak (gawss-stayk). *Nor.* Roast goose.

gâteau (gau-toe). *Fre.* A round flat buttercake, generally decorated.

gateaux (gah-toah). *Ara.* A Lebanese cake of the sponge cake family made with stiffly beaten egg whites, raisins and nuts folded into the batter, flavored with nutmeg, baked in a tube pan, and served unfrosted.

gaufre (goo-freh). *Fre.* Waffle.

gauloise (goa-lwahs). *Fre.* A garnish of cocks' combs and kidneys for clear soup.

gayette (gay-cht). *Fre.* An hors d'oeuvre; a flat sausage of pigs' liver and bacon encased in caul and cooked in an oven.

gazpacho (gahs-PAH-choh). *Spa.* A cold vegetable soup of tomatoes, garlic, olive oil, garlic.

geans (jeans). *Bri.* Wild cherries.

Gebäck (ger-BAHK). *Ger.* Pastry.

gebäcken (ger-BAHKN). *Ger.* Baked.

gebak (khuh-BAHK). *Dut.* Pastry.

gebakken (khuh-BAHK-kuh). *Dut.* Fried.

gebonden soep (khuh-BOH-den). *Dut.* Cream soup.

gebraden (khuh-BRAH-duh). *Dut.* Roast.

gebraden kip (khuh-BRAH-duh kip). *Dut.* Fried chicken.

gebraten (ger-BRAA-tern). *Ger.* Roasted.

gebunden (ger-BUHN-dehn). *Ger.* Thickened.

Gedampfte Ente (ger-DEHMPFT EHN-ter). *Ger.* Steamed duck.

Gedampfte Rinderbrust (ger-DEHMPFT RINT-err-breast). *Ger.* Wine-marinated beef slowly cooked with onions and carrots.

Gedünstete Gurke (ger-DOON-sterter goork). *Ger.* Stewed cucumbers in sour cream sauce.

Gedünstete Ochsenschlepp (ger-DOON-sterter OK-sern-sch-lehp). *Ger.* Braised oxtail.

gee choy (tze chee). *Chi.* Paper-thin rectangles of dried purple-black laver seaweed used for wrapping food.

gefilte fish (gah-FEHL-tah-fesch). *Jew.* A mixture of ground fish, eggs, and matzo meal, shaped into balls or flat loaves, and cooked in fish broth, served hot or cold.

Geflügel (ger-FLEW-gerl). *Ger.* Poultry.

Geflügelfrikassee (ger-FLEW-gerl-fri-kah-sser). *Ger.* Chicken fricassee.

Geflügelklein (ger-FLEW-gerl-klahn). *Ger.* Chicken giblets.

Geflügelleber (ger-FLEW-gerl-leh-behr). *Ger.* Chicken livers.

Geflügelragout (ger-FLEW-gerk-rah-goo). *Ger.* An Austrian stew of chicken and giblets.

gefüllt (ger-FEWLT). *Ger.* Stuffed.

Gefüllter Gänsehals (ger-FEWLT-gahns-hahls). *Ger.* Stuffed skin of goose neck.

Gefüllte Kartoffeln (ger-FEWLT kahe-TOF-ferln). *Ger.* Stuffed baked potatoes.

gegrillt (ger-GRILT). *Ger.* Grilled.

gehakt (khuh-HAHKT). *Dut.* Chopped meat.

gehaktballetjes (khuh-HAHKT-bahl-let-yus). *Dut.* Meatballs.

Geitost (YAYT-oost). *Nor.* A ewes' milk cheese with a rich brown color and sweet flavor; brick shape.

gekocht (ger-KOKHT). *Ger.* Boiled, cooked.

gekookt (khuh-KOHKT). *Dut.* Boiled.

gekristalliseerde gember (gher-KRYS-tahl-ez-zeer dah CHEHM-behr). *Dut.* Crystalized ginger.

gelado (zhe-LAH-doo). *Por.* Ice cream; frozen dessert.

gelatin (JEL-ah-ten). *USA.* A glutinous material obtained from animal bones, cartilege, tendons by boiling. See other types of gelatins: agar-agar, carrageenan, gum tragacanth, Irish moss, and rennet.

gelatina (jehl-ah-TEE-nah). *Ita, Spa.* Jelly.

gelato (jah-LAHT-to). *Ita.* Ice cream.

gelé (shay-LAY). *Swe.* Jelly.

geléa (zheh-LAY-ah). *Por.* Jelly.

gelée (zhay-LAY). *Fre.* Aspic.

gelinotte (zhay-lee-nott). *Fre.* Hazel hen.

gelo (ZHAY-loh). *Por.* Ice.

gemischt (ger-MISHT). *Ger.* Mixed.

Gemischt Kalter Braten (ger-MISHT KALT-ehr BRAA-tern). *Ger.* Assorted cold roast meats.

Gemischt Salat (ger-MISHT zah-LAAT). *Ger.* Mixed salad.

Gemüse (ger-MEW-zer). *Ger.* Vegetables.

Gemüseplatte (ger-MEW-zer plah-ter). *Ger.* Vegetable plate.

Genever (yuh-NAY-vur). *Dut.* Dutch gin. Also spelled Jenever.

genevoise (zheh-nayv-wahss). *Fre.* A sauce served only with fish that is made of salmon stock, red wine, herbs, and anchovy.

gengibre (zhehn-ZHEE-bruh). *Por.* Ginger.

genièvre (zheh-neehv). *Fre.* Juniper berry.

genip (heh-NEEP). *Spa.* A one-inch round fruit from the Caribbean Islands eaten fresh, like grapes. Sometimes called Spanish limes.

genmai cha (jehn-mah-ee chah). *Jap.* A green tea made of toasted glutinous rice. Some rice grains that have exploded and look like little popcorn are left in with the tea leaves and give the beverage a sweet and nutty flavor.

genoise (ZGEN-ah-swoy). *Ita.* A rich, moist sponge cake.

geranium (JER-rain-e-um). *USA.* A sweet-scented herb having many-flavored leaves; use in pound cakes, jellies, compotes.

geräuchert (ger-ROT-khert). *Ger.* Smoked.

German chocolate (JUHR-mun CHOK-o-laht). *USA.* A cooking chocolate that has sugar, milk, vanilla added, and has been conditioned against heat.

gerookte (her-ROKE-ter). *Dut.* Smoked.

geroosterd brood (khuh ROHS-turt broht). *Dut.* Toast.

geröstete (ger-RUR-sterter). *Ger.* Broiled or grilled.

geröstete Mehlsuppe (ger-RUR-sterter MAYL-zupper). *Ger.* Swiss gravy soup.

gerst (chehrst). *Dut.* Barley.

Gerstensuppe (GER-stehn-zupper). *Ger.* Barley soup.

geschabt (ger-SCHAHBT). *Ger.* Grated, ground, scraped.

geschmort (ger-SCHMOART). *Ger.* Braised.

Geschmorte Kalbshaxe (ger-SCHMOART KAHLP-hahkser). *Ger.* Braised veal with vegetables.

Geschnetzeltes (ger-SHNEH-tsert-terss). *Ger.* Small bits of veal served in wine sauce.

Geselchtes (ger-ZEHLKH-terss). *Ger.* South German word for smoked pork of any kind.

Gesottenes Rindfleisch (ghee-SORT-tahn-ness RHEND-flehsh). *Ger.* Boiled beef.

gestoofde (khuh-STOHG-duh). *Dut.* Stewed.

gestoofde pruimen (khuh-STOHF-duh PRIR-muh). *Dut.* Stewed prunes.

geung (jiaang). *Chi.* Ginger root.

gevogelte (her-VOH-helter). *Dut.* Poultry.

gevulde (her-VOOL-duh). *Dut.* Stuffed.

gevulde boterkoek (her-VOOL-duh BO-tur-kook). *Dut.* Buttercake with almond paste filling.

gevulde broodjes (her-VOOL-duh brote-yers). *Dut.* Rolls stuffed with salad, meats, fish, and so forth.

gevulde kool (her-VOOL-duh kohl). *Dut.* Meat-stuffed cabbage leaves.

gevulde kalfsborst (her-VOOL-duh kulfs-bawrst). *Dut.* Stuffed veal breast.

Gewürz (ger-VEWRTS). *Ger.* Spice.

Gewürzkuchen (ger-vewrts-KOOK-hern). *Ger.* Spice cakes.

ghee (khee). *Ind.* Clarified butter.

gherkin (guhr-KIN). *USA.* A small cucumber used for pickling.

ghiaccio (gee-AHT-choa). *Ita.* Ice, as for beverages; "on the rocks."

giardiniera (jee-ahrd-EEN-ehrah). *Ita.* Mixed vegetables, sliced.

gibelotte (zhee-beh-loat-teh). *Fre.* Rabbit stew with butter, onions, and potatoes.

gibier (zhee-behr). *Fre.* Game.

giblets (JIB-lets). *USA.* The edible viscera of fowl: heart, liver, gizzard, head, feet, wing tips, cocks' comb, kidneys.

gigot (zhee-goa). *Fre, Bri.* Leg of mutton.

gigot d'agneau (zhee-goa d'ah-noh). *Fre.* Leg of lamb.

gigue (zhee-gew). *Fre.* Venison or boar haunch.

gilthead (GEHLT-head). *USA.* A Mediterranean fish of the bream family, having white, fine, firm flesh.

ginepro (jee-NEH-proa). *Ita.* Juniper berry.

ginestrata (jeen-eh-STRAH-dah). *Ita.* A light, creamy, nutritious soup of chicken broth, egg yolks, butter, white wine, gentle spices.

gingelly (JIN-jeh-lee). *Ind.* Light sesame oil.

gingembre (zheen-zhehm-breh). *Fre.* Ginger.

ginger (GEHN-gher). *USA.* A cultivated spice with a pungent flavor and sweet aroma; used fresh, preserved, or dried and ground; used throughout the world to season dishes from curries to desserts.

ginger beer (GEHN-gher beer). *USA.* A nonalcoholic beverage flavored with fermented ginger.

gingerbread (GEHN-gher-bred). *USA.* A cake or cookie flavored with ginger and other spices.

ginger champagne (GEHN-gher chahm-pain). *USA.* A nonalcoholic cocktail made with ginger flavoring.

gingerroot (GEHN-gher root). *USA.* A gnarled, knobby, fibrous root with light brown skin; use grated for seasoning sauces, chicken and fish dishes, salad dressings, fruit desserts.

gingersnap (GEHN-gher-schnahp). *USA.* A crisp, thin cookie made with molasses and flavored with ginger.

ginkgo nut (GHEEN-koh nuht). *USA.* The fruit of the mature female ginkgo tree; raw nuts are white but turn pale green when cooked; mild flavor; eaten raw, grilled, deep-fried, or in one-pot dishes.

ginnan (GEEN-nahn). *Jap.* Ginkgo nut.

ginseng (zehn-sehng). *Kor.* A highly prized root used fresh for salads and to flavor soups and stews, used dried for making tea, and for many medicinal purposes.

giri (KEE-ree). *Jap.* A cut of the knife; stroke.

girolle (zhee-rol-leh). *Fre.* Chanterelle.

gishta (ISH-ta). *Ara.* Cream.

gist (jeest). *Dut.* Yeast.

gîte à la noix. (zheh-tay ah lah nwah). *Fre.* A cut of beef from the rump of the carcass. Same as silverside.

glaçage (glah-sahzhg). *Fre.* Browning or glazing.

glace (glahss). *Fre.* Cake icing; ice cream; ice.

glacé (glahs-say). *Fre.* Iced, frozen, glazed, frosted, candied, crystalized.

glacé fruit (glahs-say frwee). *Fre.* Fruit dipped in a hot syrup that has been cooked to a hard-crack stage.

glamorgan sausages (glah-MOHR-gun SAUS-ahg-jehz). *Bri.* Fried rolls made of bread crumbs and cheese and seasoned with onions and herbs; vegetarian Welsh sausages.

glass (glahss). *Swe.* Sherbet or ice cream.

glassato (glah-SAH-toh). *Ita.* Glazed.

Glasur (GLAU-seur). *Ger.* Icing.

glaze (glaz). *USA.* To make a smooth, shiny surface that can be decorated variously: stock or gravy reduced to the thickness of jelly that is used to cover meats or a thin sugar syrup on certain rolls, pastries, and confections.

glazun'ya (yee-EESH-nyee-tsoo). *Rus.* Fried eggs.

glazuur (glah-ZUHR). *Dut.* Glazed.

gliomach (glim-makh). *Iri.* Lobster.

glister pudding (GLEHS-stur PUHD-deng). *Bri.* Steamed pudding with marmalade, lemon juice, and ginger seasoning.

glögg (glurgg). *Swe.* A hot and spicy wine drink, flavored with almonds, raisins, and brandy.

glucose (GLU-kose). *USA.* Dextrose; a natural sugar widely distributed in fruits, honey and some vegetables.

Glühwein (glew-vighn). *Ger.* Mulled wine.

gluten (GLU-tun). *USA.* The tenacious and elastic substance formed when wheat flour is stirred or kneaded with a liquid.

gluten flour (GLU-tun flawr). *USA.* A starch-free, high protein flour made by washing the starch from hard wheat flour; the residue is dried and ground; gluten will not develop except in the presence of moisture and when agitated, as in kneading.

glutinous rice (GLU-tun-ous rice). *USA.* A short-grained rice that is sweet, sticky, and opaque.

glycerin (GLEH-sur-en). *USA.* A sweet, clear liquid of syruplike consistency, used to retain moisture in certain kinds of confectionery, such as cake icing, and to sweeten and preserve foods.

gnocchi (n-YOC-kee). *Ita.* A small dumpling of potato, spinach, or other ingredients, poached in water, and served in sauce, in soup or covered with grated Parmesan cheese. Discs of semolina and polenta.

gobhi (GOHB-hee). *Ind.* Cauliflower.

gobo (goh-BOH). *Jap.* Burdock root.

gochian (GOO-chee-an). *Ind.* Black beehive-shaped mushrooms from Kashmir region, similar to morels.

goed doorbakken (khoot dohr-BRAH-duh). *Dut.* Well done.

Göetta (GHER-tah). *Ger.* A molded meat dish, served sliced and fried, made of finely chopped boiled pork scraps, including heart, liver, tongue, oats, and seasonings. If made of corn meal, it is called scrapple.

gohan (GOH-hahn). *Jap.* Cooked rice, served on a plate Western style. See raisu, kome.

gold beet (gohld beet). *USA.* This vegetable looks like a red beet except the bulbs are golden-yellow; taste is a bit sweeter than the red beet; can be eaten raw or cooked.

golden buck (GOHL-dehn buhk). *Bri.* Welsh rarebit on toast, topped with a poached egg.

golden mountain oyster (GOHL-dehn MAHN-tain OEHS-ter). *USA.* A light brown, fan-shaped mushroom that has a meaty flavor.

golden oak mushroom (GOHL-dehn oak MUHSH-room). *USA.* A dark brown mushroom with a woodsy-fruity flavor and smooth velvety caps that have a light pinky-beige meat. Also known as shiitake.

golden syrup (GOHL-dehn SEHR-up). *USA.* A mild flavored residual molasses that is clarified and decolorized.

goma (GOH-mah). *Jap.* Sesame seeds, either white or coal-black.

goma abura (GOH-mah ah-BOO-rah). *Jap.* Sesame oil.

gomba (GAWM-bo). *Hun.* Mushrooms.

gombaleves (GAWM-bol-leh-vehsh). *Hun.* Mushroom soup.

gongbao rou ding (goong bao row ding). *Chi.* A dish of diced pork with hot peppers.

gongbao xiaren (goong bao sia ren). *Chi.* A shrimp dish with hot peppers.

Gonterser Bok (gun-ter-SAUR bohk). *Ger.* A Swiss dish of batter-dipped hard-boiled eggs, fried in butter.

goober (GOO-ber). *Afr.* Peanut.

gooseberry (GOOS-behr-ree). *USA.* A large green berry sometimes streaked in red; popular in France and England for use in pies, preserves, or as a sauce for mackerel in France. Also known as green gooseberry.

goosefish (GOOS-fesch). *USA.* A fish whose tailsection has firm, white flesh similar in flavor to lobster; can be sautéed, baked, broiled, poached, or cut in fingers and deep fried. Known by many names, including Monkfish.

gorchitsa (gahr-CHYEE-tsi). *Rus.* Mustard.

gorda (GOHR-dah). *Mex.* A thick cake of maize dough and lard.

gordita (gohr-DEE-tah). *Mex.* Dough of cornmeal and potato, flavored with cheese, fried in lard, and served with ground pork and guacamole.

Gorgonzola (goar-goan-DZO-lah). *Ita.* A cows' whole milk blue cheese with a rough reddish rind and a creamy white interior veined with blue-green mold; less salty than Roquefort.

gorokh (gah-ROKH). *Rus.* Peas.

gosht (gohsht). *Ind.* Meat.

Gouda (GOO-dah). *USA.* A Dutch cheese of cows' whole milk; creamy yellow, firm; young cheeses have yellow wax covering, older cured cheeses have black wax covering.

Goudsa kaas (KHOWT-suh kahs). *Dut.* Gouda cheese.

gougère (goo-zhryehr). *Fre.* A savory pastry, made in a ring, baked, then chilled; served as a light meal.

gougnettes (goo-zhneht). *Fre.* A type of doughnut sprinkled with sugar.

goujon (gou-zhawng). *Fre.* Highly esteemed fish of the carp family.

goujonette (goo-zhawng-neht). *Fre.* Deep-fried strips of breaded sole that resemble little fishes.

goulash (GOO-lahsh). *Bri.* A Hungarian stew of beef, veal or pork with onions, potatoes, tomatoes, peppers and dumplings, heavily seasoned with paprika, caraway seeds, and garlic.

govyadina (gah-VYAH-dyee-nah). *Rus.* Beef.

grädde (GREH-der). *Swe.* Cream.

gräddevåfflor (greh-der-VOF-lah). *Swe.* Sour cream waffles.

Gräddost (grahd-oost). *Swe.* A mild cheese, semisoft or hard.

graeskar (GRAIS-kahr). *Dan.* Marrow squash.

graham flour (gram flawr). *USA.* Whole wheat flour containing the bran of the wheat kernel.

graisse (grohss). *Fre.* Fat; also gras.

grana (GRAH-nah). *Ita.* Hard, dry, crumbly, long-lasting cheeses, used grated on pastas or in cooking. Parmesan is of this type.

granada (grah-NAH-dah). *Spa.* Pomegranate.

granadilla (grah-nah-DEHL-lah). *Ita.* The purple egg-sized tropical fruit whose sweet yellow flesh is eaten raw with the small black seeds, or squeezed for juice; has sweet-acid flavor. Also known as passion fruit.

granatina (grah-nah-TEE-nah). *Ita.* Pomegranate syrup.

granceole (grahn-ceh-OAL-eh). *Ita.* Large crabs, cooked in shells, and seasoned with oil and lemon.

granchi (GRAHNG-kee). *Ita.* Crabs.

grand'mère (groh-mehr). *Fre.* A garnish of pearl onions, olive-shaped potatoes, parsley, lemon juice, and browned butter.

grandville (groh-vil). *Fre.* A sauce of white wine, truffles, mushrooms, and shrimp.

granita (grah-NEE-tah). *Ita.* A fruit ice (sherbet) intentionally made so that its ice crystals have a grainy texture.

granturco (grahn-TOOR-coa). *Ita.* Corn.

granulated sugar (GRAHN-u-la-ted SCHU-gahr). *USA.* White sucrose crystals of a fine granulation that dissolve rapidly; a general purpose sugar.

grape (grap). *USA.* A vine-produced fruit that is a smooth-skinned juicy greenish-white to deep red or purple berry. Other than wine grapes, there are three types of grapes, distinguished by their use: grapes for making juice, grapes for making raisins, and grapes for the table. See specific names.

grapefruit (GRAP-froot). *USA.* A large citrus fruit with a bitter yellow rind and inner skin; highly flavored, somewhat acidic, juicy pulp.

grapefruktjuice (GRAYP-frukt-YOO-ss). *Swe.* Grapefruit juice.

grape leaves (grap leevz). *USA.* Leaves of grape vines, cleaned and packed in brine; rolled with savory stuffings; used in Greek cookery.

gras (groh). *Fre.* Fat; also graisse.

gras, au (ah groh). *Fre.* Dressed with rich meat gravy.

gras-double (groh-dubl). *Fre.* Tripe.

graslök (graiss-lurk). *Swe.* Chive.

grasshopper (GRAISS-hohp-pehr). *USA.* A flavor combination, always green; usually either a pie or a drink containing the cordials green creme de menthe and colorless creme de cocoa.

grate (grat). *USA.* To reduce to small pieces by rubbing on something rough.

gratin (GRA-tain). *Dan.* Soufflé, often cooked with vegetables.

gratin, au (GRAW-ten). *Fre.* A term for certain dishes prepared with sauce, garnish, and breadcrumbs, baked until brown, and served in the baking dish.

gratin, au (graw-tehn). *USA.* Refers to a dish prepared with cheese sauce, or having grated cheese sprinkled on top, and baked.

gratinée (grah-teen-ay). *Fre.* To brown in a hot oven or under a broiler; a food topped with breadcrumbs, cheese, or sauce.

Gratiniert (gra-teen-NEYRT). *Ger.* Covered with breadcrumbs or cheese and oven-browned.

gravad lax (GRAH-vayd lahks). *Swe.* Salmon marinated in dill.

gravlax (GRAHV-lahks). *Nor.* Raw, salt- and sugar-cured salmon fillets, seasoned with crushed dill.

gravy (GRA-vee). *USA.* A sauce made from the juices of cooked meat, usually thickened and seasoned.

grease (grez). *USA.* To rub lightly with fat.

grecque, à la (a'l a'greh-kew). *Fre.* Prepared in the Greek style; usually vegetables such as artichokes, mushrooms, cooked in olive oil, lemon juice, water, and seasonings.

green beans (grehn behns). *USA.* An edible and nutritious seed pod, 4-5 inches long, of a species of cultivated beans; bright green with about 8-10 immature beans within.

Green Goddess dressing (grehn GOHD-dehss drehss-seng). *USA.* A salad dressing made of mayonnaise, minced green onions, chives, parsley, tarragon, and anchovy fillets.

Green Goddess salad (grehn GOHD-dehss SAH-lahd). *USA.* A salad of chopped romaine, escarole, and chicory mixed with minced anchovy fillets, green onions, parsley, and tarragon; then tossed with mayonnaise, tarragon vinegar and chopped chives; served in a bowl rubbed with garlic, then topped with chicken, crab, or shrimp.

green gooseberry (green GOOS-ber-re). *USA.* Gooseberry.

green leaf letuce (green leef LETT-uhs). *USA.* A variety of lettuce whose leaves are not tightly bunched in a head.

green mango (green MAHN-go). *USA.* The unripe fruit of a tropical evergreen tree of the sumac family; pectin-rich, sour taste; basis of most Indian chutneys and pickles.

green onion (green UN-yun). *USA.* A garden vegetable with a slender white sheath for the bulb and slender, round dark green leaves; widely used in salads and as seasoning.

green peppercorns (green PEHP-pur-kornz). *USA.* Berries of the black pepper vine picked while immature; more subtle flavor than traditional black peppercorn; available freeze-dried or preserved in brine or wine vinegar.

green peppers (green PEHP-purs). *USA.* Bell peppers.

green plantain (green PLAHN-tehn). *USA.* A very hard and starchy banana-vegetable with little banana flavor and no sweetness; used as a staple starch or main dish in many parts of the world.

greens (greenz). *USA.* Plants with large, green leaves used as vegetable: Collards, dandelion greens, kale, mustard greens, and swiss chard are the major varieties.

green sauce (green saus). *USA.* Mayonnaise flavored with finely minced spinach, watercress, parsley, tarragon, which color the sauce green; mayonnaise verte.

grelhados (gray-LEEAH-doosh). *Por.* Grilled.

grelos (GRAY-loosh). *Por.* Dandelion greens.

gremolada (greh-moa-LAH-dah). *Ita.* The aromatic garnish of chopped parsley, garlic, and grated lemon zest sprinkled over osso buco.

grenade (greh-nahd). *Fre.* Pomegranate.

grenadine (GREN-a-dine). *USA.* Pomegranate syrup, used for flavoring and coloring.

grenadins (greh-nah-danh). *Fre.* Small filets of veal or fowl that are braised.

grenouilles (gruh-nuhy). *Fre.* Frog's legs.

gretskii orekh (GRYEHTS-kee-yeh ah-RYWH-khee). *Rus.* Walnut.

grib (gree-BEE). *Rus.* Mushrooms.

gribiche (gree-beesh). *Fre.* A sauce of mayonnaise, hard-boiled eggs, capers, chopped gherkins, herbs; served cold with cold fish.

griesmeelpap (GREES-mehl-pahp). *Dut.* Semolina porridge.

Gries Pudding (grees PUD-ding). *Ger.* Chilled farina pudding of Switzerland.

Griessklösschen (GREES-kloss-khern). *Ger.* Semolina dumplings.

grill (gril). *USA.* To cook by intense direct heat, over flames or embers or under a broiler.

grillades (gree-yahds). *Fre.* Small pieces of grilled meat, usually lean, boneless pork.

grillé (gree-yay). *Fre.* Grilled.

grilleret lammehoved (gril-YAYR-ert LAHM-hov-erd). *Dan.* Grilled lamb's head.

grind (grind). *USA.* To reduce to small particles or to powder form by putting food through a grinder or food chopper.

grinder (GRIND-ehr). *USA.* Hoagie.

grisfötter (GREESS-foot-ter). *Swe.* Pig's feet.

griskott (GREESS-tyurt) *Swe.* Pork; also fläsk.

grissini (gris-SEE-nee). *Ita.* Breadsticks.

grits (grehts). *USA.* Coarsely ground hulled grain, specifically hominy grits.

grive (greev). *Ita.* Thrushes, often stewed with myrtle leaves.

grives (greev). *Fre.* Thrushes; tasty birds.

groats (grots). *USA.* Hulled grain, more coarsely ground than grits.

grød (grurdh). *Dan.* Porridge.

grødaertesuppe (GRURDH-aerterr-soo-bber). *Dan.* Green pea soup.

groente (KHROON-tuh). *Dut.* Vegetables.

groentesoep (KHROON-tuh-soop). *Dut.* Vegetable soup.

grog (grohg). *Bri.* A drink made of rum, lemon, sugar, and hot water; other spirits are also used.

grönar bönar (GRO-nah BO-nor). *Swe.* Green beans.

grønlangkaal (GRURN-lahng-kawl). *Dan.* Creamed cabbage.

grønsagstromage (GRURN-saaerr-froa-maash-er). *Dan.* An elegant vegetable soufflé.

grønsaker (GRURN-ssah-kerr). *Nor, Swe.* Vegetables.

grönsakssoppa (GRON-sa-ks-SO-pa). *Swe.* Vegetable soup.

grönsallad (GRURN-sahl-ahd). *Swe.* Green salad, usually lettuce only.

groseille à maquereau (gro-zehyah mah-kar-roa). *Fre.* Gooseberry.

groseilles (gro-zehy). *Fre.* Red currants.

groselhas (groa-ssay-lee-AHOO). *Por.* Currants.

grosellas (groa-SSAY-lyahss). *Spa.* Currants.

ground beef (grahnd beef). *USA.* Beef that has been put through a meat grinder; if coarse ground, it is called chili meat.

grouper (GRU-per). *USA.* A fish of the seabass family that has firm, moist, lean flesh.

grouse (grahus). *USA.* A game bird with very delicate flesh and a pronounced pine flavor. Also known as partridge, prairie chicken.

grovbrød (GROHV-brur). *Nor.* Rye bread.

Grüne Bohnen (grew-ner BOA-nern). *Ger.* Green beans.

Grüne Erbsen (grew-ner EHR-psern). *Ger.* Green peas.

Grüne Fisolen (grew-ner fee-ZOA-lern). *Ger.* Green beans flavored with fennel.

Grüne Gurke (grew-ner GOOR-kern). *Ger.* Cucumber.

grunt (gruhnt). *USA.* A very old colonial dessert made with berries and steamed dough.

grusha (GROO-shah). *Rus.* Pear.

Grützwurst (GREWTZ-voorst). *Ger.* A smoked sausage made of buckwheat, oats, and rye groats with minced bacon.

Gruviera (groo-vee-EHR-ah). *Ita.* Mild-flavored Swiss cheese.

Gruyère (gru-yer). *Fre.* A pale yellow Swiss made cheese that has a nutlike, salty flavor, similar to Swiss but sharper; firm, smooth texture with small holes or eyes.

grytstekt (GREWT-staykt). *Swe.* Pot roast with vegetables.

gua (hwah). *Chi.* Melon.

guacamole (gua-kah-NOH-leh). *Mex.* Mashed avocado, seasoned with lime juice, finely chopped onions, chopped tomatoes, chilies.

guaiweiji (gwai wei jee). *Chi.* "Strange tasting chicken"; chicken slices marinated in soy sauce and garlic.

guajillo (gwa-HEEL-loh). *Mex.* A long, reddish brown, thin, dried, very hot chili pepper.

guajolote (gwa-hoh-LOH-teh). *Mex.* Wild turkey.

guanciale (gwan-CEE-ahl). *Ita.* Pig's cheek; a much sought after delicacy that is cured with salt and pepper in the same way as pancetta; rarer and more choice than pancetta.

guarnito (gwar-NEE-toh). *Ita.* Garnished.

guastelle (gwa-STAHL-lee). *Ita.* Rolls.

guava (GWAH-vah). *Mex.* The fruit of a tropical bush used to make pinkish-orange jellies, jams; fruit pulp is delicious, but a poor traveler. Not to be confused with the olive green, elongated egg-shaped fruit found in most of the United States, the true guava is little known outside its native habitat.

güero (GWEH-roh). *Mex.* A fairly hot, greenish yellow pepper, used fresh, toasted, or canned, but never dried. Also known as California pepper.

Gugelhopf (GOO-gerl-hupf). *Ger.* A sweet, yellow, bread-type cake containing raisins or currants baked in a fluted tube pan; the traditional Name Day cake. Sometimes spelled kugelhoph.

gui choy (jie cai). *Chi.* Mustard greens.

guimauve (gee-mov). *Fre.* Marshmallow.

guinea (GHEEN-neh). *Afr.* A fowl with delicate tasting flesh when young; resembles that of a pheasant. Also known as Bohemian pheasant and pintade.

guisado (ghee-SAH-doh). *Spa.* Stewed, ragoût, fricassee.

guisado (ghee-ZAH-doh). *Por.* Stew.

guisantes (ghee-SAHN-tehs). *Spa.* Green peas.

gujjia (goo-jee-ah). *Ind.* Crescent-shaped sweet pastry filled with nuts and coconut.

gulab (GOO-lab). *Ind.* Rosewater flavoring.

Gulasch (GOO-lahsh). *Ger.* Goulash. Also called Gulyas.

gule aerter (GOO-ler AER-terr). *Dan.* Yellow split pea soup served with salt pork.

gulerødder (GOOL-er-rurd-herr). *Dan.* Carrots.

gulrøtter (GEWL-rurt-terr). *Nor.* Carrots.

gulyás (GOO-yaash). *Hun.* Goulash.

Gulyas (GOO-lahsh). *Ger.* Goulash. Also called Gulasch.

gulyash (goo-LYAHSH). *Rus.* Goulash.

gulyásleves (GOO-yaash-leh-vehsh). *Hun.* Goulash.

gum arabic (guhm AHR-a-behc). *USA.* Vegetable gum used as emulsifier and thickener in some processed foods.

gum tragacanth (guhm TRAHG-ah-calnth). *USA.* Vegetable gum used as an emulsifier and thickener in processed foods.

gumbo (GUM-boe). *USA.* A rich, thick Cajun soup containing okra with a variety of meats, seafood, and vegetables.

gumbo filé (GUM-boe fee-LAY). *USA.* Filé powder.

Gundel palacsinta (GOON-dehl POL-lo-cheen-to). *Hun.* Pancake with nut-cream and raisin filling, flambéed.

guojiang (guop jiang). *Chi.* Jam.

guotie (guo tich). *Chi.* Fried dumpling.

gur (gour). *Ind.* A form of raw lump sugar, honey-brown in color; jaggery.

gurepufuruto (goo-REH-poo-foo-ROO-tsoo). *Jap.* Grapefruit.

gurka (GEWR-kah). *Swe.* Cucumbers.

Gurke (GOOR-kern). *Ger.* Cucumber.

gus (goos). *Rus.* Goose.

Gut Durchgebraten (goot DOORCH-ger-braa-tern). *Ger.* Well done, cooked thoroughly.

gyokuro (ryoh-KOO-chah). *Jap.* Extremely fragrant and tender, very expensive grade of green tea.

gyudon (gyoo-dohn). *Jap.* A bowl of rice with stir-fried beef and onions, topped with a sauce and served with green tea; a fast-food item in Japan.

gyümölcslét (DYEW-murl-chlayt). *Hun.* Fruit juice.

gyümölcsöt (DYEW-murl-churt). *Hun.* Fruit.

gyuniku (gyoo-nee-koo). *Jap.* Beef.

haagsche hopjes (HAHKH-skhuh HAWP-yus). *Dut.* Coffee-flavored hard candy.

haagse bluf (HAH-sexh bleuf). *Dut.* A light, fluffy dessert of egg whites and red currant juice.

haar chee meen (shah tze mian). *Chi.* Shrimp noodles; noodles colored brown and flavored with shrimp.

haas (hahs). *Dut.* Hare.

habañero (ah-bhah-NAYR-roa). *Mex.* A very hot chili pepper, green, smooth skin; also available red or yellow.

habas (AH-bhahss). *Spa.* Broad beans; fava beans.

habash (HAH-bash). *Ara.* Turkey.

habichuelas (ah-bee-CHWEH-lah). *Spa.* Kidney beans.

habichuelas verdes (ah-bee-CHWEH-lah BEHR-deh). *Spa.* String beans.

haché (hah-SHAY). *Dut.* Hashed meat.

hachée (a-she-ay). *Fre.* Sauce for minced and leftover meats; made of butter, chopped shallots, onions, tomato puree, mushrooms, capers, seasonings.

hacher (ah-shay). *Fre.* To chop; mince.

hachis (ah-shee). *Fre.* Hash.

hachis (hah-SHEES). *Dan.* Hash.

hackad (HAHK-ahd). *Swe.* Chopped.

hackad biff mid lök (HAHK-ahd bif med lurk). *Swe.* Chopped beef with onions.

hackat kalvfilet (HA-kat kahlv-fee-lay). *Swe.* Chopped veal.

Hackbraten (HAHK-braa-tern). *Ger.* Meat loaf.

hacken (HA-ken). *Ger.* Mince.

Hackfleisch (HAK-flyesh). *Ger.* Ground beef.

haddock (HAHD-dohk). *USA.* A small member of the codfish family.

Hafer (HAH-fer). *Ger.* Oats.

Haferbrei (HAH-fer-brye). *Ger.* Porridge.

haggis (HAHG-gees). *Sco.* The national dish of Scotland; sheep stomach stuffed with minced chopped liver, heart, onion, and oatmeal, then steamed like a pudding.

hagyma (HOD-ymo). *Hun.* Onions.

hahm dahn (sheen DAHN). *Chi.* Salted duck eggs; brine cured about 40 days; used hot with rice or cold as a relish.

Hahn (hain). *Ger.* Cock.

Hähnchen (HAIN-khern). *Ger.* Rooster, cockeral, as spoken in the Frankfort area.

hahni (HAHN-hi). *Fin.* Goose.

hai shen (hah sind). *Chi.* A marine creature relished as a delicacy for its gelatinous texture. Also called sea cucumber or sea slug.

hai wèi (hai wei). *Chi.* Seafood.

haizhé pí (hai dze pee). *Chi.* Jellyfish.

hajikami shoga (hah-jee-KAH-mee SHO-gah). *Jap.* "Blushing ginger"; pink, pickled ginger shoots eaten with grilled foods.

hak chih mah (hay tse mah). *Chi.* Black sesame seeds; spicy hot in taste.

hake (hak). *USA.* A small fish of the cod family whose flesh is tender, white, flaky, and easy to digest.

hakkebøf (HAHGG-er-burf). *Dan.* Chopped beefsteak, hamburger meat, ground beef.

hakket aeg og sild (HAHGG-ert ehg oa seel). *Dan.* Smørrebrød of hard-boiled eggs and smoked herring minced together.

hakusai (hah-kuh-SIGH-ee). *Jap.* Chinese cabbage. Also called wong nga bok, siu choy.

halat (HOL-lot). *Hun.* Fish.

halb durchgebraten (halp DOORCH-ger-braa-tern). *Ger.* Cooked medium-rare.

halb roh (halp roa). *Ger.* Rare, half raw.

halbran (HAHL-brahn). *USA.* A very young duck, before the age of being called a duckling.

haldi (HAHL-dee). *Ind.* Turmeric.

halewiyyaat (ha-la-wee-YEHT). *Ara.* Confectionery, candies, sweets.

half-and-half (hahlf-ahnd-hahlf). *Bri.* A drink of half porter and half pale ale.

half-and-half (hahlf-ahnd-hahlf). *USA.* A mixture of cream and milk, containing 10.5% to 18% milkfat. Also called cereal cream.

halfatányéros (HOL-fot-taan-yay-rawsh). *Hun.* Assorted fish, some breaded, some fried, served on a wooden plate, accompanied by tartar sauce.

half-mourning (hahlf-MOORN-eng). *USA.* Poached poultry and braised sweetbreads, masked with supreme sauce, and garnished with truffles placed under the skin; demi-deuil.

halib (hah-LEEB). *Ara.* Milk.

halibut (HAHL-eh-but). *USA.* A flatfish of the flounder family whose flesh is white, firm, and blandly sweet.

haliyb. (hah-LEEB). *Ara.* Milk.

hälleflundra (HAH-leh-FLUN-dra). *Swe.* Halibut.

hallon (HAH-lon). *Swe.* Raspberry.

halmajonéz (HOL-moyaw-nayz). *Hun.* An appetizer of fish with mayonnaise.

halozun (hah-loo-SOON). *Ara.* Snails.

Hälsingeost (HAHL-sing-eh-OOST). *Swe.* A semisoft cheese made of cow's and goat's milk.

halstra (HAHL-strah) *Swe.* Roast.

halstrad (HAHL-strahd). *Swe.* Broiled.

halvah (HA-la-weeh). *Ara.* A Turkish candy made of crushed sesame seeds, cooked chick-peas, and honey.

halwa (HAL-vah). *Ind.* Vegetables, lentils, nuts, fruits, cooked with sugar and ghee to consistency of plum pudding.

halwah (HAHL-wah). *Ara.* Sweets; usually candy made of crushed sesame seeds, cooked chick-peas, and honey.

halyun (hahl-YUUN). *Ara.* Asparagus.

ham (haum). *USA.* A hind leg of pork, cured and smoked.

ham (hum). *Dut.* Ham.

hamaguri (hah-MAH-goo-ree). *Jap.* Hard-shell clams.

Haman's ears (HAY-mun's eehrs). *Jew.* Ear-shaped pastries that are deep-fried and served with honey.

hamburger (HAHM-burr-ger). *USA.* A sandwich of a broiled or grilled ground beef patty on a split bun. Ground beef.

hamburgerbringa (HAHM-boo-rer-bring-ah). *Swe.* Smoked ox breast.

hamburgerryg (HAHM-boo-rer-rewg). *Dan.* Smoked loin of pork in a sauce of currant jelly, mustard, grated onion.

Hämchen (HAHM-shun). *Ger.* Pigs' knuckles and sauerkraut.

Hammel (HAH-merl). *Ger.* Mutton. Also called Hammelfleisch.

Hammelkeule (HAH-merl-kohul). *Ger.* Leg of mutton.

Hammelschulter (HAH-merl-shul-ter). *Ger.* Shoulder of mutton.

Hammelwürste (HAH-merl-voorst). *Ger.* Sausages of minced mutton, garlic, pork, seasonings.

Hammelzungen in Aspik (HAH-merl-tsun-gern im ahs-peek). *Ger.* Sheep's tongue in aspic.

hampurilainen (HAHM-poo-ril-lah-nayn). *Fin.* Hamburger.

hamu (HAH-moo). *Jap.* Ham.

hamu eggu (HAH-moo egg-oo). *Jap.* Ham and eggs.

hanagatsuo (hah-nah-GOT-soo-oh). *Jap.* Dried bonito flakes.

hanatsuki kyuri (hah-nah-tsu-KEE qoo-lei). *Jap.* Flowering baby cucumbers, used as a garnish.

Handkäse (hant-kaiz). *Ger.* A cows' skimmed milk cheese that is pungent and acidic.

hangop (hahng-AWP). *Dut.* "Hang up"; a dessert of thick buttermilk and sugar.

hangtown fry (HAHNG-town fri). *USA.* An omelet with breadcrumbed oysters and fried bacon.

hanjuku tamago (HAHN-joo-koo TAH-mah-gog). *Jap.* Soft-boiled eggs.

háoyóu gàilán (hao yoh gai lan). *Chi.* Broccoli in oyster sauce.

háoyóu niúròu (hao yoh niu row). *Chi.* Beef with oyster sauce.

hapankaali (HAH-pahn-KAA-li). *Fin.* Sauerkraut.

häränfilee (HAE-raen-fil-lay). *Fin.* Filet of beef.

häränhäntäliemi (HAE-rae-HAEN-tea-LAY-mi). *Fin.* Oxtail soup.

hara piaz (HA-rah pih-YAZ). *Ind.* Scallion.

harcsa (HOR-cho). *Hun.* Wels, an extremely large and only member of the catfish family found in Europe. Not to be confused with the wolffish, which is called catfish in Europe.

hard-ball stage (HAHRD-bahl staj). *USA.* The fourth stage of sugar crystallization: begins at 250°F and forms a firm ball between the fingers when immersed in cold water.

hard-crack stage (HAHRD-krak staj). *USA.* The sixth stage of sugar crystallization: begins at 300°F and forms brittle threads and sheets when immersed in cold water.

hard sauce (hahrd saus). *USA.* Sugar and butter creamed till fluffy and flavored with liquor.

hardtack (HAHRD-tahk). *USA.* A hard biscuit made with flour and water but no shortening or yeast. Also called sea biscuit, sea bread, ship biscuit, pilot bread, and pilot biscuit.

hare (haur). *USA.* A wild rabbit eaten for its dark meat with gamy flavor.

hare (HAA-rer). *Nor.* Hare, rabbit.

hareng (ah-rahng). *Fre.* Herring.

hareragu (HAA-rer-rahg-GEW). *Nor.* Jugged hare; rabbit stewed in red wine, onion, various vegetables and seasonings.

haresteg (HAAR-er-staigt). *Dan.* Roast hare.

haricot (ah-ree-koa). *Fre.* Bean; fresh (frais), dried (sec), white (blanc), pale green (flageolet), red kidney (rouge), green string (verte).

haricot de mouton (ah-ree-koa day moo-tom). *Fre.* Mutton stew with potatoes, turnips, but no beans.

haricots (Hahr-ee-ko). *Bri.* Dried beans.

hari gobhi (HA-ree GOHB-hee). *Ind.* Broccoli.

hari mirch (HA-ree meerch). *Ind.* Green pepper.

harina (ah-REE-nah). *Spa.* Flour.

haring (HAH-ring). *Dut.* Herring.

haringsla (HAH-ring-slah). *Dut.* Herring salad.

hart (hart). *Dut.* Heart

harusame (hah-roo-SAH-mee). *Jap.* Translucent noodles.

Harvard beets (HAHR-vuhd beets). *USA.* A dish of beets, sliced, diced or julienne, cooked in vinegar, sugar, and cornstarch.

Hase (HAA-zer). *Ger.* Hare; rabbit.

Hase im Topf (HAA-zer im tohpf). *Ger.* Potted rabbit in wine.

Hasehendl (HAA-zer-hehndl). *Ger.* Chicken, as spoken in the Frankfort area.

Haselnuss (HAA-zeri-newsser). *Ger.* Hazelnut.

Hasenbraten (HAA-zern-braa-tern). *Ger.* Roast hare.

Hasenpfeffer (HAA-zern-pfeh-ferr). *Ger.* Stew of rabbit braised in red wine flavored with pepper and spices.

Haselhühner (HAA-zerl-hoon-nerr). *Ger.* Hazel hen.

hash (hahsch). *USA.* Chopped leftover or scrap meats mixed with a sauce and seasonings.

ha-shoga (hai-SHO-gah). *Jap.* Ginger shoots.

haslett (haas-lett). *Iri.* The Irish version of the Scottish haggis.

hasselnöt (HAHSS-erl-nurt). *Swe.* Hazelnut.

hasty pudding (HA-ste PUHD-eng). *USA.* Cornmeal pudding with molasses and spices. Also called Indian pudding.

hasu (hah-SOO). *Jap.* A lotus root.

hattit kit (HEHT-teh keht). *Sco.* A high calorie drink made of buttermilk, very fresh new milk, double cream, sugar, seasoned with nutmeg.

hauki (HAHoo-ki). *Fin.* Pike.

haunch (hahnch). *USA.* Hindquarter of deer or wild game.

Hauptel Salat (HOWP-tel zah-LAART). *Ger.* Austrian wilted lettuce salad.

Hausfrauenart (hahus-FRAUHEN-art). *Ger.* With sour cream and pickles.

hausgemacht (howus-ger-MAKAHT). *Ger.* Homemade.

Havarti (haa-VAHR-tee). *Dan.* A cows' skimmed milk cheese, pale, mild, semihard, piquant flavor, many small holes.

havermout (HAH-vehr mauw-tah). *Dut.* Oatmeal.

hazel hen (HA-zehl hen). *USA.* A tender, tasty game bird, related to the grouse.

hazelnut (HA-zehl-nuht). *USA.* The nut of a hazel shrub; round or slightly oval and flat on one end, amber colored; flavor is sweet; texture firm; rich in oil, pleasant to taste; used in confectionery. Also known as filbert.

headcheese (HEHD-chez). *USA.* A jellied meat dish made of the meat of a pig's head, boiled, chopped, highly seasoned, molded, and chilled.

heavenly hash (HEAV-ehn-lee hahsh). *USA.* A dessert of vanilla wafers and whipped cream. A confection of marshmallows and nuts covered with melted milk chocolate, then cut in squares.

heavy cream (HEAV-ee krehm). *USA.* Cows' milk cream that contains 36–40% milkfat, used for whipping cream.

heavy syrup (HEH-vee SEHR-uhp). *USA.* Two parts sugar dissolved in one part water.

hechima (heh-chee-MAH). *Jap.* Sponge gourd, about a foot long, green, with deep grooves. Also known as Chinese okra or luffa.

Hecht (hehkht). *Ger.* Pike.

hedelmä (HAY-dayl-miae). *Fin.* Fruit.

hedelmäkakku (HAY-dayl-mae-KAHK-koo). *Fin.* Fruit cake.

hedelmäkeitto (HAY-dayl-mae-KAYT-toa). *Fin.* Cold fruit soup.

hedelmäsalaatti (HAY-dayl-mae-SAH-laat-ti). *Fin.* Fruit salad.

hedgehog mushroom (HEHDG-hawg MUHSH-room). *USA.* A mushroom with a sweet, hearty mushroom flavor that has a buff-orange cap with white toothlike projections under it.

Hefe (HAY-fe). *Ger.* Yeast.

Hefekranz (HAY-fer-krahnts). *Ger.* A ring-shaped cake of yeast dough with almonds and candied fruit.

Heidelbeeren (HIGH-derl-bay-rern). *Ger.* Blueberries.

Heilbot (HAYL-bawt). *Dut.* Halibut.

Heilbutt (HIGHL-but). *Ger.* Halibut.

heiss (hais). *Ger.* Hot.

helados (ay-LAH-dhoass). *Spa.* Ice cream.

heldersoep (HEL-dur-ch-soop). *Dut.* Clear soup.

helgeflundra (HEHL-yer-flewnd-rah). *Swe.* Halibut.

hellefisk (HEHL-ler-fisk). *Nor.* Halibut.

helleflynder (HAYL-er-flew-nerr). *Dan.* Halibut.

Helles Bier (HEH-lerss beer). *Ger.* Light beer.

helstekt (HEHL-stehkt). *Nor.* Fried.

hen (hehn). *USA.* A female chicken over a year old; best used stewed.

Hendel (hehndl). *Ger.* Austrian chicken.

Henne (HEHN-neh). *Ger.* Hen.

Henry IV (auhn-ray IV). *Fre.* A classic garnish of artichoke hearts, potatoes, and bearnaise.

herb (hehrb or ehrb). *USA.* An aromatic plant used for flavoring and seasoning foods.

herb salts (ehrb sawltz). *USA.* A combination of noniodized salt and crushed herbs; used for seasoning savory dishes.

herb vinegar (ehrb VEHN-ee-gahr). *USA.* Any vinegar with herbs such as tarragon or burnet placed in vinegar, and allowed to develop the flavor of the herb.

Hering (HAY-ring). *Ger.* Herring.

Hering Hausfrauenart (HER-ring hahus-FRAUHEN-art). *Ger.* Fillet of herring in sour cream with onions.

Heringskartoffeln (HAY-ring-kahr-TOF-ferln). *Ger.* Casserole consisting of layers of herring alternating with potatoes.

herkkusienikastike (HAYRK-koo-SAY-ni-KAHS-tik-kay). *Fin.* Mushroom sauce.

herkkusienikeitto (HAYRK-koos-ayni-KAYT-toa). *Fin.* Cream of mushroom soup.

hermit crab (HEHR-meht krahb). *USA.* A small crab found in vacated univalve shells; eaten deep fried or sautéed, never eaten raw.

herneet (HAYR-nayt). *Fin.* Peas.

hernekeitto (HAYR-nay-KAYT-toh). *Fin.* Green pea soup, the national dish.

hero (HEE-roh). *USA.* Hoagie.

Herrgårdsost (HAER-goar-oost). *Swe.* A hard cheese with a mild to slightly strong flavor, similar to Swiss.

herring (HEHR-rehng). *USA.* A flavorful, nutritious fish that in adult state is smoked or salted, and in young state is canned and sold as sardines.

herring caviar (HEHR-rehng kah-vee-ahr). *USA.* A caviar substitute; the roe of the alewife herring is processed and used as caviar.

Hering Rollmop (HAY-ring roll-mohp). *Ger.* Raw, filleted herring rolled around an onion or pickle, fastened with pick or clove, and packed in vinegar, served with a sauce such as horseradish, tomato or mustard; if fried before packing, known as bratrollmops.

hervir (ayr-BEER). *Spa.* To poach.

Herzogin Kartoffeln (hay-TSO-geen kahr-TOF-ferln). *Ger.* Mashed potatoes browned in the oven.

hé táo (huh tao). *Chi.* Walnuts.

hé táo zhá jipiàn (huh tao dzah jee pien). *Chi.* Deep-fried chicken with walnuts.

Hete Bliksem (HAA-tah BLENK-som). *Dut.* "Hot Lightning"; spicy mixture of potatoes, pork chops, and apples.

hickory nut (HEHK-oh-ree nuht). *USA.* A variety of walnut; the edible nut of the hickory tree; rich nut encased in a very hard shell.

hielo (YEH-loh). *Spa.* Ice.

hierbas finas (YAYR-bahss FEE-nahss). *Spa.* Mixture of herbs.

higaditos de pollo (ee-gah-DHEE-toass day POAL-lyoa). *Spa.* Chicken livers.

hígado (EE-gah-doh). *Spa.* Liver.

higos (EE-goass). *Spa.* Figs.

hijiki (HEE-gee-kee). *Jap.* A calcium-rich edible sea vegetable that resembles strands of black twine in its dried form.

hijiso (hee-GEE-soh). *Jap.* Shiso seed pods; pepper; used for seasonings.

hikiniku (hee-KEE-nee-koo). *Jap.* Ground beef.

hilloa (HIL-loah). *Fin.* Jam.

Himbeeren (HIM-bay-rern). *Ger.* Raspberries.

himmelsk lapskaus (HIM-melsk LAPS-kewss). *Nor.* "Heavenly potpourri"; fresh fruit and nuts with brandied egg sauce.

Himmel und Erde (HIM-ehl unt ert). *Ger.* "Heaven and Earth"; apples and potatoes with onions and sausage.

hina (hee-NAH). *Jap.* A young chicken, 3–4 months of age; fryer.

hindbaer (HEEN-baer). *Dan.* Raspberry.

hindbi (HEEN-bee). *Ara.* Dandelion greens.

hinojo (ee-NOU-hoh). *Spa.* Fennel.

hinta (HEN-tah). *Ara.* Wheat grain.

hirame (hee-RAH-meh). *Jap.* Flounder.

Hirn (hehrn). *Ger.* Brains.

hirondelles (ee-ron-dehls). *Fre.* Swallows.

Hirsch (heersh). *Ger.* Stag, venison.

Hirschbraten (heersh-BRAA-tern). *Ger.* Roast venison.

hirvi (HIR-vay-ni). *Fin.* Elk.

hjärta (YAHR-ta). *Swe.* Heart.

hjerte (YAIR-ter). *Dan, Nor.* Heart.

hjort (yoort). *Swe.* Deer; roebuck.

hjortetakk (YOOR-tch-tahkk). *Nor.* Special Christmas doughnuts.

hjortron (YOORT-ron). *Swe.* Artic cloudberry.

hjortstek (yoort-stehk). *Swe.* Venison steak. Also called rådjursstek.

hoagie. (HOH-ghee). *USA.* A glorified sandwich made on a long, split roll generously filled with cold cuts, cheeses, onion, lettuce, tomatoes, pickles. Also called grinder, hero, Italian sandwich, po boy, poor boy, sub, submarine.

hoagie roll (HOH-ghee rohl). *USA.* An oblong yeast-dough roll about 6 inches long, used for a glorified sandwich called a hoagie.

hoarhound (hoahr-houhnd). *USA.* An herb of the mint family that produces a bitter tonic; its stems and leaves are used to make teas, syrups, candy, and cough drops.

hochepot (osh-eh-poa). *Fre.* A thick stew of less desirable cuts of meats and winter vegetables.

hodesalat (HOO-der-ssah-laat). *Nor.* Lettuce.

hodgels (HAHD-gehls). *Sco.* Chive-flavored oatmeal dumplings boiled in meat broth.

hodge-podge (hohdg-pohdg). *Sco.* A thick stew of less desirable cuts of meats and winter vegetables.

hoecake (HO-kahk). *USA.* A pancake of cornmeal, originally cooked using a hoe as a griddle; johnny cake.

hoh laan dow (how lahn dahw). *Chi.* Edible-pod peas: snow peas, sugar pea pods, Chinese pea pods.

Hohle Schokoladenhippen (ho-leh shok-eh-LA-den-hep-en). *Ger.* Hollow tubes of chocolate filled with cream.

hoh yow (hoa yoh). *Chi.* Oyster sauce.

hoi sin jeung (hai sheen gee-ong). *Chi.* A bean sauce, reddish, slightly sweet, seasoned with garlic and chilies; canned as well as made fresh.

hoja de laurel (OA-khah day lahoo-RAYL). *Spa.* Bay leaf.

hollandaise (hol-uhn-daz) *Fre.* A classic rich sauce made of butter, egg yolks, and lemon juice or vinegar.

Holländische Sosse (HOH-lehn-dish ZOH-seh). *Ger.* Hollandaise sauce.

Holsteiner Schnitzel (HOL-shtigh-nerr SHNIT-serl). *Ger.* Breaded veal escallope topped with fried egg, may be garnished with one of the following: vegetables, bread, butter, anchovies, mussels, and smoked salmon.

homard (om-mahr). *Fre.* Lobster.

homard à l'américaine (omahr ah lah-may-ree-kehn). *Fre.* Sautéd diced lobster, flamed in cognac, simmered in wine, aromatic vegetables, herbs and tomatoes.

hominy (HOHM-e-knee). *USA.* Inner kernel of corn that has been processed to remove the outer covering, and used whole as is or ground into grits.

homogenized milk. (hoh-MAH-gen-i-zed mehlk). *USA.* A fresh, fluid milk, with 3.25% milkfat and 8.25% protein, lactose and minerals; has no cream line; fat particles are broken up so finely during the process that they remain uniformly dispersed throughout the milk. Also called homo.

höna (HUR-nah). *Swe.* Chicken.

høne (hur-ner). *Dan.* Chicken.

høne bryst (hur-ner brewst). *Dan.* White meat of chicken.

hønekødsuppe (HUR-ner-kurdh-soo-bber). *Dan.* Chicken and vegetable soup.

honey (HUHN-nee). *USA.* A sweet, viscous liquid manufactured by honey-bees; used for centuries as a sweetening agent in food and drink.

honeybun (HUHN-ee-buhn). *USA.* A flat, yeast-dough breakfast roll or "bun," basted with honey before baking.

honeydew melon (HUHN-ee-deu MELL-un). *USA.* A melon with a semi-hard, creamy yellow-green rind; flesh is delicate green, juicy, fine-grained, and sweet; used in salads and desserts; the basic ingredient in the liqueur called Midori.

hóng chá (hoong chah). *Chi.* Black tea.

hongos (OHN-goh). *Spa.* Mushrooms.

hongroise (ahng-grwah). *Fre.* In the Hungarian way; eggs, meats, fish, poultry cooked in a cream sauce seasoned with paprika.

Honig (HOA-nikh). *Ger.* Honey.

honing (HO-ning). *Dut.* Honey.

honingkoek (HO-ninh-kook). *Dut.* Honey cake.

honning (HON-ning). *Nor.* Honey.

honningkake (HON-ning-kaa-ker). *Nor.* Honey cake.

hønsekødsuppe (HRUNSS-er-kurdh-soo-bber). *Dan.* Chicken-vegetable soup.

hønsessupe (HURN-sser-ssew-pper). *Nor.* Chicken soup.

hon shimeji (hon SHEE-meh-jee). *Jap.* A mushroom that comes in clusters with small caps, and has a lobsterlike flavor; entire mushroom, cap, stem, and most of the cluster base is edible.

hons med ris (hurn maey reess). *Nor.* Chicken with rice.

hönssoppa (HONS-SOOpa). *Swe.* Chicken soup.

hon tarako (hon TAH-rah-koh). *Jap.* A product made from the roe of cod, which has been salted and dyed red; a caviar substitute.

honung (HOA-newng). *Swe.* Honey.

hopjes (HAWP-yus). *Dut.* Coffee-flavored candy.

Hoppel-Poppel (HOP-perl-POP-perl). *Ger.* Scrambled eggs with bacon or sausages and potatoes.

Hopping John (HOHP-eng Jon). *USA.* A dish of rice and black eyed peas.

hops (ahps). *USA.* The edible tips of the panicle (male plant) are broken away from the woody stem in the same manner as asparagus tips, then boiled in salted water with lemon juice, and served with butter, cream, or gravy. The ripe pistillate, or ovum-bearing catkin of the plant, is used dried to impart a bitter taste to malt liquors.

horchata (oar-CHAH-tay). *Spa.* A beverage made of almond or pumpkin seeds.

horehound candy (HORE-hownd KAN-dee). *USA.* A candy made from the aromatic plant hoarhound; shaped as balls, drops, or squares; often used to treat sore throats.

horenso (hoh-rehn-soh). *Jap.* Spinach; mild taste and sweet.

Hörnchen (HERN-shen). *Ger.* Crescent-shaped, slightly sweet rolls.

horno (OAR-noa). *Spa.* Baked.

hors d' oeuvre (ohr-durv). *Fre.* Canapé, appetizer, side dish, or relish served at the beginning of a meal.

hors d'oeuvres (awr-DER-vruh). *Dut.* Hors d'oeuvres.

horseradish (HORS-rad-disch). *USA.* A zesty-flavored herb of the mustard family; its tops can be used as a salad green; its white-fleshed roots are ground up to make a pungent, hot-tasting condiment.

hortalizas (oar-tah-LEE-thays). *Spa.* Greens.

hortclã pimenta (or-TAY-LAHN pee-MEHN-tah). *Por.* Peppermint.

hortobágyi ropstélyos (HAWR-taw-baad-yee RAWSH-tay-yawsh). *Hun.* Steak Hortobágy style: braised in a mix of stock and bacon bits and accompanied by a large semolina dumpling.

hot chocolate (haht CHOHC-oh-laht). *USA.* A tasty chocolate drink, always served hot, and usually garnished with marshmallows or whipped cream.

hotch-potch (HAHTCH-pahtch). *Sco.* A thick stew of less desirable cuts of meats and winter vegetables.

hot cross buns (haht krahs buhns). *Bri.* A round, sweet yeast roll with a white cross in icing marking the top.

hot dog (haht dawg). *USA.* A long bun split on one side only, stuffed with a boiled weiner or frankfurter, seasoned with mustard, catsup, chopped onions, pickle relish.

hot fudge (haht fujg). *USA.* A thick topping of chocolate, butter and sugar, used hot on ice cream and desserts.

hot house cucumbers (haht haus KU-kohm-behrz). *USA.* Also known as European and burpless, these cucumbers are hydroponically grown; have a mild cucumber flavor and cook like common cucumbers; excellent eaten fresh.

hot pack (haht pahk). *USA.* A canning term, referring to food that is precooked a little or fully, and packed into canning jars or cans while very hot, then sealed, and processed in a boiling-water bath.

hot pot (haht paht). *Bri.* A thick stew of less desirable cuts of meats and winter vegetables.

hot sauce (hoht saus). *USA.* Any of various commercially made seasoning sauces containing chili peppers, salt, and vinegar.

hottokeki (ah-TSOO-keh-kee). *Jap.* Hotcakes.

hotto kokoa (ah-TSOO KOH-koh-ah). *Jap.* Hot chocolate.

hovdessert (HOHVOdes-SEHR). *Swe.* Meringues with chocolate sauce.

huachinango (wah-chee-NAHN-goh). *Mex.* Red snapper.

hua jiao (hwa jiao). *Chi.* A reddish brown peppercorn that is very hot, used in dipping sauce.

hua juan (hwa juan). *Chi.* Steamed rolls.

huánggua (hwang gwa). *Chi.* Cucumber.

huáng-yóu (hwaang-yo). *Chi.* Butter.

huángyú (huang yu). *Chi.* Sturgeon.

huasheng (hwa sheng). *Chi.* Peanuts.

Hubbard squash (HUHB-bahrd squawsh). *USA.* A hard-skinned winter squash; used baked, boiled, or steamed.

huckleberry (HUCK-kle-bear-re). *USA.* An edible dark bluish-black berry resembling blueberries; has 10 large seeds (nutlets); acidic taste.

huevos (WEH-vohs). *Spa.* Eggs; huevo is singular.

huevos al horno (WEH-vohs ahl OAR-noh). *Spa.* Baked eggs.

huevos al nido (WEH-vohs ahl NEE-dhoa). *Spa.* "Eggs in a nest"; egg yolks set in small soft rolls, then fried and covered with egg white.

huevos al trote (WEH-vohs ahl TROA-tay). *Spa.* Boiled eggs filled with tuna and dressed with mayonnaise.

huevos com jamón (WEH-vohs kon khah-MON). *Spa.* Ham and eggs.

huevos duros (WEH-vohs DOO-roh). *Spa.* Hard-cooked eggs.

huevos escaljados (WEH-vohs ehs-kahl-KHAH-doa). *Spa.* Shirred eggs.

huevos flamenco (WEH-vohs flah-mehn-koa). *Spa.* Eggs baked with tomato, onion and diced ham; garnished with asparagus tips, red peppers, spicy pork sausage.

huevos fritos (WEH-vohs FREE-toass). *Spa.* Fried eggs.

huevos medio cocidos (WEH-vohs MEH-dyoh koh-see-doh). *Spa.* Poached eggs.

huevos pasados por agua (WEH-vohs pah-SSAH-dhoa por AHG-wah). *Spa.* Soft-boiled eggs.

huevos rancheros (WEH-vohs rahn-CHER-ohs). *Spa.* Eggs with a hot spicy sauce, served with tortillas.

huevos revueltos (WEH-vohs ray-BHWAYL-toass). *Spa.* Scrambled eggs.

Huhn (hoon). *Ger.* Chicken.

Hühnerbein (HEW-nerr-bine). *Ger.* Chicken leg.

Hühnerbraten (Hew-nerr BRAA-tern). *Ger.* Baked chicken.

Hühnerbrühe mit Nudeln (HEW-nerr-brew-er mit NOO-derln). *Ger.* Chicken broth with noodles.

Hühnerbrust (HEW-nerr-brust). *Ger.* Chicken breast.

Hühnerfrikassee (HEW-nerr-frec-kah-zee). *Ger.* Chicken fricassee.

Hühnerleber (HEW-nerr-LAY-berr). *Ger.* Chicken livers.

Huhn mit Käsesaus (hoon mit KAIZ-saus). *Ger.* Boiled chicken with cheese sauce; a Swiss dish.

huile (lweel). *Fre.* Oil.

huile d'olive (lweel doll-eev). *Fre.* Olive oil

huitlacoche (wee-tlah-KOH-cheh). *Mex.* A fungus that grows on green corn cobs, making a favorite stuffing for quesadillas or soup; the fungus makes the kernels grow large, black and deformed, but tastes delicious.

huître (weetr). *Fre.* Oyster.

hú-jiao-miàr (hoo-gee-ow-mee-ar). *Chi.* Pepper.

hull (huhl). *USA.* The outer covering of a seed or nut, or pith of a strawberry.

húluóbò (hoo luo bo). *Chi.* Carrots.

humble pie (UM-ble pi). *Bri.* Pie once made from sundry parts of the deer and fed to the servants at hunting feasts while the wealthy ate the venison.

Humboldt dressing (HUHM-bohlt DREHS-seng). *USA.* A dressing of crab butter, mayonnaise and seasonings; served mixed with a dish of crabs.

Hummer (HUM-merr). *Ger.* Lobster.

hummer (HOOM-merr). *Nor, Dan.* Lobster.

hummer (HEW-merr). *Swe.* Lobster.

hummer I gelé (HOOM-merr ee sheh-LAY). *Nor.* Lobster in aspic jelly.

hummeri (HOOM-mayri). *Fin.* Lobster.

Hummerkrabben (HUM-merr-krah-bern). *Ger.* Large prawns; large shrimp.

hummerstuvning (HU-mehr-STOO-veng). *Swe.* Lobster Newburg.

hummus (HUM-mus). *Ara.* A paste of mashed chick-peas with lemon juice, garlic, seasonings.

hún tún (hwen tuen). *Chi.* A wonton noodle; used as a dough wrapper in making wonton.

huo-tui (huo-tway). *Chi.* Ham.

hush puppies (huhsh PUH-pees). *USA.* A deep-fried cornmeal bread, shaped like a dumpling, seasoned with finely chopped onion; eaten with fried fish.

hussaini kabab (hoo-SIE-nee ka-BAHB). *Ind.* Ground meat shaped into thin sausages, stuffed with nuts and raisins, and panfried or broiled.

húst (hoost). *Hun.* Meat.

hutspot (HUHTS-poht). *Dut.* A dish of potatoes, onions, and carrots.

hutspot met klapstuk (HUHTS-poht meet KLAHP-stahk). *Dut.* Stewed lean beef with potatoes, onions, and carrots.

hüttenkäse (HOO-ten-kayz). *Ger.* Cottage cheese.

Hutzelbrot (HOOT-serl-broat). *Ger.* Fruit bread.

Huzarensla (hew-ZAH-ruh-slah). *Dut.* Hussars salad; a complete meal in itself consisting of bits of meat, pickles, diced apples, potatoes, and beets, and all bound together with mayonnaise.

hvalkkjøtt (VAAL-khurt). *Nor.* Whale meat.

hveteboller (VAY-teh-bohl-lehr). *Nor.* Sweet rolls.

hvide bønner (VEEDH-er BURN-err). *Dan.* Kidney beans.

hvidløg. (VEEDH-lurg). *Dan.* Garlic.

hvidløgssmør (VEEDG-lurg-ssmurr). *Dan.* Garlic butter.

hvidtøl (VEEDH-turl). *Dan.* Nonalcoholic malt beer used in øllebrød.

hvidvinssovs (VEEDH-veen-soooss). *Dan.* White wine sauce.

hvitkålsalat (VEET-kawl-ssah-LAAT). *Nor.* Cole slaw.

hvitløk (VEET-lurk). *Nor.* Garlic.

hvitting (VIT-ting). *Nor.* Whiting.

hylderbaersuppe (HEWL-derr-bear-soap-pey). *Dan.* Elderberry soup.

hyse (HEW-sser). *Nor.* Haddock.

hyssop (HEHSS-uhp). *USA.* A minty, spicy, somewhat bitter herb used sparingly in salads and fruits; use its dried flowers in soups and tisanes.

iasc (ee-ask). *Iri.* Fish; more than one fish is éisc.

ice (ics). *USA.* Glacé; water ice; made of fruit juice, sugar and water; flavored variously as lemon juice, coffee or liqueur; frozen smooth but without addition of egg white; related to granita, sherbet, spoom, spuma, but each is different.

ice cream (ics krem). *USA.* A frozen dessert of cream, milk, eggs, sugar, flavoring, with or without fruits or nuts.

ice glazing (ics GLAHZ-cng). *USA.* A method of freezing food, particularly fish, meats, and poultry, by dipping, brushing or spraying with water to form a thin shield of ice; preserves freshness and flavor.

iceberg lettuce (ICS-burg LEHT-us). *USA.* A salad lettuce with a large firm head, crisp, brittle, tightly packed; outer leaves medium green, inner leaves are pale green and chunky; the most common variety of lettuce used in the United States. Also called crisphead lettuce.

icebox pie (ICS-bohx pi). *USA.* A crusted pie with a creamy filling that is frozen or chilled until firm.

ichimi (ee-CHEE-mee). *Jap.* Red pepper flakes.

ichigo (ee-CHEE-goh). *Jap.* Strawberries.

icing (ICS-eng). *USA.* Covering for cakes, pastries, made of sugar, butter, flavorings, cooked or uncooked; used in confectionery of all kinds; interchanges with frosting.

icing sugar (ICS-eng SCHU-gar). *Bri.* Confectioners' sugar.

i dolce (ee DOAL-chay). *Ita.* Desserts.

iets vooraf (eets fohrd-aff). *Dut.* Appetizer.

ijji (ah-JEE). *Ara.* Omelet.

ijs (eys). *Dut.* Ice; ice cream.

ika (ee-KAH). *Jap.* Squid.

île flottante (eel floh-tahng). *Fre.* Floating islands: meringue "islands" floating on a sea of custard; also sliced sponge cake layered in a deep bowl, sprinkled with liqueur, spread with jam, nuts, dried fruits, topped with Chantilly Crème, decorated, then covered with a chilled vanilla-flavored custard.

im (imm). *Iri.* Butter.

imam bayildi (AH-mahm by-yahl-deh). *Ara.* A cold vegetable dish of sautéed eggplant, garlic, onions, tomatoes, and parsley.

im baile (im BA-la). *Iri.* Homemade butter.

imbiss (em-BEHSS). *Ger.* A snack.

imbottini delizia (eem-bou-TEE-nee day-LEE-tsja). *Ita.* Veal rolls stuffed with ham, cheese, and truffles.

imbottito (eem-boa-TEE-toa). *Ita.* Stuffed.

imli (IM-lee). *Ind.* Tamarind.

impanato (eem-pah-NAH-toa). *Ita.* Breaded.

impériale (eem-pay-ree-ahl). *Fre.* A garnish of truffles, cocks' comb, kidneys, sweetbreads, foie gras, and Madeira sauce.

Incanestrato (een-kah-nehs-STRAH-toh). *Ita.* A sharp, hard, grating cheese.

incasciata (een-kahs-cee-AH-tah). *Ita.* Noodles mixed with hard-boiled eggs and meat.

Indian bread (EEN-dee-un brehd). *USA.* Cornmeal bread.

Indianerkrapfen (en-dee-AHN-nehr-KRAP-fen). *Ger.* Indian Cruller Balls; a rich dessert of hollow sponge cake balls, filled with whipped cream, then rolled in chocolate icing.

Indian nut (EEN-dee-un nuht). *USA.* The edible seed from any of several pine trees. Also called chinquapin, crenata, pignola, pine nut, piñon.

Indian pudding (EEN-dee-un PUHD-eng). *USA.* An American Indian pudding of cornmeal, molasses, spices; hasty pudding.

indienne (en-dee-ahng). *Fre.* "In the style of India"; dishes usually served with boiled rice.

Indo-Chinese rice (EN-doh-CHI-nez risc). *USA.* Rice which is smaller than Indian rice, is excellent and cooks perfectly without breaking up.

indyuk (een-DYAY-kah). *Rus.* Turkey.

infuse (en-FUZ). *USA.* To steep or soak herbs, spices or vegetables in boiling water to extract their essence.

ingefaer brød (EEN-sheh-fah-eer brurdh). *Dan.* Gingerbread.

ingefära (I-nger-fae-rah). *Swe.* Ginger.

ingemaakte vruchten (een-gehr-MAAK-teh FRUHK-ten). *Dut.* Canned fruit.

ingen (ENG-ghen). *Jap.* String beans.

Ingwerbrot (INJ-vehr-broat). *Ger.* Gingerbread.

Ingwer kuche (INJ-vehr koo-chee). *USA.* A Pennsylvania Dutch ginger cake.

inhame (ee-NYAH-muh). *Por.* Yam.

inlagd sil (IN-lagd SIL). *Swe.* Pickled herring.

insalata (een-sah-LAH-tah). *Ita.* Salad.

insalata mista (een-sah-LAH-tah MEE-stah). *Ita.* Combination salad.

insalata paesana (een-sah-LAH-tah paaeh-SAH-nah). *Ita.* Potato, egg, and vegetable salad.

insalata verde (een-sah-LAH-tah vehr-day). *Ita.* Green salad; usually only one green is used (lettuce, escarole, or lamb's lettuce) and extra virgin olive oil, salt, and vinegar.

instant breakfast (EN-stahnt BREHK-fahst). *USA.* A drink with a milk basis, having nutrients added, that is drunk in place of eating usual breakfast items.

instant coffee (EN-stahnt KAWF-fee). *USA.* Brewed coffee that has been dehydrated and pulverized, stored, then can be rehydrated quickly in hot water.

instant flour (EN-stahnt flowr). *USA.* A specialty flour used in making gravies and sauces.

instant rice. (EN-stahnt rics). *USA.* Rice that has been partially cooked and split open.

instant tea (EN-stahnt tee). *USA.* Brewed tea that has been dehydrated and pulverized, stored, then can be rehydrated quickly in hot water.

interlard (EN tehr lahrd). *USA.* To lard; to thread strips of fat through meat or other flesh for the purpose of basting during cooking.

intingolo (een-teen-GOA-lou). *Ita.* Sauce.

in umido (een OO-mee-doa). *Ita.* Braising; stewing.

invert sugar (EEN-vehrt SCHU-gahr). *USA.* Simple sugar; blended from dextrose and fructose; used in candy making, soft drinks, confections.

involtini (een-voul-TEE-nee). *Ita.* Rolls.

involtini di vitello (een-voul-TEE-nee dee vee-TEHL-lou). *Ita.* Veal birds; meat rollups; scallops of meat, usually veal, stuffed, rolled, and cooked; saltimbocca.

iodized salt (I-oh-dizd sawlt). *USA.* Table salt with added iodine, an essential trace element.

iota (EEO-tah). *Ita.* Jota; a robust soup of beans, potatoes, bacon, sauerkraut slowly cooked.

iqdi safra (AH-dee SAH-frah). *Ara.* Saffron.

Irish coffee (I-rehsh CAHF-fe). *USA.* Hot sugared coffee with Irish whiskey and whipped cream.

Irish Mist (I-rehsh mehst). *USA.* Irish whiskey flavored with heather honey; a liqueur.

Irish moss (I-rehsh mahss). *USA.* A seaweed that needs to be well purified; used as an emulsifier, stabilizer, and thickener in a variety of foods; carrageenan.

Irish soda bread (I-rehsh soh-doh brehd). *USA.* A traditionally Irish free-form round bread, leavened with baking soda and buttermilk, not yeast.

Irish stew (I-rehsh steu). *USA.* A stew of meat, potatoes, and onions in thick gravy.

irlandaise (leer-lahng-daise). *Fre.* Irish style; that is, with potatoes.

is (eess). *Dan, Nor, Swe.* Ice.

iscas de figado (EESH-kahs duh FEE-gah-doo). *Por.* Thin slices of calf's liver, cooked in oil and wine, and seasoned with garlic.

Ischlertörtchen (ISH-lehr-turt-chern). *Ger.* A biscuit spread with jam.

ise ebi (ee-SEH ee-bee). *Jap.* Lobster.

isinglass (i-seng-glahs). *Fre.* A pure, transparent gelatin obtained from the air bladder of fish, particularly the sturgeon.

iskaffe (ICS-KAH-feh). *Swe.* Iced coffee.

iskiriym (ays-KREEM). *Ara.* Ice cream.

isleta bread (ees-LEH-tah brehd). *USA.* Bread shaped like a bear's claw; a Pueblo Indian product.

Ismail Bayaldi (es-mayl by-yahl-dee). *Fre.* A classic garnish of Turkish origin; sliced fried eggplant, crushed tomatoes, rice pilaf and sauce portugaise. Also known as Imam Bayildi.

ispíní (ish-PEE-nee). *Iri.* Sausages.

iste (ics-teh). *Swe.* Iced tea.

isvann (EESS-vahn). *Nor.* Ice water.

Italian meringue (ee-TAHL-ee-ahn meh-RAHNG). *USA.* Meringue made by whipping hot sugar syrup into stiffly beaten egg whites; used to lighten buttercreams, pastry, sherbets, souffles, to frost pastries.

Italian sandwich (ee-TAHL-ee-ahn SAHND-wehch). *USA.* Hoagie.

Italian sausage (ee-TAHL-ee-ahn SAW-sahg). *USA.* An Italian pork sausage in two forms, hot and sweet.

itir (AH-tahr). *Ara.* Syrup made from rose geranium leaves; rosewater or orange essence can be substituted.

ito-kanten (EE-toh AHN-ten). *Jap.* Thread agar-agar.

ivoire (ee-vwahr). *Fre.* A white supreme sauce with meat glaze for poultry.

iwashi (ee-WAH-shee). *Jap.* Sardines.

izer cookie (EHS-zehr KOO-kee) *USA.* A cookie baked on a special iron with figures and designs, much like a waffle iron.

J

jäätellö (YEF-tay-lur). *Fin.* Ice cream.

jabalí (khah-bhah-LEE). *Spa.* Wild boar.

jaboticaba (zheh-buht-eh-KOHB-eh). *Por.* A fruit, native to Brazil, with a grapelike appearance; dark maroon skin with a muscadine flavor; use fresh in salads, sherbets; cooked in cobblers, jams, jellies.

jachtschotel (YAHT-skoh-tehl). *Dut.* Casserole dish of meat, potatoes, onions; traditional hunting dish.

Jack cheese (jahk chez). *USA.* Monterey Jack cheese.

jagaimo (GAH-ee-moh). *Jap.* Potato.

Jägerart (YAG-er-art). *Ger.* In the hunter's style, with mushrooms and a wine sauce.

Jägert (YAG-ert). *Ger.* Sautéd with onions.

jaiba (HAHY-bah). *Mex.* Small, hard-shell crab.

jaiphul (JAY-fchl). *Ind.* Nutmeg.

jalapeño (hah-lah-PEH-nyoh). *Mex.* Small, plump, green chili.

jalea (khah-LAY-ah). *Spa.* Jelly.

jalousie (ZAH-luh-zee). *Fre.* Little flaky pastries made in strips, resembling a venetian blind.

jam (jahm). *USA.* Made from crushed or ground fruit; almost holds its shape, but is not jelly-firm.

jambalaya (djum-buh-LIE-yuh). *USA.* A Cajun dish of rice with ham, shellfish, chicken, sausage, beans, seasoned with vegetables and spices.

jambon (zhahng-bawng). *Fre.* Ham.

jambon d'Ardennes (zhahng-bawng dahr-dehnz). *Fre.* The famous Belgian ham of the Ardennes, served cut in very thin slices as an appetizer.

jamón (ah-NOHN). *Spa, Mex.* Ham.

jamu (JAH-moo). *Jap.* Jam.

jan hagel (yahn HEH-yehl). *Dut.* Cookies garnished with almonds.

jan in de zak (yahn een de zahk). *Dut.* Steamed pudding with currants and raisins.

jänis (YAE-niss). *Fin.* Hare.

Janssons frestelse (yahn-SOHNS FRESS-tel-seh). *Swe.* Popular Swedish casserole of potatoes, onions, and anchovies.

Japanese cucumbers (JAHP-ahn-neez KU-kuhm-behrs). *USA.* A seedless cucumber, 9 to 10 inches long with prickly skin.

Japanese eggplant (JAHP-ahn-neez EGG-plahnt). *USA.* A small, slender, purple eggplant, sweeter than the American variety; use baked, sautéed, stir-fried, grilled, or in casseroles.

Japanese rice (JAHP-ahn-neez rics). *USA.* A greyish-white, shiny short-grain rice with regular oval grains, hard, translucent with a dark mark at the center.

japonaise (zhah-pawng-ayz). *Fre.* A garnish with Japanese or Chinese artichokes and potato croquettes.

jardinière (zhar-de-nayr). *Fre.* A dish of mixed vegetables.

Jarlsberg (YAHRLZ-behrg). *Nor.* A cow's partially skim milk cheese; hard; nutty and sweet.

jarret (zhah-reh). *Fre.* A part of the leg of an animal behind the knee joint; hock or knuckle.

Javaanse Sla (yah-VAHD-sah schlah). *Dut.* An exotic Indonesian salad.

javali (jah-vah-LEE). *Por.* Wild boar.

Java rice (JAH-vah rics). *USA.* Flat, transparent, shiny rice with elongated grains.

javitri (ja-VIH-tree). *Ind.* Mace.

jazara (GA-zar). *Ara.* Carrot.

jeera (JEE-rah). *Ind.* Cumin.

jellied soup (JEL-leed soop). *USA.* A soup made from gelatinous knuckle bones, clarified and used as is or with added gelatin.

Jell-o (JEL-oh). *USA.* A trademark of General Foods Corporation for a gelatin product used for salads and desserts.

jelly (JEL-lee). *Bri.* Jell-o™; any gelatin dessert.

jelly (JEL-lee). *USA.* Soft food product made from fruit juice and thickened with gelatin or pectin; clear and firm; quiveringly, it holds its shape when turned out of the jar.

jelly bean (JEL-lee behn). *USA.* An oblong shaped candy with a chewy texture and a semifirm coating, variously flavored and colored.

jelly roll (JEL-lee rohl). *USA.* A sponge cake, baked in a special rectangular pan, spread with jelly, then rolled and sprinkled with confectioners' sugar.

Jenever (YAH-neh-vahy). *Dut.* Dutch gin. Also spelled Genever.

jerky (JER-kee). *USA.* Preserved beef that has been cut in strips and dried in the sun.

Jerusalem artichoke (jeh-RUZ-ah-leum AHR-tee-chok). *USA.* The edible tuber of a sunflower used as a vegetable. Also called sunchoke.

jets d'houblon (zjah du'blowng). *Fre.* Hop sprouts eaten as a vegetable.

jewfish (GEU-fisch). *USA.* Giant sea bass.

ji (jee). *Chi.* Chicken.

jian (jien). *Chi.* Fry, as in panfry or deep-fry.

jiang (jiang). *Chi.* Gingerroot.

jiàng niúròu (jiang niu row). *Chi.* Marinated beef.

jiàng yóu (jiang yoh). *Chi.* Soy sauce.

jiaozi (jiao dze). *Chi.* Dumpling.

jibn (GIB-na). *Ara.* Cheese.

jícama (HEE-kah-mah). *Mex.* A bulbous root with crisp white flesh.

jidàn (JEE-dan). *Chi.* Eggs; chao jidàn (tsao jee don), scrambled eggs; jianjidàn (jien jee dan), fried eggs; zhu jidàn (dzoo jee don), boiled eggs.

jiè-mo (JYEAH-mwaw). *Chi.* Mustard.

ji rou (jee row). *Chi.* Chicken meat.

ji tang (gee taang). *Chi.* Chicken soup.

jit choh (geo choo). *Chi.* A red vinegar used as a dipping sauce.

Joe Mazzetti (joh mah-ZHET-ee). *USA.* Sloppy Joe with an Italian seasoning.

Joghurt (YOA-goort). *Ger.* Yogurt.

Johannisbeer Sosse (yoh-HAH-nis-bay-rern ZO-seh). *Ger.* Red currant jelly made into a sauce.

John Dory (jon douree). *USA.* Better known as St. Peter's fish; the classic ingredient of bouillabaisse; flesh is firm, white, and finely flaked; also known as Saint-Pierre.

johnny cake (JON-nee kahk). *USA.* A cornmeal pancake.

Joinville (zwhy-veel). *Fre.* A garnish of sauce normandie, finely diced shrimp, truffles, and mushrooms; served with fillet of sole.

Jókai bableves (YAWko-ee BOB-leh-vehsh). *Hun.* Bean soup Jókai style (Jókai was a famous Hungarian writer): a mix of smoked pig's knuckles, butter beans, and carrots, seasoned with pepper, garlic, paprika, and parsley.

jolly boy (JOHL-lee boy). *USA.* A fried cake made from a cornmeal dough, baked, split in half, buttered, and served with maple syrup.

Jonagold apple (JON-ah-gohld AHP-pul). *USA.* A large, hybrid apple with yellow skin having a red blush; has a subtle tart-sweet flavor; good eaten fresh or cooked; a cross between the Jonathan and Golden Delicious apples.

jonatán alma (YAW-not-taan OL-mo). *Hun.* Jonathan apple.

jordbaer (YOOR-baer). *Dan, Nor.* Strawberry.

jordgubbar (YOORD-gew-ber). *Swe.* Strawberries.

jordnötter (YOORD-NOH-ter). *Swe.* Peanuts.

jota (ee-OA-tah). *Ita.* A robust soup of beans, potatoes, bacon, sauerkraut slowly cooked. Also spelled iota.

juan canary melon (waun ka-NARR-re MELL-un). *USA.* An oblong melon that is canary yellow; flesh is sweet and white with a tinge of pink around the seed cavity.

judia (khoo-DHEE-ahss). *Spa.* Kidney beans.

judiás blancas (khoo-DHEE-ahss BLAHN-ahss). *Spa.* White beans.

judiás verdes (khoo-DHEE-ahss BEHR-dayss). *Spa.* Green string beans.

jugged hare (JUHG-gehd hahr). *USA.* Rabbit stewed in red wine, onion, various vegetables, and seasonings.

jugo (KHOO-goa). *Spa.* Juice.

jugo de naranja (KHOO-goa day nah-RAHN-khah). *Spa.* Orange juice.

jugurttia (YOO-goort-tiah). *Fin.* Yogurt.

jujube (joo-JOO-bee). *Jap.* A fruit about the size and shape of an olive; apple-prune flavor; sweet to acidic; flesh is white and pithy; has brown skin; picked ripe; eaten fresh, candied, or dried.

julekake (YEWL-kaa-ker). *Nor.* A fancy Christmas cake.

julienne (dzhu-lee-ayn). *Fre.* Vegetables cut into thin strips.

jumble (JUHM-buhl). *USA.* A cookie with coconut, rosewater, and walnuts mixed in the dough.

Junges Huhn (YOON-gees hoon). *Ger.* Spring chicken.

Junges Zwiebeln (YOON-gees TSVEE-berln). *Ger.* Spring onions.

juniper berries (JUN-eh-purr BEHR-reez). *USA.* The fruit of an evergreen shrub of the pine family; used to add flavor to marinades, as seasoning for certain foods (sauerkraut, blackbirds, thrushs), and in the distillation of gin.

junket (JUHN-keht). *Bri.* Milk curds formed with rennet and made into a custardlike dessert.

jus (zhoo). *Fre, Dut.* Juice or gravy.

jus de viande (zhoo day vee-ahnd). *Fre.* Gravy.

juusto (YOOS-toa), *Fin.* Cheese

juzi (ju-DZE). *Chi.* Tangerine.

jú-zi (jyew-dz). *Chi.* Orange.

K

kaal (`kawl`). *Dan.* Cabbage.

kaaldolmer (koal-DULL-mah). *Dan.* Stuffed cabbage.

kaali (KAA-li). *Fin.* Cabbage.

kaalikääryleet (KAA-li-KAE-rew-layt). *Fin.* Stuffed cabbage leaves.

kaalipiiras (KAA-li-PRR-rah-kkah). *Fin.* Cabbage-filled pastry, served cold or hot.

kaas (kahs). *Dut.* Cheese.

kaassaus (KAUS-sows). *Dut.* Cheese sauce.

kabab (kah-BAHB). *Ara.* Squares of mutton braised in butter, seasoned, and served with sliced onions and parsley.

kabachok (kah-bahch'-KEE). *Rus.* Squash.

Kabeljau (KAH-behl-yow). *Ger.* Cod.

kabeljauw (kah-bul-YOW). *Dut.* Codfish.

kabis (kah-BEEC). *Ara.* Pickled, preserved.

kabocha (kah-BOW-cha). *Jap.* A deep green-skinned, turban or flattened drum shape squash, with exceptionally fine flavor, rich sweetness, and almost fiberless, yellow-orange flesh.

kabu (kah-BOO). *Jap.* Turnip.

kachauri (ka-CHAW-ree). *Ind.* Fried puffy bread stuffed with spicy bean mixture.

kachoomar (ka-CHOO-mahr). *Ind.* Chopped or sliced onions, tomatoes, and green pepper, flavored with lemon juice.

kacsa (KO-cho). *Hun.* Duck.

kadhi (kahr-HEE). *Ind.* Dumplings made with chick-pea flour and simmered in yogurt with spices and vegetables.

kaerlinghedskranse (KAYHR-lee-heths-kroan-see). *Dan.* A Danish pastry; "Love Rings."

kaernemaelk (KAYHR-nah-meylk). *Dan.* Buttermilk.

kaernemaelkskoldskaal (KEHR-neh-MELK-skolk-skol). *Dan.* Cold buttermilk soup.

kafe (KO-fyeh). *Rus.* Coffee.

kafei (kay fay). *Chi.* Coffee.

kaffee (KAHF-er). *Dan.* Coffee.

Kaffee (kah-FAY). *Ger.* Coffee; afternoon coffee with sweets and sandwiches, similar to English high tea. See Schwarzer Kaffee.

kaffee (KAH-fay). *Swe.* Coffee.

kaffee (KAWF-fee). *Dut.* Coffee.

kaffeebröd (KAH-fay-brurd). *Swe.* Coffeecake.

kaffee complet (KAWF-fee koam-PLEHT). *Dut.* Coffee, usually with whipped cream, and jam and rolls.

Kaffee Haag (kah-FAY hahk). *Ger.* Decaffeinated coffee.

Kaffeekuchen (kah-FAY-KOO-khern). *Ger.* Coffee cake.

Kaffee mit Sahne und Zucker (KAH-fay mit ZAA-ner unt TSUK-kerr). *Ger.* Coffee with cream and sugar.

Kaffee Verkehrt (kah-FAY FEHR-kert). *Ger.* Coffee with more milk than coffee.

kafta (KAHF-tah). *Ara.* Finely ground lean meat.

kage (KAA-er). *Dan.* Cake. See also flødkage, lagkage, småkage, and tørkage.

Kahlua (kah-LOO-ah). *Mex.* Coffee-flavored liqueur.

kahvi (KAHH-vi). *Fin.* Coffee. See also mustaa kahvia and maitokahvi.

kahvi kerman ja sokerin kera (KAHH-vi KAYR-mahn yah SOA-kay-riah KAY-rah). *Fin.* Coffee with cream and sugar.

kaibashira (kah-EE-bah-shee-rah). *Jap.* Scallops.

kail (kail). *Bri.* Kale.

kailkenny (KEHL-kahn-nee). *Sco.* A dish of cabbage, potatoes, leeks, and milk, similar to the Irish colcannon.

kaiseki ryori (kah-EE-seh-kee ryoh-ree). *Jap.* Originally part of the tea ceremony, now a succession of many small dishes served in a formal style. The ingredients change with the seasons and may include fowl or seafood, but no meat.

Kaiserfleisch (KIGH-zerr-flighsh). *Ger.* "Meat for the Emperor"; a special smoked pork.

Kaiser Koch (KIGH-zerr kohx). *Ger.* Emperor's Pudding; rice pudding with almonds.

Kaiserschmarren (KIGH-zerr-shmah-rern). *Ger.* Emperor's Dessert Omelet; shredded pancake with raisins served with syrup or jam.

kaitsuki nagareko (kai-IETS-soo-kee nah-GAH-lei-koh). *Jap.* Canned baby abalone in the half shell, seasoned with soy sauce.

kajiki (KAH-jee-kee). *Jap.* Swordfish.

kajmak (KA-ee-muk). *Yug.* A fluffy creamed cheese dish of feta and creamed cheeses beaten with butter, served as an appetizer with bread and roasted peppers.

kajoo (KA-joo). *Ind.* Cashew nuts.

kak (kahk). *Ara.* Hard rolls or small cakes, similar to doughnuts.

kaka (KAA-kah). *Swe.* Cake.

kakao (kah-KAH-o). *Rus.* Cocoa.

kakao (KAA-kao). *Swe.* Cocoa.

kaki (kah-kee). *Fre.* Persimmon, usually served in kirsch.

kaki (kah-KEE). *Jap.* Persimmon.

kaki (KAH-kee). *Jap.* Oysters.

kakku (KAHK-kooah). *Fin.* Cake.

kakukkfú (KOK-kook-few). *Hun.* Thyme.

kål (koal). *Swe.* Cabbage.

kål (kawl). *Dan, Nor.* Cabbage.

kala (KAH-laa). *Fin.* Fish.

kalakakot (KAH-lah-kah-kot). *Fin.* Fish cakes.

kalakeitto (KAH-lah-KAYT-toa). *Fin.* Fish soup.

kalakukko (KAH-lah-KOOK-koa). *Fin.* "Fish fowl"; a famous dish consisting of a hollowed loaf of bread filled with layers of fish and pork or bacon; somewhat fish-shaped.

kala namak (dKA-lah NEH-mek). *Ind.* Black salt.

Kalb (lahlp). *Ger.* Veal.

Kalbsbraten (KAHLP-braa-tern). *Ger.* Roast veal.

Kalbsbratwurst (KAHLP-braat-voorst). *Ger.* Veal sausage.

Kalbsbries. (KAHLP-preece). *Ger.* Sweetbreads.

Kalbsbrust (KAHLP-brust). *Ger.* Breast of veal.

Kalbfleisch (KAHLP-flighsh). *Ger.* Veal.

Kalbfüsse (KAHLP-fooss). *Ger.* Calves' feet.

Kalbsfrikassee (KAHLP-frik-ah-see). *Ger.* Veal fricassee.

Kalbschnitzel (KAHLP-shnit-serl). *Ger.* Veal cutlet sautéed in butter.

Kalbshaxe (KAHLP-hahk-ser). *Ger.* Leg of veal.

Kalbskotelett (KAHLP-kot-leht). *Ger.* Veal cutlet.

Kalbsleber. (KAHLP-lay-berr). *Ger.* Calves' liver.

Kalbsleberwurst (KAHLP- ley-berr-voorst). *Ger.* Veal liver sausage.

Kalbslende (KAHLP-lahn-der). *Ger.* Filet of veal.

Kalbsrippchen (KAHLP-rip-khern). *Ger.* Veal chop.

kåldomber (KOHL-dohl-mar). *Swe.* Stuffed cabbage.

kaldt kjøtt (kahlt khurt). *Nor.* Cold meats, cold cuts.

kale (kal). *USA.* A vegetable that has loose, ruffly, green or dusky bluish leaves; resembles a giant sprig of parsley; a member of the cabbage family, kale has a mild cabbage flavor.

kalfslapjes (kawlf-LAP-pen). *Dut.* Veal steaks.

kalfslappen (kawlfs-LAHP-pen). *Dut.* Veal cutlets.

kalfsoesters (kawlfs-OOS-tur). *Dut.* Small, very tender veal cutlets; a delicacy.

kalfsvlees (KAWLFS-vlays). *Dut.* Veal.

kalfszwezerik (KAWLF-swear-iek). *Dut.* Sweetbreads.

kali mirch (KA-lee meerch). *Ind.* Black pepper.

kalja (KAHL-yah). *Fin.* Home-brew beer; nonalcoholic.

kalkeon (kal-KOON). *Dut.* Turkey.

kalkkun (KAHLK-koonah). *Fin.* Turkey.

kalkon (kal-KOONN). *Swe.* Turkey.

kalkun (kahl-KOON). *Dan.* Turkey.

kalkunragout (kahl-KOON-raa-goo). *Dan.* Jugged turkey in a sweet-sour gravy, served with mashed potatoes or chestnut purée.

kall (kahl). *Swe.* Cold.

kalocsai halászlé (KOL-law-cho-ee HOL-leh-vehsh). *Hun.* Fish soup in red wine.

kalops (ka-LOPS). *Swe.* Scallops of beef simmered in a rich sauce seasoned with allspice and bay leaf.

kålrouletter (kawl-ru-LEHT-ehr). *Nor.* Stuffed cabbage.

kalt (kehlt). *Ger.* Cold.

Kalteschale. (KAHLT-shaaler). *Ger.* Cold fruit soup.

Kalte Speisen (kehlt SHPE-yeen). *Ger.* Cold dishes.

kalv (kaalv). *Dan, Swe.* Veal.

kalvbräss (KALV-brahs). *Swe.* Sweetbreads.

kalvbrissel (KAAL-ver-bree-sserl). *Dan.* Veal sweetbreads.

kalvekotelett (KAHLV-er-kot-ter-leht). *Nor.* Veal chop.

kalvelever (KAALV-leh-ver). *Dan.* Calf's liver.

kalvemedaljong (KAHLV-may-dahl-yoon). *Nor.* Roast veal.

kalvenyrestek (KAHLV-ern-ewrer-sstayk). *Nor.* Loin of veal.

kalvkotlett (KALV-kot-LAHT). *Swe.* Veal cutlets.

kalvkyckling (KAHLV-tyewk-ling). *Swe.* Veal birds.

kalvstek (KAHLV-stayk). *Swe.* Roast veal.

kamaboko (KAH-mah-boo-koh). *Jap.* Steamed fish cake, served cold as a side dish.

kamasu (KAH-mah-soo). *Jap.* A long slender fish called saury pike.

kaminari-jiru (KAH-mee-NAH-lei joo-loo). *Jap.* Thunder soup, with bean curd and vegetables.

kampyo (KAHM-puo). *Jap.* Dried gourd shavings, which look like strips of rawhide packaged in cellophane.

kana (KAH-nah). *Fin.* Chicken; sometimes called kananpoika. See also paistettu kana.

kananpoika (KAH-nahn-KOA-pi). *Fin.* Chicken leg.

kaneel (kah-NAIL). *Dut.* Cinnamon.

kanel (kah-NAYL). *Swe.* Cinnamon.

kani (kah-NEE). *Jap.* Crab.

kaniini (KAH-nee-ee-nee). *Fin.* Rabbit.

kanin (kah-NEEN). *Swe.* Rabbit.

Kaninchen (kah-NEEN-khern). *Ger.* Rabbit.

kanin i flødepeberrod (kah-NEEN ee FLURDH-er-pehoo-rroadh). *Dan.* Jugged rabbit in a horseradish-cream dressing with mushrooms and onions.

kanten (KAHN-tain). *Jap.* Gelatin made from seaweed; does not melt at room temperature. Also called stick agar-agar.

kao (kao). *Chi.* To roast or bake.

kao-miàn-bao (kao-mien-bao). *Chi.* Toast.

Kapaun (kah-POWN). *Ger.* Capon.

Kapern (KAA-pern). *Ger.* Capers.

kaperssovs (KAH-pehr-soavs). *Dan.* Caper sauce.

kapormártás (KOP-pawr-maar-taash). *Hun.* Dill sauce.

káposzta (KAA-paw-sto). *Hun.* Cabbage.

kappan (KOP-pon). *Hun.* Capon.

kapros túrós rétes (KOP-rawsh TOO-rawsh RAY-tehsh). *Hun.* Curds strudel with dill.

kapucineres felfújt (KOP-poot-seen eh-rehsh FEHL-fooyt). *Hun.* Mocha soufflé.

kapucyners (KAHP-u-seinus). *Dut.* Grey-brown peas.

kapusta (kah-POOS-tah). *Rus.* Cabbage.

Karamel (kah-rah-MEHL). *Ger.* Caramel.

karamelbudding (kah-rah-MAYL-booth-eng). *Dan.* Caramel pudding.

karamelrand (kah-rah-MAYL-rahn). *Dan.* Caramel custard.

karashi (kah-RAH-shee). *Jap.* Very strong dry, ground mustard; prepared by mixing with water, not vinegar.

karashina (kah-LAH-see-nah). *Jap.* Mustard cabbage; a clump of fat, apple-green stalks with darker green leaves; milder flavor than ordinary mustard greens; can be purchased pickled.

karasumi (kah-LAH-see-mee). *Jap.* A caviar substitute; the roe of mullet that has been salted.

karbonader (kar-bo-NAYTH-ehr). *Dan.* Fried pork and veal patties.

karbonader (kahr-bohn-NAHD). *Dut.* Ready-to-cook rolled roast with spices.

kardemommekaker (kahr-dehr-MAHN-meh-kak-ker). *Dut.* Cardamon-spiced cookies.

kardi (KAHR-dee). *Ind.* Yogurt-base sauce that contains curry leaves and spices.

karei (KAH-lae). *Jap.* Sole.

Karfiol (kahr-fi-OAL). *Ger.* Cauliflower.

karhu (KAHR-hoon). *Fin.* Bear.

karhunkinkku (KAHR-hoon-KINK-koo). *Fin.* Smoked bear ham.

karhunliha (KAHR-hoon-LI-hah). *Fin.* Bear steak.

kari (kah-ree). *Fre.* Curry.

kari (KAH-ree). *Ind.* Curry seasoned sauce.

karicollen (KAH-ree-koo-leng). *Ger.* Tiny steamed snails; usually purchased from pushcart vendors in Belgium.

karjalanpaisti (KAHR-yah-lahn-PAH-ste). *Fin.* A dish of mutton, pork, and veal slowly simmered together.

karljohanssvamp (kaar-yoh-HAH-niss-vahmph). *Swe.* Boletus mushroom.

karnemelk (kahr-nuh-MEL-uk). *Dut.* Buttermilk.

Karotten (kah-ROT-tern). *Ger.* Carrots.

karp (kahrp). *Rus.* Carp.

karpalo (KAHR-pah-loa). *Fin.* Cranberry.

karpalo kiisseli (KAHR-pah-loa KEES-sayli). *Fin.* Cranberry pudding.

karper (KAHR-perr). *Dut.* Carp.

Karpfen (KAHR-pfern). *Ger.* Carp.

kärrmjölk (TYARR-myurlk). *Swe.* Buttermilk.

karry (KAAR-ee). *Dan.* Curry.

karrysalat (KAR-rew-sa-LAHT). *Dan.* Curried macaroni salad.

kartofcl (kahr-TO-fyehl). *Rus.* Potatoes.

Kartoffel (kahr-TOF-fcrln). *Ger.* Potato; Kartoffelbrei (kahr-TOF-ferl-brigh), mashed potatoes; Kartoffelklösse (kahr-TOF-ferl-klurss-er), potato dumplings; Kartoffelpuffer (kahr-TOF-ferl-puff-err), potato fritters.

kartofler (kahr-TOAF-lerr). *Dan.* Potatoes.

kartoflermos (kahr-TOAF-lerr-muss). *Dan.* Potato puffs; also mashed potato stuffing.

Käse (KAI-zer). *Ger.* Cheese.

Käsekuchen (KAIZ-cr-koo-khern). *Ger.* Cheese cakes.

Käsestangen (KAIZ-er-schtanj-ehn). *Ger.* Swiss cheese twists.

Käseteller (KAIZ-er-teh-lerr). *Ger.* Cheese plate.

Käsetorte (KAIZ-er-tor-ter). *Ger.* Cheesecake.

kasha (KAH-shi). *Rus.* Groats that are hulled, crushed and cooked; buckwheat, porridge.

Kasnudeln (KAH-noo-derln). *Ger.* Stuffed noodles, either savory or sweet.

Kasseler Rippenspeer (KAH-sseh-ler RIP-pern-shpayr). *Ger.* Pork loin, cured and smoked, served on sauerkraut, with mashed potatoes, apples or red cabbage, potato dumplings, with a gravy of sour cream and red wine; a favorite German meal.

Kastanienrcis (kass-STAHN-yen-rice). *Ger.* An Austrian dessert of puréed chestnuts and whipped cream made into a very rich pudding.

kastanier (KAHS-tahn-yerr). *Dan.* Chestnut.

kastaniesovs (kah-STAHN-yer-soooss). *Dan.* Chestnut sauce, flavored with Madeira.

kastanjat (KAHS-tahn-yaht). *Fin.* Chestnuts.

kastanjer (kahss-TAHNY). *Swe.* Chestnuts.

Kastlerribchen (KAH-ssehlerr-rip-skhern). *Ger.* A Belgium dish of smoked pork loin cooked with sauerkraut, white wine, and juniper berries.

kasutado (kahs-TAH-doh). *Jap.* Custard.

kaszinó tojás (KOS-see-naw TAW-yaash). *Hun.* An appetizer of eggs with mayonnaise.

katakuriko (kah-TAH-koo-lee-koh). *Jap.* Potato starch, similar to cornstarch.

katch (kahch). *Ind.* Lamb.

kateh (kah-HEHT). *Ara.* Plain boiled rice cooked with a crust. Also called Persian-style rice.

katella (kah-TEL-lah). *Dut.* Sweet potatoes. Also called obi.

Katenschinken (KAA-tern-shin-kern). *Ger.* Smoked country ham.

Katenwurst (KAA-tern-voorst). *Ger.* Smoked sausage.

katkaravut (KAHT-kah-RAH-voot). *Fin.* Shrimp.

katrinplommen (kaht-REEN-PLOO-mon). *Swe.* Prunes.

katsuobushi (kah-TSU-oh-boo-shee). *Jap.* Dried bonito fish, one of the two essential ingredients of basic soup stock; dashi.

Katzenjammer (KAHT-sehn-jahmm-ehrn). *Ger.* Slices of cold beef in mayonnaise with cucumbers.

kavamelon (KAH-vah-mehl-uhn). *USA.* A member of the muskmelon family; taste of honeydew, texture of watermelon, size of a football.

kávét (KAA-vayt). *Hun.* Coffee.

kaviaari (KAH-viaari). *Fin.* Caviar.

kaviar (KAHV-eeahr). *Dan.* Caviar.

kaviar (kah-vee-AAR). *Nor.* Caviar.

kaviar (KAH-vi-yahr). *Swe.* Caviar.

kaviár (KOV-veeaar). *Hun.* Caviar.

kazu no ko (kah-ZOO-noh-kon). *Jap.* Herring roe.

kebab (kah-BEHB). *Ara.* Small slices of meat on skewers, and grilled or braised.

kebob (keh-BOB). *USA.* Kebab.

kechappu (keh-CHAHP-poo). *Jap.* Catsup.

kecsege (KEH-chehgah). *Hun.* Sterlet.

kecskeméti barack-puding (KEHCH-keh-may-tee BOR-rotsh-pud-ding). *Hun.* Apricot pudding with vanilla cream.

kedgeree (KUH-jree). *Ind.* A breakfast dish of curried rice, lentils, spices, fish, and hard-boiled eggs.

keema (KEE-mah). *Ind.* Ground meat.

kefir (ke-FEHR). *Rus.* Fermented camel's milk that is thick, frothy, slightly alcoholic, and healthful; slightly effervescent.

kefta (KEHF-tah). *Ara.* Mutton, chopped and spiced, then shaped into rissoles and grilled.

keditetyt ravut (KAY-teh-tewt-RA-voot). *Fin.* Boiled crayfish.

keitto (KAYT-toaah). *Fin.* Soup.

kekada (KAY-krah). *Ind.* Crab.

keki (KEH-kee). *Jap.* Cake.

Keks (KEE-kss). *Ger.* Biscuit.

kelbimbó (KEHL-beem-baw). *Hun.* Brussels sprouts.

kelp (kehlp). *USA.* Seaweed; several varieties harvested for food, dried, then processed in various ways: leaf form, thread form, sheet form; used as a cracker, for seasoning, to wrap various savory and sweet foods; konbu.

kenyér (KEHN-yeh). *Hun.* Bread.

képviselófánk (KAYP-veesh-ehl-ur-faank). *Hun.* Cream puff.

kerma (KAYR-mahn). *Fin.* Cream.

kermakakku (KEHR-ma-kahk-koo). *Fin.* Sour cream poundcake.

kermakastiketta (KAYR-mah-KAHS-tik-kay). *Fin.* Cream sauce.

kerre (KEHR-ruh). *Dut.* Curry.

kerrieryst (KEHR-ruh-rayst). *Dut.* Curried rice.

kersen (KEHR-suh). *Dut.* Cherries.

kesäkeitto (KAY-ssae-KAYT-toa). *Fin.* Summer vegetable soup.

kesar (KAY-sahr). *Ind.* Saffron.

keta (kee-TAH). *Rus.* Siberian salmon.

ketchup (KEHT-chuhp). *USA.* Catsup.

ketchupot (KEH-chur-purt). *Hun.* Catsup.

ketelkoek (KAY-tel-kook). *Dut.* Steamed pudding.

ketsup (KET-soop). *Dut.* Catsup.

kex (kayks). *Swe.* Unsweetened cracker.

khall (khahll). *Ara.* Vinegar.

khas-khas (KAS-kas). *Ind.* White poppy seeds.

khass (khass). *Ara.* Lettuce.

kheer (keerh). *Ind.* Pudding, rice pudding.

kheera (KEER-ah). *Ind.* Cucumber.

khiyaar (khi-YAAR). *Ara.* Cucumber.

khleb (KHLYEH-bah). *Rus.* Bread.

khoobani (koo-BAH-nee). *Ind.* Apricot.

khowkha (kholikh). *Ara.* Peach.

khoya (KOY-yah). *Ind.* Milk "fudge", very thick and reduced.

khren (khryehn). *Rus.* Horseradish.

khubz (khubz). *Ara.* Bread, usually Oriental bread.

khudar (khi-daar). *Ara.* Vegetable.

khyar (khyahr). *Ara.* Cucumber.

kibbi (KIHB-bee). *Ara.* Baked minced meat with cracked wheat and spices.

kidney (KEHD-nee). *USA.* One of the edible, internal organs of veal, lamb, beef; used sautéed, broiled, braised.

kidney bean (KEHD-nee behn). *USA.* A large, dark red, edible, nutritious, common bean, usually used dried.

kielbasa (keel-BAH-sah). *Pol.* Sausages of very long links of coarsely ground smoked pork, flavored with garlic.

kieli (KAY-li). *Fin.* Tongue.

kiev (kee-EHV). *Rus.* A method of preparing chicken breasts by rolling seasoned butter into pounded breast fillets, rolling in breadcrumbs, and frying or baking.

kikuna (kee-koo-NAH). *Jap.* Edible chrysanthemum leaves; have a distinct fragrance, light, astringent flavor; used fresh only.

kikurage (kee-KOO-lah-gay). *Jap.* A crinkly dried black fungus; crisp texture; use in stir-fry and lightly vinegared salads. Also known as cloud ear.

Kim (kehm). *Kor.* Toasted laver seaweed eaten like a cracker or crumbled over food.

Kim Chee (kehm chee). *Kor.* A fermented vegetable pickle, served with most meals as well as cooked in many dishes.

kinako (KEE-maj-koh). *Jap.* Soy flour made by grinding roasted soybeans; nutty and fragrant; used in many traditional sweet dishes.

king, à la (kehng, ah la) Fre. Served in cream sauce containing green pepper, pimento, and mushrooms.

king crab (keng krahb). *USA.* A large crab of the northern Pacific waters. Also called Alaska king crab, Japanese crab.

Kingdom of Fire pie (KENG-dum ouv fireh pie). *Sco.* Dish of pickled pork, rabbit, and forcemeat balls spiced with nutmeg, served in a rich gravy topped with puff pastry.

king salmon (keng SAM-mon). *USA.* Chinook, or royal chinook; most highly prized of U.S. salmon; flesh separates into very large flakes, high fat content, soft texture.

kinkku (KINK-koo). *Fin.* Ham.

kinoko (KEE-noh-koh). *Jap.* An edible fungi, with a woodsy fragrance and gentle flavor; used fresh, dried and canned.

kinome (KEE-noh-mah). *Jap.* Fragrant young leaves of the prickly ash, plucked for use as an aromatic and colorful garnish; bright, with a mild hint of mint.

kip (kip). *Dut.* Chicken; kip aan't spit (kip ahnt SPIT), broiled chicken.

Kipferl (KEEP-fell). *Ger.* A sweet, doughy, crescent-shaped roll.

kip met kerrysaus (kip mayt KEHR-ruh-sows). *Dut.* Curried chicken fricassee.

kippelever (KIP-pah-laver). *Dut.* Chicken liver.

kippensoep (KIP-puh-soop). *Dut.* Chicken soup.

kipper (KEHP-er). *Bri.* Lightly salted and smoked herring.

Kir (keer). *Ger.* A liqueur made from black currants; Cassis.

kiriboshi daikon (kee-LEE-boh-she DI-ee-kon). *Jap.* Dried daikon shavings, used to flavor savory dishes.

Kirschen (KEER-shern). *Ger.* Cherries.

Kirschwasser (KERSCH-wass-ser). *Ger.* A colorless liqueur distilled from wild cherries, and used to flavor confectionery and pastry. Often called kirsch.

kirsebaer (KEER-sser-baer). *Dan.* Cherries.

kirsebaer koldskål (KHEESH-er-baer kolt-skawl). *Nor.* Chilled cherry soup.

kirsikkat (KEER-sik-kaht). *Fin.* Cherries.

kishk (keehk). *Ara.* Yogurt and crushed wheat fermented together, dried, and ground.

kishka (KEHSH-kah). *USA.* A Jewish-American sausage made by baking meat, flour, and spices.

kissel (kee-SSYEHL). *Rus.* A berry pudding; when thinned, used as a dessert sauce.

kisu (KU-suh). *Jap.* A small white fish.

kitcheri (KITCH-er-dree). *Ind.* A breakfast dish of cooked rice, lentils, spices, with fish, hard-boiled eggs, and curry; kedgeree.

kitcheri (KITCH-er-ee). *Bri.* A breakfast dish of cooked rice, lentils, spices, with fish, hard-boiled eggs, and curry.

kited fillet (KI-ted FILL-et). *USA.* Fish cut through at the backbone, filleted but left attached at the belly.

kiwano (kee-WAHN-noh). *USA.* An oblong fruit, horned, golden-orange skin; subtle flavor of cucumbers, bananas, and limes; flat, white seeds encased in juicy green pulp with jellylike texture; eaten out of shell or added to desserts.

kiwifruit (KEE-wee-froot). *NZe.* A plum-shaped fruit with thin brown fuzzy outer covering and soft green flesh with small black seeds. Also called Chinese gooseberry and kiwi berry.

kizbara (KEHZ-bah-rah). *Ara.* Coriander.

kjeks (khehks). *Nor.* Crackers; cookies.

kjøtt (khurt). *Nor.* Meat.

kjøttboller (KHURT-bol-lerr). *Nor.* Croquettes.

kjøttfarse (KHURT-fawr-ser). *Nor.* Hamburger; ground meat.

kjøttpudding (KHURT-pewd-ding). *Nor.* Meat pudding; meatloaf.

kjøttsuppe (KHURT-ssewpper). *Nor.* Boullion; meat broth.

klabär (KLAAR-bah-rr). *Swe.* Amarelles.

Klaben (KLAH-ben). *Ger.* A white bread with nuts and dried fruits.

klarbär (KLAAR-bahr). *Swe.* Amarelles.

klejner (KLEIN-ehr). *Dan.* Crullers.

kletskoppen (KLETS-kawp-puh). *Dut.* Gingersnaps.

klipfisk (KLEEP-feesk). *Nor.* Cod that is salted and spread out on cliffs to dry, instead of rack-hung as stokkfisk.

Klopse (KLOP-ser). *Ger.* Meatballs of two or three kinds of ground meat.

Klösse (KLUR-skhern). *Ger.* Meatballs; dumplings.

klyukva (KLYOOK-vah). *Rus.* Cranberries.

kmaj (kah-MAHJ). *Ara.* Round, flat bread with a pocket; used for sandwiches, dips; Arabic pizza.

Knackwurst (KNAAK-voost). *Ger.* Plump sausages flavored with garlic; means "popping" sausage, because the casing makes a popping sound at the first bite. Also called knockwurst.

knädlach (KNAHD-lahk). *Jew.* Matzo dumplings cooked in chicken broth.

knafi (kah-NAHF-fee). *Ara.* Dough that resembles shredded wheat. Also referred to as burma dough.

knakworst (KNAAK-wurst). *Dut.* Sausage.

knead (need). *USA.* To work dough with heel of hands by folding and stretching for distribution of ingredients, as well as development of gluten, and make dough ready for rising.

kneaded butter (NEED-ehd BUHT-tehr). *USA.* Equal parts butter and flour, kneaded with the fingers; used to thicken sauces.

knish (kah-NEESH). *Jew.* Chopped chicken livers wrapped in mashed potatoes thickened with flour.

Knoblauch (KNOP-lowkh). *Ger.* Garlic.

Knoblauchwurst (KNOP-lowkh-voorst). *Ger.* Garlicky sausage with chunks of fat in it.

knockwurst (KNOHK-wohrst). *USA.* A German sausage of smoked beef and pork, used boiled, grilled and steamed, often eaten with sauerkraut. See knackwurst.

Knödel (KNUR-derl). *Ger.* Dumpling.

knoflook (KNAWF-lohk). *Dut.* Garlic.

knol (knaul). *Dut.* Turnip.

Kobe beef (KOH-bee bef). *USA.* Japanese raised steer, noted for its tenderness and flavor, attributed to the fact that the cattle are fed beer and massaged with saké.

kød (kurdh). *Dan.* Meat.

kødboller (KURDH-boal-err). *Dan.* Meatballs.

kødfars (KERTH-fahrs). *Dan.* Forcemeat.

koek (kook). *Dut.* Cake.

koekjes (KOOK-yus). *Dut.* Cakes or cookies.

kofe (KO-fyeh). *Rus.* Coffee.

koffie (KAWF-fee). *Dut.* Coffee.

koffie verkeerd (KAWF-fee VAH-kehrd). *Dut.* Coffee with more milk than coffee.

koffie zonder melk (KAWF-fee ZAWN-dur MEL-uk). *Dut.* Coffee without milk.

kofta (KOHF-tah). *Ind.* Ground meatballs simmered in sauce with spices.

kogt (koat). *Dan.* Boiled.

kohi (KOH hee). *Jap.* Coffee.

kohi keki (KOH hee KEH kee). *Jap.* Coffeecake.

kohitsuji (koh-HEE-tsoo-jee). *Jap.* Lamb.

Kohl (koal). *Ger.* Cabbage.

kohlrabi (KOHL-rah-bee). *USA.* A small, pale-green, slightly knobby, slightly sweet, turnip-shaped vegetable with collardlike leaves; tastes like fresh, crunchy broccoli stems, with a hint of radish and cucumber; usually cooked.

Kohlrouladen (KOAL-roo-laa-dern) *Ger.* Stuffed cabbage.

koi-kuchi shoya (KOO-ee koo-chee SHOH-you). *Jap.* Dark, thick, heavy soy sauce.

kokosnoten (KOH-kah-snoten). *Dut.* Coconut.

kokosnøtt (KOO-koos-noht). *Nor.* Coconut.

kokt (kookt). *Nor.* Boiled.

kola (KOA-lah). *Swe.* Toffee; caramel.

kolachy (ko-LAHCH-ee). *Cze.* Fruit-filled bun.

kolbászfélék (KAWL-baas-fay-layk). *Hun.* Sausages.

koldtbord (KOL-brurdh). *Dan.* Cold table; buffet; a great assortment of salads, cold meats and cheeses.

koldtbord (KOLT-boor). *Nor.* Cold table; varieties of fish, meat, cheeses, salads.

koldt kød (kolt kurdh). *Dan.* Cold cuts.

kolja (KOL-yah). *Swe.* Haddock.

kolje (KOL-yer). *Nor.* Haddock.

kombu (KOHM-boo). *Jap.* Kelp. See also konbu.

kome (koh-MEH). *Jap.* Uncooked rice; cooked rice served on a plate Western style is raisu; cooked rice served Japanese style in a bowl is gohan. It is the same rice!

komió (KAWM-iaw). *Hun.* Hops.

komkommers (kawm-KAWM-ur). *Dut.* Cucumbers.

Kompott (KOM-pott). *Ger.* Compote, stewed fruit.

konbu (KON-boo). *Jap.* Dried tangle seaweed; kelp; essential to dashi and various dishes.

konfeta (kahn-FYEH-ti). *Rus.* Candy.

Königinpastete (KUR-nig-gin-pahs-tay-ter). *Ger.* Pastry with savory fillings, usually meat and mushrooms.

Königinsuppe (KUR-nig-gin-zup-per). *Ger.* Soup thickened with eggs and cream; very rich.

konijn (koh-NEYN). *Dut.* Rabbit.

konnyaku (kohugn-NYA-koo). *Jap.* "Devil's tongue jelly"; a dense, gelatinous, dark brown to hazy gray cake, neutral flavor, cooked with other foods; has two filament forms: shirataki, used in sukiyaki, and konnyaku, a thicker "string".

konsome (KOHN-soh-meh). *Jap.* Consommé.

kon'yak (kah-NYAHK). *Rus.* Cognac.

kool (kuhl). *Dut.* Cabbage.

koolraap (KUHL-rahp). *Dut.* Turnips.

koosmali (KOHS-ma-lee). *Ind.* Relish made with raw grated carrots and fried black mustard seeds.

Kopfsalatherzen (KOPF-zah-laat-hehrt-zen). *Ger.* Hearts of lettuce.

Kopfsalatsuppe (KOPF-zah-laat-ZUP-per). *Ger.* Lettuce soup.

korinkake (koo-RIN-kaa-ker). *Nor.* Currant cake.

korma (KOHR-mah). *Ind.* Braise or stew.

Korn (kahrn). *Ger.* Cereal or grain; may be wheat, rye, or barley, not necessarily corn.

körsbär (CHOHSH-bahr). *Swe.* Cherries.

körte (KURR-teh). *Hun.* Pear.

korv (korv). *Swe.* Sausage.

kosher (KO-sher). *Jew.* According to Jewish dietary laws.

kosher salt (KO-shur sawlt). *USA.* A squarish-grained salt; very flavorful; used sprinkled over meats, pretzels, breads, rolls. Also called coarse salt or sea salt.

koshian (koh-SHE-ah-ung). *Jap.* Dried beans, usually red ones, already mashed and sweetened for pastry fillings; sweet bean paste or prepared red bean flour.

kosho (koh-SHOH). *Jap.* Pepper.

Kossuth cake (KAUGH-suht kahk). *USA.* A sponge cake filled with whipped cream or ice cream, then covered with icing; usually made in individual servings.

Kotelett (KOT-leht). *Ger.* Cutlet.

koteletter (koa-der-LEHT-terr). *Dan.* Chops.

kött (khurt). *Swe.* Meat.

köttbullar (KHURT-bew-larr). *Swe.* Meatballs.

köttfärs (KHURT-fahrs). *Swe.* Meatloaf; minced meat.

koud (kout). *Dut.* Cold.

koud vlees (kout flaasch). *Dut.* Assorted cold cuts.

kourabiedes (koor-ahm-bee-EHSS). *Gre.* Biscuit; cookie; usually a crescent shaped, crisp, almond and anisette flavored cookie.

krab (krahb). *Rus.* Crab.

krabba (KRA-ba). *Swe.* Crab.

krabbe (KRAHB-er). *Dan.* Crab.

krabbe (KRAHB-ber). *Nor.* Crab.

Krabben (KRAH-bern). *Ger.* Prawns.

krabbesalat (KRAHB-ber-ssah-latt). *Nor.* Crab salad made with celery, lettuce, and dill in mustard dressing.

krabbetjes (KRAHB-beht-tish). *Dut.* Pork spareribs.

kraemmerhuse med flødeskum (kray-mehr-hoo-see meth FLEHR-the-skoam). *Dan.* Airy, cone-shaped cakes filled with whipped cream and jelly.

kräfta (KREHF-tah). *Swe.* Crayfish.

Kraftbühe (KRAHFT-brew-er). *Ger.* Beef consommé.

Kraftbühe mit Hühnerfleisch (KRAHFT-brew-er mit hoon-er-flighsh). *Ger.* Chicken soup.

Krakauer (KROCK-kaur). *Ger.* Polish ham sausage.

krakelingen (KRACK-leng-en). *Dut.* Cracker, pretzel.

kransekage (KRARN-see-kah-yeh). *Dan.* Almond pastry ring.

Kranzkuchen (krahnts-KOO-kern). *Ger.* Braided sweet cake.

Krapfen. (KRAP-fen). *Ger.* Sweet fritters; doughnuts.

Krapfenchen (KRAP-fen-chen). *Ger.* Special doughnuts served at pre-Lenten carnivals.

kråsesuppe (KROA-se-soap-pay). *Dan.* Frugtsuppe with the addition of chicken giblets and apples.

Kraut (krowt). *Ger.* Sauerkraut.

Kräuterklösse (KROYT-ehr-klur-sser). *Ger.* Green dumplings, made green with spinach and herbs.

Kraut Fleckerl (kraut FLECK-erl). *Ger.* Boiled cabbage and noodle combined in a dish.

Krautkräpfli (KRAWT-kept-flee). *Ger.* Swiss spinach turnovers, similar to ravioli.

Kraut mit Eisbein und Erbensuppe (krawt mit IGHS-bighn unt EHRP-zern-zup-per). *Ger.* The German national dish of cabbage, pigs' knuckles, and pea soup.

Krautwürsteln. (KRAWY-vewrst-erln). *Ger.* An Austrian dish of stuffed cabbage, using minced beef and onions.

kreatopita (kreh-ah-TO-ppeetah). *Gre.* A meat pie wrapped in phyllo dough.

Krebs (krayps). *Ger.* Crab, crayfish.

krebs (KRAYBSS). *Dan.* Crayfish.

kreeft (krayft). *Dut.* Lobster.

krem (kraym). *Nor.* Whipped cream; custard.

Kren (krays). *Ger.* Horseradish.

Krenfleisch (KRAYN-flighsh). *Ger.* Boiled beef, sliced, and served with horseradish.

krenten (KREN-ten). *Dut.* Currants.

krentenbrood (KREN-tuh-broht). *Dut.* Raisin bread.

krentenbroodjes (KREN-tuh-broht-yus). *Dut.* Raisin buns.

kreplach (KREHP-lahk). *Jew.* Small dough turnovers with savory fillings.

kreps (krehpss). *Nor.* Tiny, tender crayfish.

Krevetten (krau-VET-ten). *Ger.* Shrimps.

Kriek-lambric (kreek LAHM-brik). *Dut.* A Belgium cherry-flavored beer.

kringlor (KRING-loor). *Swe.* Pastry twists; cracknels.

kroepoek (KREW-pook). *Dut.* Indonesian tidbit, like a huge, crunchy potato chip, but made of pulverized shrimp.

Krokette (kroh-KEH-teh). *Ger.* Croquette.

krona (KROA-nah). *Mex.* A mild red pepper.

kronärtskocka (KROO-Nahrts-KO-ka). *Swe.* Artichoke.

Kronsbeer (KOHNS-beer). *Ger.* Cranberry.

kroppkaker (KROP-KA-koor). *Swe.* Pork and potato dumplings.

kropsla (KRAHP-slah). *Dut.* Head lettuce.

kruiden (KROHW-dehn). *Dut.* Herbs.

kruidenagelen (KROHWT-nahg-ah-len). *Dut.* Cloves.

kruiden azÿn (KROHW-dehn ah-ZAYN). *Dut.* Herb vinegar.

kruisbes (KROHWT-bess). *Dut.* Gooseberry.

krusbär (KRUS-bahr). *Swe.* Gooseberries.

krydder (KREW-ther). *Dan.* Bun cut in half and baked.

kryddersild (KREW-dehr-sil). *Nor.* Spiced herring.

kryddor (KRU-door). *Swe.* Condiments.

Kryddost (KREW-dah-oost). *Swe.* Anise-flavored cheese.

kryddpeppar (KREW-dah-pay-pahr). *Swe.* Pimento; allspice.

kuàngquán shui (KWANG-chuan shui). *Chi.* Mineral water.

kuchen (KOOK-hern). *Ger.* A pastry or cake.

kudamono (koo-DAH-moh-noh). *Jap.* Fruit.

kufta (KUF-ta). *Ara.* Minced grilled meat.

kugel (KOO-ghel). *Jew.* Baked casserole or pudding.

Kugelhopf (KOO-ghel hopf). *Ger.* Puffy Swiss buns filled with whipped cream. Also spelled kugelhoph.

ku gua (koo gwah). *Chi.* Bitter melon.

kuha (KOO-hah). *Fin.* Perch-pike.

kuiken (KIR-kuh). *Dut.* Squab.

kukki (KOOK kee). *Jap.* Cookies.

kukorica (KOO-kaw-ree-tso). *Hun.* Sweetcorn.

kukuruza (koo-koo-ROO-zah). *Rus.* Maize; corn.

kulcha (KULL-cha). *Ind.* Leavened white-flour dough shaped into rounds and baked.

kulfi (KULL-fee). *Ind.* Indian ice cream made with cooked-down milk, frozen in special conical molds.

kulibyaka (KOO-lee-byah-kah). *Rus.* A hot fish pie filled with layers of salmon or fish, rice, mushrooms, herbs, onions.

kumiss (kuh-MISS). *USA.* A drink of fermented milk, thought to have some digestive benefits; originated with the Mongols; similar to laban.

kumler (KHEWM-lehr). *Nor.* Potato dumplings.

kummel (KU-mehl). *Swe.* Hake.

Kümmel (KEW-merl). *Ger.* Caraway seeds.

Kümmelsuppe (KEW-merl-zup-per). *Ger.* An Austrian soup flavored with caraway seeds.

kumquat (KUHM-kwaht). *Chi.* A small oblong fruit, resembling an orange, but is not a citrus; has a rind that is deliciously sweet and pulp that is sour; used in stuffings, cakes, muffins, sauces, syrups, preserves, and jellies.

kunafa (ku-NEH-fa). *Ara.* Fine-spun pastry stuffed with nuts.

Kurbis (KEWR-biss). *Ger.* Squash, pumpkin.

kuri (koo-REE). *Jap.* Chestnuts; Tamba chestnuts are large and pleasantly mealy; Shiba chestnuts are small, firm, sweet.

kurista (KOO-ree-tsah). *Rus.* Boiling chicken; hen.

kuro goma (KOO-roh GAH-mee). *Jap.* Black sesame seeds that have a pungent flavor.

kusa (KOO-sah). *Ara.* Summer squash.

kushary (KU-sha-ree). *Ara.* Macaroni or rice with noodles, lentils, fried onion, and a hot tomato sauce.

kushikatsu (koo-SHEE kah-tsoo). *Jap.* Pork, chicken, seafood, and vegetables skewered on bamboo sticks, breaded, and deep-fried, then eaten with salt, hot mustard, and sauces.

Kutteln (KUT-terln). *Ger.* Tripe.

kuzu (KOO-zoo). *Jap.* An excellent thickening agent; produces a sparkling, translucent sauce, adds shiny gloss to soups; has pleasant, gentle aroma.

kvaeder (KVAIDH-err). *Dan.* Quinces.

kvass (KBAH-ssoo). *Rus.* A beerlike drink, made from barley, rye, and yeast; used to flavor borsch, chlodnik; usually a grocery item as restaurants consider it inelegant.

kveite (KVAY-ter). *Nor.* Halibut.

Kwark (kwark). *Dut.* A skimmed milk cheese similar to cottage cheese.

kyabetsu (KYAH-beh-tsoo). *Jap.* Cabbage.

kyckling (TYEWK-ling). *Swe.* Chicken.

kylling (KEWL-ling). *Nor.* Chicken.

kylling (KEW-leeng). *Dan.* Chicken.

kyllingesalat (KEW-leen-ger-sah-laat). *Dan.* Chicken salad with chicken meat, macaroni, tomato slices, green peppers, olives, green peas, lettuce, and mushrooms, covered with tomato dressing.

kyllingsuppe (KEWL-ling-ssewpper). *Nor.* Chicken soup.

kyodo ryori (KYOH-doh ryoh-ree). *Jap.* Local or regional specialities: may consist of one dish or an entire meal that typifies the cooking of a particular area.

kyuri (KYOO-ree). *Jap.* Thin skinned cucumber, about 1 inch in diameter and about 8 inches long.

L

là (lah). *Chi.* Hot, peppery.

là báicàl (la bai-tsai). *Chi.* Hot pickled cabbage.

laban (LA-ban). *Ara.* Yogurt; a soured milk similar to buttermilk.

labni (LAB-hee). *Ara.* Yogurt cheese paste.

Labskaus (LAAPS-kowss). *Ger.* A stew of pickled pork or beef cooked with potatoes and onions, and sometimes pickled fish, beets, or gherkins as garnish.

là cháng (loh chaang). *Chi.* Spicy pork sausages.

Lachs (lahks). *Ger.* Salmon.

Läckerli (LEH-kerrli). *Ger.* Swiss sugar cookies with chopped nuts and bits of orange peel in the dough.

Lacksforelle (LAHKS-to-reh-ler). *Ger.* Salmon trout.

lacón con grelos (lay-CHON kon greh-loas). *Spa.* Cured pork shoulder with turnip tops.

lactic acid (LAHK-tehk AHSS-eed). *USA.* The bacteria-produced acid that breaks down lactose (milk sugar) causing the coagulation of milk and is the first step in the cheese-making process; it is also found naturally in muscle tissue and acts as a natural preservative in slaughtered meat.

lactose (LAHK-tos). *USA.* Milk sugar.

la cuite (lah kweet). *Fre.* Cooked sugar syrup in the last stage before it blackens and turns bitter.

låda (LOA-dah). *Swe.* Casserole.

là de (la de). *Chi.* Spicy.

lady apple (LA-dee AHP-pul). *USA.* A light green, mini apple with a red blush and a mild-sweet flavor; eaten fresh.

Lady Baltimore cake (LA-dee BALL-tee-mohr kahk). *USA.* A white cake filled with raisins and nuts in a boiled meringue or seven-minute icing and flavored with vanilla.

lady finger (LA-dee FENG-ger). *USA.* A pastry made from a sponge cake batter, shaped about 3-inches long using a plain pastry tip; used filled by pressing two together around a filling, or singularly to line a springform pan or mold.

Lafayette gingerbread (lah-fehy-ette JEHN-juhr brehd). *USA.* A cakelike ginger and spice bread made with the juice and rind of an orange added.

lagerblad (LAA-gerr blaad). *Swe.* Bay leaf.

lagerøl (LAA-err-url). *Dan.* Dark beer.

lagkage (LAHG-kaaer). *Dan.* A towering layer cake filled with whipped cream.

lagmi (LAHG-mee). *Ara.* Palm wine; made from the sap when the palm is dying.

lagôsta (la-GAW-shta). *Por.* Lobster.

lagôstim (lah-goush-TEEM). *Por.* Prawn.

lahm (LAH-ma). *Ara.* Meat, usually lamb or mutton.

lahm bagar (LAH-ma BA-a-ree). *Ara.* Beef.

lait (leh). *Fre.* Milk.

laitance (lay-tounce). *Fre.* Soft fish roe.

laitances d'alsoe (lay-tounce d'al-soh). *Fre.* Shad roe.

laitue (lay-tew). *Fre.* Lettuce.

làjiao fen (la-jiao fen). *Chi.* Chili pepper.

là jiao jiàng (la jiao jiang). *Chi.* Hot chili sauce; red in color, red-hot in taste; made from chili peppers, vinegar and seasonings.

làjiao yóu (la-jiao yoh). *Chi.* Pepper oil.

lakka (LAHK-kah). *Fin.* Cloudberry; used on ice cream and in making liqueur.

laks (lahks). *Nor, Dan.* Salmon.

laks øg-røraeg (lahks oa RURR-ehg). *Dan.* Salmon in scrambled eggs.

lal mirch (lahl meerch). *Ind.* Red pepper.

lam (lahm). *Dut.* Lamb.

lamb fries (lahm friiz). *USA.* Testicles of a bull, pig, or lamb; breaded and fried. Also called animelles, frivolitées, mountain oyster, prairie oyster, Rocky Mountain oyster.

Lambic (LAHM-brik). *Ger.* Austrian Gueuze on tap; a very special wheat and barley beer.

lamb's lettuce (lahmz LEHT-us). *USA.* A European plant with dark green, nutty-flavored leaves that are used for winter salads; prized by the French. Also called corn salad and mache.

Lamm (lahm). *Ger, Swe.* Lamb.

lammas (LAHM-mahss). *Fin.* Lamb, mutton.

lammesteg (LAHM-stayg). *Dan.* Roast lamb.

lammkotlett (lahm-KOT-leht). *Swe.* Lamb chop.

lammstek (LAHM-stay). *Swe.* Roast lamb.

lampaankyljys (LAHM-paan-KEWL-yewss). *Fin.* Mutton or lamb chop.

lampaanpaisti (LAHM-paan-PAHS-ti). *Fin.* Roast leg of lamb or mutton.

lamponi (lahm-POA-nee). *Ita.* Raspberries.

lamprede (lahm-PRAY-day). *Ita.* A salt- or freshwater fish resembling the eel whose fatty flesh is usually stewed.

lamsbout (LAHMZ-bout). *Dut.* Leg of lamb.

lamsvlees (LAHMZ-vlays). *Dut.* Lamb. Also called lam.

Lancashire (LANK-kah-shur). *Bri.* A full-flavored, creamy-white cow's milk cheese from England, cooked and pressed, yet soft and crumbly, used for Welsh rarebit.

Landjäger (LAUND-yea-ger). *Ger.* A smoked sausage.

ländstycke (LAHND-stayk). *Swe.* Sirloin steak.

Lane cake (lahn kahk). *USA.* A layer cake with a fluffy frosting containing coconut, chopped fruits, and nuts.

lángos (LAAN-gawsh). *Hun.* Fried doughnuts.

langoustines (lahn-ggoo-steen). *Fre.* Prawns.

langue (lahngg). *Fre.* Tongue.

languedocienne (lohn-ger-do-cee-een). *Fre.* A meat or poultry dish garnished with a mixture of sautéed eggplant, tomatoes, mushrooms and chopped parsley.

langues-de-chat (lahngg-der sha). *Fre.* Cat's tongue; a long, thin, light, dry cookie whose shape resembles a cat's tongue. Often accompanies simple desserts and sweet wines.

Languste (lahng-GOOS-ter). *Ger.* Clawless variety of lobster.

lanttu (LAHNT-too). *Fin.* Rutabaga.

laos (lohsc). *Ind.* A root of the ginger family, much used in Middle Eastern and Oriental cooking for seasoning.

lapereau (lah-peh-roa). *Fre.* Young rabbit.

lapin (lah-pang). *Fre.* Rabbit.

lapin en gibelotte (lah-pang uhn zjee-beer-loht). *Fre.* Rabbit stew.

lapja (LAHP-yuhs). *Dut.* Scallops, small slices of meat.

lapocka (LOP-paw-tsko). *Hun.* Shoulder cut of meat.

lapskojs (LOBS-couse). *Swe.* A corned beef hash.

laqtin (lak-TEEN). *Ara.* A vegetable similar to pumpkin.

laranjada (lah-rahn-ZHAH-dah). *Por.* Orangeade.

laranjas (lah-RAHN-zhah). *Por.* Oranges.

lard (lahrd). *USA.* Rendered pork fat, softer, oilier than other shortenings; used in making flaky pastry and for deep-frying.

lard (lahr). *Fre.* Bacon.

larding (LAHR-deeng). *USA.* The insertion of strips of pork fat (lardoons) into lean cuts of meat, giving the meat juiciness and flavor.

lardo (LAHR-doa). *Ita.* Salt pork.

lardo affumicato (LAHR-doa AHFF-oom-ee-KAA-toa). *Ita.* Bacon.

lardoon (lahr-doon). *Fre.* A strip of fat with which meat is larded; that is, threaded through with a needle in order to moisten the meat as it cooks.

largo (LAHR-goh). *Mex.* A long, thin, yellow-green, fairly hot chili pepper.

lasagna (lah-ZAAN-yah). *Ita.* Wide flat strips of pasta with ruffled edges; used to make a casserole known as lasagne.

lasagne (lah-ZAAN-ynay). *Ita.* A casserole of lasagna noodles layered with sauce, meat, cheese, and other fillings.

lassan (LAH-sahn). *Ind.* Garlic.

lassi (LAH-see). *Ind.* Yogurt flavored with rosewater and sugar.

latkes (LAHT-kehs). *Jew.* Potatoes grated and fried in pancakes.

letspraengt oksebryst (let-sprayngt-OAK-see-brurst). *Dan.* Corned beef.

latte (LAHT-tay). *Ita.* Milk.

Lattich (LAH-tikh). *Ger.* Lettuce.

lattuga (laht-TOO-gah). *Ita.* Lettuce.

lauch (lowkh). *Ger.* Leeks.

Laugenbrezel (LAU-ken-pret-zehl). *Ger.* A special type of pretzel.

laung (longh). *Ind.* Clove.

lauro (LAH-ooroa). *Ita.* Bay leaf.

lavender (LAH-ven-der). *USA.* An herb with highly aromatic leaves and flowers that give a bitter pungency to salads.

lavender gem (LAH-ven-dehr gem). *USA.* A delicate, sweet, pink, mini-grapefruit.

laver (LAH-vehr). *Ind.* Thin black seaweed, called sea lettuce. Called nori in Japan.

lax (lahks). *Swe.* Salmon.

laxforell (LANKS-fo-rayl). *Swe.* River trout.

laymun bussfayr (lay-MOON BOOC-fair). *Ara.* A citrus fruit found in hot climates; flavor is of lemon and grapefruit.

leather (LEH-thuhr). *USA.* A confection from early America made of dried-fruit purees mixed with brown sugar or honey, then spread on a baking sheet and thoroughly dried in a slow oven; cut in strips and usually rolled and dusted with sugar.

leavening (LEAH-vehn-eng). *USA.* A substance such as yeast, baking powder, baking soda, or egg white, used to produce gas in dough or batter to lighten and raise it.

Leber (LAY-beer). *Ger.* Liver.

Leberkäs (LAY-berr-kaizer). *Ger.* A loaf of mixed ground meats.

Leberklösse (LAY-berr-klur-zeh). *Ger.* Liver dumplings.

Leberknödelsuppe (LAY-berr-knur-derl-zup-per). *Ger.* A soup of clear meat broth with liver dumplings.

Leberspiessli (LAY-beer-speess-lee). *Ger.* A Swiss shish-kabob made of bits of liver flavored with sage and bacon, grilled on a skewer.

Leberwurst (LAY-berr-voorst). *Ger.* A smoked sausage made of ground pork liver and usually combined with ground pork or veal.

Lebkuchen (lab-KOO-cklien). *Ger.* Spiced honey cake.

lebre (LEH-bruh). *Por.* Hare.

leche (LEH-cheh). *Spa.* Milk.

lechecillas (lay-chay-THEE-liahs). *Spa.* Sweetbreads.

lechoncillo asado (loa-chee-NEE-lyoa ah-SSAH-dhoa). *Spa.* Roast suckling pig.

lechuga (leh-CHOO-gah). *Spa.* Lettuce.

lecithin (LETH-ee-ceen). *USA.* An emulsifier used in confectionery goods; keeps oil and water from separating.

Leckerli (LEH-kerr-li). *Ger.* A rectangular cinnamon flavored Swiss biscuit made with honey, dried citrus peel, almonds.

Lee cake (lee kahk). *USA.* A white cake flavored with citrus juice and rind.

leechee (LAY-chee). *Ind.* Litchi.

leek (leek). *USA.* A mild, subtle flavored onion, with broader green leaves and white bulb than the green onion or shallot; lends itself well to soups, stews; should be used cooked.

legumbres (leh-GOOM-bres). *Spa.* Vegetables.

legumbres secos (leh-GOOM-bres SEH-kos). *Spa.* Dried vegetables.

legumes (lee-GOOMZ). *USA.* Peas, beans, peanuts; eaten fresh or dry, sprouted or not; high in protein and carbohydrate value.

legumes (lay-GOO-mayss). *Por.* Vegetables.

légumes (lay-gewm). *Fre.* Vegetables.

legumi (lay-GOO-mee). *Ita.* Vegetables.

Leicester (LES-tur). *Bri.* A whole-milk cows' cheese made in large cylinders with a hard reddish-brown rind and yellow flaky moist interior; similar to cheddar.

Leichte Kraftsuppe (LICH-ter krahft-zup-per). *Ger.* Chicken and veal broth.

Leidse Kaas (LEYT-ser kahs). *Dut.* A hard Dutch cheese made from partially skimmed cow's milk flavored with cumin, caraway, and spices, then molded and pressed.

leipää (LAY-pae). *Fin.* Bread.

leitão assado (lay-TAWNG ah-SAH-doo). *Por.* Roast suckling pig.

leite (late). *Por.* Milk.

leite-créme com forófias (LAY-tuh-KREH-muh kohm fou-ROU-feeah). *Por.* Meringues in custard, similar to floating island.

lekach (LEE-kasch). *Jew.* Honey-spice cake, traditionally served for Rosh Hashanah.

lemon (LEH-mon). *USA.* The oblong acidic pale yellow fruit of the lemon tree; used for seasoning food and drink.

lemon balm (LEH-mon bahlm). *USA.* An herb with lemon-scented leaves used fresh in teas, salads, and compotes, and in making Chartreuse.

lemon cucumber (LEH-mon KU-kom-behr). *USA.* A burpless cucumber; a more delicate flavor than green-skinned varieties; about the size of a tennis ball; turns from lemon to golden-yellow as it matures; use as common cucumber.

lemon curd (LEH-mon kuhrd). *Bri.* A pastry custard of lemon juice, sugar, butter, and egg yolks.

lemongrass (LEH-mon-grahss). *USA.* An herb of lemon-scented pampas-grass-type leaves for use in tea blends, punches, and salad dressings. A must in Thai and Vietnamese cooking, especially with fish and poultry.

lemon verbena (LEH-mon vehr-BEE-nyah). *USA.* An herb of lemony flavored elongated leaves to be used fresh or dried in salad dressings, cold salads, desserts, drinks, teas.

lencse (LEHN-cheh). *Hun.* Lentils.

Lendenbraten (LEHN-dern-braa-tern). *Ger.* Roast sirloin of beef.

Lendenstuk (LEHN-dern-stayk). *Ger.* Loin.

lengpán (leng-pan). *Chi.* Coldplatter.

lengua (LEN-guah). *Spa.* Tongue.

lengua de ternera (LEN-guah deh tehr-NEH-rah). *Spa.* Calf's tongue.

lenguado (len-GWAH-do). *Spa.* Sole.

lentejas (layn-TAY-khahss). *Spa.* Lentils.

lenticchie (layn-TEEK-keeay). *Ita.* Lentils.

lentilhas (lehn-TEE-leeahs). *Por.* Lentils.

lentilles (lahng-tee). *Fre.* Lentils.

lepre (LAI-pray). *Ita.* Hare.

le rouge royal (lay roogz rah-yahl). *USA.* An uncharacteristically large thick-walled pepper with a sweet, mild taste and brilliant flame red coloring; use fresh or cooked.

leshch (lyehshch). *Rus.* Bream.

lesso (LAYS-soa). *Ita.* Boiled, or boiled meat.

letterbanket (LET-tur BAHNG-ket). *Dut.* Almond paste.

lettuce (LETT-us). *USA.* Succulent vegetable whose leaves are used mostly in salads. Lettuce is divided into five categories: butterhead, crisphead, looseleaf, romaine, and stem. See individual names.

lever (LEH-vehr). *Dan.* Liver.

lever (LAY-veer). *Swe.* Liver.

leverkorv (LAY-veer-korv). *Swe.* Liver sausage.

leverpostej (LEH-vehr-poa-stai). *Dan.* Liver pâté.

levest (LEH-vehsht). *Hun.* Soup.

liaison (lee-yeh-zon). *Fre.* The mixture of egg yolks and cream, used for thickening or binding white soups and sauces.

liángkaishui (LIANG-kai-shui). *Chi.* Cold water.

liba (LEE-bo). *Hun.* Goose.

libamáj pástértom (LEE-bom-maa PAASH-tay-tawn). *Hun.* A hot appetizer of goose liver pâté mixed with butter and béchamel sauce, spices and brandy, and served in a flaky pastry shell

libamáj rizottó (LEE-bomaa REE-zawt-taw). *Hun.* Goose liver risotto.

licorice (LICK-ah-rish). *USA.* An anise flavored herb used for flavoring candies, pastries, cough lozenges, tobacco preparations.

lichee (LEE-zhi). *Chi.* Litchi.

licuado (lee-KWA-dou). *Spa.* Fruit drink, usually citrus.

liebre (LYAH-bray). *Spa.* Hare.

Liederkranz (LEE-der-krantz). *Ger.* A soft, mild, rectangular surface-ripened cheese of Switzerland.

liégeoise (lea-zhwah). *Fre.* Garnished with juniper berries.

lien jee (lian zee). *Chi.* Lotus seeds.

lien ngow (lian ou). *Chi.* Lotus root.

lier (lee-ay). *Fre.* To blend.

lièvre (ly-ehvr). *Fre.* Hare; a rabbit.

lifit (LEF-feht). *Ara.* Turnips.

light cream (lite kreem). *USA.* Cream containing 18–30% milkfat. Also called coffee cream or table cream.

light whipping cream (lite WHEHP-eng kreem). *USA.* Whipping cream containing 30–36% milkfat.

lights (lites). *USA.* The lungs of an animal combined with other organs and meat in stews, pâté, used in countries around the world, but in the United States used in pet foods.

lihaliemi (LI-hah-LAY-mi). *Fin.* Broth; clear soup.

lihamurekepiiras (LEE-hah-moo-reh-keh-PEE-rah). *Fin.* Meat pie with sour cream crust.

lihapyörykät (LI-hah-PEWUR-rew-kaet). *Fin.* Meat ball.

lihapiirakka (LI-hah-PEER-rah-khah). *Fin.* Meat pie.

li jiàng (lee jeeang). *Chi.* Oyster sauce, used mostly in Cantonese cooking.

lima (LEE-mah). *Spa.* Lime.

lima bean (LI-mah behn). *USA.* An edible, nutritious, flat, cultivated bean; light green color; starchy texture; fibrous pod not usually edible.

limande (lee-mahngd). *Fre.* Lemon sole.

limão (lee-MOW). *Por.* Lemon.

Limburger (LEHM-buhrr-gehr). *Ger.* A soft, creamy, surface-ripened, dense, yellow pasteurized cow's milk cheese that is highly pungent; has a strong flavor and aroma.

limes (limmz). *USA.* The fruit of the lime tree; having thin rinds and green-yellow color; acidic flavor; aromatic.

limon (lee-MON). *Rus.* Lemon.

limón (lee-MON). *Spa.* Lemon.

limonad (lyee-mah-NAH-dah). *Rus.* Lemonade.

limonada (lee-moh-NAH-dah). *Por.* Lemonade.

limonade (lim-o-nah-deh). *Fre.* Lemonade.

limonmádét (LEE-maw-naadayt). *Hun.* Lemonade.

limoncillo (lee-MON-ceel-loa). *Spa.* Lemongrass.

limone (lee-MOA-nay). *Ita.* Lemon.

limpa (LEHM-pah). *Swe.* Rye bread.

limpet (LEHM-peht). *USA.* An edible marine mollusk, conical shape; eat the foot and discard the visceral hump; tastes much like oysters.

Limpin' Suzan (LEHMP-eng SU-zuhn). *USA.* A dish of red beans and rice; a corollary to Hoppin' John.

lingon (LING-on). *Swe.* Lingonberries, the fruit of the mountain cranberry.

lingua (LEEN-gwah). *Por, Ita.* Tongue.

lingua di bue (LEENG-gwah dee boo). *Ita.* Ox tongue.

linguado (leeng-WAH-doo). *Por.* Sole.

lingue di passero (LEEN-gwah dee pah-SEH-roh). *Ita.* Eggless pasta that is very flat and thin.

linguiça (leen-GWEE-sa). *Por.* Garlic-flavored pork sausage.

linguine (lynn GWEE knee). *Ita.* Flat, thin, narrow, eggless pasta.

Linse (LIN-zern). *Ger.* Lentil.

Linsensuppe (LIN-zern-zup-per). *Ger.* Lentil soup made with sausage.

linser (LIN-sserr). *Nor.* Lentils.

linser (LIN-sehr). *Dan.* Cream tarts.

Linzertorte (LIN-tser-tor-ter). *Ger.* An Austrian tart of ground hazelnut pastry filled with raspberry jam and a latticework crust.

lipeäkala (LI-ppayae-KAH-lah). *Fin.* Highly pungent, lye-soaked codfish.

litchee (LEE-chee). *Chi.* Litchi.

litchi (LEE-chee). *Chi.* A delicious, round fruit with a very sweet flavor similar to raisins; red, leathery outer covering; fresh pulp is translucent white to pale cream in color, when dried becomes brown; can be eaten alone, or combined with other fruits.

Livarot (lee-vah-roe). *Fre.* A soft, even-textured, tangy, disc shaped, cows' whole-milk cheese with a hard, shiny surface, colored yellow-brown or red.

liverwurst (LEH-vahr-worst). *USA.* A sausage of very smooth texture made of chopped liver seasoned with onions, pistachios and other spices; usually smoked.

liyí (lee-yu). *Chi.* Carp.

liymuwn (la-MOON). *Ara.* Lemon.

lìzhi (lee-dzi). *Chi.* Litchi. Also spelled lichee, lichi, litchie, lizhi, lychee.

lízi (lee-dze). *Chi.* Chestnut.

lízi (LEE-dzi). *Chi.* Pear.

lizi (leh-dzi). *Chi.* Plum.

loaf sugar (lowf SCHU-gahr). *USA.* Granulated sugars molded into loaf or rectangular shapes; used in hot drinks; crushed it makes a sparkling garnish for iced cakes.

lobhia (LHOB-hee-ah). *Ind.* Black-eyed peas.

lo bok (luo bo). *Chi.* Loh baak.

lobscouse (LAHB-skaus). *USA.* A New England beef and potato stew.

lobskovs (LAHB-skoo-oss). *Dan.* A thick stew of beef, diced potatoes, slices of carrots and onions; served with rye bread.

lobster (LAHB-stuhr). *USA.* A family of crustaceans prized for its delectable, flavorful meat, particularly the claw and tail meat, but also the coral (roe) and tomalley (liver).

lobster mushroom (LAHB-stuhr MUHSH-room). *USA.* A mushroom with a slight fish taste, these range from orange to red in color, and look like paper mache.

lochshen (LAHK-shehn). *Jew.* Noodles.

locust bean (LOH-cuhs behn). *USA.* Carob.

Lodigiano Formaggio (loa-dee-jee-AHN-oa fohr-MAHG-jee-oa). *Ita.* A hard, grating cheese.

lofschotel (LAHF-scho-tel). *Dut.* Chicory.

løg (lurg). *Dan.* Onion.

loganberry (LOW-guhn-behr-ree). *USA.* The red berry-fruit that is a hybrid of the Western dewberry and the red raspberry.

loh baak (luo bo). *Chi.* A giant white radish, squatty, and slightly fibrous; very crisp, tender, mild, and sweet; much like a turnip in flavor. See lo bok.

lohi (LOA-hi). *Fin.* Salmon.

lohipiirakka (LOA-hi-PEE-rahk-kah). *Fin.* Salmon pie.

loin (lohen). *USA.* That part of the beef between the rib and the round; contains the tenderest cuts of the sirloin and short loin.

löjrom (LURJ-room). *Swe.* Roe from tiny freshwater fish served on hard-cooked egg halves with chopped onion.

lök (lurk). *Swe.* Onion.

løk (lurk). *Nor.* Onion.

lökdolmar (LUHK-dohl-MAR). *Swe.* Stuffed onion rolls.

lok dow (lok dou). *Chi.* Tiny olive-green mung beans, used for sprouting.

löksoppa (LOHK-sop-pa). *Swe.* Onion soup.

lombata (loam-BAA-tah). *Ita.* Loin.

lombo (LOAM-boa). *Ita.* Loin.

lombo (LOHN-boh). *Por.* Loin.

lombo de vitela (LOHM-boh day vee-TEH-lah). *Por.* Veal loin.

lo mein (low mian). *Chi.* Fresh Chinese egg noodles.

lomi-lomi salmon (LOH-mee-LOH-mee SAHM-un). *USA.* A Hawaiian dish of salted salmon cooked with chopped tomatoes, Maui onions, and scallions.

lomo (LOH-moh). *Spa.* Loin.

London Broil (LUHN-dohn browl). *USA.* A boneless cut of beef from the flank that is marinated and broiled and sliced on an angle.

longan (lohng-yahn). *Chi.* "Dragon's eye"; a small, round fruit with brown skin, crispy opaque flesh, and a single large seed; similar to litchi, but not as sweet, dried or fresh-canned.

longaniza (lohn-gah-NEE-thah). *Spa.* A large sausage of pork, pimento, garlic, and majoram.

long bean (lohng behn). *USA.* A member of the Chinese green bean family, whose flavor is somewhat stronger than ordinary green beans. Also called asparagus beans, yard-long beans.

longe de veau (lonzhe der voa). *Fre.* Loin of veal.

long-grain rice (lohng-grain rics). *USA.* A basic type of rice, which separates into distinct kernels when cooked; grains are four to five times as long as wide. Many varieties include: basmati, bluebonnet, Carolina, della, jojutla, lebonnet, and newrex.

Long Island duck (lohng I-luhnd duhk). *USA.* A specially raised duck for commercial use; commonly 7 to 8 weeks old, and weighs 3 to 5 pounds.

lóngxia (loong-siah). *Chi.* Lobster.

lóngxu niú ròu (loong shee niu row). *Chi.* Thinly sliced beef served with sautéed asparagus.

lonza (LOHN-tzah). *Ita.* Cured pork loin.

looseleaf lettuce (LOOS-leef LETT-us). *USA.* A fragile, delicious salad lettuce; the loose leaves branch from a single stalk, do not bunch, vary in color; used as plate liners and garnishes. Varieties include Matchless (deer's tongue variety), Oakleaf (green and bronze), Prizehead (red-pigmented leaf), and Salad Bowl (looks like a nosegay).

lop cheeng (lah chaoong). *Chi.* Spicy pork sausages.

loquat (LOA-kwaht). *USA.* The sweet-sour apricot shaped fruit of a Japanese evergreen; has yellow-orange skin, deep orange flesh, cherrylike flavor; used cooked in jams and jellies, eaten fresh in fruit salads, or baked in desserts.

lorraine, à la (lohr-rain). *Fre.* Served with the garnish of red cabbage balls and small potatoes sauteed in butter.

lotte (lot). *Fre.* Burbot; monkfish.

lotus root (LOA-tuhs root). *USA.* Root of the Chinese lotus plant, when peeled and sliced are crisp, white, and filled with holes resembling snowflakes; may be eaten raw or cooked.

lotus seeds (LOA-tuhs seeds). *USA.* Seeds of the Chinese lotus plant that when dried are yellow in color, used in stews and desserts and roasted to make a kind of popcorn.

loup (loo). *Fre.* Sea bass.

lovage (LOHV-adj). *USA.* Celery-flavored herb whose leaves, stems, roots, and seeds are all edible.

love and tangle (lohv-and-TAHN-uhl). *USA.* Doughnuts that are twisted and entwined, then deep-fried.

love apples (lohv AHP-puhl). *USA.* A romantic term for tomatoes, because originally they were thought to have aphrodisiacal attributes.

low-fat milk (loa-faht mehlk). *USA.* Cows' milk that contains not more than 2% milk fat.

low mull (loh muhl). *USA.* A vegetable and meat stew of varying ingredients; related to mulligan stew.

lowza (lahz). *Ara.* Almond.

lox (lohks). *Jew.* Salt-cured salmon soaked in water to remove some of the salt, traditionally eaten with bagels.

lsanat (ll-SAH-naht). *Ara.* Tongue.

lubina (loo-BEE-nah). *Spa.* Sea bass.

lubyi (LLOO-bee). *Ara.* Green beans.

lü chá (lu tsah). *Chi.* Green tea.

lucullus (luh-KEHL-luhs). *Ita.* Lavish, luxurious; applies to a subterranean mushroomlike fungus used for garnishing and flavoring.

luganeaga (loo-gah-neh-AH-gah). *Ita.* Fresh pork sausage, mildly flavored with Parmesan cheese and made in long tubes, not links.

luk (look). *Rus.* Onion.

lukewarm (LUK-wahrm). *USA.* Moderately warm; approximately 100°F.

lumaca (loo-MAA-kay). *Ita.* Snail.

lumberjack pie (LUHM-behr-jahk pi). *USA.* A meat pie made of vegetables and deer meat.

lumpfish caviar (LUHMP-fisch KAHV-ee-ahr). *USA.* A caviar substitute; roe of the lumpfish salted and sold as caviar.

lump sugar (luhmp SCHU-gahr). *USA.* A granulated sugar cut into half-inch by half-inch cubes; usually used in hot beverages.

luó bo gao (luo bo gao). *Chi.* Turnip cake; a dim sum.

luó hàn zhai (law han dzai). *Chi.* "Buddha's vegetable dish"; bamboo shoots, nuts, mushrooms sautéed in soy sauce and sherry.

lutefisk (LOO-teh-feesk). *Nor.* Dried cod, soaked in lye prior to cooking; eaten with cream sauce or pork drippings.

lutefisk (LOOT-feesk). *Swe.* Stockfish, usually cod, soaked in lye prior to cooking; a Christmas specialty.

luumut (LOO-moot). *Fin.* Plums.

Luzener Alleblei (loo-ZEN-ner AHL-lee-bly). *Ger.* A Swiss vegetable and mushroom salad.

lychee (LEE-chee). *Chi.* Litchi.

Lymeswold (LIMZ-wohld). *Bri.* A new cheese, essentially a milk blue Brie with a delicate white rind and soft creamy paste with blue veining.

Lyonerwurst (LEW-oa-nayr-voorst). *Ger.* Garlic-flavored ham sausage.

lyonnaise (ly-awng-nehz). *Fre.* Seasoned with onions; generally chopped onions sautéed in butter and reduced with white wine and vinegar, then strained.

lys saus (lewss sowss). *Nor.* Any light sauce: white wine sauce, curry sauce, horseradish sauce.

M

maanz (mahz). *Ind.* Meat.

maçã (mah-SAH). *Por.* Apple.

macadamia nut (mahk-ah-DAHM-ee-ah nuht). *USA.* A round nut that is white, sweet, high in fat, and usually roasted before purchase; a fine dessert nut.

maçapão (mah-sah-PAHNG). *Por.* Marzipan.

macaron (mah-kah-rohn). *Fre.* Macaroon.

macaroni (mahc-ah-ROHN-ee). *Ita.* Tube-shaped dried pasta.

macaroni and cheese (mahc-ah-ROHN-ee ahnd cheez). *USA.* An original American dish made by layering boiled macaroni in a dish, alternating with grated or diced American cheddar or Swiss cheese then baking till the cheese melts and the top is lightly browned.

macaroon (MACK-ah-roon). *USA.* A small round cookie made of almond paste, sugar, and egg whites; in the United States usually shredded coconut is added.

macarrão (mah-kah-RROW). *Por.* Macaroni.

macarrones (mah-kahr-ROA-nehs). *Spa.* Macaroni.

macarrones con queso (mah-kahr-ROA-nehs kohn KAY-ssoa). *Spa.* Macaroni and cheese.

macãs (ma-SANSH). *Por.* Apples.

maccarello (mahk-chah-REHL-loa). *Ita.* Mackerel.

maccheroni (mahk-keh-ROA-nee). *Ita.* Large spaghetti with a hole in the middle.

mace (mayc). *USA.* A spice made from the netlike covering of the nutmeg seed that is dried to an orange-brown color, and powdered; tastes like nutmeg with a hint of cinnamon.

macédoine (mah-say-dwan). *Fre.* A mixture of various vegetables or fruits set in a galatin mold; also, a fruit salad flavored with liqueurs and syrup.

macédonia (mah-CHAY-doa-nee). *Ita.* Fruit compote flavored with maraschino liqueur.

macerate (MASS-er-rate). *USA.* To steep in liquid; usually refers to fresh fruit steeped in liqueur.

macéré (mahs-eh-ree). *Fre.* Pickled.

mache (mah-chee). *Fre.* Lamb's lettuce; spoon-shaped, rounded green leaves; a sweet hazelnut taste; used fresh in salads or cooked like spinach.

machi (MAH-chee). *Ind.* Fish.

made (MAH-day). *Fin.* Burbot.

madeleine (mad-ah-lynn). *Fre.* A classic tea cake made of flour, sugar, butter, and baked in a shell mold.

madère (mah-dehr). *Fre.* Prepared with the Spanish wine, Madeira.

maderise (mah-drees). *Fre.* Wine that has acquired a brownish color and the aroma of Madeira due to spoilage by oxidation.

madras (mahd-rahs). *Fre.* Flavored with curry or chutney.

madrilene (mah-dree-leen). *Fre.* Tomato-flavored beef consommé.

maelk (mehlk). *Dan.* Milk.

mafalde (mah-FAHL-day). *Ita.* Long strips of narrow or medium width pasta with fluted edges.

magdalenas (mahg-dah-LEH-nahs). *Spa.* Cornmeal muffins.

maggi (MADG-ji). *USA.* A concentrated seasoning sauce used to enhance the flavor of gravies, sauces for meats, as well as to make broth.

maggiorana (mad-joar-RAA-nah). *Ita.* Majoram.

magliyy (MAHK-lee). *Ara.* Fried.

magro (MAH-groa). *Ita.* Lean; a dish without meat.

mahlab (MAAH-lahb). *Ara.* A seasoning used in dough or pastries; it is a small seed of the stone of a wild cherry.

Mahón (MA-hon). *Spa.* A goat cheese from Menorca.

mahonesa (mah-oa-NAY-sah). *Spa.* Mayonnaise.

mah tai (maah tee). *Chi.* Water chestnuts.

maiale (maaee-AA-lay). *Ita.* Pork.

Maifisch (MAE-fish). *Ger.* Shad.

maigre (meh-gruh). *Fre.* A dish without meat; applied to Lenten dishes.

Mainauer (MEH-nowr). *Ger.* A semihard, whole-cream cheese.

maionese (mahee-OA-nays). *Ita.* Mayonnaise.

Mais (mighss). *Ger.* Corn.

mais (mays). *Fre.* Sweet corn.

maison (meh-zhon). *Fre.* Designates a dish of the restaurant's own special recipe.

Maisturta (MIGHSS-tuhr-tah). *Ger.* Corn pudding.

maito (MAH-toaah). *Fin.* Milk.

maitokahvi (MAH-toaah-KAH-vi). *Fin.* Coffee with hot milk.

maitre d'hotel sauce (MEH-tr doh-TEL saus). *Fre.* A yellow sauce of butter, lemon juice, parsley, egg yolk, seasonings; served on grilled meats; also, food that is quickly and plainly prepared and flavored with parsley.

maiz (mah-EES). *Spa.* Dried corn.

maize (mayz). *USA.* An American Indian word for corn.

majonnäs (mah-yoo-NAYSS). *Swe.* Mayonnaise.

Majoran (mah-yo-RAAN). *Ger.* Marjoram.

Makaroni (MAH-kah-roa-nee). *Ger.* Macaroni.

makaronilaatikko (MAH-kah-roa-ni-LAA-tik-koa). *Fin.* Macaroni stewed in milk and cream with egg yolks.

makaruni (MAAH-kah-roa-nee). *Ara.* Refers to pastas; spaghetti and macaroni.

makbus (mack-BOOC). *Ara.* Pickled or preserved in vinegar or oil.

makhan (MAH-kehn). *Ind.* Butter.

makkara (MAHK-kah-rah). *Fin.* Sausage.

mako (MA-koh). *Jap.* Shark.

makreel (mah-KRAYL). *Dut.* Mackerel.

Makrele (mah-KRAY-ler). *Ger.* Mackerel.

makrill (MAHK-ril). *Swe.* Mackerel.

Makronen (mah-KROA-nern). *Ger.* Macaroons.

makroner (mah-KRO-nehr). *Dan.* Macaroons.

maksa (MAHK-sah). *Fin.* Liver.

malaga (mah-LAH-ghah). *Spa.* A sweet sherry that is dark and heavy.

malai (ma-LIE-ee). *Ind.* Cream of all kinds: heavy, light, sour, and coconut.

malanga (mah-LAHNG-gah). *Mex.* A tuber whose stems are also peeled and cooked like potatoes; a somewhat starchier taste than ordinary potatoes; a staple in Central American countries.

malasado (mah-lah-SAH-doo). *Por.* A puff pastry made from an egg batter, deep-fried, then rolled in sugar.

malay apple (MA-la ahp-pul). *USA.* A crispy, red, pear-shaped fruit with a bland flavor.

malet kött (MAH-let choht). *Swe.* Ground beef.

malfatti (mahl-FAHT-tee). *Ita.* Gnocchi of spinach and ricotta.

malfuf (mahl-FUHF). *Ara.* Cabbage.

malfuwfa (MAL-fuf). *Ara.* Cabbage.

malk (mal). *Ara.* Salt.

malosol (mah-lah-SAWL). *Rus.* "Prepared with little salt." All types of caviar can be prepared malosol and are considered fresh caviar.

malpoora (mal-POOH-rah). *Ind.* Sweet whole wheat crepes flavored with crushed fennel.

malsouka (mahl-SOO-kah). *Gre.* Phyllo. Also known as brik, filo, yukka.

malt (mahlt). *USA.* Barley germinated by softening in water, used in brewing and distilling. Also, malt powder can be flavored, such as with chocolate, then dissolved in milk to make a beverage.

maltagliati (mahl-tahl-YAH-teh). *Ita.* Flat pasta, half inch thick, cut on the bias; used basically in bean soups.

maltaise (mahl-teh). *Fre.* Hollandaise sauce flavored with grated orange rind and the juice of a blood orange.

malt-based vinegar (mahlt-basd VEH-eh-gahr). *USA.* Fermentation of an infusion of barley malt or cereals whose starch has been converted by malt.

Malzbier (MAHLTS-beer). *Ger.* A dark and sweet low-alcohol malt beer.

mamão (mah-MOW). *Por.* Papaya.

mamey sapote (mah-mee sah-PO-tay). *Mex.* The round fruit of a Central American tropical tree with coarse, brown skin, smooth orange pulp, eaten fresh or in ice cream. Also called mammee.

mämmi (MAEM-mi). *Fin.* A rye pudding made with molasses, flavored with bitter orange and served with cream; traditional at Easter.

manapua (mah-nah-POO-ah). *USA.* A Hawaiian dough bun filled with pork, bean paste, or other stuffings, then steamed.

manche (mensh). *Fre.* The projecting bone of a chop.

Manchego (mahn-CHAY-goa). *Spa.* A ewes' milk cheese with a pale, golden curd whose rind is rubbed with olive oil after a greenish-black mold is brushed off.

manchette (mensh-ayt). *Fre.* The paper frill used to cover the projecting bone of a chop.

Mandarine (mahn-dah-REE-ner). *Ger.* Tangerine.

mandarine (mahng-dah-reen). *Fre.* Tangerine.

mandarino (mahn-dah-REE-noa). *Ita.* Tangerine.

mandarin orange (MAHN-dah-rehn OHR-rahnj). *USA.* The reddish-orange loose-skinned fruit of the spiny Chinese orange tree.

mandelbiskvier (MAN-dehl-bisk-VEE-er). *Swe.* Almond cookies.

Mandeln (MAHN-derln). *Ger.* Almonds.

mandeln (MAHN-dayl). *Swe.* Almonds.

Mandeltorte (MAHN-derl-tor-ter). *Ger.* An almond torte with a custard filling and butter icing.

mandlar (MAND-lar). *Swe.* Almonds.

mandler (MAHN-dlerr). *Nor.* Almonds.

mandler (MAHN-lerr). *Dan.* Almonds.

mandoo (MAN-du). *Kor.* Meat-filled dumplings, seasoned with soy sauce, toasted sesame seed, garlic, pepper, and onion; steamed, fried, or boiled in a broth; similar to won ton.

mandorla (MAHN-doar-lay). *Ita.* Almond.

mange-tout (monj-too). *Fre.* A pea or bean eaten with the shell on; such as sugar snap or snow pea.

mángguo (mang-guo). *Chi.* Mango.

manglam (MAHNG-luhm). *Iri.* Pie.

mango (MAHNG-go). *USA.* A flattish-oval tropical Indian fruit, when full-ripened, has deep orange or yellowish-green skin with smooth golden flesh; eaten fresh or when green is cooked in chutneys and preserves.

mangosteens (MAHN-go-steen). *USA.* A 2-3 inch fruit with an exquisite milky juice; has five or six sections; may be easily scooped out and eaten with a spoon.

mangue (mahn-gah). *Fre.* Mango.

manicotti (mahn-eh-COHT-teh). *Ita.* A thin, tubular pasta stuffed with a ricotta cheese mixture and baked in a sauce.

manioc (mah-NEE-oahk). *Spa.* Tapioca. Also called cassava, yuca.

mannagrynspudding (MAH-na-gri-ins-PU-ding). *Swe.* Semolina pudding.

mannitol (MAHN-ee-tohl). *USA.* A sweetening agent.

mano (MAHN-oh). *Mex.* A stone that is rolled over the surface of a metate to grind grains and spices.

manoa (mah-NOH-ah). *USA.* A Hawaiian salad lettuce of the butterhead lettuce family; smallish head, slightly loose leaves; darker green on outer leaves, pale green on inner leaves; holds up well in warm weather.

mansikkasoppa (MAHN-sik-kah-soh-pah). *Fin.* Strawberries with cream and sugar.

mansikkat (MAHN-sik-kaht). *Fin.* Strawberries.

mansikkatorttu (MAHN-sik-kah-TOART-too). *Fin.* Strawberry tart or pie.

mántáu (man-toh). *Chi.* Steamed buns.

manteca (mahn-TEH-kah). *Mex.* Lard.

Manteca (mahn-TEE-kah). *Ita.* A cows' milk cheese, mozzarella, wrapped around a pat of butter.

mantecado (mahn-teh-KAH-dhoa). *Spa.* A rich vanilla ice cream into which whipped cream has been folded.

manteenmäti (MAH-tayn-MAE-ti). *Fin.* Burbot caviar; a supreme delicacy.

manteiga (mahn-TAY-gah). *Por.* Butter.

manteli (MAHN-tay-lit). *Fin.* Almond.

mantelikokkare (MAHN-tay-lit-koak-kay-ray). *Fin.* Almond custard served with fruit sauce.

mantequilla (mahn-teh-KEE-yah). *Spa.* Butter.

mányú (man-yu). *Chi.* Eel.

manzana (mahn-ZAH-nah). *Spa.* Apple.

manzanilla (mahn-zah-NILL-lah). *Spa.* Chamomile tea; also, a Spanish sherry.

manzano banana (mahm-ZAHN-noh bah-NAH-nah). *Mex.* A short, stubby banana, with its flavor accented by that of strawberries and apples; eaten fresh out of hand or in salads and desserts.

manzo (MAHN-dzoa). *Ita.* Beef; manzo arrosto (MAHN-dzoa ahr-ROA-stoa), roast beef; manzo brasiato (MAHN-dzoa brah-SAA-toa), braised beef; manzo salato (MAHN-dzoa sah-LAH-toa), corned beef; manzo stufato (MAHN-dzoa stoo-FAH-toa), beef stew; manzo uso (MAHN-dzoa OO-soa), pot roast.

maple syrup (MAH-puhl seh-ruhp). *USA.* Syrup made from the sap of the sugar maple tree, used for flavoring.

mápó dòufù (MA-po doh-FOO). *Chi.* Beancurd with minced pork in hot sauce.

maque choux (MAHCK-shoo). *USA.* A Cajun corn dish, sweet and highly seasoned.

maquereau (mah-ker-roa). *Fre.* Mackerel.

maräng (ma-RANG). *Swe.* Meringue.

maraschino (mahr-ah-SKEE-noh). *Fre.* A flavoring for beverages and confectionery made from oils extracted from the crushed seeds of the Royal Anne cherry; a favorite flavoring of the Middle East.

marasquin (mah-rah-skeen). *Fre.* A delicately flavored white liquor, used for flavoring.

marble (MAHR-buhl). *USA.* A term used to describe the small, white flecks of fat throughout muscle tissue, generally favored in beef for tenderness and taste. In pastry it denotes light and dark dough swirled together to resemble marbled stone.

marcassin (mahr-kahs-sang). *Fre.* Young wild boar.

marchand de vin (mah-shon day vang). *Fre.* A red wine sauce flavored with chopped shallots, parsley, and butter; similar to bordelaise; served on grilled meats.

marchpane (mahrch-payn). *Fre.* Marzipan.

marechale (mahr-shahl). *Fre.* Small cuts of poultry or meats, dipped in beaten egg, rolled in bread crumbs, fried in butter, and garnished with sliced truffles, green peas, or sometimes asparagus tips.

maree (mah-rer). *Fre.* All saltwater fish and shellfish.

marennes (mah-rehyn). *Fre.* A variety of small oyster.

margarine (mahr-jah-rehn). *Fre.* A butter substitute (oleomargarine) made from vegetable oils and ripened skim milk churned to spreading consistency, usually fortified with vitamin A. Also called oleo.

marguery (mahr-gew-rey). *Fre.* Hollandaise flavored with oyster or fish essence.

Maribo (MAH-ree-boa). *Dan.* A soft, mild, long, oblong cheese of cows' milk with yellow wax coating and a white interior with small holes.

Marie Louise (mah-ree loo-eez). *Fre.* A classic garnish of artichoke hearts filled with mushroom puree and soubise.

marignan (mah-ree-yawng). *Fre.* A rich, rum-syrup-soaked yeast dough pastry with apricot glaze and filled with Chantilly creme.

marigold (MAHR-ee-gold). *USA.* A plant whose dried centers are sometimes used as a color substitute for saffron, and the young leaves used in salads; not an herb, but used as an herb.

Marille (mah-RIL-lern). *Ger.* Apricot.

marinade (mah-ree-nahd). *Fre.* A preparation of oil, herbs, vinegar or wine, in which food is steeped before cooking, or serving, to flavor, moisten and soften it.

marinara (mahr-ah-NAHR-rah). *Ita.* A spicy tomato sauce that is prepared quickly from few ingredients but never includes cheese.

marinate (MAH-ree-nate). *USA.* The act of steeping food in a marinade.

marinato (mah-ree-NAA-toa). *Ita.* Pickled, marinated.

mariné (mah-ree-nay). *Fre.* Marinated, pickled.

marinière (mah-ree-nehr). *Fre.* Seafood cooked with parsley, chopped shallots, butter in white wine and garnished with mussels.

mariniert (mahrin-NEERT). *Ger.* Pickled.

Marinierter Hering (mahrin-NEERT HAY-ring). *Ger.* Pickled herring.

mariscos (mah-REES-kohs). *Spa.* Shellfish; shrimp or scallops.

maritozzo (mah-ree-TOHZ-zoh). *Ita.* Breakfast bun.

marjolaine (mahr-zho-lehn). *Fre.* Sweet marjoram. Also, a pastry of meringue with almond and filbert layered with chocolate, praline, and buttercream.

marjoram (mah-JOR-rum). *USA.* An herb with a warm, sweet fragrance, and delicate oreganolike flavor; use with meats, egg dishes, soups, vegetables. Also called sweet marjoram.

Mark (mahrk). *Ger.* Marrow.

Markklösschen (mahrk-KLURSK-hern). *Ger.* Bread dumplings mixed with beef marrow; served with clear soups.

Marlborough pie (MAHRRL-burr-rou pi). *USA.* An applesauce and cream pie, thickened with eggs and sugar, flavored with nutmeg and sherry; baked to a gelled texture.

marmalade (MAHR-mah-laid). *Bri, USA.* A clear, sweetened, tender citrus jelly in which pieces of the fruit and rind are suspended.

marmelad (mar-meh-LAHD). *Swe.* Marmelade.

marmelade (mahr-mer-lahd). *Fre.* A thick, sweetened, jellylike puree of fruit or onion.

Marmelade (mahr-meh-LAA-der). *Ger.* Jam.

marmellata (mahr-mayl-LAA-tah). *Ita.* Marmelade; jam.

marmite (mahr-meet). *Fre.* A pure vegetable extract, used to make a strong, rich stock for meat soups; also, a cooking pot.

Marmorkuchen (mahr-mor-KOOK-hern). *Ger.* Marblecake.

Maroilles (mah-wahee). *Fre.* A square cows' milk cheese with a reddish rind, yellow interior, creamy flavor, rich and tangy, strong aroma.

Maronen (mah-RAH-nehn). *Ger.* Chestnut.

marquise (mahr-quehss). *Fre.* A fruit ice with whipped cream folded in.

marquq (mahr-KOOK). *Ara.* Very thin, round, flat bread, rolled like Italian pizza dough.

marron (mahr-awng). *Fre.* A cultivated chestnut used in stuffings, pastries.

marroni (mahr-ROA-nee). *Ita.* Chestnuts.

marrow (MAHR-row). *Bri.* A long, large summer squash.

marrow (MAHR-row). *USA.* The soft connective tissue in the hollow of long bones, used in osso bucco and bordelaise sauce.

marrow bones (MAHR-row bonz). *USA.* The long bones of beef and veal, cut in short pieces to poach or braise to solidify the marrow for use in certain dishes or to eat as a delicacy.

Marsala (mahr-SAH-lah). *Ita.* A wine similar to Madeira.

marsepein (MAHR-seh-pain). *Dut.* Marzipan.

marshmallow (MAHRSH-mahl-loh). *USA.* A confection made from corn syrup, sugar, egg whites, and gelatin beaten to a light, spongy, creamy consistency.

marzipan (MAHR-zee-pahn). *USA.* An Arabian confection of almond paste, sugar, and egg whites, often colored and shaped into various fruits, flowers, animals.

masa (MAH-sah). *Mex.* Dough made from corn flour.

masa harina (MAH-sah ah-REE-nah) *Mex.* Dehydrated corn flour.

masala (ma-SAH-la). *Ind.* A blend of seasonings and spices.

masar dal (MA-sahr dahl). *Ind.* Pink lentils.

Mascarpone (mahz-KAHRR-poan). *Ita.* A thick, velvety, rich, soft cows' milk cheese that has a delicate sweet flavor, and is served with fruit and pastries like cream; has the texture of whipped cream.

mash (mahsh). *USA.* To crush food until its original form is entirely lost.

mask (mahsk). *USA.* A French term meaning to cover food completely; such as, a sauce over food before serving, or to put merignue on a pie.

maslina (mahs-LYEE-ni). *Rus.* Olives.

maslo (MAH-sloh). *Rus.* Butter.

masquer (mahsk). *Fre.* To mask.

massa (MAH-sah). *Por.* The word for a number of spaghetti products.

massepain (mah-sah-pahng). *Fre.* Marzipan.

Mastgeflugel (MAHST-ger-flew-gerl). *Ger.* Specially raised grain-fed poultry of exceptionally fine quality.

matar (MA-tehr). *Ind.* Chick-peas.

matcha (mah-CHAH). *Jap.* A powdered tea used for the famous Japanese tea ceremony.

maté (MAH-ta). *Spa.* The leaves and shoots of a South American holly rich in caffeine used to make the aromatic beverage, yerba maté. Also referred to as yerba maté.

matelote (mah-ter-lot). *Fre.* A stew of freshwater fish usually and red or white wine. Also pochouse.

matignon (mah-tee-yawng). *Fre.* A blend of minced vegetables used as a base, or for seasoning; similar to mirepoix, which is diced.

Matjesherring (MAHT-yeh-hay-ring). *Ger.* Young virgin herring that has not yet spawned; of high quality.

matjessill (MAAT-yehs-sil). *Swe.* Marinated herring fillets, served with sour cream and chives.

matsutake (maht-soo-TAH-kee). *Jap.* Pine mushrooms; dark brown with thick, meaty stem; scented with the fragrance of pine woods.

mattha (MAH-tah). *Ind.* Yogurt drink flavored with salt, roasted cumin, and fresh mint leaves.

matzo (MAHT-sah). *Jew.* Flat, unleavened bread eaten during Passover. Also spelled matzoh.

matzo meal (MAHT-sah mehl). *Jew.* Meal made of matzo to be used in breading food as well in various dishes served during Passover.

Maui onion (MAHOO-we UN-yun). *USA.* A mild, sweet Hawaiian onion; golden brown bulb with white flesh; eaten raw in salads, or cooked in soups, stews.

Maultaschen (MAHUL-teaschen). *Ger.* A savory dish of ground pork, veal, and spinach wrapped in noodle dough and served in gravy.

maward (MAHW-wahrd). *Ara.* Rose water; a flavoring used in confectionery.

mawzat (mahw-oo-ZEHT). *Ara.* Meat shanks; the leg portions of beef or lamb.

May wine (mai vighn). *Ger.* A spring punch made of white wine lightly sweetened and flavored with woodruff, then chilled and served with strawberries.

mayonnaise (may-o-nayz). *Fre.* A basic cold sauce that is an emulsion of egg yolks seasoned with vinegar and mustard with oil gradually added to make a thick sauce.

mayonnaise verte (may-o-nayz vehrt). *Fre.* Mayonnaise flavored with finely minced spinach, watercress, parsley, or tarragon, which color the sauce green.

Maytag Blue (MAY-tahg bloo). *USA.* A blue-veined, tangy, smooth-textured cheese made with the milk of holstein-friesian cows from the farmlands of Newton, Iowa; rarely seen elsewhere.

maza (MAZ-zah). *Ara.* Appetizers or hors d'oeuvres.

mazahir (mah-ZAH-hehr). *Ara.* Orange blossom essence.

mazat (MAHS-lah). *Rus.* Oil.

mazzancolle (mats-tsan-KOL-lee). *Ita.* Large prawns.

mead (meed). *Fin.* A fermented drink of water, honey, malt, and yeast.

mealie crenchie (MEEL-ee KREN-chee). *Bri.* Oatmeal flakes fried in bacon fat; served with eggs and bacon at breakfast. Also called mealie greachie.

meatballs (MEET-bawlz). *USA.* Ground meat shaped into globular shapes, varying in size from half-inch to one inch.

meat birds (meet burdz). *USA.* Very similar to veal birds; slices of meat filled with savory stuffing, rolled, skewered or tied, browned in fat, and braised.

meat grades (meet gradz). *USA.* Grades of beef as designated by the U.S. Department of Agriculture: Prime (prym), from young, specially fed cattle, well marbled; tender, fine flavor and texture; usually aged. Choice (choys), high quality, with somewhat less marbling than prime; tender, good flavor; Good (guhd), still a relatively tender grade, with a higher ratio of lean; less juiciness and flavor; Standard (STAHN-dahrd), from low-quality young animals, virtually no marbling; bland flavor; not tender. Commercial/Utility (kom-MEHR-shuhl/u-TEHL-ee-te), meat from old animals; better flavor than Standard; tough.

meat loaf (meet lohf). *USA.* A dish made of ground beef, bread crumbs, and seasonings, baked in a deep rectangular pan, turned out on platter, and served.

medaglioni (may-dah-LYOA-nee). *Ita.* Filet of beef.

médallion (may-dah-yawng). *Fre.* A small circular slice of meat or poultry.

medisterpølse (meh-DEES-terr-purl-sserr). *Dan.* Pork sausage.

medium batter (MEE-dee-uhm BAHT-tehr). *USA.* A flour mixture that contains 1½ parts flour to 1 part liquid; such as thick gravies, pie fillings.

medium white sauce (MEE-dee-uhm whit sahus). *USA.* A roux-liquid mixture that contains a fat-flour ratio of two tablespoons each to one cup liquid, such as used in soups and thin gravies.

medlar (MEHD-lehr). *Bri.* Loquat.

meen see jeong (mee soh GEE-ong). *Chi.* Salty yellow or brown bean sauce.

Meerrettich (MAYR-reh-tikh). *Ger.* Horseradish.

meetha (MEE-tah). *Ind.* Sweet.

Mehlpüt (MAYL-pewt). *Ger.* A dessert of stewed pears with dumplings.

Mehlspeise (MAYL-shpigh-zer). *Ger.* A flour-based pancake or dumpling used to make a dish such as strudel.

mehu (MAY-hoon). *Fin.* Juice.

mein (meen). *Chi.* The general word for noodles.

méizi (may-dzi). *Chi.* Prunes.

mejillones (may-khee-LYOA-nayss). *Spa.* Mussels.

mejorana (meh-khoa-RAH-nah). *Spa.* Marjoram.

mel (mayl). *Por.* Honey.

mela (MAY-lah). *Ita.* Apple.

melaço (may-LAH-soo). *Por.* Molasses.

melagrana (may-lahg-RAH-nah). *Ita.* Pomegranate.

melancia (meh-lahn-SEE-ah). *Por.* Watermelon.

mélanger (may-lon-zhay). *Fre.* To mix or blend; mélange: a mixture.

melanzana (may-lahn-TSAA-nay). *Ita.* Eggplant.

melão (mel-OWN). *Por.* Melon.

melba toast (MEHL-bah toast). *Bri.* Very thin slices of bread, toasted very dry.

melboller (mehl-BOAL-er). *Dan.* Dumplings.

melidzanes (meh-lee-DZAH-nah). *Gre.* Eggplant.

melk (MEL-uk). *Dut.* Milk.

melkbrood (MEL-uk-broht). *Dut.* Milk bread; as opposed to bread made with water.

melkchocolade (MEL-uk-zhoh-ko-lah-duh). *Dut.* Chocolate made with milk.

meloen (muh-LOON). *Dut.* Melon.

melon (MELL-un). *USA.* An edible gourd, such as a muskmelon or watermelon; variable in size; vine grown; usually eaten raw and fresh. Well-known varieties are cantaloupe, casaba, crenshaw, honeydew, juan canary, Persian, Santa Claus.

melón de verano (meh-LOHN day bay-RAH-noa). *Spa.* Cantaloupe.

Melone (may-LOA-ner). *Ger.* Melon.

melt (mehlt). *USA.* To liquify by heating.

Melton Mowbray pie (MEHL-tun MAHW-bree piy). *Bri.* A double-crust pork pie, served cold.

menestra (may-NAYS-trah). *Spa.* Stew.

Menggu kao ròu (MENG-goo kao row). *Chi.* Mongolian barbecue; beef and fresh vegetables grilled in barbecue sauce.

mente (MAYN-tah). *Ita.* Mint.

menthe (mahngt). *Fre.* Mint.

menu (men-you) *Fre.* The bill of fare.

menudillos (mah-noo-DHEE-lyahss). *Spa.* Giblets.

menudo (meh-NOO-doh). *Spa.* Tripe and corn stew.

merga (MEHR-aw). *Ara.* Stock of mutton and/or chicken, strongly spiced; drunk when the weather is very cold or when a person is sick.

meringue (mah-RANG). *USA.* Light pastry, made of egg whites and sugar, then filled with cream or custard; also used as a pie topping.

merlan (mahr-lahng). *Fre.* Whiting.

merlano (mayr-LAA-noa). *Ita.* Whiting.

merluche (mehr-lusch). *Fre.* Stock fish, haddock; dried or smoked.

merluza (mayr-LOO-thah). *Spa.* Hake.

merluzzo (mayr-LOOT-tsoa). *Ita.* Cod.

mero (MEH-roa). *Spa.* Rock bass.

mesimarja (MAY-ssi-MAHR-yah). *Fin.* An Artic brambleberry, the honeyberry; used to make a very sweet liqueur.

Mesost (MAYSS-oost). *Swe.* Amber-colored, sweet whey cheese.

mesquite (mess-SKEET). *Mex, USA.* A wild scrub tree of southwestern United States and Mexico, with distinctively fragrant wood highly prized for open-fire cooking of meats.

messicani (mes-see-KA-nee). *Ita.* Stuffed veal rollups; saltimbocca.

mesticanza (may-stee-KAHN-zah). *Ita.* A mixture of small, tender salad greens.

metate (meh-TAH-teh). *Mex.* A stone with a concave upper surface used for grinding grains and spices using a mano.

methi (MAHT-hee). *Ind.* Fenugreek.

metso (MAYT-soa). *Fin.* A game bird. Also called capercaillie.

Mettwurst (MEHT-voorst). *Ger.* Smoked pork sausage of coarse texture with red skin.

meunière (meh-nyair). *Fre.* Lightly floured, sauteed, and served in butter with lemon slice.

Mexi-bell pepper (MEX-ee-behl PEHP-pehr). *USA.* A mildly hot bell pepper that can be red or green or a combination of both.

Mexican saffron (MEX-ee-kahn SAHF-frohn). *Mex.* Safflower.

mexilhão (mesheel-YOwnsh). *Por.* Mussels.

mezcal (mehs-KAHL). *Mex.* Distilled liquor made from agave (century plant).

mezzani (medz-DZAHN-nee). *Ita.* Long, narrow, tube-shaped pasta.

m'habia (mm-hah-lah-BEE-ah). *Ara.* Cake made of milk, semolina, pistachio nuts, walnuts, and pine nuts.

m'hamsa. (mm-HAHM-sah). *Ara.* Soup with pasta and tomatoes.

miànbao (mien-bao). *Chi.* Bread.

miàntiáo (mien-tiao). *Chi.* Noodles.

miche (meesh). *Fre.* Loaf.

midollo (meh-DOHL-lah). *Ita.* Marrow.

mie (mee). *Fre.* The soft interior part of a loaf of bread.

miel (myehl). *Fre.* Honey.

miele (mee-AY-lay). *Ita.* Honey.

mifàn (mee-fan). *Chi.* Rice.

mignon (mehn-yuon). *Fre.* A small cut of beef; a medallion.

mihli (MOOH-lee). *Ara.* Assorted sweets made with phyllo.

mihshi (MEH-she). *Ara.* Stuffed meats or vegetables.

mi jiu (MEE choo). *Chi.* Yellow rice wine.

mijoter (mee-zho-tay). *Fre.* To simmer.

mikado (meh-KAH-doh). *Fre.* Japanese style.

mikan (MEE-kahn). *Jap.* Tangerine.

milanaise (me-lahn-ayz). *Fre.* A classic garnish; implies the use of pasta and cheese with a suitable sauce, often béchamel.

Milch (milkh). *Ger.* Milk.

milho (MEEL-yoh). *Por.* Corn.

milk (melk). *USA.* The fluid secreted by the mammary glands of cows, ewes, used as a food. See sweet milk.

milk chocolate (melk CHOK-oh-laht). *USA.* Chocolate with sugar, milk, and vanilla added; used for candy, icings, pies, and puddings.

milk punch (melk punch). *USA.* Any of various low-proof alcoholic drinks of milk, sugar and liquor; streamlined versions of egg nog.

milk shake (melk shakah). *USA.* A drink of milk and ice cream, blended to a thick consistency.

mille-feuille (meel-fey). *Fre.* Puff pastry.

mille foglie. (MEEL-le FOL-yeh). *Ita.* Puff pastry.

millet (MEHL-eht). *USA.* Tiny, hulled grain, high in protein, may be cooked with rice or in place of rice; a staple food in many parts of the world.

milt (mihlt). *Dut.* Male fish sperm gland when filled; usually prepared like roe.

Milzwurst (MEELTZ-voorst). *Ger.* Bavarian veal sausage.

mimosa (meh-MOH-sah). *USA.* A garnish of finely chopped hard-boiled egg or egg yolk.

Mimosa (mie-MO-sah). *USA.* A brunch drink of champagne and orange juice.

mince (mincz). *USA.* To chop food into very small pieces; not as fine as grinding, but finer than chopping. See also chop, cube, and dice.

mince (mincz). *Bri.* Ground beef; hamburger.

mincemeat (MINCZ-meet). *Bri.* A finely chopped mixture of fresh or dried fruits, mainly apples, and raisins, spices, nuts, rum or brandy, and suet.

Mineralwasser (min-ner-RAAL-vah-sserr). *Ger.* Mineral water.

mineral water (MEHN-ruhl WAH-tehr). *USA.* Water with naturally occurring, or artificially impregnated, mineral salts or gases.

minestra (men-ah-STRA-ah). *Ita.* A thin soup served as the first course.

minestrone (mee-nah-STROH-nay). *Ita.* A thick, hearty vegetable soup in a meat broth with pasta; a meal in itself.

mint (meant). *USA.* An aromatic Mediterranean herb divided in two basic groups, spearmint, and peppermint, with diverse culinary uses for sauces, beverages, confections, vegetables, and flavoring liqueurs.

miqli (MEHC-lee). *Ara.* Fried.

Mirabeau (meer-ah-boa). *Fre.* A garnish for grilled meats of anchovy fillets, pitted olives, tarragon, and anchovy butter.

mirabelle (meer-ah-behl). *Fre.* A small, highly aromatic golden plum used in preserves, tarts, and a colorless fruit brandy.

mirchi (MEER-chee). *Ind.* Chili peppers.

mirepoix (meer-pwa). *Fre.* A mixture of diced vegetables, herbs and fat, for flavoring brown soups and sauces, also braised meats; similar to matignon, which is minced.

mirin (MEH-rehm). *Jap.* A sweet, syrupy, thin, golden-colored rice wine used for cooking, not drinking.

mirliton (MEER-lee-tohn). *USA.* Chayote.

miroton (mehr-rohl-tawng). *Fre.* A stew of meat and onions in brown gravy.

mise en place (meez on plas). *Fre.* "The preparation is ready up to the point of cooking."

mish mish (mesh mesh). *Ara.* Apricots.

mishwi (MASH-wee). *Ara.* Grilled.

miso (mee-SOH). *Jap.* Fermented soy bean paste used as a thickener for many soups, barbecue sauce, and in salad dressing; comes in two forms: mild white or pungent brick-red.

misoramen (mee-SOH-rah-mehn). *Jap.* A white curled noodle containing miso bean paste.

misoshiru (mee-SOH-shee-roo). *Jap.* Soup made with miso bean paste.

misticanza (mee-stee-CAHN-tsa). *Ita.* Mixed salad.

mistki (MEEST-kee). *Ara.* Arabic gum; used as emulsifiers and thickeners in certain processed foods such as ice cream, candy, commercial sauces; mustica.

misto (MEE-stoa). *Ita.* Mixed.

mithai (mit-HIE-ee). *Ind.* Sweets.

mitsuba (mee-TSOO-bah). *Jap.* Trefoil; a member of the parsley family; flavor between sorrel and celery; attractive light green color; used to add flavor and color accent; a type of clover.

miúdos (mee-OO-dahsh). *Por.* Giblets.

mix (mehx). *USA.* To combine two or more ingredients by stirring or blending.

mixed grill (mehxd grehl). *Bri.* Various grilled meats, such as beef steak, lamb chop, pork chop, and kidneys served with fried potatoes, grilled mushrooms, and tomatoes.

mizu (mee-zoo). *Jap.* Water.

mjölk (myurlk). *Swe.* Milk.

mjuka småfranska (MYU-ka SMO-FRAN-ska). *Swe.* Soft rolls.

Mjukost (MYEW-kah-oost). *Swe.* A soft, white, bland cheese.

mlabbas (mm-LAB-bahs). *Ara.* Sugar-coated almonds.

mlukhiyyi (mm-loo-HEEYE). *Ara.* Green leafy vegetables, similar to spinach. Also known as Jew's mallow.

mnaqish (mah-roh-QUEESH). *Ara.* Flat tarts.

mnazli (mm-NAH-zah-lee). *Ara.* Stew; refers to dishes made with eggplants or other vegetables as the basic ingredients.

mocha (MOH-kah). *USA.* A flavoring of coffee infused with cocoa or chocolate. Originally, a fine, superior Arabian coffee .

mochi (moh-CHEE). *Jap.* Sweet rice cakes.

mochi-gome (moh-CHEE goh-MEH). *Jap.* A special sticky glutinous rice used for certain dumplings, noodles, in red rice and sweet rice cakes.

mochiko (moh-chee-KO). *Jap.* A rice flour made from mochi-gome, used as thickening agent.

mochomos (moh-CHOH-mohs). *Mex.* Meat that has been cooked, shredded, then crisply fried.

mock duck (mahk duhk). *Iri.* A dish of pork tenderloin filled with poultry stuffing, chopped apple, and cooked under a topping of chopped onion and rashers of bacon.

moelle (mwahl). *Fre.* Beef marrow; used as a garnish or spread.

moh gwah (moh gua). *Chi.* The Chinese fuzzy melon; sweet-flavored with gray-green, fuzzy skin.

môhlo (MOHL-yoh). *Por.* Gravy; sauce.

môhlo de maças (MOHL-yoh der mas-ANSH). *Por.* Applesauce.

Mohn (mon). *Ger.* Poppyseed.

Mohnbrötchen (mon-BRURT-khern). *Ger.* Poppyseed rolls.

Mohnkipfel (MON-kip-ferl). *Ger.* Poppy-seed crescent rolls.

Mohrenköpfe (MOA-rern-kopf). *Ger.* Moors' heads; a genoise cake baked in a special half-round mold, then filled with chocolate pudding, then the halves joined together and covered with whipped cream.

Mohr Im Hemd (moar em hehmt). *Ger.* An Austrian dessert of chocolate pudding in whipped cream.

Mohrrüben (MOAR-rew-bern). *Ger.* Carrots.

moisten (MOY-sehn). *USA.* To add liquid.

moka (mauka). *Fre.* Mocha.

molako (mah-lah-KAH). *Rus.* Milk.

molasses (moh-LASS-esz). *USA.* The thick dark to light brown syrup remaining after sucrose crystallization.

mold (mohld). *USA.* To mix or knead into a required consistency or shape.

mole (MOH-leh). *Mex.* An elaborate sauce, made of various ingredients depending on the dish with which it is served.

moleas de vitela (MOH-lehss der vee-TEl-a). *Por.* Veal sweetbreads.

molecche (moh-LEHK-kee). *Ita.* Soft-shelled crabs.

mòli hua chá (MAW-lee hua tsah). *Chi.* Jasmine tea.

molinillo (moh-lee-NEE-yoh). *Mex.* Carved wooden beater used to make Mexican hot chocolate.

mollusc (moh-lysk). *Fre.* Mollusk.

mollusk (MAHL-uhsk). *USA.* Shellfish, such as clam, crab, lobster, oyster, shrimp, snail, or squid.

molto cotto (moal-toa KOT-toa). *Ita.* Cooked thoroughly; well done.

monégasque (moh-neh-gahsk). *Fre.* A salad of nonats, tomatoes, and rice.

monégasque, à la (moh-neh-gahsk, ah lah). *Fre.* In the style of Monaco; with tomatoes and rice.

mongo-ika (MOHN-goh ee-kah). *Jap.* Cuttlefish.

Mongolian hot pot (mohn-GOA-lee-uhn haht paht). *USA.* A Chinese one-dish meal composed of various pieces of seafood, poultry, and meat cooked individually in simmering stock and served with sauces; shuan yang rou.

monkey bread (MUHNC-key brehd). *USA.* A sweet bread made of separate pieces of bread dough randomly piled in a tube pan and baked. Nuts, currants, or cinnamon and sugar are sometimes added.

monkfish (MUHNCK-fish). *USA.* Goosefish, whose tailsection is firm white flesh similar in flavor to lobster; can be sauteed, baked, broiled, poached, or cut in fingers and deep fried. Also known as frogfish, sea devil, and angler.

monosodium glutamate (mow-noh-SOH-dee-uhm GLU-tah-mate). *USA.* MSG; a crystalline salt used as a taste intensifier and enhancer; widely used in Oriental cooking.

monstera (mon-STAIR-a). *USA.* Ceriman.

Montasio (mohn-TAH-zee-oa). *Ita.* A cows' whole-milk cheese that is firm and pale yellow with a smooth rind, has scattered holes and is made in large wheels. When young it is a good table cheese with a mild, nutty flavor; when old it is a good, pungent grating cheese.

Mont Blanc (mon blon). *Fre.* A classic dessert of chantilly creme and chestnut puree.

Monte Bianco (moan-teh bee-AWHN-ko). *Ita.* A classic dessert of chantilly creme, chestnut puree, chocolate, and rum.

monter (mohn-teh). *Fre.* To whip cream or egg whites to give volume.

monter au beurre (mohn-teh oa burr). *Fre.* To enrich a sauce with butter.

Monterey Jack (MOHN-tehr-ray Jahk). *USA.* A cow's whole-milk cheese that is pale, creamy and bland; the skimmed-milk version is harder and stronger.

montmorency (mo-mo-rahn-cee). *Fre.* Prepared with cherries.

montone (moan-TOA-nay). *Ita.* Mutton.

Montpensier (mo-pahn-cee-a). *Fre.* A garnish of sliced truffles, green asparagus tips, artichoke hearts, and Madeira sauce.

montreuil (mohn-hoia). *Fre.* With peaches.

Montreuil (MOHN-treall). *Ger.* Fish poached in white wine, served with large potato balls and shrimp sauce.

moolee (MO-lee). *Ind.* In coconut sauce.

moorkoppen (MOHR-kop-pen). *Dut.* Filled tarts with cream.

Moors' heads (muhrz hehdz). *USA.* A genoise cake batter baked in a special half-round mold, then filled and the halves joined.

moo shu zoh (moo shee zoh). *Chi.* A rolled pancake stuffed with shredded pork stir-fried with scallions, egg, and cloud ears.

moqua (MOH-gwah). *Chi.* Fuzzy melon.

morangos (moh-RAHN-gohss). *Por.* Strawberries.

mørbrad (MURR-braa). *Dan.* Pork tenderloin.

mørbradøf (MURR-braa-urf). *Dan.* Pork filet.

Morcheln (MOHR-chaund). *Ger.* Morels.

morcilla blanca (moar-THEE-lyah BLAHN-kah). *Spa.* A sausage made of chicken, bacon, hard-boiled eggs, and parsley.

morcilla negra (moar-THEE-lyah NAY-grah). *Spa.* A sausage made of pork, pig's blood, garlic, spices.

more (MO-ray). *Ita.* Blackberries.

morel (moh-RELL). *USA.* A wild mushroom with a honeycomblike cap that resembles a pine cone; creamy tan to brown to black; used either dried or cooked; has a nutty flavor.

morena (mohr-REE-nah). *Spa.* Brown bread.

Morgenrot (MOHR-gahn-roat). *Ger.* "Red Dawn"; a chicken broth soup with tomato puree and bits of chicken.

morille (mo-reey). *Fre.* Morel.

morkov (mahr-KOV). *Rus.* Carrots.

mörkt rågbröd (mohrkt ROG-brohd). *Swe.* Toast.

mornay (mohr-nay). *Fre.* Béchamel sauce with butter, grated Parmesan and Gruyère cheese, and egg yolk; a classic sauce.

morötter (MOO-ROH-terr). *Swe.* Carrots.

morozhense (mah-RO-zhi-nah-yeh). *Rus.* Ice cream.

mortadela (mohr-tah-DEH-lah). *Por.* Bologna.

mortadella (mohr-tah-DELL-lah). *Ita.* A sausage of ground pork with white cubes of fat, coriander, pistachio nuts, and wine.

morue (mo-rew). *Fre.* Salt cod.

moscada (mos-KAH-dah). *Spa.* Nutmeg.

Moscht (mohst). *Ger.* Swiss apple cider.

moskovitaeg (mo-SKO-vit-egg). *Dan.* Hard-boiled egg with mayonnaise.

mosselen (MAWS-suh-luh). *Dut.* Clams, mussels.

Most (must). *Ger.* Fruit juice or cider.

mostaccioli (mo-stash-chee OA-lee). *Ita.* Hollow, tubular pasta cut obliquely about 2½″ long.

mostard (MAWS-turt). *Dut.* Mustard.

mostarda (mohss TAHR dah). *Por.* Mustard.

mostarda di frutta (mohss-TAHR-dah dee FROOT-tah). *Ita.* A mustard-flavored syrup with various preserved fruits, eaten with bread or cold meat, like chutney.

mostaza (moas-TAH-thah). *Spa.* Mustard.

mosterd (MAWS-turt). *Dut.* Mustard.

moulange (moul-ahng). *Fre.* The act of molding, such as ice cream or butter.

moule (mool). *Fre.* Mussel. Also, a mold.

moules à l'Escargot (mool ah l'ehs-kahr-goa). *Fre.* A Belgian dish of mussels stuffed and prepared to look like snails.

mountain oyster (MAUNT-n ouy-stur). *USA.* Testicles of a bull, pig, or lamb, breaded and fried. Also called animelles, frivolitées, lamb fries, prairie oyster, Rocky Mountain oyster.

moussaka, mousaka (moo-SOCK-kah). *Gre.* A dish of eggplant, lamb, tomatoes, and white sauce.

mousse (moos). *Fre.* A sweet or savory dish lightened with beaten egg whites and frothy cream.

mousseline (moos-leen). *Fre.* A sauce, usually mayonnaise or hollandaise, or a dish with beaten egg whites or whipped cream folded in.

moutarde de Meaux (moo-tahrd der moa). *Fre.* Mustard from Meaux made with partly crushed seeds.

mouton (moo-ton). *Fre.* Mutton.

mowz (mokz). *Ara.* Banana.

moyashi (mo-YAH-shee). *Jap.* Bean sprouts from the tiny, olive-green mung bean.

Mozzarella (mots-ah-REHL-lah). *Ita.* A fresh, unsalted, white, moist cheese with a delicate flavor, eaten sliced or in baked dishes; rindless; sometimes smoked.

mqania (mm-AH-nec). *Ara.* Sausage.

mrabba (mm-RAHB-bah). *Ara.* Jam.

MSG (m-s-g). *USA.* Monosodium glutamate; a flavor enhancer.

muffin (MUFF-ehn). *Bri.* A flat yeast bread baked on a griddle.

muffin (MUFF-ehn). *USA.* A raised, quick bread made of various flours, with fruits or nuts, baked in a mold in an oven.

muhennettu (MOO-hayn-nayt-too). *Fin.* Stewed.

muhennos (MOO-hayn-noas). *Fin.* Stew.

muikku (MWEEK-koo). *Fin.* Tiny freshwater fish related to the salmon.

muisjes (MIRS-yus). *Dut.* Small anise-flavored sugar pellets eaten on a sandwich.

mulard (mew-lahrd). *Fre.* A hybrid duck bred for its meat and liver.

mulato (moo-LAH-toh). *Mex.* A large, brown, dried, pungent chili pepper.

mulberry (MUHL-behr-ree). *USA.* A purplish-black berry that resembles the raspberry in appearance, whose flavor is a cross between a raspberry and boysenberry, used as a fruit in salads, and in jams, jellies, preserves, and syrups.

mull (muhl). *USA.* To make a hot drink of cider, wine, or ale by heating and adding sugar and spices.

mullet (MULL-et). *USA.* The name of various fish found throughout the world, of which the red mullet found in the Mediterranean is the most highly prized, with the silver mullet of the Gulf and South Atlantic coasts of the United States also desirable.

Mulligan stew (MUHL-ee-gahn stu). *Iri.* A meat-vegetable stew thickened with okra. Also known as burgoo.

mullagatanni (mool-ah-sa-TAH-nee). *Ind.* Black pepper and broth; the origin of Mulligatawny soup.

mulligatawny (mul-ee-ga-TAW-nee). *USA.* A rich soup of chicken or lamb stock flavored with spices and curry, and served with rice, diced meat, lemon, and cream.

multer (MEWL-terr). *Nor.* Cloudberry.

mulukhiyya (moo-loo-KHEE-yah). *Ara.* Vegetable soup with rice and meat.

muna (MOO-nah). *Fin.* Egg; hyydytetyt munat (HEW-day-tay-tewt MOO-naht), poached egg; munakokkeli (MOO-nah-KOAK-kay-li), scrambled eggs; muna kova (MOO-nah KOA-vah), hard-boiled eggs; muna pehmeä (MOO-nah PAYH-mayea), soft-boiled eggs.

muna ja pekonia (MOO-nah yah PAY-roa-yah). *Fin.* Bacon and eggs.

munchies (MUHN-chees). *USA.* Any snack food such as popcorn, potato chips, pretzels, trail mix.

Munchner (MUENCH-nehrn). *Ger.* Designates the dark, malty beers found in Munich, Germany.

mung bean (muhng been). *Ind.* Various dried beans, rich in protein, and used at virtually every meal in Asia.

mung dal (muhng dahl). *Ind.* Split mung beans.

munk (mewngk). *Swe.* Doughnut.

munkar (MUNG-kar). *Swe.* Dumplings.

Munster (muhn-stur). *Fre.* A cows' whole-milk cheese that is round with a smooth orange rind, pale yellow soft interior with cracks, and a light salty flavor that gets tangy with age.

Murazzano (moo-rahz-ZAHN-noh). *Ita.* A cylindrical cheese with no rind and a dense white interior that ages to pale yellow, made mostly of ewes' milk.

Mürbeteig (MOOR-bay-tike). *Ger.* A rich, sweet egg tart dough; a tender paste for fresh fruit and nut-filled fillings.

Murcott orange (muhr-KOT oranj). *USA.* A hybrid orange resulting from an orange and tangerine cross.

mure (mewr). *Fre.* Blackberry or mulberry.

murgh (moorgh). *Ind.* Chicken.

Murol (mehr-hoyl). *Fre.* A wheel-shaped cows' milk hard cheese with a pinkish rind and a hole in the center.

muscadine (MUHS-kah-dine). *USA.* A white grape with a musky flavor used for raisins as well as table grapes.

muscat (muhs-kaht). *Fre.* A white or black grape with a musky flavor used for wine.

Muscheln (MU-sherln). *Ger.* Shellfish, such as scallops, clams, mussels.

muscoli (moos-KOA-lee). *Ita.* Mussel.

mush (muhsh). *USA.* A thick porridge made with cornmeal boiled in water or milk that when cooled can be sliced and fried.

mushimono (moo-SHEE-mo-no). *Jap.* Steamed food.

mushroom (MUHSH-room). *USA.* A complex fleshy fruiting body of an edible fungus that consists typically of a stem bearing a cap; countless varieties throughout the world; many are listed in this volume.

Muskatnuss (mus-KAHT-nuss). *Ger.* Nutmeg, mace.

muskmelon (MUHSK-mehl-un). *USA.* A sweet, musky-odored netted melon, also called cantaloupe and winter melon.

muslin bag (MUHS-lehn bahg). *USA.* A bag of loosely-woven muslin in which spices and herbs are tied, then placed in cooking liquids to impart flavors, then removed and discarded.

muslinger (MOOS-leen-gerr). *Dan.* Mussels.

mussel (MUHS-suhl). *USA.* A mollusk with a dark blue-black or light brown elongated shell, popular in Europe.

mussla (mewss-lah). *Swe.* Mussel, clam.

Must (moos). *Ger.* Juice of fruit, especially grapes, before and during fermentation.

mustaa kahvia (MOOS-tah KAHHH-viah). *Fin.* Black coffee.

mustard (MUHST-urd). *USA.* A seasoning made from powdered mustard seeds and a liquid blended into a paste.

mustard greens (MUHST-urd greens). *USA.* Green leafy vegetable for table use.

mustard seeds (MUHST-urd seeds). *USA.* Two basic varieties of the mustard family are dried for use as seasonings: white or yellow seeds that have a mild flavor, and dark brown or black seeds that have a pungent taste; used whole, crushed, ground and powdered.

mustawiy (MEHSS-tah-wee). *Ara.* Cooked well-done.

mustikka (MOOS-tik-kah). *Fin.* Blueberry.

mustikkakeitto (MOOS-tik-kah-KAYT-toa). *Fin.* Blueberry soup, a dessert.

mustikkapiiras (MOOS-tik-kah-PEE-rah-kah). *Fin.* Blueberry tart or pie.

mutton (MUTT-uhn). *USA.* The flesh of mature sheep, has rich flavor and is dark red in color.

muttonfish (MUTT-uhn-fisch). *USA.* One of the names for the ocean pout fish, whose flesh is sweet, white, and has few bones.

muy hecho (mwee AY-choa). *Spa.* Well-done, as referring to steak.

myaso (my-AH-ssah). *Rus.* Meat.

mylta med grädde (MUL-ta mah GRAHDE). *Swe.* Cloudberry compote with cream, a northern Swedish dessert.

myrtilles (meer-teey). *Fre.* Blueberries.

Mysost (MEWSS-oost). *Nor.* A firm, dense cows' milk cheese that is dark brown and sweet.

mystery meat (MYSS-tree meet). *USA.* A college-cafeteria term for any meat item covered with a sauce or gravy, rendering it unidentifiable.

N

naawr mai (noah mee). *Chi.* A special sticky, glutinous rice used for certain dumplings, noodles, and pastries.

naba (NAH-bah). *Spa.* Rutabaga.

nabos (NAH-bohss). *Spa, Por.* Turnips.

nacho (NAH-choh). *Mex.* Tortilla chips with melted cheese, topped with green chilies, chopped or sliced.

Nachspeise (NAAKH-shpigh-zer). *Ger.* Dessert.

naganegi (nah-GAH-nee-gee). *Jap.* Long onion, 14–16 inches long, of which only the white part is used.

nage (nahj). *Fre.* Cooked in a stock of white wine, carrots, onions, shallots, and herbs.

nagerechten (nawh-her-RES-ten). *Dut.* Desserts.

naiyóu báicài (nai-YOU-BAI-tsai). *Chi.* Chinese cabbage in cream sauce.

näkkileipää (NAEK-ki-LAY-pae). *Fin.* A hard, crisp bread.

namak (NAH-mak). *Ind.* Teardrop-shaped bread made with leavened dough and baked.

naméko (nah-MEE-koh). *Jap.* A tiny, delicate, slippery mushroom with a button top; usually canned; used in soups.

nam pla (nahm pla). *Thi.* Pungent salty fish sauce.

nam prik (nahm preek). *Thi.* Pungent salty fish sauce with chilies served hot as a dipping sauce.

nana (nah-NAH). *Ara.* Green mint leaves.

nantua sauce (nahn-tew saus). *Fre.* Béchamel sauce reduced with cream, beaten with crayfish butter, and garnished with crayfish tails.

Napfkuchen (napf-KOOK-hern). *Ger.* Light yeast cake with raisins.

Naples biscuit (NA-puls BEHS-keit). *USA.* A light dessert or tea biscuit, resembling a ladyfinger.

napoleon (nah-pohl-yuhn). *Fre.* A dessert of puff paste spread with pastry creme, stacked in layers, sometimes iced.

napoletana (nah-poa-lay-TAA-nah). *Ita.* Made meatless with tomatoes, garlic, onion, and olive oil.

napolitain (nah-po-lee-tahng). *Fre.* A genoise spread with jam, then spread with Italian meringue, then more jam.

napolitaine à la (nah-po-lee-tahn ah lah). *Fre.* Scallops of veal dipped in beaten eggs, then covered with breadcrumbs mixed with grated Parmesan, fried, and served with spaghetti, topped with tomato sauce sprinkled with Parmesan.

naranja (nah-RAHN-jah). *Spa.* Orange.

nargisi kofta (NEHR-geh-see KOF-tah). *Ind.* Meatballs stuffed with whole eggs, fried, cut in half to expose the egg, and simmered in onion gravy.

narial (NAH-ree-el). *Ind.* Coconut.

nasello (nah-SEHL-loa). *Ita.* Coalfish; a food fish related to whiting.

nashi (nah-SHEE). *Jap.* Pears; several varieties; applelike in shape and crispness, light yellow to brown in color, and a tart juiciness.

nasi goreng (NAH-see GOH-reng). *Dut.* An Indonesian dish of fried rice cooked with various spices and ingredients, including chicken, shrimp, meat, onions, garlic, shrimp paste, chilies.

nasturtium (nahs-TUHR-shuhm). *USA.* An herb whose blossoms and leaves have a peppery flavor that enhances salads and sandwiches. Its seeds can be pickled and are much like capers.

nasu (NAH-soo). *Jap.* Eggplant.

natillas (nah-TEE-yah). *Spa.* A soft runny custard made from ewes' milk, sweetened and flavored with cinnamon and lemon.

nattmat (NAHT-awt). *Swe.* "Night food"; offered just before a party breaks up.

natur (nah-TOOR). *Ger.* Plain, simple, ungarnished.

naturale (nah-too-RAHL). *Ita.* Plain, simple, ungarnished.

naturel (nah-tewr-erl). *Fre.* Plain, simple; plainly and simply prepared.

Naturschnitzel (nah-TOOR-schneet-zehl). *Ger.* Unbreaded veal cutlet.

naudanliha (NAH-oo-dahn-LI-haa). *Fin.* Beef.

nauris (NAH-oo-riss). *Fin.* Turnip.

naval orange (NA-vahl oranj). *USA.* A thick-skinned, seedless orange with easy-to-peel rind, and a navallike protrusion on the blossom end; a good table fruit.

navarin (nah-veh-rahng). *Fre.* A stew of turnips with lamb or mutton, onions, and potatoes.

navet (nah-veh). *Fre.* Turnip.

navy bean (NAH-ve bean). *USA.* A small, white, common bean used dried in such dishes as navy bean soup, Boston baked beans, cassoulet.

nayyi (nah-HEE). *Ara.* Raw, in reference to food.

neapolitan ice cream (nee-oh-POHL-ee-tuhn ics krehm). *USA.* Chocolate, vanilla, and strawberry ice cream layered in a mold to display the ribbon of three flavors.

nectarine (NEHK-ter-reen). *USA.* Actually a peach with smooth, slick skin, and flavor that is a cross between peach and plum.

neeps (nehps). *Sco.* Turnips.

négi (NAH-gee). *Jap.* Scallion, onion, leek.

négresse (nay-grehss). *Fre.* Chocolate mousse topped by whipped cream.

negrítas (nay-GREE-tahs). *Spa.* Chocolate mousse topped by whipped cream.

negus (nee-GAHS). *Ara.* A warm wine punch with lemon, spices, and sweetened with sugar.

neige (nehzh). *Fre.* Snow; white of eggs beaten to a froth or snow.

nepaul pepper (NAH-paul PEHP-pehr). *USA.* A red pepper of the same characteristic as cayenne; has a sweet pungent flavor.

neslesuppe (nehs-leh-SEWP-peh). *Nor.* Nettle soup; tastes like spinach soup.

nesselrode (nehs-sehl-ROHD). *USA.* A frozen custard pudding, topped with whipped cream, flavored with chestnut puree mixed with candied fruits.

nettles (NET-teul). *Irl.* A coarse herb with stinging hairs; when picked young and cooked, the nettles have no sting; similar to spinach in taste.

Neufchâtel (neu-cho-tel). *Fre.* A soft, uncooked, cows' milk cheese similar to cream cheese, but containing less fat and more moisture.

New Bedford pudding (neu BEHD-fohrd PUHD-deng). *USA.* A pudding made from cornmeal, flour, eggs and flavored with molasses.

Newburg (NEU-berg). *USA.* A thick cream sauce with egg yolk and sherry in which lobster, shrimp, or various seafoods are served.

New England boiled dinner (neu EHNG-land boild DEN-nehr). *USA.* A one-dish dinner with corned beef, cabbage, potatoes, carrots and other vegetables cooked together and served with horseradish or mustard. Chicken sometimes replaces the corned beef.

New England clambake (neu EHNG-land KLAM-bak). *USA.* See clambake.

New Zealand spinach (neu ZEE-lund SPEHN-nehch). *USA.* A vegetable with a mellow taste when cooked and a flavor similar to garden grass with a tang when raw; leaves are dark green with slight fuzz; best when cooked, but add raw to salads.

ng heung fun (ng hung fon). *Chi.* Five-spice seasoning; the Cantonese name for the blend of ground cloves, fennel, licorice root, cinnamon, and star anise.

niboski (nee-BO-shee). *Jap.* Dried sardines for making stock.

niçoise (knee-qwau). *Fre.* Chopped tomatoes sauteed in olive oil with garlic, capers, anchovies, black olives, sliced lemon.

nierbroodje (NEER-broht-yuh). *Dut.* Kidney patty.

nievwe haring (NEW-ah HAHR-reng). *Dut.* Fresh herring.

nigauri (nee-GOHW-oo-lee). *Jap.* Chinese bitter melon; balsam pear.

nigiri zushi (nee-GEE-lei zoo-she). *Jap.* A type of sushi that consists of rice balls topped with various ingredients such as fish or shrimp.

niku (NEE-koo). *Jap.* Meat.

nimboo (NIM-boo). *Ind.* Lime, limon.

nimono (nee-MOH-noh). *Jap.* Simmered or braised food.

ninaa (ni-NEH). *Ara.* Mint; an important seasoning in Middle Eastern cookery.

ningméng (ning meng). *Chi.* Lemon.

ninjin (NEEN-jeen). *Jap.* Carrot.

nioi (nee-O-ee). *USA.* A Hawaiian seasoning made with chili peppers, water, and salt, used in various dishes.

Niren (NEE-rern). *Ger.* Kidneys.

niú ròu (niu row). *Chi.* Beef.

njure (NYEW-rer). *Swe.* Kidney.

nkhaat (nn-HAH-aht). *Ara.* Lamb or beef brains.

nocchette (noh-KOYT-teh). *Ita.* Small bow tie pasta used in soups.

nocciole (noat-CHO-lay). *Ita.* Hazelnut.

noccioline Americane (noat-CHO-leen ah-mahr-EE-cahn). *Ita.* Peanuts.

noce moscata (NOA-chay moa-SKAA-tah). *Ita.* Nutmeg.

noci (NOA-chee). *Ita.* Walnuts.

Nock (nokh). *Ger.* Dumpling.

Nockerl (NOKH-rehl). *Ger.* Dumplings.

nødder (NURDH-err). *Dan.* Nuts.

Noeuds de Bruges (nuh day broogz). *Fre.* "Bruges Knots," a delicious, fragile Belgian pastry.

noga (NOH-hah). *Dut.* Nougat.

nogada (noh-GAH-dah). *Mex.* Walnut sauce; usually served with poblano chilies stuffed with shredded pork and garnished with pomegranate seeds.

noisette (nooa-zet). *Fre.* Hazelnut; also a cut of meat from the rib of a lamb, trimmed, rolled, tied in a small round shaped like a hazelnut (about ½″ in diameter), and served as an individual portion.

noisette potatoes (nooa-ZET poh-TA-tohz). *USA.* Potatoes shaped like hazelnuts and browned in butter; the American version of pommes noisette.

noix (nwah). *Fre.* Walnut.

noix de coco (nwah day ko-koa). *Fre.* Coconut.

noix de veau (nwah day voa). *Fre.* Cut of veal from the tenderloin.

noix muscade (nwah mew-skahd). *Fre.* Nutmeg.

Nøkkelost (NUR-ker-loost). *Nor.* A hard cheese based on the Dutch Leyden and similarly flavored with caraway and cumin.

nonat (no-naht). *Fre.* A very small Mediterranean fish, usually deep-fried.

nondairy creamer (nohn-DAHR-ree KREEM-mehr). *USA.* A manufactured creamer containing no milk or cream, usually using palm or coconut oil instead.

nonfat milk (nohn-faht melk). *USA.* Cows' milk containing less than ½% milkfat. Also called skim milk.

nonpareille (nuhn-pah-reel). *Fre.* A small flat disk of chocolate covered with white sugar pellets. Also small sugar pellets of various colors.

noodles (NOO-dlehs). *USA.* A type of pasta, long, flat like a ribbon, and of varying widths and thicknesses.

nopale (no-PAHL). *Mex.* The fleshy oval parts of a cactus, eaten with scrambled eggs or in salad.

nopalitos (no-pah-LEE-toes). *Mex.* Cactus leaves used in salads.

noques (noa-chee). *Fre.* Gnocchi.

noques (nohks). *Fre.* A light, sweet Austrian dessert of egg-shaped meringues, poached in milk, and served in a custard sauce. Also known as Snow Eggs.

noquis (NOA-kee). *Spa.* Gnocchi.

nori (NOH-ree). *Jap.* A seaweed; thin, black sheets of sea lettuce, used lightly toasted as a cracker, as a wrapper for sushi, or crumbled over rice and noodle dishes.

norimaki zushi (noh-ree-MAH-kee ZHU-shee). *Jap.* A type of sushi that consists of rice and an assortment of colorful ingredients rolled pinwheel fashion inside a wrapping such as a sheet of nori seaweed or a sheet of cooked egg.

normande (nor-muhnd). *Fre.* A classic sauce of fish veloute with oyster liquor, mushrooms, egg yolks, cream and butter; with oysters, mussels, shrimp, mushroom caps, and truffles added, it becomes a classic garnish.

Normande, à la (nor-muhnd). *Fre.* Implies that the flavor of apple has been introduced into the dish.

norvégienne (nor-vayzh-yehn). *Fre.* A sauce of mashed hard-boiled eggs, seasoned with vinegar and mustard and beaten with oil into a thick sauce.

Norway haddock (NOHR-way HAHD-duhk). *USA.* One of the names for ocean perch.

Norway lobster (NOHR-way LOHB-stuhr). *USA.* A saltwater crayfish.

nostrano (noh-STRAH-noh). *Ita.* Homegrown.

noten (NO-tuh). *Dut.* Nuts.

nötkött (NOHT-chot). *Swe.* Beef.

nøtteterte (NURT-teh-tehr-teh). *Nor.* Nut layer cake.

nougat (noo-gah). *Fre.* A confection made of roasted nuts, usually almonds, and honey or syrup.

nougatine (noo-gah-teen). *Fre.* Can be any of several confections such as almond brittle or nougat combined with chocolate; a vague term.

nouilles (noo-yuh). *Fre.* Noodles.

nova (NOH-veh). *USA.* Cold-smoked salmon, eaten like lox with cream cheese and bagels.

nouvelle cuisine (noo-vehl-lee koo-szeen). *Fre.* The movement toward fresher, lighter foods, served in smaller portions; prepared by classic French techniques.

noyau (nwah-yoh). *Fre.* The stone of a fruit; a liqueur flavored with peach or nectarine kernels.

noz (nosh). *Por.* Walnut.

Nudeln (NOO-derln). *Ger.* Noodles of a stiff paste made with flour and eggs, rolled out very thin, cut up in thin strips and boiled, and served as a garnish, or fried and served as a sweet.

Nudelschöberl (NOO-derl-shor-berl). *Ger.* Austrian noodle pie, usually served with meat.

nudlar (nood-lahr). *Swe.* Dumplings.

nuez (new-ez). *Spa.* Walnut or nut.

nuka (noo-KAH). *Jap.* Rice bran; one of the basic pickling media in Japan.

nun's toast (nuhnz tohst). *USA.* Hard-boiled eggs with milk gravy, served over toast.

nuò mi zóngzi (nuo mee DZONG-dze). *Chi.* A dish of lotus leaves stuffed with sweet rice and meat.

Nur Hier (noor heer). *Ger.* "Only Here"; a solid, black bread sold only in Hamburg.

Nuss (NEW-sser). *Ger.* Nut, walnut.

nut meal (nuht meel). *USA.* Finely ground dry nuts used as a flour substitute in many Torten.

nutmeg (NUHT-mehg). *USA.* The dried seed found inside the tropical fruit of the nutmeg tree, which is ground and used to flavor a wide range of sweet and savory dishes.

nuts (nuhtz). *USA.* A generic term referring to the edible nut of a given tree. Varieties listed in this volume are: almonds, Brazil nuts, filberts (hazelnuts), peanuts, pecans, pistachios, walnuts.

nymphes à l'aurore (nehf ay l'ohr-ohr). *Fre.* A beautiful, shimmery dish; frog legs poached in white wine, covered with pink chaud-froid sauce, garnished with chopped aspic.

nypon (NEW-poan). *Swe.* Rose hips; used in jellies, soups.

nyponsoppa (NU-pon-SOHP-pa). *Swe.* Rose-hip soup.

nyrer (NEW-rerr). *Dan, Nor.* Kidney.

nyrøket laks (NEW-rurkt lahks). *Nor.* Smoked salmon.

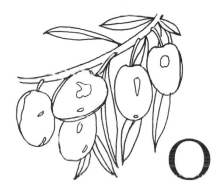

oatmeal (OUHT-meel). *USA.* Coarse ground oats, used in baking or as hot cereal.

oats, rolled (ouhts, rold). *USA.* Hulled oats ground to a meal, steamed to gelatinize starch, rolled into flakes, then dried, allowing much shorter cooking time.

oboro konbu (o-BOL-o KOHM-boo). *Jap.* A form of konbu which is soaked in vinegar and shaved the width of the leaf to form a thin sheet.

O'Brien (oh-BRYN). *USA.* A garnish of sautéed bacon, onions, red and green peppers usually served over a potato dish.

Obst (oapst). *Ger.* Fruit.

Obstsauce (OAPST-saus). *Ger.* A sweet-sour fruit sauce made to accompany roasted meats.

Obstsuppe (OAPST-zup-per). *Ger.* Soup of pureed fruits.

Obsttorte (OAPST-tor-ter). *Ger.* An open fruit tart, glazed and usually garnished with whipped cream or meringue and almonds.

oca (OH-kah). *Ita.* Goose.

ocha (oh-CHAH). *Jap.* Green tea.

Ochs (ahks). *Ger.* Ox, beef; rindfleisch.

Ochsenbraten (AHK-sern-braa-tern). *Ger.* Roast beef.

Ochsenlende (AHK-sern-lehn-dern). *Ger.* Beef filet.

Ochsenmausalat (AHK-sern-maw-zah-laa-ter). *Ger.* Salad of cold beef, onions, vinegar.

Ochsenniere (AHK-sern-neer). *Ger.* Beef kidney.

Ochsenschwanz (AHK-sern-shvnz). *Ger.* Oxtail.

Ochsenzunge (AHK-sern-tsun-ger). *Ger.* Ox tongue.

octopus (OHK-tah-pus). *USA.* A sea mollusk of flavorful but tough meat, often smoked, stewed or marinated; used mainly by Oriental and Mediterranean cultures.

oeil d'anchois (uhy d'on-shwah). *Fre.* An hors d'oeuvre of raw egg yolk surrounded by anchovies and chopped onion; literally "eye of anchovy."

oester (OOS-turs). *Dut.* Oyster.

oeufs (uhfs). *Fre.* Eggs; oeufs à la coque mollet (uhfs ah lah kok mol-leh), soft-boiled eggs; oeufs à la coque (uhfs ah lah kok), boiled eggs; oeufs au plat (uhfs oa plah), fried eggs; oeufs brouillés (uhfs broo-yay), scrambled eggs; oeufs bûcheronee (uhfs boo-cher-rohn), beaten eggs poured over slices of ham on toast and baked; oeufs chasser (uhfs shah-ser), scrambled eggs with chicken livers; oeufs durs (uhfs dewrz), hard-boiled eggs; oeufs en cocotte (uhfs uhng koh-koht), eggs poached in a casserole; oeufs farcis (uhfs fahr-see), stuffed eggs; oeufs frits (uhfs free), fried eggs; oeufs en gelée (uhfs uhng zhel-ah), eggs poached and chilled in aspic; oeufs justine (uhfs zjos-steen), hard-cooked eggs stuffed with mushrooms in cream sauce, coated with breadcrumbs and fried in butter; oeufs pochés (uhfs poh-shay), poached eggs; oeufs pochés bénédictine (uhfs poh-shay bay-nay-dehk-teen), eggs poached and served on a creamed salt-cod base (not Eggs Benedict); oeufs poêles (uhfs pwahl), eggs sunny-side up; oeufs rossini (uhfs roh-zee-nee), egg yolks baked on a meringue of whites; oeufs sur le plat (uhfs syr ler pla), baked eggs.

oeufs à la neige (uhfs ah lah nehzh). *Fre.* Snow eggs, which are egg-shaped meringues, poached in sweetened milk, drained, and served with a custard sauce.

offal (OWF-fuhl). *USA.* Internal organs or trimmings removed from the skeletal meat, such as brains, heart, sweetbreads, liver, kidneys, pancreas, spleen, tripe, tongue, headmeat, tail, blood, skin, feet, horns, intestines; carrion; can mean inedible waste.

ofentori (oh-fehn-TOH-ree). *Ita.* A Swiss dish of mashed potatoes flecked with diced bacon.

Ohio pudding (oh-HI-oh PUHD-deng). *USA.* Mashed sweet potatoes, carrots, and squash mixed with brown sugar, bread crumbs, and light cream, baked until firm; served with sauce of butter, confectioner's sugar, cream, and lemon juice.

ohraryynipuuro (oah-rah-rew-nee-POO-roa). *Fin.* Thick barley porridge eaten with cream and sugar.

oie (wah). *Fre.* Goose.

oie à l'instar de Visé (wah a'lehn-stahr day veh-say). *Fre.* A Belgian speciality of roast goose in a rich cream and garlic sauce; a gastronomic triumph of Visé.

oignon (ohn-nawng). *Fre.* Onion.

oignon cloute (ohn-nawng kloo-teh). *Fre.* Onion studded with cloves.

oiseau (wah-zoh) *Fre.* Bird.

oiseaux sans tête (wah-zoh seh teht). *Fre.* Meat birds; meat scallops stuffed, rolled, and cooked.

oison (wah-zyoh). *Fre.* Gosling.

okara (o-KAH-lah). *Jap.* Soybean pulp that is the by-product of tofu-making; crumbly, white, high in protein; provides bulk and roughage; use with vegetables, in salads, and soups.

okayu (o-KAI-yoo). *Jap.* Rice gruel.

okra (OH-kra). *USA.* A tropical plant from Africa whose seed pods are used as a vegetable or as a thickener for gumbos and soups.

oksebryst (OAKS-er-stayg). *Dan.* Beef brisket.

oksefilet (OAKSS-er-fil-lay). *Nor.* Filet of beef.

oksekødsuppe (OAKS-er-kurdh-soob-ber). *Dan.* Beef soup.

oksesteg (OAKS-er-stayg). *Dan.* Roast beef.

oksestek (OAKSS-ers-stayk) *Nor.* Roast beef.

oksetunge (OK-seh-toong-eh). *Dan.* Beef tongue.

Öl (url). *Ger.* Oil.

öl (url). *Swe.* Beer.

øl (url). *Dan, Nor.* Beer.

olie (O-lee). *Dan, Dut.* Oil.

oliebollen (O-lee-bawl-luh). *Dut.* Doughnuts, usually filled with currants and raisins.

olijfolie (oh-LIF-oh-lee). *Dut.* Olive oil.

olijven (oh-LIV-vahn). *Dut.* Olives.

olio (OL-yoa). *Ita.* Oil.

Oliven (o-LEE-veh). *Ger.* Olives.

olive oil (AHL-leev oul). *USA.* Important cooking oil pressed from olives; basic oil in Italian cooking. Most common grades are: **Extra virgin:** first cold press from superior quality olives; contains no cholesterol; less than 1% acidity; light, delicate taste; clear greenish color. **Superfine virgin:** second cold press from superior quality olives; less than 1.5% acidity; clear greenish color. **Virgin:** third cold press from olives of superior quality; contains no cholesterol; 1-3% acidity; light taste. **Refined:** has higher acidity; limpid yellow color; contains no cholesterol. **100% pure:** pressed from blended olive varieties; a mixture of refined and 5–10% virgin; contains no cholesterol. **Pomace** (POH-muhs): a hot press after the third press, higher acidity, stronger flavor. **Sansa** (SAHUN-zah): a low grade oil; hot pressed, high acidity, very strong flavor.

oliver (oo-Ll-ver). *Swe.* Olives.

olives (o-LEE-vay). *Ita.* The fruit of the olive tree; used brined or preserved in oil.

olives (AHL-leevez). *USA, Bri.* The fruit of the olive tree, used brined or preserved in oil. Also meat birds; a small slice of meat wrapped around a savory filling.

Olivet (oh-lee-veh). *Fre.* A cows' milk cheese similar to Camembert, eaten fresh.

Olivet Bleu (oh-lee-veh bluhr). *Fre.* Olivet cheese matured for a month, having a delicate blue rind.

olivette (oh-lee-vay). *Fre.* Refers to food cut oblong shaped and about ⅜ inch in diameter.

olivette di vitello (oh-LEE-veh dee vee-TEHL-loa). *Ita.* Veal birds; veal scallops stuffed, rolled, and braised.

olivetti (oh-lee-VEE-tee). *Ita.* Meat birds.

olja (OL-yah). *Swe.* Oil.

olla Gitana (ohl-lah jee-TAH -nah). *Spa.* An all-vegetable, no meat stew; gypsy stew.

olla podrida (ohl-lah poh-DREE-dah). *Spa.* A stew of different meats, mainly pork, and cabbage, chick-peas, tomatoes.

øllebrød (URL-er-brurdh). *Dan.* Soup made with black bread and nonalcoholic malt beer.

olut (OA-loot). *Fin.* Beer.

omenalumi (OH-meh-na-LOO-mee). *Fin.* Apple-snow dessert.

omelet (OUM-let). *USA.* Beaten eggs cooked in butter in an omelet pan until set; usually filled with a wide variety of seasonings and fillings; can be savory or sweet.

omelette (oum-let). *Fre.* Omelet.

omelette à la norvégienne (oum-let ah lah nor-vay-zhyehn). *Fre.* Baked Alaska.

omena (OA-may-nah). *Fin.* Apple.

omenasose (OA-may-nah-SOA-ssay). *Fin.* Applesauce.

omuretsu (oh-MOO-reh-tsoo). *Jap.* Omelet.

onion (UN-yun). *USA.* The generic name for the edible bulbs of the lily family; numerous varieties worldwide. See under specific name.

onion rings (UN-yun rengs). *USA.* Slices of large onions, separated into rings, dipped in batter, and deep fried.

ontbijtkoek (awnt-BAY-tuh-kook). *Dut.* A breakfast spice cake.

oolong (OO-lohng). *Chi.* An amber-colored, partially fermented tea.

operatärta (OO-peh-ra-TOR-ra). *Swe.* Creamy layer cake.

opgerolde koek (oh-per-ROLD kook). *Dut.* Rolled-up cake.

orange (AWH-rehnj). *USA.* The globular fruit of the orange tree; peel is a bright orange; pulp is segmented, juicy, sweet, slightly acidic.

orange flower water (AWH-rehnj flawr wah-tuhr). *USA.* Liquid distilled during the extraction of essential oil from bitter orange blossoms and used as a flavoring; principal flavoring extract of the Middle East.

orange pekoe (AWH-rehnj PEE-koh). *USA.* A superior grade of tea from India or Ceylon with leaves slightly larger than pekoe.

orange roughy (AWH-rehnj RUFF-fee). *USA.* A fish of the South Pacific found in New Zealand waters; has firm white flesh and a bland taste; is sold in fillets and can be baked, broiled, pan-fried, or poached.

orange sauce (awh-rehnj saus). *Fre.* Demi-glace with orange, and sometimes lemon, juice and julienne orange zest.

orata (oa-RAA-tah). *Ita.* Large, fine fish found along the Riviera.

oregano (oh-REG-gun-oh). *USA.* An herb similar to marjoram, more pungent; wild marjoram; popular in Italian cookery.

Oregon grapes (OHR-ree-gohn grapz). *USA.* Barberries.

oreilles (oh-rehy). *Fre.* Ears of slaughtered animals.

organic (oar-GAHN-iek). *USA.* Anything grown without artificial or chemical fertilizers or pesticides.

orge (orj). *Fre.* Barley.

orientale (o-ryon-tahl). *Fre.* Seasoned with curry or saffron, and sometimes garnished with rice-stuffed tomatoes.

Oriental garlic (ORE-ee-en-tahl GAR-lick). *USA.* An exotic name for common garlic.

origan (ko-ree-gahng). *Fre.* Oregano.

origano (oa-REE-gahg-noa). *Ita.* Oregano.

orly (ohr-lee). *Fre.* A dish of sliced fish or meat dipped in a rich batter and fried in fat. Also horly.

ormer (OHR-mehr). *Bri.* Abalone.

orre (O-rrer). *Swe.* Black grouse.

ørred (URR-erdh). *Dan.* Trout.

ørret (URR-eht). *Nor.* Trout.

ortolan (ort-o-lahng). *Fre.* A small, nearly extinct bird, prized for its flavor; it is plucked, usually boned, but not drawn, as its entrails are considered delicious.

oscietr (ahs-syee-TREE). *Rus.* Roe of the white sturgeon, the world's very best caviar.

oseille (oh-zehj). *Fre.* Sorrel.

ossenhaas (AWS-suh-hahs). *Dut.* Filet of beef.

ossestaartsoep (OS-ses-staht soup). *Dut.* Oxtail soup.

osso bucco (O-so BOO-ko). *Ita.* Veal shank or shin bones slowly braised with carrots, tomatoes, onions, celery, garlic, white wine, stock, and garnished with a mixture of chopped parsley, garlic, and grated lemon zest called gremolada.

ost (oost). *Swe, Nor, Dan.* Cheese.

østers (URSS-tersh). *Dan, Nor.* Oysters.

ostkaka (OOST-kaw-kah). *Swe.* Puddinglike cheesecake that is baked in a mold.

ostras (OS-trahss). *Spa, Por.* Oysters.

òstriche (O-stree-kay). *Ita.* Oysters.

ostron (OOST-ron). *Swe.* Oyster.

ostronläda (OOST-ron-LOA-dah). *Swe.* Escalloped oysters.

ou (oh). *Chi.* Lotus root.

ouaouaron (ooah-ooah-RROWN). *USA.* Cajun word for frog.

ouzo (OO-zo). *Gre.* A sweet anise-flavored liqueur.

ovenfry (UH-vehn-fri). *USA.* A method of cooking meats by dredging in seasoned flour, rolling in melted fat, placing on sheet pans and baking in a hot oven; results in browning without turning.

ovoli (oa-VAWL-lee). *Ita.* A highly prized mushroom that resembles an egg; has a bright orange cap; eaten raw as a salad.

ovos (AH-vohss). *Por.* Eggs; ovos cozidos (AH-vohss koh-ZEE-dohss), hard-boiled eggs; ovos estrelados (AH-vohss ess-tray-LAH-dohss), fried eggs; ovos mexidos (AH-vohss meh-SHEE-dohss), scrambled eggs; ovos pochê (AH-vohss poh-SHAY), poached eggs; ovos quentes (AH-vohss KEN-tayss), soft-boiled eggs.

ovos moles (AH-vohss MOH-layss). *Por.* Egg yolks mixed with sugar, and used as a sauce or filling; or can be molded, cooked in rice water, and sprinkled with cinnamon.

ox (ooks). *Swe.* Beef.

oxbringa (OOKS-bringah). *Swe.* Beef brisket.

oxfilé (OOKS-fil-lay). *Swe.* Beef filet.

Oxford pudding (OOKS-ford puhd-deng). *Bri.* Apricot tart masked with meringue.

Oxford sauce (OOKS-ford saus). *Bri.* Red currant jelly dissolved with port, flavored with shallots, orange zest and mustard; an accompaniment for game.

oxidation (OOKS-ee-da-shun). *USA.* Exposure to oxygen, generally causing a darkening of the product, as well as a deterioration of freshness.

oxkött (OOKS-tyurt). *Swe.* Beef.

oxrulader (OOKS-roo-la-der). *Swe.* Piquant rolled beef.

oxstek (OOKS-stayk). *Swe.* Roast beef.

oxsvanssoppa (OOKS-svans-SO-pa). *Swe.* Oxtail soup.

oxtail (OOKS-tahl). *Bri.* Tail of beef; excellent in soups and stews because of high percentage of gelatin.

oxtunga (OOKS-toong-er). *Swe.* Beef tongue.

oyster (OEHY-stur). *USA.* A bivalve mollusk with a rough, irregular shaped shell; eaten raw or prepared in numerous ways: stews, dressings, soups, baked, fried, sautéed.

oyster crab (OEHY-stur krahb). *USA.* A tiny, ½ inch crispy, pink crab found living in the shell of a live oyster; may be eaten raw, sautéed, or deep-fried.

oyster mushroom (OEHY-stur mush-rohm). *USA.* Has oyster-shell shape; is grey-brown with a delicate flavor and texture; tastes peppery when raw; use with veal, chicken, pork chops, hamburger or steak; also use in omelets and stews.

oyster plant (OEHY-stur plahnt). *USA.* Salsify

oyster sauce (OEHY-stur saus) USA. A thick paste consisting of oysters, salt, and seasonings; li jiang.

Oysters Bienville (OEHY-stur bee-en-vell). *USA.* Oysters with béchamel sauce of green peppers, onions, cheese, and bread crumbs; originated in New Orleans.

Oysters Rockefeller (OEHY-sturs ROK-ee-fehl-lehr). *USA.* Oysters on the half shell, resting on a bed of rock salt, each topped with pureed seasoned spinach, then quickly browned.

paalaeg (poh-LAYGH). *Dan.* "Something laid on"; that which is put on buttered bread, such as cold meats or salads, to make open-face sandwiches.

paan (pahn). *Ind.* Betel leaves, used as a vegetable by stuffing with spices and nuts; used as a digestive agent.

paani (PAH-nee). *Ind.* Water.

paaskebryg (poah-skeh-BREHRG). *Dan.* A high alcoholic content dark beer.

pachadi (PAH-cha-ree). *Ind.* Vegetables and yogurt flavored with mustard seeds.

paella (pah-AY-lyah). *Spa.* A rice dish cooked with a variety of meats, sausage, shellfish, game; assorted vegetables including peas and tomatoes; flavored with garlic, onions, and saffron; exact ingredients vary widely.

pære (PAER-err). *Dan.* Pear.

pagello (PAH-jahl-loa). *Ita.* Red snapper.

paglia e fieno (PAL-ya ee FYE-noh). *Ita.* "Straw and hay" fettucine; half green, made with spinach, and half white, made with egg only; served simply with melted butter and Parmesan cheese, or sometimes with reduced cream and Parmesan.

pähkinäkakku (PAEH-kin-nae-KAHK-koo). *Fin.* A very rich cake made with ground walnuts, served covered with whipped cream.

pähkinäpaisti (PAEH-kin-nae-PAH-sti). *Fin.* A meatless meaty-tasting patty made of ground nuts and rice.

paillarde de veau (pahy-lahrd der voa). *Fre.* Grilled veal scallop.

paillettes (pahy-leht). *Fre.* Pastry straws; can also be potatoes cut in very thin strawlike shreds.

pain (pang). *Fre.* Bread, loaf.

pain à la Greque (pang ah lah grehs). *Fre.* Belgian-Greek bread; rich little cakes.

pain à l'anglaise (pang ah l'ahng-glehz). *Fre.* Bread sauce, a sauce of milk thickened with bread crumbs.

pain bis (pang beez). *Fre.* Brown bread.

pain complet (pang kohm-pleh). *Fre.* Whole grain bread.

pain de Genes (pang day zheh-nehz). *Fre.* Genoa cake, a rich almond pound cake.

pain de mie (pang day my). *Fre.* Sandwich bread.

pain d'epice (pang d'eh-spehs). *Fre.* Gingerbread.

pain de seigle (pang day sehgl). *Fre.* Rye bread.

pain de veau (pang day vooh). *Fre.* Belgian veal loaf.

pain fourré (pang foo-reh). *Fre.* Small rolls, filled like sandwiches.

pain grillé (pang grehj). *Fre.* Toast.

pain mollet (pang moh-leh). *Fre.* Soft bread.

pain noir (pang nwahr). *Fre.* Black bread made of rye, wheat, and buckwheat.

pain perdu (pang per-dru). *Fre.* French toast as made in France from stale bread, usually sweetened, with cinnamon added.

pain tôti (pang toa-tee). *Fre.* Toast.

pain trouvé (pang truh-veh). *Fre.* "Found Bread"; A Belgian dish of French toast topped with béchamel sauce, chopped ham, and Parmesan cheese.

paio (pah-EE-oo). *Por.* Meaty garlic sausage.

paistettu kana (PAHS-stayt-too KAH-nah). *Fin.* Fried chicken.

paisteutut sienet (PYE-steh-toot SEE-yen-ett). *Fin.* Fried mushrooms.

paistinperunat (PAHS-steern-pay-roo-naht). *Fin.* Fried potatoes.

paj (pay). *Swe.* Pie.

pakode (pah-KOOH-ray). *Ind.* Fritters.

pakoras (pah-KOOH-rayz). *Ind.* A spicy fritter, served hot as an appetizer or snack.

palacsinta (POL-lo-cheen-to). *Hun.* Crepe.

palak (PAH-lek). *Ind.* Spinach.

palatte knife (PAHL-laht knif). *USA.* A wide, flexible spatula used for spreading butter or icing.

Palatschinke (pah-lah-TSHIN-kern). *Ger.* Pancakes with sweet or savory fillings.

pale (pael). *Nor.* A young, very bony fish of the cod family.

paleron de boeuf (pah-ler-ron der burf). *Fre.* Marinated chuck roast.

paling (PAH-ling). *Dut.* Eel.

palm (pahlm). *USA.* A large family of tropical trees and shrubs; many of its parts are edible.

palm butter (pahlm BUHT ter). *USA.* Palm oil.

palm cabbage (pahlm CAHB-bahge). *USA.* The terminal head of a type of the edible palmetto; eaten as a vegetable. Also called swamp cabbage.

palm heart (pahlm hahrt). *USA.* New buds or shoots of the palm tree.

palmier (pahlm-ay). *Fre.* A pastry made from strips of a puff pastry, sprinkled with sugar, folded, sliced, and baked; looks like a palm leaf.

palm oil (pahlm ouyl). *USA.* Oil extracted from parts of the palm tree.

palm wine (pahlm wyne). *USA.* Wine made from the sap of a dying palm tree; called lagmi.

paloise (pahl-wahz). *Fre.* Béarnaise sauce flavored with mint instead of tarragon.

palombe (pahl-lomb). *Fre.* Dove; wild pigeon.

palourde (pah-loord). *Fre.* Clam.

Pampelmuse (PAHM-perl-moo-zwe). *Ger.* Grapefruit.

pamplemousse (pahng-pler-moos). *Fre.* Grapefruit.

pan (pahn). *Spa.* Bread.

panache (pah-nach). *Fre.* Used to describe salad, fruit, ice cream; means mixed colors.

panade (pah-nahd). *Fre.* Culinary paste of flour and water or soaked bread, used for preparing forcemeat, mousse or stuffing; can also be a peasant soup of water, stock, or milk thickened with bread.

panais (pah-neh). *Fre.* Parsnip.

panato (pah-NAH-toa). *Ita.* Coated in breadcrumbs, then fried.

pancake (PAHN-kak). *USA.* A batter cake cooked on a griddle or pan. Usually served in stacks with melted butter and syrup.

pancetta (pahn-CHEHT-tah). *Ita.* Unsmoked bacon cured with spices, salt and pepper; may be rolled or flat.

pancetta affumicata e uova (pahn-CHEHT-tah ahf-foo-mee-KAA-tah ay WAW-vah). *Ita.* Bacon and eggs.

panchporan (PAHUNCH-por-rahn). *Ind.* A five-spice seasoning: whole cumin seeds, whole black mustard seeds, whole fennel seeds, whole kalonji, and whole fenugreek seeds, mixed in equal portions. See wu hsiang fun; five-spice seasoning.

pancit (PAHN-ceet). *Phi.* Pasta, usually in shape of noodles, often stir-fried with chopped meats, seafood, vegetables. Also dough wrappers that are stuffed with savory fillings.

pancotto (pahn-KOT-toa). *Ita.* A Milanese soup made of stale bread.

panderkager (PAHN-er-kaa-err). *Dan.* Pancakes.

pan di genova (PAA-nay dee jayn-oa-vay). *).* *Ita.* Almond cake.

pan di natale (PAA-nay dee nah-TAA-lay). *Ita.* "Christmas bread"; a soft sweet yeast dough with candied fruits, nuts, raisins, pine nuts added, made into varying shapes and textures.

pan di Spagna (PAA-nay dee SPAA-nah). *Ita.* A sponge cake filled with cream or jam and soaked with liqueur.

pandorato (pahn-doh-RAH-toa). *Ita.* Bread dipped in an egg-milk batter, usually stuffed with a savory filling, and deep-fried; French toast.

pandoro (pahn-DOH-roa). *Ita.* A cake traditionally served at Christmastime; very light in texture, like a sponge cake, and is shaped like an octagonal cone.

pandours (pahn-doers). *Bri.* A variety of oyster found in the Firth of Forth.

pandowdy (pahn-DOW-dee). *USA.* A cobbler of sliced apples, cider, spices, brown sugar or molasses, and butter, covered with biscuit dough, then baked.

pan drippings (pahn DREHP-pengs). *USA.* The browned bits of meat and fat left in the pan after roasting, frying; used as basis for pan gravy, adding flour and liquid.

pan pepato (PAA-nay pay-PAH-toa). *Ita.* A cake made with nuts, raisins, almonds, chocolate, and hazelnuts and flavored with nutmeg and pepper.

pan broil (pahn-brouyl). *USA.* A method of cooking meat, uncovered, using a very hot heavy iron skillet, searing and browning the meat on the bottom side, then turning at once to sear and brown the other side; liquid is never added.

pan dressed (pahn-drehsd). *USA.* Refers to a gutted and scaled fish with head and fins removed, ready for sautéing or deep-frying.

pan-fry (pahn-fri). *USA.* To cook in a skillet in small amount of fat.

pané (pah-nay). *Fre.* Breadcrumbed.

pane (PAA-nay). *Ita.* Bread.

pane bianco (PAY-nay bee-AHNG-koa). *Ita.* White bread.

pane bolognese (PAY-nay boa-loa-nays). *Ita.* Corn bread.

pane di frumento (PAY-nay dee froo-MEHN-toa). *Ita.* Whole wheat bread.

pane di segala (PAY-nay dee say-GAH-lah). *Ita.* Black rye bread.

paneer (pah-NEER). *Ind.* Chenna, Indian cheese, compressed into a cake and cut in small pieces; also chhena.

pane grattugiato (PAY-nay graht-too-AH-toa). *Ita.* Bread crumbs; pangrattato.

pane scuro (PAY-nay SCHOO-roa). *Ita.* Dark bread.

pane tostato (PAA-nay to-STAA-toa). *Ita.* Toast.

panettone (pahn-EHT-tohn). *Ita.* A cylindrical-shaped yeast-dough cake with sultana raisins and candied lemon peel, eaten at breakfast; traditional at Christmas.

Panfisch (PAHN-fish). *Ger.* Minced fish and onion in mashed potatoes.

panforte (pahn-FOHR-teh). *Ita.* Fruitcake; a flat, very rich cake containing walnuts, almonds, hazelnuts, honey, candied fruits, lots of spices.

pangrattato (pahn-grah-TAH-to). *Ita.* "Grated bread"; breadcrumbs produced by drying stale bread in the oven, then processing in a food processor until the texture of coarse sand.

pángxiè (pong sieh). *Chi.* Crab.

panino (pah-NEE-noa). *Ita.* A biscuit; roll.

panna (PAHN-nah). *Ita.* Cream.

panna montana (PAHN-nah moan-TAH-nah). *Ita.* Whipped cream.

pannbiff med lök (PAHN-bif mit lurk). *Swe.* Chopped steak with onions.

pannekoeken (PAHN-nuh-koo-kuh). *Dut.* Pancakes.

pannequet (pahn-nuhr-kahy). *Fre.* Small crepe filled with sweet or savory filling and folded in quarters.

Pannerone (pahn-nay-ROAN-nay). *Ita.* An unsalted cows'-milk cheese; pale yellow, creamy; delicate, slightly tangy, flavor. Also called White Gorgonzola.

panning (PAHN-neng). *USA.* To cook a vegetable in a tightly covered skillet, using a small amount of fat; no water is added.

pannkakor (PAHN-kaa-koor). *Swe.* Pancakes.

pannkakor med sylt (PAN-KAH-koor mah SULT). *Swe.* Large, thin pancakes with jam.

pannukakku (PAHN-noo-KAHK-koo). *Fin.* Oven-baked pancake used for dessert.

panocha (pah-NOH-chah). *Mex.* A candy made of brown sugar, milk, butter, and nuts. Also spelled penuche.

pantostato (paa-nay-to-STAA-toa). *Ita.* Toasted bread.

panucho (pah-NOO-choh). *Mex.* A small tortilla fried until puffed-up, filled with savory filling, then fried until crisp.

panure (pahn-nyr). *Fre.* Golden breadcrumb crust.

panurette (pahn-oo-rett). *Fre.* Grated rusks, used for crumbs and for lining the inside of molds.

panvis (PAHN-vees). *Dut.* Casserole of dried codfish, onions, potatoes.

panzanella (pahn-tsah-NAYL-lah). *Ita.* A vegetable and anchovy salad, served with stale bread that has been soaked in water, squeezed dry, fried in olive oil.

panzarotti (pahn-tsah-RAWT-tee). *Ita.* Deep-fried cheese-stuffed noodle crescents.

pão (pan). *Por.* Bread.

pap (pahp). *Dut.* Porridge.

papa (PAH-pah). *Mex.* Potato.

papad (PAH-per). *Ind.* Lentil wafers.

papain (pah-PAI-un). *USA.* An enzyme from the papaya, used for tenderizing meats.

papatzul (pah-paht-SUHL). *Mex.* Egg-stuffed tortilla with pumpkin seed.

papaw (PAW-paw). *USA.* Papaya.

papaya (pah-PAHY-yah). *USA.* A large pear-shaped tropical fruit with orange flesh, black seeds, skin turns yellow when ripe; unripe, it is cooked as a vegetable; ripe, eaten raw as a fruit; when cooked, leaves resemble spinach.

papeeta (pa-PEE-tah). *Ind.* Papaya.

papillon (pah-pee-yawnh). *Fre.* A butterfly-shape cookie of flaky pastry.

papillote (pah-pee-joht). *Fre.* A paper frill used to dress the bone-end of chops or crown roast.

papillote, en (pah-pee-joht, ahng). *Fre.* Baked in a greased paper wrapper.

papos de anjo (PAH-pahsh deh AHN-zhoo). *Por.* Small egg cakes served with syrup.

pappa al pomodoro (pah-pah al pohm-oh-DOH-roa). *Ita.* A Tuscan soup made of stale bread.

pappardelle (pahp-pahr-DEHL-leh). *Ita.* Long, flat, broad egg noodles with crimped edge; traditionally served with hare cooked in a rich wine sauce; fettuccine, tagliatelle.

paprika (PO-pree-ko). *Hun.* Red pepper; sweet, brilliant scarlet color, and slight pungent odor.

paprikas (PAH-pree-kahs). *Dut.* Green peppers; capsicum.

paprikas csirke (PO-pree-ko CHEER-kae). *Hun.* A dish of chicken braised with garlic, onions, sour cream, and paprika. Also made with meat or fish.

papu (PAH-poo). *Fin.* Bean.

paquette (pah-kett). *Fre.* Mature lobster roe, dark greenish-black in color, about to be laid. Also refers to the female lobster carrying such roe.

Paradeiser (pah-rah-DIGH-zerr). *Ger.* Tomato.

paratha (pa-RAHT-ha). *Ind.* Griddle-fried flaky whole wheat bread.

parboil (PAHR-boyl). *USA.* To boil briefly; a preliminary cooking procedure.

parboiled rice (PAHR-boyld rice). *USA.* Rough rice soaked in warm water under pressure, steamed, and dried before milling, thus gelatinizing the starch in the grain, which ensures a separateness of grain.

parch (pahrch). *USA.* To cook in dry heat until slightly brown.

pare (pair). *USA.* Cut off the outside peeling or covering, usually with a knife.

pareve (parv). *Jew.* Kosher; containing no meat or milk, therefore suitable to be eaten with either.

parfait (par-fay). *Fre.* A cold or frozen dessert of layers of fruit, syrup, nuts, and whipped cream.

parfait (par-FAY). *USA.* A dessert of ice cream, layered with sauces and whipped cream served in a tall narrow glass.

Paris-Brest (pah-ree brehst). *Fre.* A dessert of creamy puff pastry rings filled with praline creme topped with sliced almonds, or chantilly cream topped with fresh strawberries.

parisersmørgaas (par-rea-ser-SMEHR-goahs). *Dan.* Scraped raw beef slightly grilled on toast with egg.

Parisienne (pa-ree-zyan). *Fre.* "After the fashion of Paris"; elaborately garnished.

Parker House Rolls (PAHR-kehr howus rolz). *USA.* A yeast roll folded in two halves before baking; originated at the Parker House in Boston in nineteenth century.

parmentier (pahr-mahng-tee). *Fre.* Containing potatoes in some form.

Parmesan (PAR-meh-szan). *USA.* A cow's skim-milk cheese shaped in large, squat cylinders; pale yellow with a golden rind; dense, grainy, sweet, fragrant, mellow; young, it is a table cheese; aged at least two years, a sharp grating cheese; use freshly grated over many dishes.

parmigiana (par-mee-ZHAN-ah). *Ita.* Veal, chicken, or eggplant covered with tomato sauce, mozzarella cheese and Parmesan cheese, then browned in an oven or broiler.

Parmigiano (pahr-mee-JAA-noa). *Ita.* Parmesan.

päron (PAH-ron). *Swe.* Pear.

parrilla (pahr-REE-lyah). *Spa.* Grill.

parrillada di pescado (pahr-REE-lyah-doh dee pays-KAH-dhoa). *Spa.* Mixed seafood grill with lemon.

parsa (PAHR-sah). *Fin.* Asparagus.

parsley (PAHRS-lee). *USA.* A flavorful herb whose root, stem, and leaves have a high vitamin A-carrying factor; valuable as an agent for blending the flavors of other herbs and having the power to destroy the scent of garlic and onion; used raw or cooked.

parsley root (PAHRS-lee ruht). *USA.* A vegetable similar in shape to a carrot topped with green leaves; tastes somewhat like celery; eaten fresh or cooked.

parsnips (PAHRS-nehps). *USA.* A root vegetable of the carrot family, usually served boiled and buttered.

parson's nose (PAHR-son's nohz). *USA.* The tailpiece of a bird. Also pope's nose.

partans (PAHR-uns). *Bri.* Large, tasty crabs.

partridge. (PAHRT-tredg). *USA.* A medium size game bird with delicate flesh; the American ruffed grouse, bobwhite, quail, pheasant; a general term.

pasa (PAH-sah). *Mex.* Raisin.

pasa ciruela (PAH-ssahss thee-RWAY-lahss). *Spa.* Prune.

pasha (PAH-sha). *Fin.* Cheesecake of Russian origin.

pasilla (pah-SEHL-lah). *Mex.* A very hot, long, dark brown chili pepper.

pass (pahss). *USA.* To cause to go through a sieve or strainer.

passas (PAH-sahss). *Por.* Raisins.

passata (pah-SAH -tah). *Ita.* Puree.

passatelli in brodo (pah-sah-TELL-lee en BRAW-doa). *Ita.* A pasta of parmesan, eggs, and breadcrumbs forced through a tool to form strands that are cooked and served in meat broth.

passato (pahs-SAH-toa). *Ita.* Creamed.

passer (pah-say). *Fre.* "To pass" a sauce, soup, vegetable or meat, means to run it through a sieve or strainer or cheesecloth. Also means to slightly fry over a quick fire to form a crusty surface on meats or vegetables intended to be finished by another method of cooking.

passion fruit (PAH-shun froot). *USA.* Purple egg-sized tropical fruit whose sweet yellow flesh is eaten raw with the small black seeds, or squeezed for juice; has sweet-acid flavor. Also called purple granadilla.

pasta (PAHS-tah). *Ita.* A dough composed chiefly of flour, water, and sometimes eggs, and made into many shapes and sizes; see also the following varieties of pasta: agnolini, cannelloni, cappelletti, conchiglie, ditali, farfelle, fettuccine, gnocchi, lasagne, maccheroni, pasta asciutta, pasta in brodo, ravioli, rigatoni, spaghetti, tagliatelle, tortellini, vermicelli, ziti.

pasta al uovo (PAHS-tah ahl WAW-voa). *Ita.* Egg pasta.

pasta ascuitta (PAHS-tah a-SHOOT-toa). *Ita.* Dry or plain pasta; can be stuffed or in sauce; not served in broth; general term for cooked pasta.

pasta e fagioli (PAHS-tah ay fah-JOA-lee). *Ita.* A soup of pasta, white beans, and salt pork.

pasta foglia (PAH-syah FOL-yah). *Ita.* Puff pastry.

pasta frolla (PAHS-tah FROH-lah). *Ita.* Short pasta.

pasta in brodo (PAHS-tah een BRAW-doa). *Ita.* Pasta cooked in soup.

pasta primavera (PAHS-tah pree-mah-VEH-rah). *USA.* A dish of pasta made with a sauce of spring vegetables.

paste (paast). *USA.* Soft, smooth mixture made of dry ingredients and a liquid.

paste (paast). *Bri.* Anything that spreads easily, such as sandwich paste.

pastei (PAHS-tay). *Dut.* Meat pie; creamed chicken or meat in pastry shell.

pasteijes (PAHS-tay-yers). *Dut.* Pastry shells.

pastéis (pahsh-TAYISH). *Por.* Cakes; used for either sweet cakes or savory such as codfish cakes.

pastej (PAHS-tay). *Swe.* Pie.

pastel (pahs-TAYL). *Spa.* Pastry, cake, pie, pâté.

pastél (pash-TEL). *Por.* Pie, tart, pastry.

pastélinho (pahsh-tay-LEE-nyoo). *Por.* Small pie.

pastelitos (pah-stehl-EE-tohs). *Mex.* Cookies; little cakes.

pastèque (pah-stehk). *Fre.* Watermelon.

Pastete (pas-TAY-teh). *Ger.* Pie.

pasteurize (PAHS-tuhr-riz). *USA.* Partial sterilization of perishable food products such as meat, fish, or milk with gamma ray radiation.

pasticcini (pahs-teet-CHEE-nee). *Ita.* Savory or sweet pies; usually layers of pasta with a savory filling; timbales.

pastillage (pahst-tee-ahz). *Fre.* A paste of sugar, water, and gum tragacanth used in the past to make various shapes; used for elaborate table decorations.

pastina (pahs-STEE-nah). *Ita.* Small pasta used in soups.

pastis (pahs-tihs). *Fre.* An anise-flavored liqueur.

pastrami (pah-STRAH-me). *Jew.* A highly seasoned smoked beef prepared from shoulder cuts; used very thinly sliced.

pastry flour (PA-stre flawr). *USA.* Milled of soft wheat; fine granulation; low gluten; excellent for quick breads and pastries.

pasty (PA-stee). *Bri.* A Cornish turnover with various fillings, usually of meats or vegetables.

pata (PAH-toa). *Spa.* Duck.

patakukko (PAH-tah-kook-ko). *Fin.* "Pot fowl"; a casserole of small freshwater fish and salt pork baked under a rye crust.

patata (pah-TAH-tah). *Spa.* Potato; patata fritas (pah-TAH-tahss FREE-tahss), fried potatoes, french fries.

patata (pah-TAA-tay). *Ita.* Potato; patata fritte (pah-TAA-tay FREET-tay), fried potatoes, french fries; patata lesso (pah-TAA-tay LAYS-soa), boiled potatoes; patata stacciate (pah-TAA-tay stah-CHA-tay), mashed potatoes.

patate (pah-TAA-tay). *Ita.* Sweet potato.

pâte (paht). *Fre.* Pastry; paste, pasta, dough or batter.

pâté (pah-tay). *Fre.* A rich savory spread or mixture made from food finely ground to paste consistency; can be anything from almonds to pig's head.

pâte à choux (paht ah sho). *Fre.* Cream puff pastry made by stirring flour into boiling water and butter then adding eggs. When cooked, the pastry puffs up, making a cavity that can be filled with flavored cream or custard as in eclairs and cream puffs.

pâte à croissant (paht ah cro-sawng). *Fre.* Pastry dough for croissants.

pâte d'amandes (paht dah-mahngd). *Fre.* Almond paste, marzipan.

pâte de compagne (paht der kon-pa-nyee). *Fre.* A pastry with a coarse, crumbly texture.

pâte de foie gras (pah-tay d'fwah-grah). *Fre.* A well-known delicacy prepared from the livers of fat geese.

pâte en terrine (paht een tehr-reen). *Fre.* "Cooked in an earthenware dish."

pâte feuilletée (paht fuhy-leh-tay). *Fre.* Puff-paste; many thin layers; "thousand leaves".

pâte levée (paht leh-vay). *Fre.* Raised or leavened dough.

pâte sucrée (paht sew-kra). *Fre.* Sweet dough used for pie shells, pastry shells, and so forth.

patinho (pah-TEE-nyoo). *Por.* Young duckling.

patis (pah-teesc). *Phi.* Fermented fish sauce that is salty and pungent.

patisserie (pah-teess-ree). *Fre.* A pastry shop, or a piece of pastry.

Patna rice (paht-NAH rics). *USA.* Rice with semi-hard, semi-transparent, slightly shiny grains; milky white and slightly cylindrical in form.

pato (PAH-toh). *Spa, Por.* Duck.

pato bravo (PAH-toh BRAH-voh). *Por.* Wild duck.

patrijs (pah-TRAYS). *Dut.* Partridge.

patty pan (PAH-te pahn). *USA.* A yellow or white, round summer squash with a scalloped edge. Also known as cymling squash.

patty shell (PAH-te schel). *USA.* A puff paste or pastry shell or case for serving individual portions of creamed mixtures.

paunce bourré (pons boo-RAY). *USA.* A Cajun dish of stuffed pork stomach.

paupiettes (po-pee-ette). *Fre.* Slices of meat or fish rolled with forcemeat or vegetables.

pausnaya (PAH-yoos-nah-yah). *Rus.* Pressed caviar.

pavé (pau-va). *Fre.* Designates a square or rectangular shape; indicates a dish chilled in a square mold and garnished; a sponge cake in a square shape, spread with buttercream and garnished.

pavo (PAH-bhoa). *Spa.* Turkey.

pavot (pah-vo). *Fre.* Poppy seed.

pawpaw (PAU-pau). *USA.* The edible fruit of a North American tree of the custard-apple family; yellow skin; smoky taste.

payasam (PIE-ya-sahm). *Ind.* A pudding made of mung beans, coconut milk, and peas.

paysanne, à la (pahy-sahn). *Fre.* "Peasant style"; with potatoes, carrots, onions, and bacon.

peach (peech). *USA.* The mostly round fruit of the peach tree; downy, golden skin with reddish blush; an indention from bloom end to stem end on one side; fragrant, juicy, firm flesh; use fresh out of hand or in salads, stewed, jam, preserves, juice; two types: freestone and clingstone, which are canned commercially.

peach Melba (peech MEHL-bah). *USA.* A dessert of peaches poached in vanilla-flavored syrup, served over ice cream, and topped with raspberry puree.

peaman (PEE-mahn). *Jap.* Green bell peppers.

peanut (PEE-nuht). *USA.* The seed or seed-containing pod of a South American leguminous herb; fibrous hourglass-shape shell, usually containing two nuts; highly nutritious; a staple food in Africa, an important crop in India and China.

peanut butter (PEE-nuht BUTT-ehr). *USA.* The resultant product when peanuts are crushed to a paste with a mortar and pestle or in a blender; a smooth, creamy, spreadable product.

peanut flour (PEE-nuht flawr). *USA.* Peanuts ground to a fine powder. Contains sixteen times the protein value of wheat; used to enrich flours.

peanut maki (PEE-naht-tsoo mah-kee). *Jap.* A sesame-studded crisp cracker, wrapped around a whole peanut.

peanut oil (PEE-nuht oul). *USA.* The oil extracted from the peanut during processing; very light in texture and color; very mild flavor that does not mask other flavors.

pea pods (pee pohds). *USA.* Snow peas; Chinese pea pods.

pear (paher). *USA.* The fleshy oblong fruit of the pear tree; larger on the bloom end; slick, smooth skin that may be yellow-green, green, reddish-green, or red; sweet, softly-granular aromatic flesh. Some varieties are bartlett, red bartlett, bosc, comice, forelle, and seckel.

pearl barley (pehrl BAHR-lee). *USA.* Hulled and polished barley; looks like pearls; used in soups or like rice.

pearl rice (pehrl rics). *USA.* Rice that is a little shorter than medium grain rice; more tender and clings as it cooks.

peas (peez). *USA.* The edible seedpod of various leguminous vines; three main types: English peas, which are usually eaten with seeds, or peas, removed from the pods; snow peas; and snap peas, which are both eaten pod and all.

peber (PAH-ooerr). *Dan.* Pepper.

pebernødder (PEH-ber-NUEH-dor). *Dan.* "Pepper nuts"; a variety of Christmas cookie.

peberrod (PEH-ooer-roadh). *Dan.* Horseradish.

pecan (pea-KAHN). *USA.* The oblong, light brown, thin-shelled, oval nut of the pecan tree; an important nut in the United States; uncommon elsewhere.

pêche (pehsh). *Fre.* Peach.

pêche Melba (pehsh mehl-bah). *Fre.* Peach Melba.

pecho de ternera (PAY-choo day tehr-NAY-rah). *Spa.* Breast of veal.

pechuga (peh-CHOO-gah). *Spa.* Chicken breast.

Pecorino (pay-koa-REE-noa). *Ita.* A hard cheese made from ewes' milk.

Pecorino Romano (peck-oh-REE-noh rah-MAH-noa). *Ita.* A ewes' whole-milk cheese round in shape, white or very pale yellow interior, dense, with a yellow brown rind; sharp, salty, and intense.

Pecorino Siciliano (peck-oh-REE-noh see-sill-ee-AHN-oa). *Ita.* A ewes' milk cheese that is hard, and made pungent by the addition of peppercorns; good for grating.

pectin (peck-ten). *Fre.* Various water-soluble substances that bind plant cells, particularly in apples, quinces, citrus, currants, and yield a gel used in jelly-making to "set" the jelly.

peda (PEH-ray). *Ind.* Milk fudge molded into small pillows and garnished with pistachio nuts.

peel (peal). *USA.* Strip off, by pulling or cutting, the outside covering of a food.

peertjes (PAYR-tyus). *Dut.* Cooking pears.

peixe (PAY-shay). *Por.* Fish.

Peking duck (PEA-keng duhk). *USA.* An elaborate Chinese dish made from specially reared ducks; a finger-food. Beijing kao ya.

pekoe (PEE-ko). *Ind.* A superior grade of black tea from India and Ceylon, made from the first three leaves on the spray of the tea bush.

pekonia (PAY-koa-niah). *Fin.* Bacon.

Pellkartoffeln (PEHL-kahr-tof-ferln). *Ger.* Potatoes boiled in their skins.

peltopyy (PAYL-toa-pew). *Fin.* Grey partridge.

pemmican (PEM-eh-kan). *USA.* A dried meat product made of lean meat pounded fine, mixed with melted fat, and sometimes berries, flour, molasses, and suet, pressed into cakes; used as emergency rations and by North American Indians and settlers.

penchenè (pee-ROZH-niyeh). *Rus.* Tea cakes; cookies.

penne (PEHN-neh). *Ita.* Pasta tubes cut on the diagonal.

Penrod (pahng-ro). *Fre.* Anise-flavored liqueur.

penuche (peh-NOO-chee). *Mex.* A fudgelike candy made with brown sugar, cream, nuts; poured into a pan to cool, then cut in squares. Also called panocha.

pepe forte (PAY-pay FOUR-tay). *Ita.* Chili pepper.

pepe nero (PAY-pay nee-roh). *Ita.* Black pepper.

peper (PAY-pur). *Dut.* Pepper.

peperkoek (PAY-pur-kook). *Dut.* Gingerbread.

pepermunt (PAY-pur-moont). *Dut.* Peppermint.

pepernoten (PAY-pur-no-tuh). *Dut.* Tiny, spicy ball-shaped cakes served on December 5, the eve of St. Nicholas Day.

peperonata (pay-pay-roa-NAH-tah). *Ita.* A dish of sweet peppers cooked in olive oil with tomatoes, garlic, onions; served cold.

peperoncino (pay-pay-rohn-CEE-noa). *Ita.* A hot red chili pepper used dried or fresh.

peperoni (pay-pay-ROA-nee). *Ita.* Bell peppers, red or green.

pepe rosso (PAY-pay ROAS-soa). *Ita.* Red pepper.

pepininhos de conserva (pay-pee-nee-nyoos duh kon-SAYR-vah). *Por.* Pickles.

pepino (pe-PEE-noo). *Por.* Cucumber.

pepino (peh-PEE-noh). *Spa.* A small, oval fruit with a delicate, sweet cucumber-melon flavor; skin is pale yellow with purple stripes; eaten fresh.

pepita (peh-PEE-tah). *Spa.* Pumpkin seed.

peppar (PAH-pahr). *Swe.* Pepper.

pepparkakor (PEH-pahr-kah-koor). *Swe.* Gingersnap cakes.

pepparrot (PEH-pahr-root). *Swe.* Horseradish.

pepper (PEP-per). *Ind.* Black pepper is the dried, unripened fruit of a tropical semiwoody vine. White pepper is exactly the same fruit with the outer black covering removed.

pepperoncini (peh-pehr-rohn-CEE-nee). *USA.* Mild chili peppers used in salads; green, 2-3 inches long.

pepperoni (pep-pehr-ROW-nee). *Ita.* A sausage of beef and pork, highly seasoned with hot red peppers.

pepperpot (PEH-pehr-poht). *USA.* A highly seasoned stew or soup made from tripe.

pepperpot (PEH-pehr-poht). *Spa.* A highly seasoned West Indies stew or soup made with meat, seafood, vegetables, as well as cassava juice.

pepper sauce (PEH-pehr saus). *USA.* Traditional sauce served with venison; poivrade.

pepperrot-saus (PEHPP-ehr-root sows). *Nor, Dut.* Horseradish sauce.

peppers (PEH-pehrs). *USA.* A generic term for the seedpods of various pepper bushes; two main types: mild or sweet-fleshed such as the bell peppers, and hot or pungent-fleshed such as the various chili peppers; colors vary from green to yellow to red to purple to black (when dried).

pêra (PAY-rah). *Por.* Pear.

pera (PEH-rah). *Spa.* Pear.

pera (PAY-rah). *Ita.* Pear.

percebes (pehr-THAY-bhayss). *Spa.* A type of shellfish; goose barnacles.

perch (purch). *USA.* Various related and unrelated freshwater and saltwater fish, including the white perch, yellow perch, snappers of coastal West Africa, snook, walleye.

perche (pehrsh). *Fre.* Perch; a fresh- and saltwater fish.

perciatelli (pay-chaa-TEHL-lee). *Ita.* Long, tubular pasta.

perdiz (pehr-DEETH). *Spa.* Partridge.

perdreau (pehr-droa). *Fre.* Young partridge.

perdrix (pehr-dree). *Fre.* Partridge.

perejil (PEHR-eh-jeel). *Mex.* Parsley.

peren (pee-AHR-en). *Dut.* Pears.

périgourdine (pehr-ree-go-deen). *Fre.* Garnished with truffles.

périgueux sauce (pehr-ree-goh saus). *Fre.* Truffle sauce made with Madeira wine.

Perilla (peh-REE-lyah). *Spa.* A cows' milk cheese firm in texture and mild in flavor. Also known as teta.

periwinkle (pear-e-WEN-kle). *Bri.* A small snaillike mollusk eaten uncooked or roasted in the shell.

perle (perl). *Fre.* Pearl; refers to the shape of any vegetable cut and shaped round and small.

perleløge (payr-LER-lurg). *Dan.* Pearl onions.

Perlhuhn (PEHRL-hoon). *Ger.* Guinea hen.

pernice (payr-NEE-chay). *Ita.* Partridge.

perry (PEHR-ree). *USA.* Pear cider.

Persian melon (PURR-szhun MELL-un). *USA.* A melon with a dark green rind with fine brown netting; globular in shape with thick, bright pink-orange flesh.

Persian-style rice (PURR-szhun-styl rics). *USA.* An Arabian dish of plain boiled rice with a crust, kateh.

persika (PAER-shi-kah). *Swe.* Peach.

persil (pehr-see). *Fre.* Parsley.

persilja (POER-silyah). *Swe.* Parsley.

persillade (payr-se-yad). *Fre.* Served with or containing chopped parsley.

persille (pear-SILL-eh). *Dan.* Parsley.

persillé (pehr-ssay). *Fre.* Designates beef of the highest quality, well marbled with fat; also, green-veined cheeses; sprinkled with parsley.

persimmon (purr-SEHM-mun). *USA.* A large, orange, globular fruit that is edible when fully ripe, but extremely astringent when unripe; kaki.

peru (pay-ROO). *Por.* Turkey.

peruna (PAY-roo-nah). *Fin.* Potato.

perzik (PEHR-zik). *Dut.* Peach.

pesca (PEH-skah). *Ita.* Peach.

pescada (paysh-KAH-dah). *Por.* Haddock.

pescadilla (pay-skah-DHEEL-yah). *Spa.* Whiting.

pescado (pays-KAH-dhoa). *Spa.* Fish.

pescado a la sal (pays-KAH-dhoa ah lah sahl). *Spa.* Whole fish baked in rock salt.

pesca noce (PEH-skah NOA-chay). *Ita.* Nectarine.

pesce (PAY-shay). *Ita.* Fish.

pesce persico (PAY-shay PEHR-see-koa). *Ita.* Perch.

pesce San Pietro (PAY-shay saun pec ET troa). *Ita.* John Dory.

pesce spada (PAY-shay SPAA-dah). *Ita.* Swordfish.

pêssego (PAY-say-goh). *Por.* Peach.

pesto (PES-to). *Ita.* A sauce of basil, garlic, parsley, pine nuts or walnuts, and romano or parmesan cheeses mixed together in virgin olive oil.

petersilie (pay-terr-ZEE-lier). *Ger.* Parsley.

petite marmite (peh-tee mahr-meet). *Fre.* A clear consommé in which is cooked lean meat, a whole chicken, marrow bones and vegetables for flavor; served with croûtes spread with marrow and sprinkled with grated cheese.

petite sèches (peh-tee say-shay). *Fre.* Little cream biscuits.

petit four (pee-tee foor). *Fre.* Small fancy cake covered with icing and highly decorated.

petit lait (pee-tee lot). *Fre.* Whey.

petit pain (pee-tee pahn). *Fre.* Very small roll scooped out and stuffed with various savory purees, served as side dish or appetizer.

petits pois (per-tee pwah). *Fre.* Spring peas; fine, very small peas with a delicate flavor.

petits pois princesse (per-tee pwah pran-ses). *Fre.* Snow peas.

Petit-Suisse (per-tee-sweess). *Fre.* A cows' milk cheese, mild in flavor, shaped in small cylinders.

petticoat tails (PEHT-tee-koat tails). *USA.* Thin shortbread cakes, with scalloped edge to resemble petticoats.

petti di pollo (PEHT-tee dee POAL-loa). *Ita.* Chicken breasts.

petto (PEHT-toa). *Ita.* Breast, brisket, chest.

peultjes (PERLT-yers). *Dut.* A vegetable similar to snowpeas; podded peas; young early peas.

pez espada (payth ays-PAH-dhah). *Spa.* Swordfish.

pezzo (PEHT-soa). *Ita.* Chunk, piece.

Pfannkuchen (PFAN-eh-kook-hern). *Ger.* Pancake.

Pfeffer (PFEH-ferr). *Ger.* Pepper.

Pfefferkuchen (PFEH-ferr-kook-hern). *Ger.* Spice cake, similar to gingerbread, traditional at Christmastime.

Pfefferminz (PFEH-ferr-mints). *Ger.* Peppermint.

Pfeffernüsse (pfeh-ferr-NEW-sser). *Ger.* Spicy ginger cookies.

Pfefferpothast (pfeh-ferr-PO-tahast). *Ger.* A stew of beef ribs and onions, seasoned with pepper and lemon.

Pfifferlinge (PFIF-ferr-ling-er). *Ger.* Chanterelle.

Pfirsich (PFEER-zikh). *Ger.* Peach.

Pflaume (PFLOW-mern). *Ger.* Plum.

Pfnutli (FRU-dlee). *Ger.* Swiss apple fritters.

pheasant (PHEH-szehnt). *USA.* Any of a variety of game birds with colorful plumage and characteristic long tail feathers.

Philadelphia cheesesteak (phehl-ah-DEHL-phee-ah CHEEZ-stehk). *USA.* A crisp Italian-style roll covered with thin slices of beef, cheeses, and other condiments, including sautéed onions.

Philadelphia eggs (phehl-ah-DEHL-phee-ah ehgs). *USA.* Two split muffins topped with cooked white chicken meat, poached eggs, and hollandaise sauce.

philpy (PHEHL-pee). *USA.* A rice bread with origins in South Carolina.

phool gobhi (POOL GO-bhee). *Ind.* Cauliflower.

phosphated flour (PHAHS-fa-ted flowr). *USA.* A wheat flour with salt and leavens added; has short storage life since the leavens will lose their potency.

phyllo (PHEE-loh). *Gre.* Leaf-thin sheets of dough, made from flour and water; used for sweet and savory dishes by layering with fillings; similar to the French mille-feuille. Also called brik, fllo, malsouka, yukka.

physalis (PHYS-sah-lihst). *USA.* A fruit about the size of a large grape; smooth-skinned and golden-yellow; encased in a thin, papery husk; sweet flavor; called ground-cherry; used in sauces and dessert toppings.

piadina (pee-ah-DEE-nah). *Ita.* A soft type of flat bread, usually eaten with salami or prosciutto; also may be filled with sautéed spinach or with ricotta.

piaz (pih-YAZ). *Ind.* Onion.

picada (peh-CAH-dah). *Mex.* A small round of tortilla dough filled with a savory stuffing and cooked; an appetizer or entrée; garnacha.

picada (peh-CAH-dah). *Spa.* Minced, shredded or ground meat; hash.

picadillo (peh-kah-DEHL-loa). *Spa.* A salad of orange, onion, green pepper, and shredded salt codfish.

picadillo (pee-kah-DEE-yoh). *Mex.* Mixture of meat and other ingredients used as filling or stuffing.

picado (pee-KAH-doh). *Por.* Hash.

picante (pee-KAHN-ta). *Ita, Spa.* Piquant; hot, spicy, sharp.

picatostes (pee-kah-TOAS-tehz). *Spa.* Deep-fried slices of bread.

piccata (peek-KAA-tah). *Ita.* Veal scallop.

piccioni (peet-CHOA-nay). *Ita.* Squab.

Pichelsteiner (PIK-herl-shtigh-nerr). *Ger.* A hearty meat and vegetable stew.

pichón (pee-CHON). *Spa.* Pigeon; squab.

pickerel (PEHK-er-ol). *USA.* A long, slender fish of the pike family; has soft flesh and a needlelike bone structure. Erroneously called Walleye.

Pickert (PEH-kert). *Ger.* Peasant bread, made of potato or wheat flour.

pickle (PEH-kehl). *USA.* Any food preserved in brine or syrup and vinegar.

pickling cucumbers (PEHK-leng KU-kom-bers). *USA.* A short, small, hard and spiny cucumber with a tart flavor, especially good for making dill pickles.

pickling salt (PEHK-leng sawlt). *USA.* A pure salt that is free from additives that cloud pickling liquid, available in granulated and flake forms.

picnic ham (PEHK-nik haum). *USA.* A front leg of pork, cured and smoked; sometimes mistaken for ham because of similar flavors.

picón (pee-KOHN). *Por.* A pungent, blue-veined cheese made of goats' milk; same as the Spanish cabrales.

pí dàn (pee dahn). *Chi.* Thousand-year-old eggs; duck eggs preserved in a clay casing made of ashes, lime, salt, and strong tea, rolled in rice husks, and buried for three months; the yolks turn greenish-brown, the whites black-purple. Also known as hundred-year-old eggs.

pie (pi). *USA.* A sweet or savory dish baked in a pastry crust, with a filling; with or without a crust top; may have a crumb, pastry, or meringue topping; may also have a top, but no bottom crust.

piémontaise, à la (pee-a-mohng-tez). *Fre.* A garnish for meats of rice, timbales or mounds, mixed with grated white truffles.

pierna de cordero (PYEHR-nah day koar-DAY-roa). *Spa.* Leg of lamb.

pieterman (PEET-ur-mahn). *Dut.* Stingfish.

pigeonneau (pee-zhon-noa). *Fre.* A young squab bred for the table.

piggvar (PIG-varr). *Swe.* Turbot.

piggvar (PIG-vahr). *Nor.* Turbot.

pig-in-a-blanket (pehg-en-a-BLANH-keht). *USA.* Sausage wrapped in dough and baked.

pignola (pihg-NOH-loa). *Ita.* Pine nut.

pihvi (PIH-vi). *Fin.* Beefsteak.

piimä (PEE-mae). *Fin.* Buttermilk; a very popular drink in Finland.

piirakka (PEE-rah-kkah). *Fin.* A dish of meat or fish and rice cooked in pastry.

píjiu (PEE-jiu). *Chi.* Beer.

Pikante sosse (pee-KAHN-tah ZO-seh). *Ger.* A spicy, piquant sauce.

pike (pik). *USA.* A large, elongated, long-snouted fish, whose sweet, white flesh is used in many fine dishes; found in cooler northern waters.

pilaf (pih-LAHF). *Tur.* A dish made of seasoned rice, served with meat, poultry, or shellfish. Also pilauf, pilau, pilau, pilaw.

pilchard (PILL-chahrd). *USA.* A small fish of the herring family found along European coasts; a sardine.

pili-pili (PEHL-ee PEHL-ee). *Afr.* Powdered dried chilies.

pilot biscuit (PI-loht BISC-kit). *USA.* Hardtack.

pilot bread (PI-loht brehd). *USA.* Hardtack.

pilsner (PILLZ-nuhr). *USA.* A high quality lager beer; pale golden, lower in alcohol and calories than American beer.

pilsner (PILS-nerr). *Dan.* Light lager beer.

Pilze (PILT-ser). *Ger.* Mushroom.

Pilzschnitzel (PILT-ser-shnit-serl). *Ger.* An Austrian nonmeat cutlet made with mushrooms, carrots, and peas.

piman (PEE-mahn). *Jap.* Bell pepper; used in nontraditional cooking; used in grilled foods and deep-fried foods.

pimenta (pee-MEN-tah). *Por.* Pepper.

pimenta (pee-MYAYN-tah). *Spa.* Pepper.

piment doux (pee-mahng doo). *Fre.* Sweet pepper.

pimentos (pee-MYAYN-toass). *Spa.* Sweet red peppers; the seed pod from which allspice comes; a sweet red pepper pod used in salads, vegetable dishes, as garnish.

pimento cheese (pee MEHN-to cheez). *USA.* A sandwich spread, or filling, made of cheese, usually cheddar, American, or cream cheese, to which ground pimentos have been added.

pimentón (pee-mayn-TON). *Spa.* Paprika.

piments verts (pee-mahngs vehr). *Fre.* Green peppers.

pimienta (pee-MYEHN-tah). *Spa.* Black pepper.

pimiento dulce (pee-MYAYN-toa DOOL-thay). *Spa.* Hot red pepper.

Pimm's Cup (pehmz kup). *Bri.* The brand name of a starter for various highballs; Pimm's #1 has gin and bitters, #2 has whisky, #3 has brandy, and #4 has rum.

piña (PEE-nyah). *Spa.* Pineapple.

pinaattiohukaiset (PEE-natt-tee-yo-hoo-KYE-sett). *Fin.* Spinach pancakes.

pinch (pehnch). *USA.* As much as you can hold between the thumb and first finger, that is, a pinch of salt.

pinda (PEHN-daas). *Dut.* Peanuts

pindakaas (PEHN-dah-kaas). *Dut.* Peanut butter.

pineapple (PINH-ahp-pul). *USA.* The multiple fruit of the pineapple plant; has rich, succulent flesh with a slightly acid taste; must be peeled; use raw or cooked.

pineapple guava (PINH-ahp-pul GWUA-vah). *USA.* A slightly bumpy, thin skinned, green South American fruit with a cream-colored, slightly soft flesh, like a pear; tart and perfumy; use fresh in salads or make into preserves. Also known as feijoa.

pine nut (pine nuht). *USA.* The edible seed of the cone from the pine tree. Also known as chinquapin, crenata, Indian nut, pignola, piñon.

píngguo (PING-guo). *Chi.* Apple.

Pinkel (PIH-kehrl). *Ger.* A smoked sausage of groats, onions, and bacon.

pink sauce (pehnk saus). *USA.* A mayonnaise-based sauce colored pink with catsup and served with shrimp.

pinnekjøtt (pee-neh-SHUTT). *Nor.* Salt-cured mutton chops steamed on peeled birch twigs.

pinole (pah-NOH-lah). *USA.* Sweetened corn that has been dried, ground, and spiced; sometimes used to make a chocolate drink.

pinoli (pee-NO-lee). *Ita.* Pine nuts.

piñon (PEEN-yohn). *Spa.* Pine nut.

pintada (peen-TAH-dah). *Spa.* Guinea hen.

pintade (pang-tahd). *Fre.* Guinea hen.

pintadeau (pang-tah-doa). *Fre.* Young guinea cock.

pinto bean (PEN-toe bean). *USA.* A common dried bean, mottled reddish color, used alone or as an ingredient in many stewed dishes.

piperade (pee-pehr-rohd). *Fre.* Tomatoes, green bell peppers, and onions cooked in olive oil, with beaten egg and ham or bacon added.

pipian (pee-PYAHN). *Mex.* A red sauce of sesame and pumpkin seeds ground with spices and peanuts or almonds; served on chicken.

pipikaula (PEE-pee-kah-OO-lah). *USA.* A dish of beef jerky and soy sauce, of Hawaiian origins.

piquant (pee-kahnt). *Fre.* Highly seasoned; sharp.

piquante (pee-kahnt). *Fre.* "Agreeably stimulating to the palate"; a classic sauce of chopped shallots reduced with white wine and vinegar, demi-glace added, strained, then garnished with gherkins, parsley, chervil, and tarragon.

piquin (pe-KEEN). *Mex.* A very small, very hot, dark green chili pepper.

piri-piri (pee-ree-pee-ree). *Por.* A sauce made from hot red chili peppers and olive oil.

pirog (pee-roh). *Fre.* Canoe-shaped.

pirog c limon (peer-ROHG s lyee-MO-nahm). *Rus.* Lemon tart.

pirogi (peer-ROHG-gheey). *Rus.* Large pastries cut into servings.

piroshki (peer-ROSH-keey). *Rus.* Small turnovers or dumplings filled with a savory or sweet stuffing.

pisang goreng (PEE-sang HOH-reng). *Dut.* Fried or baked bananas, Indonesian-style.

Pischingertorte (PEESH-eng-er-tor-ter). *Ger.* An Austrian torte made of round wafers filled with chocolate hazelnut cream, covered with chocolate icing.

piselli (pee-SEHL-lee). *Ita.* Peas.

piselli alla romana (pee-SEHL-lee AHL-lah roa-MAA-nah). *Ita.* Peas cooked with butter, onion, and ham.

pissaladière (pee-sah-lah-daere). *Fre.* A pizzalike tart made with onions, black olives, anchovies, and tomatoes arranged decoratively.

pissenlit (pee-sehn-lee). *Fre.* Dandelion greens; best eaten before flowering or after frost.

pista (PIH-stah). *Ind.* Pistachio.

pistache (pee-stash). *Fre.* Pistachio nut.

pistacchio (pee-STACH-cheo). *Ita.* Pistachio nut.

pistachio (peh-STASCH-ee-oh). *USA.* Kernel of the nut of the turpentine tree, green in color and delicate in flavor; shells are naturally tan, but sometimes dyed pink-red or green; used as flavoring and garnishing.

pisto (PEES-toa). *Spa.* A vegetable dish of chopped tomatoes, zucchini, onion, red or green peppers stewed together. Also called samfaina and frito de verduras.

pistolets (pees-sto-la). *Fre.* Crusty rolls; popularly used for sandwiches.

pistou (pees-too). *Fre.* A rich, garlic-flavored vegetable soup, made of green beans, potatoes, tomatoes, and vermicelli.

pit (peht). *USA.* To remove pits from fruits.

pita (PEE-tah). *USA.* A Middle Eastern round, flat bread slit open to form a pocket; used with endless varieties of fillings.

pitepalt (PEE-teh-palt). *Swe.* Potato dumplings stuffed with pork.

Pithiviers (pee-tee-vee-a). *Fre.* An almond cake, a large round of puff pastry with almond paste filling, decorated in pinwheel or rosette pattern.

pito-ja-joulupuuro (PEE-to-ya-YO-loo-poo-roh). *Fin.* Whole-grain barley pudding cooked in milk and served with rose-hip or raisin puree.

piviere (pee-vee-EH-ray). *Ita.* Plover.

pivo (PEE-voh). *Rus.* Beer.

pizelle (peets-TSEH-leh). *Ita.* Deep-fried pizza dough; eaten plain, with tomato sauce, sautéed vegetables, or cheese; also a cookie baked on an intricately patterned iron called a pizelle iron. Cookie can be rolled conically for filling with pastry creams or ice cream.

pizza (PEAT-zah). *Ita.* An open-faced pie spread with all manner of savory foods.

pizza di ricotta (PEAT-zah dee ree-KOAT-tah). *Ita.* Cheesecake.

pizzaiola (peat-zee-OHL-ah). *Ita.* A pizza sauce of fresh tomatoes, herbs and garlic; served with steak, fish, or leftover boiled meat dishes.

pizz figliata (peetz feel-YAH-tah). *Ita.* A sweet with honey and nuts.

plaice (plas). *Bri.* A fish with fine-textured, delicate, white flesh; eaten fresh or smoked; a member of the flounder family.

plank (plahnk). *USA.* To bake or broil, meat or fish, on a board of hard wood that seasons the food on it.

plantain (plahn-TAYNE). *Spa.* A fruit similar to the banana, with a high starch and low sugar content, making it suitable for savory cooking; when cooked, a staple food in Central and South America.

plantano (PLAH-tah-noh). *Spa.* Banana.

plantation shortcake (plahn-TAY-shun SHORT-kake). *USA.* Hot cornbread square served with a rich, creamy chicken or ham sauce on top.

plättar (PLAH-tar). *Swe.* Small, thin pancakes.

Plättchen (PLETCH-chen). *Ger.* Pretzel.

pletzlach (plehtz-lohk). *Jew.* Pastry squares with apricot or plum filling; traditional for Passover.

pleurotus mushroom (PLU-roh-tuhs MUHS-room). *USA.* Oyster mushroom.

plie (plee). *Fre.* Plaice; a flatfish similar to sole and flounder.

Plinz (pleenz). *Ger.* Fritter, pancake.

plommegrøt med fløtemelk (PLWM-meh-grurt may FLUR-ter-mehlk). *Nor.* Pudding made of groats, plums, and cream.

plommon (PLOO-mon). *Swe.* Plum.

plommonkompott (PLOO-mon-kom-POT). *Swe.* Plum compote.

plommonpudding (PLOO-mon-PU-ding). *Swe.* Plum pudding.

plommonspäckad fläskkarré (PLOO-mon-SPAH-kad FLASK-ka-RE). *Swe.* Loin of pork with prunes.

plover (PLO-vehr). *USA.* A European shore bird whose eggs are highly prized for their delicious taste.

pluck (pluk). *USA.* The heart, liver, lungs, and windpipe of an animal.

plum (pluhm). *USA.* The edible fruit of a plum tree; round to oval smooth-skinned fruit with oblong seed; flesh is softly-firm and juicy; color ranges from yellow to a blackish-purple or blue; eat raw or cooked.

plum duff (pluhm duhf). *Bri.* A less fancy version of plum pudding made with raisins or currants.

plum pudding (pluhm PUHD-deng). *Bri.* A steamed dessert of various dried fruits and suet, often flamed with brandy. Traditional at Christmas and not a plum in it.

plum sauce (pluhm saus). *USA.* A thick Chinese sweet-sour sauce made of plums, apricots, vinegar, and sugar; Suan mei jiang; duck sauce.

plum tomato (pluhm toh-MAH-toe). *Ita.* Shaped like a plum, slightly stronger flavored than ordinary tomatoes; widely used in Italian cooking.

pluvier (ploo-vay). *Fre.* Plover.

poach (poch). *USA.* To cook in an open pan at simmering point, with sufficient liquid to cover.

poblano (poh-BLAH-noh). *Mex.* A large, dark green, mild tasting chili pepper.

po boy (poh boy). *USA.* Hoagie.

poché (po-shay). *Fre.* Poached.

pochouse (po-shooz). *Fre.* A freshwater fish stew made with wine; matelote.

poco hecho (POA-koa AY-choa). *Spa.* Cooked rare; undercooked.

podina (puh-DEE-nah). *Ind.* Mint.

poffertjes (PUF-fer-jees). *Dut.* Puffy fritters.

poi (POH-ee). *USA.* A Hawaiian paste preparation made of breadfruit, banana, sweet potato, or taro; a staple of the native Hawaiian diet.

point, à (pwan, ah). *Fre.* "To the perfect point"; rare for steak; peak of ripeness for fruit and cheese.

poire (pwahr). *Fre.* Pear.

poireau (pwah-roa). *Fre.* Leek.

pois (pwah). *Fre.* Peas.

pois à la française (pwah ah lah fron-sez). *Fre.* Peas braised with lettuce, spring onions, parsley, butter, a pinch of sugar, and a little water.

pois casses (pwah kahs). *Fre.* Split peas.

pois chiches (pwah chee-ches). *Fre.* Chick-peas.

poisson (pwahs-sawng). *Fre.* Fish.

poisson brun (pwahs-sawng brang). *Fre.* "Brown fish," seasoned with many herbs and wine; a Belgian dish.

poitrine (pwah-treen). *Fre.* Chest, breast, brisket.

poitrine de porc (pwah-treen der por). *Fre.* Pork belly.

poivrade (pwahv-rahd). *Fre.* Pepper sauce; the traditional sauce served with venison.

poivre (pwahvr). *Fre.* Pepper; spicy, pungent.

poivron (pwahv-rawng). *Fre.* Allspice; pimento.

poke (pok). *USA.* A Hawaiian dish of marinated fish in various sauces such as chopped seaweed, Maui onions, chili.

Pokel (PUR-kerl). *Ger.* Pickle.

pokeweed (POK-weed). *USA.* A wild, leafy plant whose young leaves and shoots are edible and are cooked like spinach and asparagus.

polenta (poa-LEHN-tah). *Ita.* A cornmeal pudding that is cooled, sliced and fried, grilled or baked with other foods, especially cheese; an Italian specialty.

polentagrøt (poo-LEHN-tah-grurt). *Nor.* Cornmeal pudding.

polished rice (PAWL-eshed rics). *USA.* Any rice that has had the outer aleurone layer removed.

pollame (poal-LAA-may). *Ita.* Poultry.

pollastrino (poal-lah-STREE-noa). *Ita.* Spring chicken.

pollo (POH-yoh). *Ita, Spa.* Chicken.

pollock (POHL-luhk). *USA.* A fish of the cod family.

polonaise (poh-loh-neh). *Fre.* A garnish of hard-boiled eggs, breadcrumbs, and parsley, mixed in melted butter.

polpetta (poal-PAYT-tay). *Ita.* Meat patty, croquette, meatball.

polpettine di spinaci (poal-payt-TEE-nay dee spee-NAA-chee). *Ita.* Spinach dumplings.

polpettone (poal-payt-TOA-nay). *Ita.* Meat loaf.

polpo (POAL-poa). *Ita.* Squid or octopus.

pølse (PURLSS-err). *Nor.* Sausage.

pølser (PURL-sserr). *Dan.* Sausages.

Polsterzipfel (pohstl-ZEF-fehl). *Ger.* An Austrian jam-filled turnover.

pomace (POHM-asc). *USA.* The dry or pulpy residue remaining after the liquid has been extracted during the cider- or wine-making process.

pomegranate (PAHM-ah-gran-ate). *USA.* An ancient fruit with leathery skin and red fibrous pulp in which many red, glistening, refreshingly acid seeds are embedded, that when removed are used in various savory and sweet dishes. The juice of the seeds is used to make grenadine, a syrup used in mixed drinks.

pomelo (POHM-eh-loh). *USA.* The largest of the citrus fruits; native to Southeast Asia; similar to the grapefruit, but slightly pointed at one end; sweeter than grapefruit; skin is yellow and slightly bumpy; flesh ranges from pink to rose.

pomfret (POHM-freht). *Ind.* Nonoily firm-fleshed fish similar to flounder.

pomme (pom). *Fre.* Apple.

pommes de terre (pomz der tehr). *Fre.* Potatoes; prepared countless ways in France, including: Anna (pomz ahn-nah), Potatoes Anna, a dish of layered potato slices, seasoned with salt and pepper, dotted with butter, baked in a casserole until brown and crisp on the outside, soft on the inside; au lait (pomz oa leh), creamed potatoes; bouilli (boo-yee), boiled potatoes; farcies (fahr-see), stuffed potatoes; frites (free), french fried potatoes; paille (pye), potato "straws", deep-fried, match-stick size potatoes; parisienne (pomz der pah-ree-zyang), small oval shaped potatoes sauteed in butter; purée (py-reh), mashed potatoes.

pommes novelles (pomz noo-vehl). *Fre.* New potatoes.

pomodoro (poam-oa-DAW-roa). *Ita.* Yellow tomato.

pompano (POHM-pah-noh). *USA.* A silvery fish whose rich white meat is a delicacy cooked many ways.

pompelmo (poam-PAYL-moa). *Ita.* Grapefruit.

pompelmoes (PAWM-pul-moos). *Dut.* Grapefruit.

Pont-l'Évêque (pon l'ay-vek). *Fre.* A cows' milk cheese with a square golden rind, a full aroma, and a rich creamy texture and taste.

poori (POOH-ree). *Ind.* Puffy deep-fried bread, made from various combinations of flours, semolina, and mashed potatoes.

poor boy (poor boy). *USA.* Hoagie.

poor knights of Windsor (poor nites of WEHND-suhr). *Bri.* Sliced bread soaked in sherry, dipped in egg batter, fried in butter, and served with cinnamon and sugar; a British version of French toast.

popcorn (POHP-korn). *USA.* An Indian corn whose kernels on exposure to dry heat burst open to form a light, crispy, white starchy mass.

pope's nose (pops nohz). *Bri.* The rump, or tail piece, of a bird. Also called parson's nose.

popover (POHP-ohv-er). *USA.* A hollow quick bread shaped like a muffin and made from a light batter of eggs, flour, and milk; texture resembles Yorkshire pudding.

poppy seed (POHP-pee seed). *USA.* The tiny, black, dried seed of the Mediterranean poppy plant, used in pastries, breads, salad dressing.

pop tart (pohp tahrt). *USA.* A commercially made pastry, similar to a turnover, but thinner, having various fillings; usually heated in a toaster that "pops" up, hence the name; can be heated in an oven or microwave.

porc (por). *Fre.* Pork.

porcella (poar-CHAYL-lah). *Spa.* Suckling pig.

porchetta (poar-KAYT-tah). *Ita.* Suckling pig.

porcini (poar-CHEE-nee). *Ita.* A wild mushroom with a thick fleshy cap and stem; boletus.

porco (POHR-koh). *Por.* Pork.

porgy (POR-gee). *USA.* A saltwater fish related to the bream, found throughout the world; has delicate, moist, sweet flesh and many sharp bones.

pork (pohrk). *USA.* The flesh of swine when dressed for food; can be red or white meat, depending on how the swine is slaughtered.

porkkana (POARK-kah-nah). *Fin.* Carrot.

pörkölt (PURR-kurlt). *Hun.* Goulash made with pork or lamb.

poron (POA-roan). *Fin.* Reindeer.

poronkäristys (POA-roan-KAE-ris-tewss). *Fin.* Paper-thin slices of braised reindeer meat.

poronkieli (POA-roan-KAY-li). *Fin.* Reindeer tongue.

porridge (POHR-rij). *USA.* A term used worldwide for a soft food made by boiling cereal or grain, usually oatmeal, in milk or water until thickened; may or may not be flavored with sugar, salt, butter, raisins, and various other ingredients.

porro (POA-roa). *Ita.* Leek.

porsaankyljys (POAR-saan-KEWL-yewss). *Fin.* Pork chops.

porter (POR-tehr). *Iri.* Dark beer, not as strong or dark as stout.

porterhouse (POR-tehr haus). *USA.* A large, superior beef steak cut from the thick end of the short loin to contain a T-shaped bone and a large piece of tenderloin as the tail.

porto, au (por-toa). *Fre.* A sauce of veal stock, port, orange juice, lemon juice, shallots, orange zest, lemon zest, and thyme.

Port Salut (port sah-laht). *Fre.* A cow's whole-milk cheese; mellow to robust flavor similar to Gouda; semisoft, smooth elastic texture; creamy white to yellow.

portugaise (pohr-tay-geh). *Fre.* A sauce of chopped onions, chopped tomatoes, tomato sauce, meat glaze, chopped parsley, and garlic.

portugaise, à la (ah lah pohr-tay-geh). *Fre.* Stuffed tomatoes with chateau potatoes and portugaise sauce.

posset (PUH-seht). *Bri.* A punch dating to the Middle Ages made of milk, eggs, wine or ale, lemon juice, spices, and sugar; with whipped cream folded in, today it is eggnog.

posta de carne (POUSH-tah duh KAHR-nuh). *Por.* Slice of beef, not a steak.

postej (poh-STY). *Dan.* Pâté or paste.

postre (POHS-treh). *Spa.* Dessert.

potage (pot-ahzh). *Fre.* Soup; a few of the many French soups include: **bonne-femme** (bon fahm), leek and potato soup; **condé** (kawng-day), kidney-bean soup; **julienne** (zhew-lyehn), shredded vegetables soup; **parmientier** (pahr-mahng-tyay), potato soup; **pistou** (pee-stoo), provençal vegetable soup; **printanier** (prahn-tahng-yea), vegetable soup; **Saint-Cloud** (sahn klood), pureed green peas and lettuce, served with croutons; **velouté** (ve-loo-tay), cream soup; **de tomates** (der to-maht), tomato; **de volaille** (der vo-lahy), chicken.

potaje *Spa.* A thick soup or stew.

potatis (po-TAA-tiss). *Swe.* Potatoes; kokt (kookt), boiled potatoes; stekt (staykt), fried potatoes; sturvad (STEW-vahd), creamed potatoes; -mos (-MOOS), mashed potatoes.

potato (pah-TAH-toh). *USA.* The edible, starchy tuber of the potato plant; four types classified as: russet, long white, round white, round red.

potato chips (pah-TAH-toh chehps). *USA.* Very thin slices of raw potatoes that are fried, either homemade or commercially prepared.

potato flour (pah-TAH-toh flowr). *USA.* Made from potatoes that have been cooked, dried, and ground; used in breadmaking to keep bread moist; used to thicken soups and gravies; good in cakes, particularly sponge cakes. Also called potato starch.

potato skins (pah-TAH-toh skeenz). *USA.* The skin and adhering portion of a cooked potato after the pulp has been scooped out.

potato snow (pah-TAH-toh sno). *USA.* Potatoes that have been boiled, dried, then sieved, and not mixed in any way.

potato starch (pah-TAH-toh starch). *USA.* Potato flour.

pot-au-feu (po-toa-fur). *Fre.* An economical and wholesome broth made by cooking vegetables and meat together in water, then serving the meat and vegetables as the main course while using the resulting broth as soup.

pot de creme (poa der krehm). *Fre.* Individual covered cups filled with custard or mousse.

potée (po-tay). *Fre.* A thick soup of pork, potatoes, and cabbage.

poteter (poo-TAY-terr). *Nor.* Potatoes

poteter salat (poo-TAY-terr sah-LAAT). *Nor.* Potato salad.

potetkaker (poo-TAY-terr-kaa-kerr). *Nor.* Potato pancakes.

potiron (po-teer-awng). *Fre.* Pumpkin.

potlikker, pot liquor (POHT-lick-ker). *USA.* The broth in which greens and vegetables have been cooked.

potpie (POHT-pie). *USA.* A savory dish of meat or poultry with vegetables in gravy, baked in a deep dish covered with piecrust.

potpourri (poo-purr-reh). *Fre.* A stew of various kinds of meats and spices.

pot roast (poht rohst). *USA.* A large cut of meat used for braising.

pot roasting (poht ROHST-eng). *USA.* A method of slowly braising large cuts of meat in a tightly covered pot.

potted meat (POHT-ted meet). *Bri.* The English equivalent of French pâté.

potted shrimps (POHT-ted shrehmps). *Bri.* An hors d'oeuvre of small shelled shrimp, seasoned with nutmeg, warmed, and preserved in clarified butter a few days.

pouding (poo-deng). *Fre.* Pudding.

poularde (pool-ahrd). *Fre.* A fattened hen.

poule (pool). *Fre.* A stewing chicken, one too old for other cooking methods.

poule-au-pot (pool-oa-po). *Fre.* Stewed chicken served with reduced pot liquor and vegetables.

poulet (poo-leh). *Fre.* A young spring chicken, used for frying or broiling, weighing up to four pounds.

poulpe (poolp). *Fre.* Squid or octopus.

poultry (POL-tre). *USA.* All domestic fowl kept for eggs or meat.

pound cake (pownd kahk). *USA.* A rich cake originally made using one pound each of sugar, butter, eggs, flour.

pour batter (pohr BAHT-ter). *USA.* A batter that contains 1 part flour to 1 part liquid; such as used for cream puffs, timbale cases, crepes, popovers, dip batters. Also called thin batter.

pousser (poo-say). *Fre.* To rise, as in yeast dough.

poussin (poos-sang). *Fre.* A very young chicken; spring chicken; a fryer.

powdered eggs (PAHW-dehrd ehgs). *USA.* Beaten eggs which have been dried and pulverized into powder form; used basically in commercial food manufacturing.

powdered sugar (PAHW-dehrd SHU-gahr). *USA.* Very finely ground sugar with cornstarch added; quick dissolving. Also known as confectioners' sugar, and in England and France, as icing sugar.

powsowdie (puh-SUH-dee). *Sco.* Sheepshead broth.

pozole (poh-SOH-leh). *Mex.* A thick soup laced with chunks of ham and hominy, topped with shredded lettuce and fried tortilla strips, and served with salsa.

praire (prehr). *Fre.* Thick-shelled clam; quahog.

prairie chicken (PREH-ree CHEH-kehn). *USA.* Grouse of the open plains of the West.

prairie oyster (PREH-ree OEHY-sturs). *USA.* Testicles of a bull, pig, or lamb; breaded and fried. Also called animelles, frivolitées, lamb fries, mountain oyster, Rocky mountain oyster.

praline (prah-leen). *Fre.* The flavoring of burnt almonds in caramel syrup.

praline (PRAY-leen). *USA.* A fudge-type candy made of brown sugar, cream, and pecans; made in 3–4 inch patties.

praties (PRAHT-teez). *Iri.* Potatoes.

pratos de carne (PRAH-too day karn). *Por.* Meat dishes.

pratos frios (PRAH-too FREE-oo). *Por.* Cold dishes; buffet.

Prätost (PREHST-oost). *Swe.* A cows' milk cheese.

prawn (praun). *USA.* A very large shrimp.

precooked rice (pre-KOOKD rics). *USA.* Rice that is milled, enriched, completely cooked and then dehydrated. Also called quick cooking and instant rice.

prei (pry). *Dut.* Leek.

Preiselbeeren (PRIGH-zerl-bay-rern). *Ger.* Cranberrylike berries.

preserves (prc-SERVZ). *USA.* Whole or large pieces of fruit in a thick syrup that sometimes is slightly jellied.

presifted flours (pre-SEFTD flowrs). *USA.* Wheat flours ground to pulverization and sifted; gives different texture to baking.

Pressburger Beugel (PRRES-buhr-gehr BOY-gerl). *Ger.* A rich Austrian pastry filled with ground walnuts.

pressgurka (PRAYSS-gewr-kah). *Swe.* Cucumber salad or relish.

Presskopf (PRRES-kopf). *Ger.* Headcheese.

pressure cookery (PREH-shur KOOK-ree). *USA.* Cooking by steam under pressure, to increase the temperature and shorten the cooking period; done in a special pot called a pressure cooker.

presunto (pray-ZOON-toh). *Por.* Smoked ham.

pretzel (PRET-zehl). *USA.* A brittle, glazed kind of cracker, tied in a loose knot like a rope, and sprinkled with coarse salt.

prezzemolo (preht-TSAY-moa-loa). *Ita.* Parsley.

prickly pear (PREHK-lce pair). *USA.* A general term for the edible fruit of certain cactus whose interior flesh is sweet and mild; used mainly for dessert and candy.

primavera (prec moh-VAY-rah). *Ita.* A garnish of raw or blanched spring vegetables.

prime meat (prim meet). *USA.* The top grade of beef. See meat grades.

primeurs (preem-oor). *Fre.* Early fruit or vegetables.

princesse (pran-ses). *Fre.* A garnish of asparagus tips and sliced truffles in cream sauce. Also asparagus tips stuffed in artichoke bottoms.

prinskorv (PRENS-korv). *Swe.* Small sausages.

printanier (prahn-tahng-yea). *Fre.* Spring vegetable soup.

printanière (prin-tan-yey). *Fre.* Garnished with spring vegetables.

processed cheese (PRO-cessd cheez). *USA.* Cheese made by blending several batches of different cheeses using emulsifiers, then packaging in plastic while still hot.

profiterolles (pro-fee-ter-rol). *Fre.* Small puffs of choux paste filled with cream or custards; can be a sweet or a savory.

prosciutto (pro-SHOOT-toh). *Ita.* Dry-cured spiced ham, not smoked.

protose steak (PRO-tohs stehk). *USA.* A vegetable protein substitute for steak; eaten at certain times when meat is prohibited by kosher dietary laws.

provençale (pro-van-syahl). *Fre.* Cooked with garlic, parsley, and tomatoes in olive oil.

Provolone (pro-vah-LOH-nee). *Ita.* A cows' milk cheese with a buttery color, a buttery, mellow to sharp, smoky and salty taste.

prugna (PROO-nyah). *Ita.* Plum.

pruim (prirm). *Dut.* Plum.

pruna (PROO-nah). *Ita.* Prune.

prune (prewn). *Fre.* Plum.

prune (proon). *USA.* A dried plum.

pruneau (prew-noa). *Fre.* Prune.

psito arni (psee-TOSS ahr-NEE). *Gre.* Roast lamb.

ptarmigan (TAHR-meh-gehn). *USA.* A Scandinavian grouse with feathered feet.

puchero (poo-CHEH-roa). *Spa.* Meat boiled in an earthenware pot.

pudding (POOD-ding). *Dut.* Pudding.

pudding (PUHD-deng). *USA.* A dessert of a soft, thick, creamy consistency.

pudim de ovos (poo-DEE day AW-vohss). *Por.* Egg pudding.

pudim flan (poo-DEE flahn). *Por.* Caramel custard.

pudin (poo-DEEN). *Spa.* Pudding.

puerco (PWEHR-koh). *Spa.* Pig; pork.

puerros (PWAYR-roass). *Spa.* Leeks.

Puffer (POO-fehr). *Ger.* Pancake; fritter.

puff pastry (puhf PAH-stree). *USA.* Flaky, rich pastry, made by enclosing butter in the dough, rolling thin, folding, rolling, turning many times to produce many leafy thin layers.

puit d'amour (pwee d'ah-moor). *Fre.* A small round pastry usually filled with cream or jelly; fruit is also used.

pulla (POOL-lah). *Fin.* Braided yeast cake.

pullao (poo-LAW-oo). *Ind.* Pilaf.

pullet (PUHL-et). *USA.* A young chicken hen, weighing up to four pounds, used for frying or broiling.

pulpo (POOL-poa). *Spa.* Squid or octopus.

pulque (POOL-keh). *Mex.* Distilled sap of agave (century plant).

pulse (puhls). *USA.* Dried, edible seeds of legumes, such as peas, lentils, chick-peas, beans.

pultost (PEWLT-oost). *Nor.* A rindless cows' milk cheese, soft and caraway flavored.

pummelos (PUHM-mehl-lohz). *USA.* Chinese grapefruit.

pumpa (PEWM-pah). *Swe.* Pumpkin.

Pumpernickel (POOM-pehr-neh-kehl). *Ger.* A dark, slightly sour, coarse textured rye bread.

pumpkin (PUM-kehn). *USA.* A usually large, round, yellow-orange fruit of the gourd family that is cultivated as a food.

punajuuri (POO-nah-YOO-ri). *Fin.* Beetroot.

punajuurikeitto (POO-nah-YOO-ri-KAYT-toa). *Fin.* Borscht; beet soup.

punajuuri salaati (POO-nah-YOO-ri SAH-laa-ti). *Fin.* Beet salad.

punch (puhnch). *USA.* A beverage mixture, alcoholic or nonalcoholic, made from a variety of ingredients, usually fruit based.

punchero (puhn-CHER-oh). *Mex.* A one pot dish of meats, vegetables, legumes, served broth first, then meats and vegetables.

Punschtorte (PUNSH-tor-ter). *Ger.* Rum cake.

puntarelle (poon-tah-REHL lea). *Ita.* A special Roman salad green, served only in winter; very long stalks with needlelike serrated leaves that curl when cut; served with oil, vinegar, salt, anchovy, and crushed garlic.

puppadam (PA-pa-rahm). *Ind.* Puffy lentil wafers.

puree (pur-ray). *Fre.* Food that is passed through a sieve to achieve a smooth consistency.

puri (POOH-ree). *Ind.* Another spelling for poori.

purjo (PEWR-yoo). *Swe.* Leeks.

purple granadilla (PUHR-pul grahn-nah-DEHL-lah). *USA.* The purple egg-sized tropical fruit whose sweet yellow flesh is eaten raw with the small black seeds, or squeezed for juice; has sweet-acid flavor. Also called passion fruit.

purslane (PURSC-leen). *USA.* An herb with succulent, fleshy leaves that have a tart, vinegary taste; good in sandwich spreads and in soups.

puss pass (POOSS-pass). *Nor.* Stew of mutton, carrots, potatoes, and cabbage.

pútáo (poo-tao). *Chi.* Grapes.

pútaogan (poo-tao-GAN). *Chi.* Raisins.

pútáojiu (poo-tao-JIU). *Chi.* Wine.

putt i panna (pewt ee PAHN-nah). *Swe.* "Tidbits in a pan"; chunks of meat, sausages, and fried potatoes topped with a fried egg.

puuro (POO-roa). *Fin.* Porridge; used as main dish or dessert; may be oats, rice, or rye.

pyramide (pee-ra-meed). *Fre.* A generic name for goats' milk cheese; is very white, soft, crumbly, delicately flavored.

pyy (pew). *Fin.* Hazel hen.

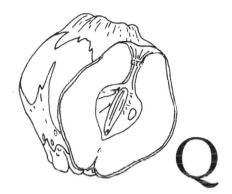

qarnabit (ar-na-BEET). *Ara.* Cauliflower.

qasbi (AHUS-bee). *Ara.* Liver.

qatayif (a-TAA-yif). *Ara.* Tiny pancakes, layered with nuts, syrup, and cream.

qdemi (DAH-mee). *Ara.* Roasted and unsalted garbanzo beans.

qiaokelì (chiao-ke-lee). *Chi.* Chocolate.

qiézi (chieh-dzi). *Chi.* Eggplant.

qíncài (ching-tsai). *Chi.* Celery.

qingcài dòufù tang (ching-tsai doh-foo tong). *Chi.* Vegetable soup with beancurd.

qing jiao (ching jiao). *Chi.* Green pepper.

qingjiao niúròu (ching-jiao niu-row). *Chi.* Shredded beef with green peppers.

qingyú (ching-yu). *Chi.* Mackerel.

qingzheng (ching-dzeng). *Chi.* To steam food.

qing-zheng quán yú (ching-dzeng chuan yu). *Chi.* Whole fish steamed.

qìshui (chi-shui). *Chi.* Soft drink.

quaglia (KWAH-lyah). *Ita.* Quail.

quahog (KO-hahg). *USA.* A thick-shelled clam found in the New England coastal waters.

quail (kwal). *USA.* A small migratory game bird found the world over and prized for its delicious flavor; bobwhite.

quaking custard (KWAK-eng KUHS-tahrd). *USA.* A shivering, quivering cream custard, usually garnished with egg whites; originated in New England.

Quark (kwark). *Ger.* A cows' skim milk cheese, soft, runny; a type of cottage cheese eaten with fruit, salads, or used in cooking.

Quarkklösse (KVAHRK-klurs-ser). *Ger.* Sweet cottage cheese dumplings.

quartre-épices (ka-truh ay-pee-say). *Fre.* A spice mixture of ground ginger, nutmeg, cloves, and cinnamon when used with sweet, or white pepper when used with savory dishes. Also called four spices.

quartre-quarts (ka-truh kar). *Fre.* A pound cake made of four ingredients in equal parts: sugar, butter, eggs, and flour.

quasi de veau bourgeoise (kwa-zi da vo boars-zwah). *Fre.* A casserole of veal rump braised with pork, calf's foot, and vegetables.

quassia-amara (kahs-se-ah-ah-mah-rah). *Fre.* An aperitif made by the decoction of the bark, wood, or root of the Surinam tree, native to South America.

queen of puddings (kween of PUHD-engs). *Bri.* A pudding of custard and breadcrumbs, spread with strawberry jam, covered with meringue, then lightly browned.

Queensland nut (KWEENZ-lund nuht). *Aus.* Macadamia nut, a native of Australia, now grown in Hawaii.

queijadas de sintra (kayee-SHAH-dahsh duh SEEN-trah). *Por.* Rich cakes made with cheese, almonds, eggs.

queijo (KAY-zhoh). *Por.* Cheese.

queijo de Azeitão (kayee-ZHOO duh AH-layn-tawng). *Por.* A strong-tasting, but delicious cheese; very creamy when fresh.

queijo do Alentejo (kayee-ZHOO doo-AH-layn-tay-zhoo). *Por.* A ewe- and goats' milk cheese; savory, salty.

queijo Flamengo (kayee-ZHOO flah-MAYN-goo). *Por.* Portugese version of Edam cheese.

quemada (keh-MAH-tha). *Mex.* Burnt milk; caramel-colored.

quenelles (kern-ehl). *Fre.* A light dumpling made of various forcemeats, bound with eggs, shaped variously, poached in broth, and served as an entree with a butter sauce or as a garnish to soup.

quente (kent). *Por.* Warm; hot.

quesadilla (keh-sah-DEE-yah). *Mex.* A turnover made by stuffing a tortilla with a savory filling and frying or broiling.

queso (KEH-soh). *Spa.* Cheese.

Queso blanco (KEH-so BLAHN-ko). *Spa.* A cows' milk cheese that is smooth, rindless, and eaten fresh with fruit or matured.

queso de cerdo (KEH-so day THEHR-doh). *Spa.* Headcheese.

quetsch (ketch). *Fre.* A plum used to make tarts and other confections; the juice is distilled into a colorless liqueur used to make brandies.

queue (kuh). *Fre.* Tail.

queue de boeuf (kuh day buhf). *Fre.* Oxtail.

queue d'écrevisses (kuh d'ay-kruh-vees). *Fre.* Crayfish tails.

quiche (keesh). *Fre.* An open, savory custard tart using a base of egg custard and cheeses with infinite variations.

quiche Lorraine (keesh lo-rehn). *Fre.* Quiche with bacon or ham added to the custard.

quick bread (kwik brehd). *USA.* Breads made with a quick-acting leavening agent, such as baking soda or baking powder, that permit immediate baking, such as biscuits, muffins.

quince (kwenc). *USA.* A fruit of the rose family that resembles a hard-fleshed yellow apple and is used in jellies, marmalades, and preserves.

quinoa (KEEN-wah). *Spa.* A nutritious grain that is the seed of the pigweed, native to the Andes; use same as barley, rice, oats.

Quitte (KVIT-ter). *Ger.* Quince.

Quittengelee (KVIT-ter-zher-LAY). *Ger.* Quince marmalade.

R

rabaçal (rah-bah-SAHL). *Por.* A Pombal cheese.

rabadi (RA-bhree). *Ind.* Milk thickened by reduction.

rabanadas (rah-bah-NAY-dahs). *Por.* A fried bread dessert.

rabanetes (rah-bah-NAY-tay). *Por.* Radishes.

rábano (RAH-bah-noh). *Spa.* Radish.

rábano picante (RAH-bhah-noa pee-KAHN-tee). *Spa.* Horseradish.

rabarber (rah-BAHR-berr). *Dan, Swe.* Rhubarb.

rabarbergrød (rah-BAHR-berr-grurdh). *Dan.* Rhubarb pudding or sauce.

rabarbra (rah-BAHR-brah). *Nor.* Rhubarb.

rabbit (RAH-beht). *USA.* Small member of the hare family; both domesticated and wild; has white flesh, less fat and sweeter taste than chicken; prepared similar to chicken. Also called hare.

råbiff (raw-BIFF). *Swe.* Raw beef; steak tartar.

Rachel (rah-shell). *Fre.* A garnish for tournedos: bone marrow and bordelaise sauce.

racine (ra-seen). *Fre.* Root vegetable.

rack (rahk). *USA.* A cut of lamb or veal from the rib section; served whole, in seven rib chops, or as crown roast.

Râclette (rahk-leht). *Fre.* A variety of Swiss cheese fondue made by melting a big piece of cheese by the fire and scraping off the softened cheese onto a plate of potatoes cooked in their jackets, accompanied by a glass of very heavy white wine.

radicchio (rah-DEEK-kee-oa). *Ita.* Red chicory; looks like a miniature head of red cabbage with white stalks and veins; bittersweet, satiny, crisp; used as a salad green or cooked vegetable.

radici (rah-DEE-cee). *Ita.* Radishes. Sometimes called ravanélli.

Radieschen (rah-DEES-khern). *Ger.* Radishes; red, white, purple, black; mild to very hot.

radijis (rah-DEYS). *Dut.* Radish.

radis (rah-dee). *Fre.* Radish.

radish (RAAH-dish). *USA.* A root vegetable; small, round with red outer peel and white interior; ranges from slightly- to fiery-hot taste; eaten raw; seeds used for sprouts.

rädisor (REH-dis-soor). *Swe.* Radishes.

rådjurssadel (REH-dis-soor-saa-dayl). *Swe.* Saddle of venison roasted.

rådjursstek (RO-yuussh-STEK-kah). *Swe.* Venison steak. Also called hjortstek.

rädyr (RAW-dewr). *Nor.* Venison.

rafano (rah-FAH-noh). *Ita.* Horseradish.

raffinade (ra-fee-nahd). *Fre.* Refined sugar.

raggmunkar (RAG-MUNG-kahr). *Swe.* Potato pancakes.

ragout (ra-goo). *Fre.* A rich, highly seasoned stew of meats, poultry or fish, browned or not browned, with or without vegetables.

Ragoût fin (rah-GU fehn). *Ger.* A delicate combination of organ meats such as sweetbreads and brains, cooked with mushrooms in a wine cream sauce, often served in a puff pastry shell.

ragù (rah-GOO). *Ita.* A sauce made of olive oil, butter, meat, and garlic.

ragù Bolognese (rah-GOO boa-loa-NAY-zay). *Ita.* A meat sauce of ground beef, pork, and ham sauteed in butter and oil with chopped vegetables, and simmered with milk, white wine, and tomatoes; often used for pasta.

Ragusano (rah-goo-SAHN-oa). *Ita.* A rectangular cows' milk cheese; delicate and sliceable when young, firm and sharp when aged; sometimes smoked.

Rahm (rahm). *Ger.* Cream.

Rahmschnitzel (RAHM-shnit-serl). *Ger.* A Swiss dish of veal scallops in cream.

rai (RAH-ee). *Ind.* Mustard.

raie (reh). *Fre.* Skate, a fish of the ray family; the edible portions are the "wings," which have a firm white meat so similar to sea scallops in texture and flavor that it has been used as a substitute for many years.

raifort (ray-for). *Fre.* Horseradish.

raisin (reh-zang). *Fre.* Grape.

raisin (RA-zehn). *USA.* Dried grapes; eaten as dessert; used in breads, cakes, cookies, confections, as well as in savory dishes.

raisin de Corinthe (reh-zang day kor-enth). *Fre.* Currants; used in baked goods, puddings.

raisin sec (reh-zang sehk). *Fre.* Dried grapes; same as raisin.

raisu (RAH-ee-soo). *Jap.* Cooked rice served in a bowl Japanese style. See kome, gohan.

rajas (RAH-khahs). *Mex.* Strips of poblano chili pods fried with onions and potatoes or tomatoes.

rajma (RA-jeh-mah). *Ind.* Red kidney beans.

räkor (RAI-kor). *Swe.* Prawns; shrimp.

rakørret (RAH-ker-ret). *Nor.* Trout that has been salted down and cured, a Norwegian speciality.

ramekin (RAHM-eh-kehn). *Bri.* A small cheese tart. Also a small flameproof dish.

ramen (RAH-mehn). *Jap.* White curled noodles used in soups.

ramequin (ram-e-kin). *Fre.* A small flameproof dish.

ramequins (rah-mer-kang). *Fre.* Tiny cheese pies.

ramp (rahmp). *USA.* A wild leek; member of the onion family; looks like a scallion; has a strong flavor.

rampion (RAHM-pe-yon). *USA.* A plant whose tuberous root is eaten raw or cooked and whose leaves are eaten like spinach.

ram tulsi (rahm TOOL-see). *Ind.* White basil.

ranchero (rahn-CHEH-roh). *Spa.* Country style.

rane fritte (RAH-neh FREE-teh). *Ita.* Fried frogs' legs.

rankins (RAHN-keens). *USA.* A cheese pudding that is a type of souffle because beaten egg whites are incorporated in the dish.

rapa (RRA-pah). *Ita.* Turnip.

raparperi (RAH-pahr-payri). *Fin.* Rhubarb.

rape (rahp). *USA.* A European herb of the mustard family whose seeds yield an oil used in the Mediterranean and Middle East countries for salads and frying.

rapé (RAH-pay). *Spa.* An ugly-looking fish whose tailsection is a delicacy; white, firm flesh; known as monkfish or goosefish.

râpé (rah-pay). *Fre.* Grated cheese; commonly used abbreviation for fromage râpé.

râper (rah-pay). *Fre.* To grate, especially cheese.

rapini (rah-PEE-nee). *USA.* A vegetable with dark green chardlike leaves on a stalk; a slightly bitter flavor; serve as vegetable by steaming, or added raw to salads. Also known as broccoli rabe and choysum.

rapphøne (RAHP-hur-ner). *Nor.* Partridge.

rårakor (ROH-rah-koor). *Swe.* Lacy potato pancakes.

rarebit (RAHB-biet). *Bri.* Hard Cheddar-type cheese melted with beer or milk and seasonings, served over toast; Welsh rarebit.

rasam (REH-sahm). *Ind.* Spicy lentil broth: tart, tamarind-flavored; either drunk at the start of a meal, or eaten with rice.

rasedar (reh-seh-DAHR). *Ind.* Vegetables in thin gravy.

rasher (RAH-shehr). *Bri.* A single thin slice of bacon or ham.

ras malai (RAHS ma-LIE-ee). *Ind.* Dessert of cheese dumplings in pistachio-flecked cream sauce.

raspberries (RAZ-behr-reez). *USA.* A fleshy, dark-purple or red berry grown on various bramblelike plants.

raspings (RAHS-pehngs). *USA.* Bread crumbs prepared from oven-dried crusts.

ratafia (raht-ah-FEE-ah). *USA.* The essence of bitter almonds; a macaroon; a small airy biscuit made of beaten egg whites, sugar, butter, and ground almonds.

ratafia (rah-tahf-FEE-ah). *Ita.* A sweet liqueur made by marinating black cherries in sugar.

ratatouille (rat-ah-too-e). *Fre.* A stew of diced eggplant, tomatoes, green peppers, zucchini, onions, and garlic, cooked in olive oil.

raton (reh-toyn). *Fre.* A kind of cheesecake.

Räucherall (ROY-kher-raal). *Ger.* Smoked eel.

ravanélli (rah-vah-NAHL-lee). *Ita.* Radishes. Also called radici.

ravigote (rah-vee-goht). *Fre.* A classic richly-flavored, cold green herb sauce made with capers, chopped onions, and herbs; as a classic sauce served hot, it is velouté with white wine, shallot butter, and herbs.

ravioli (rav-vee-OH-lee). *Ita.* Small pasta squares stuffed with forcemeats, spinach, or cheeses.

raw (raugh). *USA.* Uncooked, fresh.

rawbi (RAH-bee). *Ara.* A starter or culture for making yogurt.

raw pack (raugh pahk). *USA.* A term used in canning of foods; boiling syrup, juice, or water added to raw foods in the canning jars or cans, then processed in a boiling-water bath.

raw sugar (raugh SCHU-guhr). *USA.* Processed from cane; U.S. Department of Agriculture notes that it is "unfit for direct use as a food ingredient because of the impurities it ordinarily contains."

razza (RAHT-tsah). *Ita.* Skate; of the flatfish family.

Rebhuhn (REHP-hoon). *Ger.* Partridge.

Reblochon (roh-blo-shahng). *Fre.* A cows' milk cheese that is rich, soft, and has a delicately fruity flavor; disc shape; gold rind.

recette (ruh-set). *Fre.* Recipe.

rechauffé (ray-sho-fay). *Fre.* Leftover food that is recooked or remade.

recheio (ray-SHAY-yoh). *Por.* Stuffing.

reconstitute (ree-KON-ste-toot). *USA.* To restore concentrated foods to their original state, usually by adding a liquid.

red banana (rehd bah-NAN-nah). *USA.* A short, squat banana with a sweeter taste than a yellow banana; peel is purple-red when ripe; flesh is creamy white with a tinge of light pink.

red bartlett pear (rehd BART-lett pair). *USA.* A bell-shaped, sweet tasting pear with red or red-over-green skin and white flesh; eaten fresh out of hand.

red beans and rice (rehd behnz ahnd rics). *USA.* A specialty of southern Louisiana where red kidney beans are cooked with ham hock and served over rice.

red currants (rehd KUHR-rahnts). *USA.* Small red, semitransparent berries; pleasant, sour flavor; use for jellies, preserves, syrups, sauces; add to baked goods such as muffins, breads.

redeye gravy (REHD-ey GRAV-e). *USA.* Ham gravy made by deglazing the utensil in which the ham was cooked, using ice water or coffee with a little brown sugar as the liquid.

redfish (REHD-fesch). *USA.* One of the names for ocean perch.

red flannel hash (rehd FLAHN-nul haesh). *USA.* Made from leftovers of a New England boiled dinner, by chopping the beets, potatoes, turnips, cabbage, corned beef, then browning together in a skillet.

red herring (rehd HEHR-eng). *USA.* Herring left whole and ungutted, then heavily salted, and cold-smoked for three weeks until it becomes deep red in color and hard.

redikker (REHD-di-kerr). *Nor.* Radishes.

red-leaved chicory (rehd-leevd CHICK-er-rey). *USA.* A lettucelike plant used in salads; spectacular crimson color; livens up salad taste; much used in northern Italy.

red mullet (rehd MUHL-leht). *USA.* Rouget; a very desirable Mediterranean fish; white, sweet, delicate flesh.

red onion (rehd UN-yun). *USA.* A fancy edible bulb of the lily family whose flesh is a light pinkish-white with the outer layer of each ring a maroon color; used widely in salads and as garnishes.

red perch (rehd purch). *USA.* One of the names for ocean perch.

red potatoes (rehd poh-TA-toas). *USA.* A round potato with white flesh and a pinkish-red skin.

red sauce (rehd saus). *USA.* Any Italian-style tomato sauce or tomato-flavored clam sauce.

red seedless watermelon (rehd SEED-lehss WAH-tehr-mehl-lon). *USA.* A melon about the size of a basketball that has all the characteristics of a watermelon but contains no seeds.

red snapper (rehd SNAHP-pehr). *USA.* A saltwater fish, abundant around Florida and the Gulf of Mexico; best known of the species; rose-red in color, carmine fins; white, succulent, sweet flesh.

red stew (rehd steu). *Chi.* Meat cooked without browning in liquid that is half soy sauce and half water, seasoned with ginger, scallions, and curry; meat is colored during cooking.

reduce (re-DUCS). *USA.* To boil down, evaporating liquid from a cooked dish to thicken its consistency and concentrate its flavor.

reduction sauce (ree-DUHK-shun saus). *USA.* A sauce that is thickened by the evaporation of liquid during very slow simmering to achieve more richness and subtlety of taste and flavor.

réduire (ray-dweer). *Fre.* To reduce a liquid.

ree (reh). *Dut.* Venison.

Réforme, à la (reh-fohr-ma, ah lah). *Fre.* A garnish of julienne strips of ham, truffles, carrots, hard-boiled egg whites in poivrade sauce; usually served with breaded and fried lamb chops.

refresh (ree-FREHSH). *USA.* To make cold under running water.

refried beans (RE-frid beans). *USA.* Frijoles refritos; dried pinto or pink beans cooked, mashed, and added to bacon drippings, then cooked until thickened and drippings are absorbed.

refrigerator cookies (ree-FREHG-ehr-a-tor KOOK-ees). *USA.* Cookie dough that is prepared, rolled, and wrapped, then stored in the refrigerator to chill until ready to bake; facilitates very thin slicing.

Regensburgerwurst (RAY-gerns-bur-gerr-voorst). *Ger.* A short, fat pork and beef sausage.

réglisse (ray-glees). *Fre.* Licorice.

Reh (ray). *Ger.* Venison.

Rehrücken (RAY-rew-kern). *Ger.* Saddle of venison.

rehydrate (ree-HI-drate). *USA.* To restore water lost during drying process, usually by cooking or soaking.

reine, à la (rehn, ah lah). *Fre.* Garnished with chicken in some form.

reinette (reh-neh). *Fre.* Russet apple.

reinsdyr (RAYNSS-dewr). *Nor.* Reindeer.

reinsdyrstek (RAYNSS-dewr-sstayk). *Nor.* Reindeer steak.

Reis (righss). *Ger.* Rice.

Reisauflauf (righss-OWF-lowf). *Ger.* Rice pudding.

rejemad (RIGH-er-mahdh). *Dan.* Smørrebrød delicacy of mounds of tiny pink shrimps.

rejer (RIGH-err). *Dan.* Shrimps.

reker (RAY-kerr). *Nor.* Shrimps.

relish (REHL-esh). *USA.* A spicy, often pickle-base condiment used as a spread or as a side dish.

rellenos (rreh-YEH-nohs). *Spa.* Stuffed, stuffing.

remolacha (ray-moa-LAH-chah). *Spa.* Beet.

remoulade (ray-moo-LAHD). *Fre.* A classic sauce of mayonnaise to which chopped gherkins, capers, parsley, spring onions, chervil, chopped tarragon, and anchovy essence are added; served with a cold dish or used as salad dressing.

Renaissance, à la (reh-nee-zsahnce, ah lah). *Fre.* With spring vegetables.

render (WREHN-der). *USA.* To melt down, or free fat from connective tissue, at low heat.

renkon (LEHNG-kong). *Jap.* Fresh lotus root.

rennet (WREN-neht). *USA.* An enzyme from the stomach lining of calves, kid or lamb that coagulates the casein of milk; vegetable rennets have the same property.

rensdyrstek (RAYNSS-dewr stayk). *Nor.* Roast reindeer.

renstek (RAYN-syayk). *Swe.* Roast reindeer.

renverser (ron-vehr-say). *Fre.* To unmold on a plate.

repollo (ray-POAL-yoa). *Spa.* Cabbage.

Rettich (REH-tikh). *Ger.* Radish.

reuben (ROO-behn). *USA.* A sandwich of sliced corned beef and Swiss cheese on rye bread that has been spread with Russian dressing, then topped with sauerkraut and grilled.

revbensspjäll (RAYV-bayns-spyehl). *Swe.* Roast spareribs.

revenir (ruh-vuh-neer). *Fre.* To brown.

Rhabarber (rah-BAHR-berr). *Ger.* Rhubarb.

Rheinlachs (RINE-lahks). *Ger.* Rhine salmon, a real delicacy. Also called Rheinsalm.

Rheinsalm (RINE-zahlm). *Ger.* Rhine salmon. Also called Rheinlachs.

rhubarb (RUE-barb). *USA.* A plant with thick reddish stalks used in pies, tarts, compotes, and jams; only the stalks are edible.

rib (rehb). *USA.* On a beef carcass, that part of the forequarter between the chuck and the loin; used whole as a standing rib roast or cut into individual rib chops.

ribbe (REEB-beh). *Nor.* Rib pork chops.

ribes (REE-bays). *Ita.* Currants.

ribollita (ree-bohl-LEE-tah). *Ita.* A famous bean soup made with black cabbage, a very dark-colored vegetable with elongated leaves.

ricci (REE-chee). *Ita.* Sea urchins; a shellfish.

ricciarelli (reech-chah-REHL-lee). *Ita.* Almond cookies; biscuits.

rice (rics). *USA.* A semiaquatic member of the grass family; its edible seed is the staple grain for over half the world's population; basically divided into long-grain, medium-grain, and short-grain; very low in fat, high in gluten, but does not give an elastic paste. See also the following varieties of rice: Arwa Chawal, Basmati, brown, Carolina, converted, glutinous, Indo-Chinese, instant, Japanese, Java, Patna, Persian-style, Piedmont, polished, Roman, unpolished, and wild.

rice (rics). *USA.* To force potatoes and other vegetables and fruits through a tool that has small holes called a ricer, so that the food resembles grains of rice.

rice flour (rics flowr). *USA.* Makes a close but delicately textured cake in recipes heavy in eggs; not to be confused with the waxy rice flours known as sweet flour or mochika.

Richelieu (risch-eh-lou). *Fre.* A large sweet pastry made in cake layers spread with apricot jam and frangipane cream, then iced with white fondant flavored with maraschino and decorated with angelica.

Richelieu, à la (risch-eh-lou, ah lah). *Fre.* A classic garnish for meat; stuffed tomatoes and mushrooms, braised lettuce and potatoes lightly roasted in butter.

ricotta (ri-COT-toh). *Ita.* Not a cheese, but a by-product of the cheesemaking process; made from leftover whey of other cheeses (ewe or cow), sometimes enriched with cream; bland, sweet, and dry; eaten fresh or cooked.

riekko (RAYK-koa). *Fin.* Ptarmigan; Scandinavian grouse.

rigaglie (rah-GAHG-lee). *Ita.* Giblets.

rigatoni (rehg-ah-TONE-e). *Ita.* Macaroni with fat ribs.

rigodon (reh-gah-dohn). *Fre.* A custard tart served either warm or cold, either savory with ham or bacon or sweet with fruit puree.

riisi (REE-ssi). *Fin.* Rice.

rijst (rayst). *Dut.* Rice.

rijstaffel (RAYS-tah-ful). *Dut.* Javanese rice table: an elaborate feast with rice as the focal point and dozens of side dishes including meat and seafood dishes, fried, steamed savory foods, vegetables, fruit, chili dishes, sauces and marinades; hot, cool, spicy, bland.

rillauds (ree-yo). *Fre.* A preparation of pork, cut into very small pieces, gently cooked in lard with seasonings, cooled; NOT pounded.

rillettes (ree-yeht). *Fre.* A preparation of pork, cut into very small pieces, gently cooked in lard with seasonings, cooled and pounded in a mortar.

rillons (ree-yahng). *Fre.* A preparation of pork, finely chopped, cooked in fat and seasoned with salt and pepper; served hot or cold.

rillots (ree-yo). *Fre.* Rillauds.

rimmad skinka (RI-mad SHING-KAH). *Swe.* Salted ham.

rimmat kött (RI-mat choht). *Swe.* Salt meat.

Rind (rint). *Ger.* Beef.

Rinderbraten (RINT-err-braa-tern). *Ger.* Roast beef.

Rinderbrust (RINT-err-brust). *Ger.* Beef brisket.

Rinderleber (RINT-err-lay-berr). *Ger.* Beef liver.

Rinder Rouladen (RINT-err roo-LAA-dern). *Ger.* Beef rolls, stuffed and braised.

Rinderwurst (RINT-err-voorst). *Ger.* A type of beef sausage, pressed into a block, fried with apples, and eaten with toast.

Rindswurst (RINTS-voorst). *Ger.* Beef sausage.

riñones (ree-YNOS-nayss). *Spa.* Kidneys.

rins (reess). *Por.* Kidney.

ripieno (rip-YEN-noa). *Ita.* Stuffing.

Ripp (rip). *Ger.* Rib.

Rippchen (RIP-chern). *Ger.* Pork chops, but can be any chops.

Rippenbraten (RIP-pern-braa-tern). *Ger.* Roast loin.

Rippenspeer (RIP-pern-shpayr). *Ger.* Pork ribs; sparerIbs.

Rippenstück (RIP-pern-shtewk). *Ger.* Beef ribs.

ris (reess). *Dan, Nor, Swe.* Rice.

ris à l'amande (REE ah-lah-mahnd). *Dan.* Rice pudding with whipped cream and chopped almonds served with cherry sauce.

ris d'agneau (ree dah-noa) *Fre.* Lamb sweetbreads.

ris de veau (ree der vo). *Fre.* Veal sweetbreads.

risengrød (REA-sen-grehrth). *Dan.* Porridge, or soup made with rice.

risengrynsklatter (rea-sen-grewns-KLAT-ter). *Dan.* Rice fritters.

risengrynslapper (rea-sen-grewns-SLAHP-per). *Nor.* Pancakes.

risgrøt (REESS-grurt). *Nor.* Rice pudding.

risgryn (REESS-gruhn). *Swe.* Rice; also ris.

risgrynsgröt (REESS-gruhns-groht). *Swe.* Rice pudding.

risi e bisi (REE-see eh BEE-see). *Ita.* Rice and peas cooked in broth with onion, parsley, and Parmesan. Also called risi bisi.

riso (REE-sos). *Ita.* Rice.

risoles (ree-SOH-lehs). *Mex.* Fritters.

risotto (ree-SOT-toa). *Ita.* Rice cooked in butter with chopped onions to which stock is added until absorbed; then various savory foods are added.

rissole (ree-sall). *Fre.* A mixture of minced fish or meat, enclosed in pastry, half-moon shaped, and fried; a puff-pastry fritter or turnover.

rissolé (ree-sohl). *Fre.* Food such as potatoes that has been fried.

ristet (RIS-teht). *Nor.* Roasted, grilled, fried.

ristet brød (RIS-teht brut). *Nor.* Toast.

ristet brød (REES-tert brurdh). *Dan.* Toast.

ristet torskerogn (REES-tert TOARS-ker-roan). *Dan.* Fried roe.

rivierkreeft (re-VEE-krehft). *Dut.* Crayfish.

riz (ruzz). *Ara.* Rice.

riz (ree). *Fre.* Rice.

riz à l'impératrice (ree ah l'eim-peh-rah-tres). *Fre.* A vanilla flavored rice pudding with candied fruits and custard cream.

rizards (REH-zahrds). *Sco.* Currants. Also rizzerberries.

riz sauvage (ree so-vazh). *Fre.* Wild rice.

roast (rost). *USA.* To cook uncovered by exposing to dry heat; in an oven, on a spit, on or near hot embers or stones.

roast (rost). *USA.* A cut of meat suitable for roasting.

roast beef (rost beef). *USA.* A cut of beef from the chuck, or the hindquarter cuts of rump, round, or tip that has been roasted.

roaster (rohst-tehr). *USA.* As a food, refers to a chicken of either sex, under eight months old and weighing 3½ to 5 pounds. Also see broiler, fryer, stewing chicken, capon, stag chicken, and cock.

Robiola (ro-bee-O-lah). *Ita.* A soft cow's or ewes' milk cheese, rectangular or disc shaped, reddish thin rind, smooth and even paste.

robusta (ro-BUS-tah). *USA.* A coffee bean used mostly in commercial blends of coffee and in instant coffee, high in caffeine, inferior in taste to arabica.

Rochen (RO-khehn). *Ger.* Skate, a saltwater fish.

Rock Cornish game hen (rahk KORN-esh gam hehn). *USA.* A crossbreed chicken with succulent flesh.

rock crab (rahk krahb). *USA.* A cousin of the Dungeness crab.

Rockefeller (RAHK-ah-fell-eh). *USA.* A garnish, usually for oysters, of creamed spinach with breadcrumbs, chopped bacon, seasonings, herbs.

rocket (RAH-kett). *Ita.* A peppery, piquant tasting aromatic herb used in salads; not to be confused with the poisonous weed also called rocket. Also known as arugula, rugola, misticanza.

rockfish (RAHK-fehsh). *USA.* A fish of the Pacific, sometimes mistakenly called red snapper; has firm, delicate flesh that is lean and used extensively by the Chinese.

rock salt (rahk sawlt). *USA.* A nonedible, unrefined salt used as a base for baking potatoes, heating oysters on the half shell, freezing ice cream; use is based on its ability to retain heat and cold.

Rocky mountain oyster (RAH-kee moun-tane OYU-stur). *USA.* Testicles of a bull, pig, or lamb; breaded and fried. Also known as animelles, frivolitées, lamb fries, mountain oyster, prairie oyster.

rocky road (RAH-kee rohd). *USA.* A confection, can be candy, ice cream, cake, pie, made of milk or dark chocolate mixed with marshmallows and nuts.

rodaballo (roa-dhah-BHAH-lyoa). *Spa.* Turbot.

rödbetor (RUR-bay-toor). *Swe.* Beets.

rode kool (RO-yuh kohl). *Dut.* Red cabbage.

rødgrød med fløde (rohth-GROH meh FLUH-theh). *Dan.* "Red gruel" with cream; pudding of thickened raspberry and currant juices eaten with sweet cream.

rødgrot (RUR-grot). *Nor.* Pudding made of currants and raspberries.

rødkaal (RURTH-kohl). *Dan.* Red cabbage.

rødkål (RUR-kawl). *Nor.* Red cabbage.

rödkål (RURD-koal). *Swe.* Red cabbage.

rødspaette (RUR-spaider). *Dan.* Plaice.

rödspätta (RUR-speh-tah). *Swe.* Plaice.

roe (ro). *USA.* Eggs of fish and shellfish.

roebuck (ro buhk). *USA.* Male roe deer; venison.

rogani gosht (RO-gah-nee gohsht). *Ind.* Rich meat dish made with cream, usli ghee, and spices.

rogan josh (RO-gahn joosh). *Ind.* Lamb braised in yogurt and cream with Moghul spices.

Rogen (RO-gehn). *Ger.* Fish roe.

røget (ROI-ert). *Dan.* Smoked.

røget sild (ROI-ert seel). *Dan.* Smoked herring.

Roggenbrot (RO-gehn-brot). *Ger.* Rye bread.

roggerbrood (RAWKH-uh-broht). *Dut.* Rye bread.

rognoni (roa-NYOA-nee). *Ita.* Kidneys.

rognons (ro-nyawng). *Fre.* Kidneys.

roh (ro). *Ger.* Raw.

Rohkost (RO-kohst). *Ger.* Raw vegetables; crudités.

Rohkost tomaten (RO-kohst tom-MAA-tern). *Ger.* Savory stuffed tomatoes.

roi (RO-ee). *Ind.* A local Calcutta fish.

rojões (ROU-zehngsh). *Por.* Pork prepared with white wine, paprika, and potatoes.

røket fisk (RUR-ket-fisk). *Nor.* Smoked fish.

rökt (rurkt). *Swe.* Smoked.

roll (rohl). *USA.* A small piece of variously shaped baked yeast dough; a bread product.

rollatini (rohl-lah-TEE-nee). *Ita.* Small slices of meat stuffed and rolled; saltimbocca.

rollè (rol-LEH). *Ita.* Slices of meat stuffed and rolled.

rolled oats (rold ouhts). *USA.* Separate flakes formed by rolling the groats with hulls removed and steaming them; thinness of flake determines regular or quick-cooking; popular for adding flavor to cookies; also used as a hot breakfast cereal.

rollmop (rohl-mohp). *Fre.* An hors d'oeuvre of fillet of herring rolled around a gherkin and skewered.

Rollmop (ROL-mops). *Ger.* A pickled herring rolled around a tiny sour onion.

rollo (ROHL-loh). *Spa.* A slice of meat stuffed and rolled.

roly-poly pudding (ROH-lee POH-lee PUHD-deng). *Bri.* Suet pastry spread with jam, rolled in shape of sausage, steamed or baked.

rom (rom). *Swe.* Roe.

romaine (roh-MAHNE). *USA.* . A salad lettuce with firm, thick, narrow leaves; cos lettuce, romaine lettuce.

Roman rice (RO-mahn ris). *USA.* A variety of rice that has dull, greyish-white grains.

Romano (roh-MAHN-oh). *Ita.* A round, ewes' whole-milk cheese, white or very pale yellow paste, dense, with a yellow brown rind; sharp, salty and intense. Same as Pecorino Romano.

romarin (roa-mah-rang). *Fre.* Rosemary.

romavaya baba (RO-mah-vah-yah BAH-bah). *Rus.* Rum cake.

rombo (ROAM-boa). *Ita.* Turbot.

romfrommage (ROM-froa-maa-sher). *Dan.* Creamy rum-flavored dessert.

rømmegrøt (ROHM-meh-greht). *Nor.* Sour cream porridge.

rømmekolle (rohm-meh-KOHL-lee). *Nor.* Yogurtlike dessert of clabbered cream and zwieback crumbs.

rømmesalat (rohm-meh-sah-LAHT). *Nor.* Lettuce with dressing of sour cream.

Roncal (ron-KAHL). *Spa.* A hard, close-grained, pungent ewes' milk cheese.

rookspek (ROHK-spek). *Dut.* Bacon.

rookvlees (ROHK-vlays). *Dut.* Smoked chipped beef.

rookwurst (ROHK-voorst). *Dut.* Smoked sausage.

room (rohm). *Dut.* Cream.

roomeiersaus (rohm-AY-uh-sows). *Dut.* Sour cream sauce with eggs, served on fish.

roomijs (ROHM-ays). *Dut.* Ice cream.

roomkaas (ROHM-kahs). *Dut.* Cream cheese

rooster (Roo-stur). *USA.* An adult male domestic fowl, cock.

Roquefort (rowk-fort). *Fre.* A celebrated cheese of ewes' milk, with thin orange rind, ivory interior, blue-green veining; salty, sharp, creamy taste; a unique cheese in that powder-fine breadcrumbs containing a spiral greenish mold are mixed with the curds.

roquette (roh-kay). *Fre.* Rocket, a salad herb.

rosbif (ros-beef). *Fre.* Roast beef.

rosbif (ROS-beef). *Ita.* Roast beef.

rosbife (rohz-BEE-fay). *Por.* Roast beef.

rosefish (ROHZ-fesch). *USA.* One of the names for ocean perch.

rose hips (rohz hehps). *USA.* The fruit of certain rose plants, high in vitamin C, used in making jellies and syrup.

rosemary (ROHZ-mahr-ee). *USA.* An herb with narrow, glossy dark green needlelike leaves that are grayish white underneath; enhances the flavor of pork and lamb.

Rosenkohl (ROA-zern-koal). *Ger.* Brussels sprouts.

rosenkohl (ROASS-ern-kawl). *Dan.* Brussels sprouts.

rosette (roh-zet). *Fre.* Thin, rich batter made into fancy shapes using a special iron and fried in deep fat.

rose water (ROZ-wah-tehr). *USA.* An oil extracted from the petals of roses, used as a flavoring.

Rosinen (ro-ZEE-nern). *Ger.* Raisins.

rosmarino (roaz-mah-REE-noa). *Ita.* Rosemary.

rosolio (roz-soh-LEE-oa). *Ita.* A very sweet traditional liqueur; delicate taste.

Rossini (roh-see-nee). *Fre.* A classic garnish for small cuts of meat; slices of foie gras sauteed in butter, thick slices of truffles, and stock blended with Madeira.

rostat bröd (ROS-taht brurd). *Swe.* Toast.

Rostbraten (ROAST-braa-tern). *Ger.* Roast beef.

Rostbratwurst (ROAST-braat-voorst). *Ger.* Roasted ham sausage.

Rösti (RUR-shtee). *Ger.* A Swiss dish of shredded potatoes fried in a pancake.

Röstkartoffeln (RURST-kahr-tof-ferln). *Ger.* Home-fried potatoes.

Rotbarbe (ROAT-bahrb). *Ger.* Red mullet.

Rote Grütze (RO-dah GRUT-zeh). *Ger.* A fruit pudding made with farina, heavy cream, fruit juice and sugar; tapioca may be used in place of farina.

Roterübe (ROA-ter-rewb). *Ger.* Beet.

roti (RO-tee). *Ind.* Flat bread.

rôti (roa-tee). *Fre.* Roasted.

rôtir (ro-teer). *Fre.* Toast; a toasted slice of bread.

Rotkohl (ROAT-koal). *Ger.* Red cabbage.

Rotkraut (ROAT-krowt). *Ger.* Red cabbage with apples and vinegar.

rotmos (ROOT-mooss). *Swe.* Mashed turnips.

Rotwein (ROAT-vighn). *Ger.* Red wine.

ròu (row). *Chi.* Meat.

rouelle (rwehl). *Fre.* A fairly thick slice of veal, across the leg.

rouennaise (rwah-nayz). *Fre.* A red wine reduced bordelaise sauce with shallots and pureed raw duck livers.

rougail (ROO-guye). *USA.* A highly spiced Creole condiment that accompanies Creole dishes served with rice.

rouget (roo-heh). *Fre.* Red mullet; a very desirable fish found in the Mediterranean; white, sweet, delicate flesh.

rouille (roo-yuh). *Fre.* A spicy mayonnaise with red pepper and garlic; served with fish.

roulade (roo-lahd). *Fre.* Slices of meat rolled around a filling, then browned, and slowly braised.

Rouladen (roo-LAA-dern). *Ger.* Beef rolls.

round (rownd). *USA.* The part of the beef hindquarter between the rump and the tip; used in various cuts, such as top round, bottom round, top sirloin, or left whole to braise or roast.

roux (roo). *Fre.* A thickener for sauces; a mixture of butter or fat and flour, cooked for varying lengths of time depending on its use; white roux, blond roux, and brown roux.

rova (ROO-vah). *Swe.* Turnip.

rowanberry (roa-uhn-behr-ree). *Fre.* Fruit of the rowan tree; makes a bright red, tart jelly served with venison, game, lamb.

royale (rwah-yal). *Fre.* Molded custard, flavored but not sweetened, used as garnishes in clear soups.

royal icing (ROHY-yahl l-ceng). *USA.* A glazing icing made of confectioners' sugar, egg white, and lemon juice; used for wedding cakes, special cakes, pastry writing; dries hard. Sometimes called royal glaze and Swiss meringue.

royan (wah-yahng). *Fre* A large sardine.

rozijnen (roh-ZI-en). *Dut.* Raisins.

Rübe (rewb). *Ger.* Turnip.

rubyaana (rihbb-YAHN). *Ara.* Persian Gulf shrimp.

ruchetta (ru-KET-tah). *Ita.* Rocket, a salad herb.

rucola (roo-CHOA-lah). *Ita.* Rocket, a salad herb. Also ruchetta.

rue (roo). *Ita.* An herb used for flavoring some brandies.

rugbrød (ROO-brurdh). *Dan.* Dark rye bread.

rugde (REWG-der). *Nor.* Woodcock.

rugola (roo-GOA-lah). *Ita.* Rocket, a salad herb. Also roquette, rucola, ruchetta.

ruh (rooh). *Ind.* Essence.

ruibarbo (rwee-BHAHR-boa). *Spa.* Rhubarb.

rulader (REW-lah-derr) *Swe.* Beef roll.

rull (rooll). *Nor.* Spiced beef roll.

rullepølse (ROO-luh-PUL-seh). *Dan.* Spiced and larded meat roll of veal, beef, or lamb.

rullesild (REWL-leh-sill). *Nor.* Rolled herring.

rumaki (roo-MAH-kee). *Jap.* An appetizer of chicken livers and waterchestnuts wrapped in bacon then broiled.

rump (ruhmp). *USA.* The cut of beef above the round, from the hindquarter.

rundergehak (RHUN-der-her-HAHK). *Dut.* Chopped or ground beef.

rundstykker (ROONN-stewk-kewh). *Nor.* Roll.

rundvlees (ROONT-vlays). *Dut.* Beef.

ruote (RWO-tah). *Ita.* Wheel-shaped pasta.

rusinat (ROO-ssin-naht). *Fin.* Raisins, sultanas.

rusk (ruhsk). *USA.* Slices of a special bread, rebaked, used for breadcrumbs, appetizers, as hard toast.

russe (roos). *Fre.* "With strawberries," as in Charlotte russe.

russe, à la (roos ah lah). *Fre.* Served with sour cream.

russin (roo-sin). *Swe.* Raisin.

rustica, alla (roor-STEE-kah). *Ita.* Anchovies, cheese, garlic, oregano in a sauce served with spaghetti.

rutabaga (roo-tah-BAHG-gah). *USA.* A yellow turnip.

ryba (RI-boo). *Rus.* Fish.

rye flour (ryi flowr). *USA.* Fine granulation; usually combined with wheat flour because rye flour gluten provides stickiness but lacks elasticity; breads made largely from rye flour are moist, compact, made with sourdough leavener.

rye meal (ryi meal). *USA.* Coarsely ground whole-rye flour.

rygeost (REW-eh-oast). *Dan.* Smoked cream cheese.

rype (REW-ber). *Dan.* Grouse, ptarmigan.

rype (REW-per). *Nor.* Grouse, ptarmigan.

rype i fløtesaus (REW-per ee FLUR-ter-ssowss). *Nor.* Ptarmigan in cream sauce, a Norwegian delicacy.

S

saag (sahng). *Ind.* Greens: spinach, collard greens, beet greens, escarole, mustard greens, fenugreek greens.

Saankäse (zahn-KAI-zer). *Ger.* A Swiss cows' milk cheese with a mellow fragrant flavor; hard, large orange discs; dessert or grating cheese.

saba (sah-BAH). *Jap.* Mackerel.

sabayon (sa-by-on). *Fre.* A cream mousse made of egg yolks, flour, sugar, wine or other alcoholic flavorings, beaten over heat while thickening; zabaglione.

sablé (sab-leh). *Fre.* A shortbread; a delicate small biscuit or cake.

sabzi (SAHB-zee). *Ind.* Vegetables.

saccharin (SAH-kehr-rehn). *USA.* A noncaloric sugar substitute; an artificial sweetener 350 times sweeter than sugar.

Sachertorte (ZA-kher-tor-teh). *Ger.* A very rich world-famous Austrian chocolate cake layered with apricot jam and covered with chocolate icing.

sacristain (sahc-chrees-stahng). *Fre.* A spiral shaped puff pastry, flavored with cheese or almonds and sugar.

sadaf (sah-DOHF). *Ara.* Oyster.

saddle (SAH-duhl). *USA.* The cut from the whole carcass of meat from the end of the rib section to the legs on both sides.

safflower oil (SAHF-flawr oyl). *USA.* Oil from the seeds of the safflower plant; light in flavor, high in polyunsaturates.

saffron (SAHF-fron). *Ita.* An herb of an autumn-blooming crocus whose orange-red stigmas are harvested by hand and dried; used for delicately coloring dishes, as well as seasoning.

safran (sahf-rahng). *Fre.* Saffron.

Safran (zah-FRAAN). *Ger.* Saffron.

Saft (zahft). *Ger.* Juice, gravy.

Saftbraten *Ger.* Beef stew.

sage (saj). *USA.* An herb of the mint family with a delicate flavor used to season dressings, pork, goose, cheese, chowder.

Sage Derby (saj DAHR-bee). *Bri.* A sage flavored cheese; flaky, mild, marbled with sage.

sago (SAY-go). *USA.* A starch made from the trunk of Indian palms, used as a thickening agent; pearllike beads, similar to tapioca.

sahlab (SAH-bab). *Ara.* A starch extracted from tubers of any of various orchids and used like tapioca; cornstarch may be substituted; also, a hot milky drink topped with chopped nuts and shredded coconut.

Sahne (ZAH-neh). *Ger.* Cream.

Sahnenkuchen (ZAH-neh-koo-kern). *Ger.* Cheese cake.

Sahnequark (ZAH-neh-kvark). *Ger.* Cream cheese.

saignant (seh-nyahng). *Fre.* Rare, as for meat.

saigneux (say-noo). *Fre.* Neck of veal or lamb.

Sainte-Maure (san-mo-reh). *Fre.* A log-shaped ewes' milk cheese with soft white interior, white rind.

Saint-Pierre (san-pyehr). *Fre.* John Dory, a very tasty ugly-looking fish.

saisir (seh-zeer). *Fre.* To sear.

Saiten (zye-ten). *Ger.* One of many varieties of sausages.

saj (sahjg). *Ara.* Paper-thin bread baked over a metal dome on an open fire.

sakana (sah-KEE-nah). *Jap.* Fish.

sake (SAH-keh). *Jap.* Salmon.

saké (sah-KAH). *Jap.* Sweet or dry white rice wine.

sal (sahl). *Spa, Por.* Salt.

salad (SAHL-ehd). *USA.* A dish of mixed raw, fresh vegetables or fruits, usually served with a dressing; can also be made of meats, fish, poultry, seafood, cheeses, eggs, pasta.

salada (sa-LAH-da). *Por.* Salad.

salad dressing (SAHL-ehd DREHS-eng). *USA.* A liquid mixture, either cooked or uncooked, normally containing either vinegar or mayonnaise, and seasonings.

salade de pissenlit (sah-lahd duh pee-sehn-lee). *Fre.* Wilted dandelion greens salad.

salade verte (sah-lahd vehrt). *Fre.* Green salad.

salado (SAH-doh). *Spa.* Salty, salted.

salambo (sahl-lahm-bo). *Fre.* A small pastry filled with kirsch-flavored creme filling and iced with caramel.

salame di fegato (sah-LAA-may dee fay-GAH-toa). *Ita.* Liverwurst.

salami (sah-LAHM-mee). *Ita.* A highly spiced sausage, often smoked; used as a sandwich meat or cold cut.

Salat (za-LAHT). *Ger.* Salad.

salata (sah-LAH-tchss). *Gre.* Salad of raw fresh vegetables.

salatagurker (sah-LAA-tah-GEWR-kehr). *Nor.* Dill pickles.

Salbei (ZAL-bye). *Ger.* Sage.

salchichas (sahl-CHEE-chahs). *Spa.* Sausages.

sale (SAA-lay). *Ita.* Salt.

salé (sa-lay). *Fre.* Salted.

salées au fromage (sah-layz o fro-mazh). *Fre.* Cheesecake.

salgado (sahl-GAH-doo). *Por.* Salted.

Salisbury steak (SAHLS-buhr-ree stehk). *USA.* A seasoned beef patty, broiled.

salladsås (SAH-lahd-soass). *Swe.* Salad dressing.

Sally Lunn (SAHL-ee Luhn). *Bri.* A kind of tea cake, slightly sweet and raised with yeast

Salm (zahlm). *Ger.* Salmon.

salmagundi (sal-mah-GUN-de). *Bri.* A carefully arranged salad; greens, pickles, hard-boiled eggs, anchovy, chopped meats, onions.

salmão (sal-MEOWN). *Por.* Salmon.

salmon (SAHM-un). *USA.* A salt- and freshwater fish; firm, rich, flavorful meat; very pale to deep orange-red colored flesh; many species, but chinook, sockeye, coho, and Atlantic are best; lox is a salmon product.

salmone (sahl-MOA-nay). *Ita.* Salmon.

salmone affumicato (sahl-MOA-nay ahf-foo-mee-KAA-toa). *Ita.* Smoked salmon.

salmonette (sahl-moa-NAY-tayss). *Spa.* Red mullet.

salpicão (SAHL-pee-kahng). *Por.* Smoked ham roll.

salpicon (sal-pee-cone). *Fre.* A mince of poultry, game, or vegetables, bound with a sauce; used as a stuffing or filling.

salsa (SAHL-sah). *Ara.* Sauce.

salsa (SAHL-sah). *Por.* Parsley.

salsa (SAHL-sah). *Spa.* Seasoned sauce; used for dipping or as a condiment.

salsa borracha (SAL-sah bow-RAA-cah). *Mex.* "Drunken sauce"; made with tequila, orange juice, onion, pasilla chilies.

salsa de tomate (SAHL-sah day toh-MAH-tay). *Spa.* Catsup.

salsa francesa (SAHL-sah FRAHN-theh-sah). *Spa.* French dressing.

salsa inglesa (SAHL-sah een-GLAY-sah). *Spa.* Worcestershire sauce.

salsicce (sahl-SEET-chay). *Ita.* Sausages.

salsicha (sahl-SEE-shash). *Por.* Sausage.

salsifis (sahl-suh-fee). *Fre.* Salsify; oyster plant.

salsify (SAHL-sah-fee). *USA.* A plant whose root is eaten boiled or sauteed; called oyster plant.

salt (sawlt). *USA.* Sodium chloride; an edible crystalline compound, abundant in nature, and used for seasoning or preserving food. See also coarse salt, cooking salt, flake salt, iodized salt, kosher salt, pickling salt, rock salt, sea salt, table salt.

saltfiskballer (sahlt-fisk-BOOL-lehr). *Nor.* Dumplings of potatoes and fish.

saltimbocca (sahl-teem-BOAK-kah). *Ita.* Veal scallop with prosciutto braised in butter and Marsala.

saltpeter (SAWLT-pee-tehr). *USA.* Potassium nitrate; gives flavor and red color to meat.

salt potato (sawlt poh-TAH-toh). *USA.* A small new potato that has been soaked or boiled in brine; a specialty of Syracuse, New York.

salva (SAL-vah). *Por.* Sage.

salvia (SAHL-veeah). *Ita.* Sage.

Salz (zahlts). *Ger.* Salt.

Salzburger Nockerl (zaltz-BOOR-gehr nokh-rehl). *Ger.* Light, airy dessert dumplings.

Salzgebäck (zahlts-ger-BAHK). *Ger.* Salty cracker; pretzel.

Salzgurken (zahlts-GOOR-kern). *Ger.* Dill pickles.

Salzkartoffeln (ZAHLTS-kahr-tof-ferln). *Ger.* Plain boiled potatoes.

samak (SAH-mak). *Ara.* Fish.

sambaar (SAHM-bahr). *Ind.* A very, very chili-hot stew of large split peas (dals) and vegetables served with rice.

sambusik (sahm-BOO-sek). *Ara.* A nut filled cookie; nut moons.

samni (SAHM-nee). *Ara.* The equivalent of butter.

samosa (sa-MO-sah). *Ind.* A stuffed savory deep-fried pastry cone.

samphire (sahm-FEHR). *USA.* A salad green, grown wild or under cultivation; bacile.

Samsø (SAHM-sur). *Dan.* A cows' whole-milk cheese, large round, golden yellow; scattered holes; nutty, mild flavor.

sanamura (sah-nah-MOOR-rah). *Ara.* Herring.

sanbusak (sahn-BOO-sahk). *Tur.* A thin yeast dough turnover filled with minced meat, pinenuts, onions, and cinnamon.

sandia (sahn-DEE-ah). *Spa.* Watermelon.

sandkage (sahnd-KAH-gheh). *Dan.* Sand cake, rich with eggs, butter, sugar.

sandre (sahn-drah). *Fre.* Large perch.

sandwich (SAHN-wehch). *USA.* Two slices of bread, usually, filled with any variety of meats, cheeses, fillings, relishes, jellies, butters, vegetables, lettuce.

sang chow (sehn tso). *Chi.* A light-colored soy sauce.

sanglier (sahng-glyay). *Fre.* Wild boar.

sangria (sahn-GREE-ah). *Spa.* A punch made of mostly wine, flavored with brandy, Cointreau, and fruits; best chilled.

sangue (SAHNG-gooay). *Ita.* Rare, as for meat.

San Pedro (sahn PEH-droh). *Spa.* Better known as St. Peter's fish; the classic ingredient of bouillabaisse; flesh is white, firm and finely flaked.

sansho (SAHN-sho). *Jap.* A greenish-brown ground spice called "Japanese pepper"; tangy but not hot.

San Simon (sahn see-MOHN). *Spa.* A semihard cow's milk cheese that is pear-shaped and bland; sometimes smoked.

Santa Claus melon (SAN-tah klaus MELL-un). *USA.* A melon that resembles a small watermelon with a mottled yellow and green rind; has pale green flesh that tastes similar to honeydew. Also known as Christmas melon.

santola (san-TOL-ah). *Por.* Crab.

santola gratinada (san-TOL-ah grah-tee-NAH-dah). *Por.* Deviled crab.

sap (sahp). *Dut.* Juice.

sapodilla (sahp-o-DEHL-lah). *USA.* A round fruit with thin, brown leathery skin and flesh from honey-blonde to deep red-brown and tastes similar to maple sugar; eat out of hand or in salads and ices.

saporoso (sa-poh-ROA-soa). *Ita.* Relish.

sapsis (SAHP-sehs). *USA.* A bean porridge.

saracen corn (SAH-rah-cen korn). *USA.* Buckwheat.

Sarah Bernhardt (sa-rah burn-hahrt). *Fre.* Served with puree of foie gras.

sarapatel (sah-rah-pah-TELL). *Por.* Liver and bacon.

Saratoga potatoes (sah-rah-TOH-gah poh-TAH-tohs). *USA.* Potato chips. Also called Saratoga chips because they originated in Saratoga, New York.

sarcelle (sahr-sehl). *Fre.* Wild duck.

sarde (sahr-DEH). *Ita.* Sardines. Also sardelle, sardine.

sardelle (sahr-DEH-leh). *Ita.* Sardines. Also sarde, sardine.

Sardelle (zar-DE-leh). *Ger.* Anchovy.

sardin (sar-DIN). *Swe.* Sardine.

sardine (sahr-DEE-neh). *Ita.* Sardelle, sarde.

Sardinen (zar-DEE-nee-en). *Ger.* Sardines.

sardines (sahr-DEENZ). *USA.* Very young herring.

sardinha (sar-DEEN-yash). *Por.* Sardine.

sarsoon (sahr-SOHN). *Ind.* Mustard greens.

sås (soass). *Swe.* Sauce.

sasage (sah-SAH-geht). *Jap.* Very thin, very long green beans; taste is stronger than ordinary green beans. Also known as asparagus beans, dow ghok, long beans, yard-long beans.

sashimi (sah-SHEE-mee). *Jap.* Sliced raw fish.

sassafras (SAHS-sah-frahs). *USA.* An aromatic tree of the laurel family whose bark is dried and used as a flavoring for root beer; the bark is also pounded to make filé powder, an essential ingredient in gumbos.

satsuma-imo (sah-TSOO-mah-ee-moh). *Jap.* Sweet potato.

sato imo (sah-TOE ee-moh). *Jap.* Field yams.

Saubohnen (zow-BOA-nern). *Ger.* Broad beans.

sauce (saus). *USA.* A liquid dressing or topping for food; can be very simple, such as melted butter, or very complicated with many ingredients. There are several basic sauces from which all others are made: **béchamel** (bay-shah-mehl), basic white sauce: white roux and milk; **espagnole** (es-spon-yole), basic brown sauce: brown roux and a brown stock. **mayonnaise** (mah-ohn-aiz), basic yellow sauce: raw egg yolks, oil, and lemon juice or vinegar; for cold sauces; **tomato** (toa-may-toa), basic red sauce: blond roux and tomato purée; **vinaigrette** (vee-nay-greht), basic clear sauce: oil and vinegar; **volouté** (ve-loo-tay), basic blond sauce: white roux and light stock (chicken, fish, or veal).

Any combination of two or more basic sauces creates a compound sauce, of which there are countless variations; listed here are a few well-known sauces (simple and compound) with a hint as to their contents: **aïoli** (ah-oa-lee), garlic mayonnaise; **allemande** (ahl-mange), velouté base thickened with egg yolks; **américaine** (ah-may-ree-kehn), white wine, brandy, garlic, shallots, tomatoes, shrimp or lobster flavoring; **béarnaise** (bayr-naiz), a creamy sauce flavored with vinegar, white wine, tarragon, shallots, and egg yolks; **bercy** (burr-cee), velouté based on fish stock with shallots, white wine, butter; **beurre blanc** (berr blank), butter, shallots, white wine, vinegar; **beurre noir** (berr nohr), browned butter, lemon juice and/or vinegar; **bordelaise** (boar-deh-laiz), boletus mushrooms, shallots, red wine and beef marrow; **bourguignone** (boor-gee-nyawng), red wine and herbs; **bread sauce** (brehd saus), consommé, shallots, finely diced ham, breadcrumbs fried in butter as the roux; **brown gravy** (brahwn gra-vee), beurre noir, au jus, Harvey or Worcestershire sauce, and catsup; **chasseur** (sha-sehr), mushrooms, onions, shallots, herbs, wine; **chaud-froid** (sho-fro), dressing containing gelatine; **diable** (dee-ahbl), white wine, shallots, thyme, demi-glace, parsley, hot peppers; **duxelles** (dews-sehl), with mushrooms; **financière** (fee-non-syehr), Madeira wine, truffles, olives, mushrooms; **fines herbes** (feen zehrb), with herbs; **florentine** (flor-en-teen), with spinach; **hollandaise** (hah-lohn-daiz), raw egg yolks, butter, and lemon juice; **indienne** (ahn-dyen), curry sauce; **lyonnaise** (lyi-ohn-naiz), with onions; **madère** (mah-dehr), with Madeira wine; **marinière** (mah-rahn-yeh), white wine, mussel broth thickened with egg yolks; **Mornay** (mohr-nay), cheese sauce; **mousseline** (moos-ser-leen), mayonnaise with cream; **moutarde** (moo-thard), mustard sauce; **normande** (nohr-mond), with mushrooms, eggs, and cream; **Périgueux** (pay-ree-go), with goose- or duck-liver puree and truffles; **poivrade** (pwah-vrahd), pepper sauce; **porto** (por-toh), with port wine; **provençale** (por-van-syahl), with onions, tomatoes, garlic; **ravigote** (rah-vee-goht), a classic sauce used hot or cold of chopped capers, chives, parsley, tarragon, chervil; **rémoulade** (rue-mah-lahd), sauce flavored with mustard and herbs; **Robert** (rah-burt), espagnole base with sautéed finely diced onions, consommé, vinegar, and fine mustard; **Russian** (Ruhsh-uhn), mayonnaise with puree of caviar and lobster, mustard; **Soubise** (sue-beese), onion-cream sauce; **suprême** (sew-prehm), rich, delicately flavored thickened chicken broth made with heavy cream, **Swedish** (swee-desh), mayonnaise with apple puree, grated horseradish, or mustard; **tartare** (tahr-ter), mayonnaise flavored with mustard and herbs; **verte** (vehrt), mayonnaise with spinach, watercress and herbs; **Vincent** (vehn-sawng), mayonnaise with purée of green herbs, chopped hard boiled egg yolks; **Yorkshire** (york-shur), espagnole base with red currant jelly, port, cinnamon, orange juice and peel.

saucijsjes (so-SAY-shus). *Dut.* Sausages.

saucisse (so-sees). *Fre.* Fresh, small sausage.

saucisson (so-see-son). *Fre.* Large cured sausage.

Sauerbraten (zow-er-BRAH-ten). *Ger.* Beef marinated in spicy vinegar, pot-roasted, and served with gingersnap gravy.

Sauerkraut (SOUR-kraut). *Ger.* A kind of pickled cabbage, made by chopping cabbage that is salted then fermented in its own juice.

sauerkrout (SOUR-krot). *Eng.* Sauerkraut.

sauge (soazh). *Fre.* Sage.

saumon (soa-mawng). *Fre.* Salmon.

saunf (sohnf). *Ind.* Anise; fennel.

Saure Rahmsauce (ZOY-re RAHM-sous). *Ger.* Sour cream dressing used for salads and vegetables.

Saure Sahne (ZOY-re ZAH-neh). *Ger.* Sour cream.

saus (sows). *Dut.* Sauce.

sausage (SAU-sahg). *USA.* A highly seasoned minced or ground meat filling stuffed into a casing.

sauté (saw-TAY). *USA, Fre.* Cook in an open pan in a small amount of fat to tenderize and sear in flavor.

sauté pan (saw-tay). *Fre.* A shallow, thin-bottomed cooking pan, traditionally made of copper.

sauter (so-tay). *Fre.* Toss over the fire, in a saute pan or frying pan, using little butter or fat.

sauvage (so-vazh). *Fre.* Wild, undomesticated.

sával (SAH-vahl). *Por.* Shad.

savarin (sah-vah-rahng). *Fre.* A ring-shaped yeast dough cake soaked in flavored syrup, with rum or kirsch added, and filled variously.

savoiardi (sahr-WAHR-dee). *Ita.* Lady fingers.

savories (SAY-vor-ees). *Bri.* A course presented before the fruit and after the sweet to cut the sugar taste before the port is served; similar to hors d'oeuvres, but a little larger.

savory (SAY-vor-re). *USA.* Food that is not sweet.

savory (SAY-vor-re). *USA.* An herb of the mint family; combines well with other herbs, especially those used with poultry; indispensable for vegetable cookery; has a particular affinity for beans of every sort.

savoyarde (sahv-wah-yahd). *Fre.* With cheese and potatoes.

savoy cabbage (sah-voy KAHB-ahgj). *USA.* A hardy cabbage, in season throughout the winter; a milder flavor than common cabbage, improved by frost; has large, wrinkled leaves that are either purple or cream-colored laced with green trim. Also called salad savoy.

savu (SAH-voo). *Fin.* Smoked.

saya éndo (SAH-yah ehn-DOE). *Jap.* Edible-pod peas. Known as sugar snap peas, snow peas, or Chinese pea pods.

sbanikh (sa-BEH-nikh). *Ara.* Spinach.

sbrisolona (sbree-suh-LOH-nah). *Ita.* A famous flat and crisp cake, made with a combination of white flour, cornmeal, and chopped almonds.

scald (skahld). *USA.* Heat liquid to just below boiling, about 185°F, and either pour over food or dip food into.

scallion (SKAL-yun). *USA.* Young onion pulled while the tops are green and tender and the bulb undeveloped; green onion.

scallop (SKAH-lop). *USA.* To cover with sauce or milk and breadcrumbs and bake in a casserole. Also called escallope.

scallopine (skol-a-PEE-nee). *Ita.* Small flat pieces of veal, sauteed and served in sauce.

scallops (SKAH-lohps). *USA.* Marine mollusks whose edible part is the adductor muscle; has a radially ribbed hinged shell.

Scamorza (skah-MOR-dzah). *Ita.* A white cheese made of cows' whole milk, pear-shaped and a smooth, thin rind.

scampi (SCAM-pee). *Ita.* Saltwater crayfish, pale in color, quite large. Also called Dublin Bay prawn, langoustine, and Norway lobster.

scarola (skah-ROH-lah), *Ita* Escarole.

Schabzieger (SHARB-zeh-ger). *Ger.* A pungent cows' skimmed-milk cheese from Switzerland; hard, green, cone shaped, flavored with blue melilot clover.

Schalotten (sha-LO-tern). *Ger.* Shallots.

Schaltiere (SHAHL-tee-reh) *Ger.* Shellfish.

Schaum (showm). *Ger.* Mousse, froth, foam.

Schaumrollen (SHOWM-eo-lehn). *Ger.* Puff-pastry rolls filled with whipped cream.

Schaumwein (SHOWM-vighn). *Ger.* Sparkling wine, champagne.

Schellfisch (SHEL-fish). *Ger.* Haddock.

schelvis (SKHEL-vis). *Dut.* Haddock.

schiacciata (skya-CHAH-tah). *Ita.* A bread, rolled out thin like pizza dough, seasoned only with oil and salt, sometimes rosemary, sage, sliced onions or small pieces of olives are added.

Schildrötensuppe (SHILT-krur-ten-zoo-peh). *Ger.* Turtle soup.

Schinken (SHING-kehn). *Ger.* Ham.

Schlachtplatte (SHLAKHT-plah-ter). *Ger.* Plate of cold meats and sausages.

Schlag (shlahk). *Ger.* With cream.

Schlagsahne (SHLAHK-zah-neh). *Ger.* Whipped cream.

Schlegel (SHLAY-gehl). *Ger.* Drumstick.

Schmalz (shmahltz). *Ger.* Melted fat, lard, grease.

Schmalzgebackenes (SHMAHLTZ-ger-braa-tern). *Ger.* Fried food.

Schmand (shmahnd). *Ger.* Sour cream.

Schmierkäse (SHMEER-kaiz). *Ger.* A soft, odorous cheese.

Schmorfleisch (SHMOR-flighsh). *Ger.* Spiced meat.

Schnapps (shnahps). *Ger.* A liquor distilled from grain or potatoes and flavored variously; served very cold.

Schnitte (shnit). *Ger.* A chop or steak.

Schnittlauch (SHNIT-lowkh). *Ger.* Chives.

Schnitzel (SHNIT-sehl). *Ger.* A cutlet or scallop.

Schöbrunner Lunch (SHUR-broo-nehr). *Ger.* Ham and vegetable pie.

Schokolade (sho-ko-LAH-deh). *Ger.* Chocolate.

Schokoladeneis (shok-kol-LAA-dern-ighss). *Ger.* Chocolate ice cream.

schol (skhawl). *Dut.* Plaice, flounder, a flatfish.

Schöpsenschlegel (SHURP-zehn-shlay-gerl). *Ger.* Roast leg of lamb.

schorseneren (scors-seh-NAH-en). *Dut.* A slim, black root vegetable.

Schotensuppe (SHO-ten-zup-per). *Ger.* Fresh green pea soup.

Schrotbrot (SHROAT-broat). *Ger.* Whole wheat bread.

Schüblig (SHOOB-lerg). *Ger.* A Swiss sausage made in St. Gallen.

Schulter (SHOOL-ter). *Ger.* Shoulder.

Schupfnudeln (SHOOPF-noo-dehln). *Ger.* Thick, heavy noodles.

Schwamm (shvam). *Ger.* Mushroom.

Schwärtelbraten (SHVART-ehl-braa-tern). *Ger.* Roast leg of pork, cooked with sauerkraut and dumplings, served with sour cream.

Schwartzbrot (SHVART-broat). *Ger.* The famous black bread; gets its color from black molasses.

Schwartzwälder Kirschtorte (SHVARTS-vehl-derr KEERSH-tor-ter). *Ger.* Rich chocolate cake with cherry filling between layers and on top of icing; from the Black Forest.

Schwarzer Kaffee (SHVART-ser KAH-fay). *Ger.* Black coffee.

Schwarzfisch (SHVARTS-fish). *Ger.* Carp.

Schwarzsauer (SHVARTS-zoe-ehr). *Ger.* A stew of goose giblets and blood with dried apples, prunes, and pears.

Schwarzwürste (SHVARTS-voorst). *Ger.* Pork sausage black with pig's blood.

Schwarzwurzeln (SHVARTS-voor-tseln). *Ger.* Salsify; oyster plant.

Schwein (shvine). *Ger.* Pork.

Schweinebauch (SHVINE-eh-baux). *Ger.* Pork belly.

Schweinebraten (SHVINE-braa-tern). *Ger.* Roast pork.

Schweinekeule (SHVINE-eh-koy-leh). *Ger.* Leg of pork.

Schweinekotelett (SHVINE-eh-kot-let). *Ger.* Pork chop.

Schweineohren (SHVINE-eh-o-rehn). *Ger.* Crisp, sweet, very thin pastry.

Schweinepfeffer (SHVINE-eh-pfe-fehr). *Ger.* Highly seasoned pork.

Schweinerippchen (SHVINE-eh-rip-khern). *Ger.* Spare ribs.

Schweinerucken (SHVINE-eh-roo-kern). *Ger.* Pork tenderloin.

Schweineschenkel (SHVINE-eh-sheng-kerl). *Ger.* Roast pork leg.

Schweinsjungfernbraten (shvines-yoong-fern-BRAA-tern). *Ger.* A very tasty strip of pork roasted until skin is crunchy; an Austrian dish.

Schweinskarre (SHVINES-kah-ree). *Ger.* Smoked pork chops.

Schweinssulz (SHVINES-zoolz). *Ger.* Jellied pork.

Schweizerkase (SHVITES-ehr-kay-ze). *Ger.* Swiss cheese.

sciroppo (shee-ROAP-poh). *Ita.* Syrup.

scone (scahn). *Sco.* Quick bread usually containing currants.

score (skohr). *USA.* Make shallow slits on the surface of meat, lengthwise and crosswise.

scorzonera (skor-tho-NAY-rah). *Spa.* Black-skinned salsify that is peeled immediately after cooking to preserve its color.

Scotch broth (skotch brawth). *Sco.* A soup of vegetables, barley, and lamb.

Scotch egg (skotch ehg). *Sco.* Hard-cooked egg, encased in sausage, and fried.

Scotch woodcock (skotch WOOD-kock). *Bri.* Creamy scrambled eggs on toast with anchovies.

scottadito (skoa-tah-DEE-toa). *Ita.* "Burning fingers"; small cutlets on the bone; eaten with the fingers while very hot, hence the name.

scramble (SKRAHM-bul). *USA.* To prepare eggs or mixture containing eggs by stirring while cooking until mixture sets.

Scrapple (SKRAHP-ehl). *Ger.* Pork scraps, including heart, liver, and tongue, boiled together, chopped, seasoned with pepper, sage, salt; thickened with cornmeal; serve sliced and fried. If made with oats it is called Goetta.

scratchins (SKRAHT-chens). *Bri.* Cracklings.

scrod (skrohd). *USA.* A marketing term for young cod under 2½ pounds; schrod (spelled with an h), indicates that the fish is a young haddock.

scungilli (skoon-JEEL-lee). *Ita.* Conches; flavor similar to scallops.

scuppernong (SKUHP-pehr-nong). *USA.* A table grape of the muscadine class.

sea bass (cee bahss). *USA.* An edible fish of the bass family, with firm white meat and a delicate flavor derived from feeding chiefly on crabs, shrimp and mollusks. Also called black sea bass.

sea biscuit (cee behs-keht). *USA.* Hardtack.

sea bread (cee-brehd). *USA.* Hardtack.

Seabutt (ZAY-but). *Ger.* A tasty European flatfish of the flounder family. Also known as barbue, brill.

sea cucumber (cee QU-kum-ber). *USA.* Hai shen; a sea creature that looks like a large fat slug; when gutted, boiled, and dried, it shrinks and becomes firm, resembling a cigar butt; must be soaked in water for several days before using; mostly used in Oriental cooking.

sea fennel (cee FEHN-nul). *USA.* Samphire; an edible seaweed with the taste of fennel.

seafood (cee food). *USA.* Edible shellfish or saltwater fish.

sea kale (cee kale). *USA.* A plant that grows wild and under cultivation; has thick, glaucous basal leaves; nutty flavor; use as salad green.

sea moss (cee mohss). *USA.* An edible seaweed, principally used in Oriental cooking.

sea pie (cee pi). *USA.* A stew of New England origins made of pork, veal, or fowl mixed with sweet dried apples, molasses, and dumplings.

sear (seer). *USA.* Brown meat quickly at a very high temperature until it is cooked.

sea salt (cee sawlt). *USA.* A squarish-grained salt; very flavorful, used sprinkled over meats, rolls, pretzels, breads. Also called kosher salt and coarse salt.

sea slug (cee sluhgh). *USA.* Sea cucumber.

seasoned salts (CEE-szond sawltz). *USA.* A compound of vegetable salts, spices, and usually monosodium glutamate.

seatrout (CEE-traut). *USA.* Weakfish.

sea trout (cee trauwt). *USA.* A brown trout from the Atlantic waters, succulent pink flesh. Also called salmon trout.

sea urchin (cee UHR-chen). *USA.* A spiny marine animal that looks like a large pin cushion; the cream- to orange-colored roe is a delicacy.

seaweed (CEE-weed). *USA.* Vegetation of the ocean waters. See carrageenan, dulse, faht choy, gee choy, hijiki, Irish moss, kelp, konbu, laver, nori.

séché (sesh). *Fre.* Dried.

séco (SAY-koo). *Por.* Dried.

sedano (SEH-dah-noa). *Ita.* Celery.

Seekrabben (ZAY-kra-bern). *Ger.* Crabs.

Seezunge (ZAY-tsun-ger). *Ger.* Sole.

sel (sehl). *Fre.* Salt.

sel'd (syehld). *Rus.* Herring.

selderie (SEL-duh-ree). *Dut.* Celery.

self-rising flour (sehlf-RI-zeng flawr). *USA.* An all-purpose flour with salt and a leavening agent added; if used for pastry, texture will be spongy, rather than flaky.

selha chawal (SEHL-ha CHAH-vel). *Ind.* Converted rice.

selleri (SAH-lea-REE). *Swe.* Celery.

selleri (SEHL-er-ree). *Dan.* Celery.

Sellerie (ZE-leh-ree). *Ger.* Celery.

selters (SEHL-tehrs). *Nor.* Mineral water.

seltzer (SEHL-szur). *USA.* Plain, natural or manmade effervescent mineral water.

selvaggina (say-lvahd-JEE-nah). *Ita.* Venison; game.

sem (saym). *Ind.* Green beans.

sembel (sem-bay). *Jap.* A small, crispy rice cracker.

semifreddo (se-mee-FRAYD-doh). *Ita.* A chilled or frozen mousselike dessert, including cream, custard, cake, and fruit.

semifrío (se-mee-FREE-oa). *Spa.* Semitreddo.

semisweet chocolate (SEHM-ee-sweet CHOK-o-laht). *USA.* A slightly sweetened chocolate used in candy making because of its sheen when melted; also used for icings, sauces, and fillings.

semlor (SAHM-loor). *Swe.* Buns eaten during Lent.

semmel (ZEH-merl). *USA.* Breakfast yeast roll from the Pennsylvania Dutch.

Semmelkloss (ZEH-merl-klos). *Ger.* Bread dumpling.

semolina (sehm-oh-LEE-nah). *USA.* A creamy-colored, granular, protein-rich durum wheat flour used commercially for all types of pasta.

senap (SAY-nahp). *Swe.* Mustard.

senape (SAY-nah-pay). *Ita.* Mustard.

Senf (zehnf). *Ger.* Mustard.

Senf Kartoffeln (zehnf kahr TOF-fer ln). *Ger.* The Austrian version of escalloped potatoes in mustard sauce.

sennep (SEHN-erp). *Dun.* Mustard.

sepple (SAYP-pee-ah). *Ita.* Cuttlefish.

serendipity berry (sehr-ehn-DIP-pee-tee BEHR-ree). *USA.* A small edible red berry, native to Africa, that contains the sweetest substance known to man; 1000 times sweeter than sucrose.

seroendeng (scah-ROON-dang). *Dut.* Indonesian fried coconut with peanuts.

Serra (SER-rah). *Por.* A ewes' milk cheese; yellow rind; creamy white with a runny interior when young; pungent, hard, and crumbly when aged.

serrano chili (sehr-RAHN-noh). *Mex.* A very hot green chili pepper; used fresh, canned, and pickled; the tiniest and hottest of chilis.

Serviettenklösse (zar-vee-E-tern-klur-skhern). *Ger.* "Napkin dumpling"; a bread dumpling cooked in a tied napkin to hold its shape; when served it is surrounded with cooked pears, string beans and bacon in a sweet-sour sauce.

sesame (SEHS-eh-me). *USA.* The small somewhat flat seeds of the sesame plant; a mild nutty flavor that is strongest when toasted; used as a flavoring agent and a source of oil. Also called benne seeds; when crushed, called tahini.

sesame oil (SEHS-eh-me ohul). *USA.* Oil extracted from sesame seeds; bland nutty flavor; clear, pale yellow color.

sesos (SAY-sohs). *Spa.* Brains.

set (sceht). *USA.* To allow to stand until congealed, as in gelatin.

setas (SAY-tahss). *Spa.* Mushrooms.

seven-minute icing (SEHV-en MEN-ute l-ceng). *USA.* A very fluffy icing made of cooking egg whites, sugar, corn syrup, and cream of tartar in the top of a double boiler; this is a never-fail icing.

seviche (sah-VEESH). *Spa.* Raw fish "cooked" by chemical reaction when marinated in lime juice.

Seville orange (seh-VEEL oranj). *USA.* A bitter orange with a thin skin that is much used in the making of marmalade, and used to lend piquancy to meat, fish dishes, and various drinks.

sevruga (see-VROO-gah). *Rus.* The smallest, yet most prolific of the sturgeons which produce small, dark gray to black caviar of exceptionally fine flavor.

sfarjal (SFAFR-jahl). *Ara.* Quince.

sfogliata (sfog-lee-AHT-tah). *Ita.* Puff pastry.

sformato (sfor-MAH-toa). *Ita.* Pie, pudding.

sgombro (ZGOAM-broa). *Ita.* Mackerel.

shaay (shayy). *Ara.* Tea.

shabu-shabu (shah-BOO-shah-bOO). *Jap.* Meat and vegetables cooked at table in stock, served with seasoned sesame sauce; one-pot cooking; similar to sukiyaki.

shad (shahd). *USA.* A fish of the herring family; flesh has a distinctive, rich, sweet flavor; roe is poached, broiled or sauteed, has nutty flavor and served with bacon and lemon.

shaddock (SHAD-dock). *USA.* The largest of the citrus family; has thick, coarse skin and fibrous, dry, sweet pulp. Also known as pomelo and pummelo.

shagou dòufù (shah-guo doh-foo). *Chi.* Beancurd, or tofu, in casserole.

shakuwlaata (sho-ko-LAA-tah). *Ara.* Chocolate.

shallot (SHALL-lawt). *USA.* A small onionlike bulb with a papery brown covering; has mild, onion-garlic flavor; use sautéed, braised or steamed with vegetables, chicken, or fish.

shamme kabab (SHAH-mee ka-BOHB). *Ind.* Ground meat and yellow split peas, flavored with mint, gingerroot, and spices, shaped into small patties and fried.

shammoama (sham-MEHM). *Ara.* Melon.

shamouti (sha-MOO-tee). *USA.* An orange that is fragrant, sweet and juicy; easy to peel, no naval. Also known as Jaffa.

shandy (SHAHN-dee). *Bri.* Beer mixed with lemonade.

shandygaff (SHAHN-dee-gahf). *Bri.* Beer mixed with gingerbeer.

shank (shahnk). *USA.* That part of the leg between the knee and ankle.

shao (shao). *Chi.* Braising.

shao mài (shao my). *Chi.* Steamed pork dumpling.

sharbat (shahr-BAHT). *Ara.* Beverages.

shark (shahrk). *USA.* An ocean fish whose edible dense, delicate flesh is not popular in the United States but is used throughout the world.

shark fin (shahrk fehn). *USA.* Yú chi; savored for its gelatinous texture; used for special occasions and banquets in China.

sharon fruit (SHA-rohn froot). *USA.* A sweet-tasting fruit resembling the persimmon; seedless; eaten like an apple or peach.

shawirma (sha WIR-mah). *Ara.* Spiced lamb or veal grilled on a vertical spit; gyros.

she-crab soup (SHE-krahb soop). *USA.* A soup of South Carolina origin, made with the roe and meat of the female blue crab; flavored with cream, Worcestershire sauce, and sherry.

shellfish (SHEHL-fesch). *USA.* Any kind of seafood with a shell, such as shrimp, crab, scallop.

shell steak (shehl stake). *USA.* A boneless, tender steak, cut from the strip loin of beef.

sheng cài (sheng tsai). *Chi.* Lettuce.

shepherd's pie (SHEH-pard's pie). *USA.* A pie of cubed or ground meat, covered with mashed potatoes.

shepherd's purse (SHEH-pahrd's puhrs). *USA.* A European wild green of the mustard family.

sherbet (SCHUR-beht). *USA.* A frozen dessert made of sugar and water, fruit juice or puree, flavoring such as coffee, liqueurs; may have added beaten egg white, milk or cream.

shichimi (SHECHEE-mee). *Jap.* Seven-spice mixture; red pepper (togarashi) flakes, sansho pepper pods, flakes of dried mandarin orange peel, black kelp seeds, dark green nori seaweed bits, white sesame seeds, and white poppy seeds.

shiitake (SHEE-tah-keh). *Jap.* Mushroom; has woodsy-fruity flavor; dark brown, thick, smooth velvety caps, flesh is firm, cap edges curl under; inner meat is light pinky beige.

shio (shee-OH). *Jap.* Salt.

ship biscuit (shehp BEHS-keht). *USA.* Hardtack.

ship caviar (shehp KAHV-ee-ahr). *USA.* The roe or eggs of a hybrid sturgeon resulting from a cross between the osietr and the sevruga; is particularly firm, and produces an excellent caviar; in short supply.

shiraita konbu (shee-LAH-ee-tak KONG-uh-boo). *Jap.* The remaining core of the konbu leaf after shaving for oboro and tororo; looks like a very fine square of ecru-colored silk; is moistened with vinegar and used as an edible wrapper; has a unique, delicate, sweet ocean taste.

shirataki (shee-RAH-tah-kee). *Jap.* Translucent noodles made using arum root.

shiratamako (shee-RAH-tah-mah-ko). *Jap.* A flour made from raw glutinous rice, and used in making refined sweet confections.

shiriyyi (shah-REE-yee). *Ara.* Vermicelli.

shirona (SHEE-rohn-nah). *Jap.* Chard cabbage; consists of a clump of snow-white stalks ending in wide, dark-green leaves.

shirred eggs (sheerd eggs). *USA.* Eggs broken into a cup, covered with cream and crumbs, and baked.

shiru (shee-rou). *Jap.* Soup of all kinds.

shirumono (shee-rou-moh-noh). *Jap.* Soup.

shish kabob (shish kah-BAHB). *USA.* Cubes of meat and vegetables cooked on a skewer.

shiso (shee-SO). *Jap.* A pepper leaf used fresh, dried, or powdered; beef-steak plant; member of the mint family.

shízi (shi-dzi). *Chi.* Persimmon.

shi zi tóu (shi dzi toh). *Chi.* Large minced pork meatballs.

shizuoka no ume shiso zuke (shee-ZOO-o-kah no OO-meh she-SO ZOO-kee). *Jap.* Tiny pickled plums with shredded magenta colored ginger and pepper leaves.

shoga (SHOH-gah). *Jap.* Fresh gingerroot.

shoga sembei (SHOH-gah SEM-bey). *Jap.* A small, crispy rice cracker coated with ginger-flavored sugar.

shoofly pie (SHOO-fli pi). *USA.* A very sweet pie of Pennsylvania Dutch origin made of molasses and brown sugar.

shore dinner (shor DEHN-ner). *USA.* A dinner consisting mainly of seafoods.

shortbread (SHOHRT-brehd). *Sco.* A rich pastry of butter, flour, and sugar; cut in round shape and baked to a golden brown.

short cake (shohrt kahk). *USA.* A cake of biscuitlike dough, spread with sliced or crushed fruit, and topped with whipped cream.

shortening (SHORT-ehn-eng). *USA.* Fat suitable for frying and baking.

short-grain rice (SHOHRT-graan rics). *USA.* A type of rice which is higher in starch, wetter, and stickier than medium or long-grain rices when cooked; some varieties are Japanese, Indo-Chinese, Piedmont.

short loin (shohrt loin). *USA.* The cut of beef from which the porterhouse, T-bone and club steaks are cut.

shortnin' bread (SHORT-nehn brehd). *USA.* A quick bread made with butter or lard; of Southern origins.

shorva (SHOOR-wah). *Ind.* Soup.

shòu de (shou de). *Chi.* Lean, as in meat; lacking fat.

shoyu (SHOH-yoo). *Jap.* A lightly salted and sweet soy sauce made from toasted wheat; bright taste and aroma.

shproti (SHPRO ti). *Rus.* Sprats.

shred (shrehd). *USA.* Cut into thin pieces using the large holes of a grater.

shrimp (shrehmp). *USA.* An edible crustacean of many species and varying sizes found throughout the world; flesh has crisp texture and sweet taste; preparation varies widely.

shrub (shrub). *Bri.* An old-fashioned homemade fruit cordial, sometimes alcoholic.

shuàn yàngròu (shwan YANG-row). *Chi.* Mongolian hot pot; various pieces of seafood, poultry, and lamb cooked individually in a communal pot of simmering stock that is placed in the middle of the table; it is served with sauces, and the rich stock is consumed afterward; a kind of Chinese fondue.

shuck (shuhk). *USA.* To remove the outer shell or husk of a food, such as oyster shell or corn husk.

shuiguo (shui-guo). *Chi.* Fruit.

shuiguo zhi (shui-guo dzih). *Chi.* Juice.

shui jiao (shui jiao). *Chi.* Boiled dumpling.

shungiku (SHURNG-gee-kaok). *Jap.* A vegetable, garland chrysanthemum, having notched leaves; used like spinach; kikuna.

shurba (SHUR-ba). *Ara.* Soup.

sianliha (SI-ahn-LI-haa). *Fin.* Pork.

sienet (SIAY-nayt). *Fin.* Mushrooms.

sienisalaatti (SEE-yen-ee-sa-LAAT-tee). *Fin.* Mushroom salad.

sieve (sehv). *USA.* Rub or press food through a sieve with a spoon.

sift (schft). *USA.* Shake a dry ingredient through a sieve to remove lumps and aerate dry ingredients.

sigtebrød (SIG-teh-brehrth). *Dan.* Light rye bread.

sik (sehk). *Swe.* Whitefish.

sikkar (SUK-kar). *Ara.* Sugar.

silakka (SEE-llahk-kah). *Fin.* Baltic herring.

sild (seel). *Nor.* Herring.

sild (seel). *Dan.* Baltic herring.

sildeboller (SEEL-er-boa-lerr). *Nor.* Herring balls.

sildegryn (SEEL-er-grewn). *Nor.* Herring soup.

sildesalat (SEEL-er-sah-laat). *Nor.* Herring salad.

sill (seel). *Swe.* Herring other than that from the Baltic.

sillgratäng (SEEL-grah-TANG). *Swe.* Herring casserole with potatoes, onions, and cream.

silli (SEE-li). *Fin.* Herring.

sillsalat (SEEL-sa-LAHT). *Swe.* Herring salad with fruit and vegetables.

silq (silk). *Ara.* Swiss chard.

silvano (seel-VAH-noa). *Ita.* Chocolate meringue tart.

silverside (SIL-vehr-side). *Bri.* A cut of beef from the crown of the rump.

silversides (SIL-vehr-sides). *USA.* A term for many species of little fish such as tiny herring, anchovies, whitebait; any tiny, silver fish.

silver threads (SIL-vehr threds). *USA.* A name for Japanese translucent noodles.

sima (SEE-ma). *Fin.* Lemon-flavored mead.

simmaq (sehm-MAHK). *Ara.* Tart, ground seasoning from seed of sumac tree.

simmer (CIM-ehr). *USA.* To cook in a liquid just below the boiling point when bubbles form and slowly break just below the surface.

simnel (SEHM-nul). *Bri.* Spice cake filled with dried fruits, candied fruit peel, spread with apricot jam, almond paste; lavishly decorated.

simsim (SEHM-sehm). *Ara.* Sesame seeds.

sinaasappelen (SEE-nahs-ahp-pul). *Dut.* Oranges.

singe (sehnj). *USA.* To brown or color. Also to finish cleaning a plucked bird by passing bird over a flame to remove any downy feathers remaining.

Single Gloucester (sehn-gull GLOUGH-stehr). *Bri.* A cheese of part-skim, part-whole cow's milk; half as large as Double Gloucester; mild taste.

sippet (SEHP-peht). *USA.* A crouton; croûte, a small piece of bread used for dipping in soup.

sipuli (SI-ppooli). *Fin.* Onion.

sipulipihvi (SI-ppooli-PIH-vi). *Fin.* Beefsteak with onions.

sirloin (SUR-lohn). *USA.* A cut of beef from between the short loin and the round, from the hindquarter.

sirloin tip (SUR-lohn tehp). *USA.* The top part of the sirloin.

sirop (see-ro). *Fre.* Syrup.

sitron (si-TROON). *Nor.* Lemon.

sitronfromasje (si-TROON-froo-MAH-ski). *Nor.* Lemon pudding.

sitruuna (SIT-roo-nah). *Fin.* Lemon.

sitruunakohokas (SIT-roo-nah-KOA-hoa-kahss). *Fin.* Lemon soufflé.

siu choy (saoh chee). *Chi.* Celery cabbage; consists of a solid, oblong head of wide, celerylike stalks ending in frilly, pale-green leaves; has a delicate celery-cabbage taste.

siyami (see-YAHM-mee). *Ara.* Refers to Lenten foods, or dishes without meat; vegetarian.

sjömansbiff (SHUR mahns-bif). *Swe.* Beef stew; beef baked with potatoes and onions.

sjø-ørret (SHUR-ur-reht). *Nor.* Sea trout.

sjötunga (SHUR-tewng-ah). *Swe.* Sole.

sjøtunge (SHUR-tewn-ger). *Nor.* Sole.

skaldjur (SKAAL-yewr). *Swe.* Shellfish.

skärbönor (skahr-BUR-noor). *Swe.* French beans.

skarpsås (SKAHRP-soass). *Swe.* Piquant mustard sauce.

skate (skat). *USA.* A flatbodied, diamond-shaped relative of the shark, whose "wings" are edible after being skinned; best poached; highly prized in France, Italy, Japan, and China. Also called ray.

skewer (SKU-ehr). *USA.* To thread food on a long pin for broiling or roasting.

skim (skehm). *USA.* To remove surface fat or foam from a liquid mixture.

skim milk (skehm mehlk). *USA.* Cows' milk which contains less than ½% milk fat. Also called nonfat milk.

skinka (SKIN-kah). *Swe.* Ham.

skinkbullar (SKINK-bul-lahr). *Swe.* Ham and potato balls.

skinke (SKEEN-ker). *Dan.* Ham.

skinkestek (SKEEN-ker-stayk). *Nor.* Roasted fresh ham.

skinkfärs (SKINK-fehrs). *Swe.* Ham mousse.

skinklåda (SKINK-loa-dah). *Swe.* Ham omelet.

skirlies (SKUR-leez). *Sco.* Oatmeal slightly stirred around with suet and onions.

skirret (SKEHR-eht). *USA.* A vegetable; similar to a carrot; always peel after boiling to retain flavor; remove the inner hard core before serving.

skirt steak (skehrt stake). *USA.* The boneless part of the lower forequarter covering the diaphram from which the short plate is removed.

sköldpadda (SHURLD-pahd-ah). *Swe.* Turtle.

sköldpaddssoppa (SHOHLD-pads-SO-pah). *Swe.* Turtle soup.

skorpor (SKOR-purr). *Swe.* Rusks.

skyr (skeer). *Ice.* Curdled milk, formerly known by that name over most of Scandinavia, now found only in Iceland.

sla (slah). *Dut.* Salad; lettuce.

slagroom (SLAH-room). *Dut.* Whipped cream.

slaked lime (SLAKD lime). *USA.* Calcium hydroxide; a firming agent used in making pickles; not to be confused with rock lime, which is not edible.

släpärter (slah-PAER-turr). *Swe.* Peas in pod.

slapjack (SLAHP-jahk). *USA.* A kind of broad flat pancake.

slata (SAH-lah-tah). *Ara.* Salad.

slätvar (SLAIT-vaar). *Swe.* Brill.

slice (slics). *USA.* To cut food into broad, thin pieces.

sliver (SLEH-ver). *USA.* To cut into long, slender pieces.

sloe (slo). *USA.* A wild European plum, small, dark, and astringent; from the blackthorn tree; used for flavoring sloe gin, and making preserves.

sloke (slok). *Bri.* Laver; a purplish-brown seaweed with semitransparent leaves; used to make jelly.

sloppy joe (SLOH-pee joh). *USA.* A sandwich with a filling made of ground beef, seasonings, tomato sauce, served on a split bun.

slottsstek (SLOHTS-steyk). *Swe.* Pot roast.

slumgullion (sluhm-GUHL-yuohn). *USA.* A term for disgusting or makeshift food or drink.

slump (sluhmp). *USA.* A dessert of cooked fruit with a dumplinglike top and served with cream.

småbröd (SMOA-brurd). *Swe.* Little cakes, cookies.

småkage (SMAW-kaaer). *Dan.* Biscuits to the world, cookies to United States.

små köttbullar (smo SHIRT-bool-lahr). *Swe.* Small meatballs.

småländsk ostkaka (SMO-lahndsk OOST-KAH-ka). *Swe.* Curd cake from Småland province.

Smältost (SMEHLT-oost). *Swe.* A very mild, runny cheese, mostly used in cooking.

småltsill (SMOHLT-seel). *Swe.* "Melted" sill herring.

smasill (SMAA-sil). *Swe.* Pilchard; a small fish of the herring family; a sardine.

småvarmt (smo-VAHRMT). *Swe.* The hot part of the smörgåsbord.

smelt (smlt). *USA.* A small silvery fish eaten whole or gutted, floured and fried.

smetana (smyee-TAH-nyee). *Rus.* Sour cream.

smid (smeed). *Ara.* Grain similar to semolina or farina; used for cake and filled-cookie dough.

smitane (smee-tahn). *Fre.* Chopped onions sautéed in butter, sour cream added; cooked, strained, and flavored with lemon; a classic sauce.

Smithfield ham (SMEHTH-feeld hahm). *USA.* Ham from hogs in Virginia that have been fattened on peanuts, cured, salted, smoked, and aged; uncooked.

smoked (smokd). *USA.* Meat cured by hanging over a low, steady heat, using wood chips and chemical components to add flavoring.

smoothie (SMOO-thee). *USA.* A thick beverage made of fruit pulp, juice, and ice, blended until smooth using a blender.

smör (smurr). *Swe.* Butter.

smør (smurr). *Dan.* Butter; Denmark makes the finest butter in the world.

smørbrød (SMURR-brur). *Nor.* Open-face sandwiches with meat, fish, cheese spread.

smörgås (SMURR-goass). *Swe.* Sandwich.

smörgåsbord (smur-gohs-BOARD). *Swe.* "Bread and butter table"; arrangement of many hot and cold foods on a table in an attractive fashion, traditionally accompanied by aquavit.

smørrebrød (SMURR-er-brurdh). *Dan.* An open-face sandwich with all kinds of fish, meat, and vegetable fillings, and sauces.

smothered (SMUH-therd). *USA.* Braised; cooked in gravy or sauce in a covered pot.

smultringer (SMEWLT-ring-ehr). *Nor.* Doughnuts.

smultron (SMEWL-tron). *Swe.* Wild strawberry.

snack (snahk). *USA.* Food item eaten in a hurry, or between meals, such as candy, potato chips, pretzels.

snail (snal). *USA.* A land-dwelling gastropod mollusk; a delicacy; usually canned already prepared for the table; escargot.

snap beans (snahp beehn). *USA.* String beans; a bean grown primarily for its green pods, used as a vegetable when young and tender.

snaps (snahps). *Swe.* A clear, potent (40% alcohol) brandy, served icy cold; drunk with smørrebrød. Same as Akvavit.

sneeuwballen (SNEE-uh-bahl-lehn). *Dut.* A cream puff pastry often filled with raisins or currants.

snickerdoodle (SNEHK-ehr-doo-dle). *USA.* A cookie of New England origins flavored with cinnamon and sugar; originally made with dried fruits and nuts.

snijbonen (SNAY-bo-nuh). *Dut.* Haricot or kidney beans.

snip (snep). *USA.* Cut into very small pieces with scissors.

snitbønner (snit-BEHRN-nehr). *Dan.* French green beans.

snöripa (SNORI-pa). *Swe.* Ptarmigan; Scandinavian grouse.

snow cone (sno kohn). *USA.* A confection of scraped ice or freshly fallen snow, drizzled with flavored syrups; usually served in a cone-shaped paper cup.

snow eggs (sno eggs). *USA.* Meringue shaped with a spoon to resemble eggs, poached in sweetened milk, served with custard sauce; the classic French dessert, oeufs à la neige.

snow peas (sno peez). *USA.* Peas cultivated to have thin, flat pods with underdeveloped peas to be eaten whole; mange-tout in French, meaning "eat-all."

soba (so-BAH). *Jap.* A noodle made of buckwheat flour.

sobremesas (sawbr-MEZA). *Por.* Desserts.

socker (SOK-kerr). *Swe.* Sugar.

sockerdricka (sok-kerr-DRI-kah). *Swe.* Sweet lemonade.

sockerkaka (sok-kerr-KAA-kah). *Swe.* Sponge cake.

sockeye salmon (SOHK-i SAHM-mon). *USA.* A delicately flavored, red fleshed fish of the salmon family; firm, tasty; used for everything from sandwiches to cooked dishes.

socles (sou-kleh). *Fre.* Stands of fat or rice used to raise entrees; lending height.

soda (SO-dah). *USA.* A leavening agent; bicarbonate of soda; when moistened it produces carbon dioxide to aerate and lighten dough.

soda (SO-dah). *USA.* Flavored, colored carbonated water, such as root beers, cola drinks, cream sodas; endless varieties.

sød frugtsuppe (surdh FROOGY-soob-ber). *Dan.* Sweet fruit soup.

sodium bicarbonate (SO-dee-um bi-KAR-boh-nate). *USA.* Baking powder; soda; a leavening agent for doughs and batters.

soep (soop). *Dut.* Soup.

soezen (SU-szehn). *Dut.* Large cream puffs.

soffritto (so-FREE-toe). *Ita, Spa.* A mixture of chopped carrots, onions, celery and parsley, fried in oil or butter; used to flavor soups, sauces and meat dishes. Also sofritto, battuto.

soft-ball stage (sawft-bahl staj). *USA.* The second stage of the crystallization process: begins at 234°F, a small quantity of syrup dropped into chilled water forms a ball that does not disintegrate, but flattens out of its own accord when picked up with the fingers.

soft-crack stage (sawft-krahk staj). *USA.* The fifth stage of the crystallization process: begins at 270°F, a small quantity of syrup dropped into chilled water will separate into hard threads, which, when removed from the water, will bend.

soft dough (sawft doh). *USA.* A flour mixture that contains 3 parts flour to 1 part liquid; just stiff enough to be rolled on a lightly floured board, such as used for biscuits, drop cookies, yeast breads.

soft drop batter (sawft drahp BAHT-tehr). *USA.* A flour mixture that contains 2 parts flour to 1 part liquid, such as used for muffins or cakes.

soft-shell crab (sawft-shehl krahb). *USA.* A blue crab, while molting, has a new shell so soft and thin that it is edible.

sògliola (SAW-lyoa-lah). *Ita.* Sole.

soh mui jeong (su maae GEE-ong). *Chi.* Canned plum sauce; a spicy accompaniment to roast duck. Also called duck sauce.

sole (sohl). *Fre.* A fish of the flatfish family whose flesh is firm, white and delicate; related to the flounder.

solho (SOU-lyoo). *Por.* Plaice.

solomillo (soh-loh-MEE-yoh). *Spa.* Pork tenderloin steak.

sølvkake (SURLL-kar-ki). *Nor.* "Silver cake"; a coconut and lemon flavored light cake.

solyanka (sol-YAHN-kah). *Rus.* Freshwater fish boiled with onions, olives, cucumbers, vinegar, dill, and sour cream.

somen (SO-mehn). *Jap.* Thin, round, fine, hairlike wheat noodles.

songhua dàn (soong-hwa dan). *Chi.* Preserved duck eggs; actually preserved for 100 days. Also known as thousand-year-old eggs, hundred-year-old eggs.

songzi huángyú (soong-dzi huang-yu). *Chi.* Yellow croaker garnished with pine nuts.

sonth (sawnt). *Ind.* Ground dried ginger.

sooji (SOO-jee). *Ind.* Farina; semolina.

sookha dhania (SOO-kah TAH-nee-yah). *Ind.* Coriander seeds.

soon geung (sehn GEE-ong). *Chi.* Pickled gingerroot.

sôpa (SOH-pah). *Por.* Soup.

sopa coada (SOP-pah KOAH-dah) *Ita.* A famous soup made of bread and boned roast pigeon.

sôpa de feijão (SOH-pah der fay-ZHOW). *Por.* Bean soup.

sopa de legumbres (SOA-pah day lay-GOOM-brayss). *Spa.* Vegetable soup.

sopa de pescado (SOA-pah day pays-KAH-dhoa). *Spa.* Fish soup.

sopaipilla (soh-pahy-PEE-yah). *Mex.* A puffy fried bread.

sopari (soo-PAH-ree). *Ind.* Betel nut.

sopa seca (SOH-pah SEH-kah). *Mex.* A starchy casserole dish.

sope (SOH-peh). *Mex.* Round antojito of tortilla dough cooked and filled with a savory stuffing; garnacha; picada.

soppa (SO-ppah). *Swe.* Soup.

sorbet (sor-BAY). *Fre.* A water ice with fruit or liqueur flavor. Also an iced Turkish drink.

sorbetto (sohr-BEHT-toa). *Ita.* Sherbet.

sorghum (SOR-guhm). *USA.* A syrup made from the sweet juice of the stem of the sorgo plant; thinner and more sour than cane molasses; can be substituted for molasses.

sorghum flour (SOR-guhm flawr). *USA.* Used to thicken soups; contains no gluten. Also called milo maize.

sorrel (SAU-rul). *USA.* A leafy green, lemony-tasting plant similar to spinach, used in salads, purees, soups, sauces.

sorsapaisti (SOAR-sah-PAH-ee-sti). *Fin.* Roasted wild duck.

sorvêtte (sohr-VAY-tay). *Por.* Sherbet, ice cream.

Sosse (ZOH-sah). *Ger.* Sauce.

søtsuppe (SURT-sewp-peh). *Nor.* Sweet fruit soup.

sottaceri (soat-tah-CHAY-tee). *Ita.* Pickled vegetables.

sottaceto (soat-tah-CHAY-toa). *Ita.* Pickled.

søtunge (SUR-toon-ger). *Dan.* Sole.

sötvattenfisk (SURT-vah-tern-fisk). *Swe.* Freshwater fish.

soubise (soo-beecs). *Fre.* A white sauce containing onions; served with meat entrees; implies onions are a main ingredient in the composition of a dish.

souchets (soo-shay). *Fre.* Flatfish, as flounder or sole, sliced, and boiled in seasoned water.

soufflé (soo-flay). *Fre.* A light fluffy baked dish with beaten egg white; may be savory or sweet.

soup (soop). *USA.* A liquid food made with a meat, vegetable, or fish stock as base and usually having pieces of solid food such as meats, vegetables, or pastas.

soupe (soop). *Fre.* A hearty, robust peasant vegetable soup, usually served with bread.

sour cream (sahur krehm). *USA.* Cows' cream allowed to sour, either naturally or with the introduction of bacteria; very heavy and thick.

sourdough (SAHUR-doh). *USA.* Dough leavened with a fermented starter culture.

soused (sahusd). *USA.* Pickled in brine or vinegar.

souvlakia (sohv-LAH-kee-ah). *Gre.* Meat marinated in olive oil, lemon juice, and herbs, then grilled.

sowans (SU-ehnz). *Bri.* Nutritious smooth gruel made of the inner husks of oat grain.

soybean (SAWEE-behn). *USA.* A very nutritious legume, extremely important in Asia; used fresh, dry, sprouted, and processed in innumerable ways.

soybean curd (SAWEE-behn kuhrd). *USA.* Tofu.

soybean flour (SAWEE-behn flowr). *USA.* Made from very lightly toasted soybeans or raw beans; is nutty tasting and fragrant; retains the fat in the beans; sweetened with sugar, it is used in many Oriental sweets.

soybean low-fat flour (SAWEE-behn lo-faht flowr). *USA.* Made from soybeans from which the fat has been largely removed.

soybean oil (SAWEE-behn oyl). *USA.* A pale yellow oil extracted from the soybean, usually a liquid.

soy flour (sawee flawr). *USA.* There are two types of soy flour: soybean low-fat flour and soybean flour; causes heavy browning of the crust.

soy meal (sawee mehl). *USA.* Coarse ground soy beans, used as extender for meats.

soy milk (sawee mehlk). *USA.* A product made from dried soybeans soaked in water, crushed, and boiled.

soy sauce (sawee saus). *USA.* A condiment made of fermented soybeans and flour; used extensively in Japanese and Chinese cooking.

Spaetzle (SPET-zel). *Ger.* Fine noodles made when batter is pressed through a colander into boiling broth or water.

spagetti (spa-GAH-tee). *Swe.* Spaghetti.

spaghetti (spah-GEHT-tee). *Ita.* The world renowned cordlike Italian pasta, intermediate in size between macaroni and vermicelli, that comes with a bewildering variety of sauces. Some well-known sauces include: **al aglio e olio** (ahl AH-lyoa ay O-lyoa), with olive oil and garlic; **amatriciana** (ah-mah-tree-CHAAN-nah), with bacon, fresh tomato sauce, and onion; **bolognese** (boa-loa-NYAY-zay), in tomato and meat sauce; **buro, al** (ahl BOOR-roa), with butter; **carbonara** (kah-boa-NAA-rah), with raw egg, grated goats' milk cheese, bits of ham or salt pork; **con carne** (kon KAHR-nee), with meat; **carrettiera** (kahr-rayt-tee-AY-rah), with tuna, mushrooms, tomato puree, freshly ground pepper; **marinara** (mah-ree-NAA-rah), with tomatoes, olives, garlic, clams, and mussels; **pesto** (PAY-stoa), with basil leaves, garlic, cheese, and sometimes pine kernels and marjoram; **pommarola** (poam-mah-RAW-lah), with tomatoes, garlic, basil; **puttanesca** (poot-tah-NAY-skah), with capers, black olives, parsley, garlic, olive oil, black pepper; **ragù** (rah-GOO), similar to bolognese; **con le vongole** (kon lay VOAN-goa-lay), with clams and parsley sauce.

spaghettini (spagh-eht-TEE-nee). *Ita.* Thin spaghetti.

spalla di vitella (SPAHL-lah dee vee-TEHL-lah). *Ita.* Veal shoulder.

spanakopita (spah-nah-KOP-pee-tah). *Gre.* Spinach cheese pie.

spandauer (spun-DOW-er). *Dan.* "Envelope"; a pastry in the shape of a square envelope.

Spanferkel (SHPAAN-fehr-kerl). *Ger.* Suckling pig.

Spanische Windtorte (shpaa-NISCH wehnd-TOR-ter). *Ger.* A meringue shell, elaborately decorated with swirls, filled with berries, and covered with whipped cream; Spanish Windtorte.

Spanish lime (SPAHN-nish lym). *USA.* A fruit similar to a lychee or longan; has tough, green-brown skin and milky-colored pulp; eaten by removing skin and sucking the sweet-acid pulp away from the seed.

Spanish onion (SPAHN-nish UN-yun). *USA.* A sweet, yellow globe onion; used raw or cooked.

spareribs (SPAHR-rehbs). *USA.* A cut of pork from the rib section; usually broiled or barbequed.

Spargel (SHPAAR-gerl). *Ger.* Asparagus; usually white, which is much favored.

sparling (SPAHR-leng). *USA.* Smelt.

sparris (SPAH-riss). *Swe.* Asparagus.

Spätzle (SHPEHTS-ler). *Ger.* Small, handmade noodle or dumpling; usually pressed through a colander.

Speck (shpehk). *Ger.* Bacon; lard.

spegepølse (SPIGH-er-purl-sser). *Dan.* Salami.

Speiseeis (SCHPAI-zeh-ighss). *Ger.* Ices.

spekemat (SPEH-keh-MAHT). *Nor.* Salt-cured meats.

spekeskinke (SPAYK-shin-ker). *Nor.* Cured ham; a kind of prosciutto.

Spekulatius (shpehk-oo-LAAT-siuss). *Ger.* Sweet almond cookie.

spelt (spelt). *Ita.* A hard wheat with the husk; used for soups, both thick and thin.

spenat (speh-NAAT). *Swe.* Spinach.

Spencer steak (SPEHN-sur stayk). *USA.* A steak cut from the rib section of beef. Also called Delmonico steak.

spettekaka (SPA-te-KAH-ka). *Swe.* A towering cake of eggs and sugar specially baked on a spit; a specialty of southern Sweden.

spèzie (SPE-tsye). *Ita.* Spices.

spezzatino (spay-tsah-TEE-noa). *Ita.* Stew.

spice Parisienne (spics pahr-REE-see-ahn). *USA.* Épices composes; a classic French combination of herbs and spices for seasoning, consisting of dried thyme, bay leaves, basil, sage, coriander, mace, black pepper.

Spickgans (SPEEK-gahns). *Ger.* Smoked breast of goose.

spiedino (spee-ay-DEE-noa). *Ita.* Skewered meat or prawns.

Spiessbraten (SHPEES-braa-tern). *Ger.* Meat roasted on a spit.

spigola (SPEE-goa-lah). *Ita.* Sea bass.

spinach (SPEHN-ich). *USA.* A dark green plant with edible leaves, used in salads, and cooked as a vegetable.

spinaci (spee-NAA-chee). *Ita.* Spinach.

Spinat (shpee-NAAT). *Ger.* Spinach.

spinazie (spee-NAH-zee). *Dut.* Spinach.

spiny rock lobster (SPI-nee rohk LOHB-stur). *USA*. A lobster, smaller than the Northern lobster, found in Australia and New Zealand where it is called crayfish.

spitskool (SPETZ-kohl). *Dut*. Chinese cabbage.

split peas (spleht pez). *USA*. Dried, hulled peas which are split apart; used mostly in soups.

sponge (spung). *USA*. A batter that has yeast added.

sponge cake (spuhng kahk). *USA*. A light textured cake whose leavening is eggs only; contains very little or no shortening.

spoom (spoom). *Fre*. An ice or sherbet, made of fruit juice or wine such as champagne, port, muscatel, sherry, port, when frozen has Italian meringue added to the mixture; served in sherbet glasses.

spoon bread (spoon bred). *USA*. Cornbread baked in a casserole and served with a spoon.

spotted dog (SPOHT-tehd dohg). *Bri*. A steamed suet pudding containing raisins. Also spotted dick.

spraengt oksekød (sprehngt OAKS-ser-kurdh). *Dan*. Corned beef.

sprag (sprahg). *USA*. A large cod.

spränged (spraing'd). *Swe, Dan*. "Burst" or cured; refers to meat that has been set in brine prior to cooking.

sprats (sprahtz). *USA*. Small fish similar to herring.

Springerle (SPRING-ehr-lee). *Ger*. Anise cookie dough rolled out, stamped with wooden mold or roller into quaint little designs, and baked; a Christmas tradition.

spring onion (sprehng UN-yun). *USA*. Scallion.

spring roll (sprehng rohl). *USA*. Chun juan; a thin pastry wrapper stuffed with various fillings, rolled up, deep-fried.

spritärter (spree TAER terr). *Swe*. Green peas.

spritsar (SPREET-sahr). *Swe*. Almond butter cookies.

Spritzwasser (SPREETZ-vahs-serr). *Ger*. Soda water.

Sprotten (SHPROT-tern). *Ger*. Sprats.

sprout (sprowt). *USA*. A dried bean that has germinated; used by removing the hulls and using the new growth as a vegetable, either raw or lightly cooked.

spruce beer (sprucs behr). *USA*. A beverage made from spruce twigs and leaves boiled with molasses or sugar, and fermented with yeast.

spruiten (SPRIR-tyus). *Dut*. Brussels sprouts.

spud (spuhd). *USA*. Potato.

spuma (SPOO-mah). *Ita*. A dessert ice with Italian meringue folded in; frothy; mousse.

spumoni (spoo-MOH-nee). *Ita.* A rich ice cream containing candied fruits and nuts, of different colors and in layers, usually flavored with brandy.

squab (squahb). *USA.* A young pigeon; flesh is tender, dark, not gamy.

squash (squahsh). *USA.* The fruit of plants of the gourd family; several types: soft-shelled summer type such as zucchini and yellow summer squash, hard-shelled small winter type such as turban and butternut, and hard-shelled large winter type such as calabaza, hubbard, and spaghetti squash.

squid (squehd). *USA.* A mollusk with a long body and ten arms; popular in Orient and Mediterranean countries.

srikhand (shree-KAHND). *Ind.* Dessert made with drained yogurt, sugar, nuts, and saffron.

Stachelbeere (STAH-kherl-bay-rern). *Ger.* Gooseberry.

stag chicken (stahg CHEH-kehn). *USA.* A male chicken that is too old to roast but makes a well-flavored addition to the stock pot. Also see broiler, capon, cock, fryer, hen roaster, stewing chicken.

stamppot (STAHM-poht). *Dut.* Mashed potatoes and meat mixed into vegetables.

Stangen (STAHN-gehn). *Ger.* Stick-shaped pastries, sweet or savory. Also Stangerl.

star anise (staur ah-NEESC). *USA.* An Oriental shrub that forms a star-shaped pod holding dark, shiny brown seeds; sweet and extremely aromatic; used in many oriental foods, meats, curries, confections, pickles; ba jiao.

starfruit (STAHR-froot). *USA.* A Malaysian fruit, pale yellow with five pointed ridges forming a star when sliced across; carambola.

stark senap (stark SAY-nah). *Swe.* Hot mustard.

steack (stehk). *Fre.* Steak.

steak and kidney pie (stak and KEHD-knee pie). *Bri.* Pieces of beef and kidney flavored with onion, mushroom, oysters; baked in a suet crust.

steack au poivre (stehk oa pwahvr). *Fre.* Sautéed beef steak seasoned liberally with peppercorns.

steam (steem). *USA.* To cook food by the heat and vapor given off by boiling water, with or without pressure.

steamed pudding (steemd PUHD-eng). *USA.* A mixture of bread crumbs, sugars, milk, shortening, eggs, raisins, spices placed in a mold with a tight-fitting lid; then baked in a pan with boiling water to create steam, which give this cake a puddinglike texture.

steep (steep). *USA.* Cover with boiling liquid and let stand to extract flavors and colors.

steg (staig). *Dan.* Joint of meat. Also roasted.

stegt kylling (stehkt SHEWL-leng). *Dan.* Braised chicken.

Steinbutt (SHTIGHN-but). *Ger.* Turbot.

Steinpilz (SHTIGHN-pilz). *Ger.* Boletus mushroom; cèpe.

stekt (staykt). *Swe.* Fried.

stem lettuce (stehm LETT us). *USA.* A Chinese variety of lettuce in which the stem or seedstalk is the edible part, use like a water chestnut to give crunch to a dish. Also called celtuce.

sterlet (STEHR-leht). *USA.* The Russian sterlyad (stehr-lyahd), an almost extinct species of sturgeon, relatively small, but highly esteemed for its roe; the legendary "gold" caviar of the Czars, rarely seen outside the Soviet Union.

stew (stu). *USA.* To cook in just enough liquid to cover.

stewing chicken (STU-eng CHEH-kehn). *USA.* A chicken usually over 10 months old that profits by an extended moist cooking method. Also see broiler, capon, cock, hen roaster, rooster and stag chicken.

sticky buns (STEH-kee buhnz). *USA.* A sweet roll flavored with cinnamon and brown sugar; allowed to rise in a pan lined with brown sugar and melted butter, then baked.

stiff but not dry (stehf buht noht dri). *USA.* Refers to egg whites beaten just until they stand in peaks, still glossy and moist-looking, and not too fine-grained.

stiff dough (stehf doh). *USA.* A flour mixture that contains 4 parts flour to 1 part liquid; just stiff enough to be kneaded without sticking to a lightly floured board, such as pie crust, rolled cookies.

stiffen (STEHF-fen). *USA.* To cook meat, poultry, or fish by briefly heating in butter, or liquid without color, until just cooked.

stifle (STI-fuhl). *USA.* A New England stew of salt pork and seafood or vegetables.

Stilton (STILT-uhn). *Bri.* One of the world's great blue cheeses; made of uncooked cows' milk injected with Penicillium roqueforti mold causing the blue veining; creamy paste, brownish crust, moist, slightly crumbly; not dry or salty.

Stint (shtint). *Ger.* Smelt; a tasty, tiny fish.

stir (ster). *USA.* To mix food using a circular motion.

stirabout (STUHR-ah-bout). *Iri.* Name of an Irish dish similar to Scotch porridge.

stir-fry (STER-fri). *USA.* To cook quickly over medium-high heat, using a tossing-stirring motion.

stirrup cup (STUHR-uhp kuhp). *Bri.* Same as "one for the road" or "night-cap"; a host's signal that this is the last drink.

stoccafisso (stoak-kah-FEES-soa). *Ita.* Dried fillets of cod; stockfish.

stock (stahk). *USA.* Liquid in which meats or vegetables are cooked.

Stoemp Mé Spek (stump meh spehk). *Ger.* Cabbage and potatoes mashed together and sprinkled with fried diced bacon.

stokkfisk (STOHK-fesk). *Nor.* Unsalted, rack-dried cod. Also called tørrfisk. When salted and spread out on a cliff to dry it is called klippfisk.

Stollen (SCHTOL-lehrn). *Ger.* A long-shaped yeast bread filled with various dried fruits, sprinkled with confectioners' sugar; traditional at Christmas.

stone crab (stohn krahb). *USA.* A coastal Atlantic crab, especially from Florida, with large claws that have very fine white meat.

Stor (shturr). *Ger.* Sturgeon.

stör (stur). *Swe.* Sturgeon.

stout (stohwt). *Bri.* A dark, strong, very alcoholic ale brewed from toasted malt; the sweetest of all beers.

stoved (stohvd). *Sco.* Simmered on top of the stove.

stovies (stoh-veez). *Sco.* Boiled potatoes.

Stracchino (strah-KEE-no). *Ita.* A fresh, rindless, uncooked cheese whose paste is buttery, smooth, and delicate.

stracciatella (strah-chee-ah-TEL-lah). *Ita.* Stock thickened with a paste of egg, cheese, and semolina.

stracotto (strah-KOT-toa). *Ita.* Meat stew slowly cooked for several hours; a pot roast.

strain (strahn). *USA.* To separate liquids and solids by passing through a strainer.

strasbourgeoise (strahs-buhrzh-wah). *Fre.* A garnish of sauerkraut, chopped bacon, and sautéed slices of goose liver.

strawberries Romanoff (STRAHW-behr-reez ROH-mahn-nohff). *USA.* Strawberries flavored with orange-flavored liqueur and served with Creme Chantilly.

strawberry (STRAHW-behr-ree). *USA.* The fruit of the strawberry plant; conical shape, flesh with tiny seeds sprinkled on skin; berry topped with green leafy cap.

strawberry shortcake (STRAHW-behr-ree SHORT-kahk). *USA.* A dessert made of biscuit dough with sliced strawberries and whipped cream.

straw mushroom (strahw MUHSH-room). *USA.* Oriental mushrooms cultivated on rice straw; have very fleshy conical caps that enclose long, thin stems; among the world's tastiest mushrooms.

streusel (STRU-sehl). *USA.* A sprinkling for baked goods; usually of a mixture of flour or breadcrumbs, sugar, butter and spices.

Streuselkuchen (stru-sehl-KOO-kern). *Ger.* A yeast cake topped with cinnamon-sugar crumbles.

string beans (strehng behnz). *USA.* A vine cultivated for its long, slender, edible green bean pods; used as a vegetable.

striped bass (stripd bahss). *USA.* A fish of the Western Atlantic that lives in the sea, then migrates to freshwater to spawn; white flesh, flaky, firm, with a delicate flavor; a popular table fish.

strip loin (strehp lowen). *USA.* A cut from the top of the beef short loin that is tender and boneless; usually cut in steaks.

stroganoff (STRO-gan-off). *Rus.* Sauteed beef strips served in a sour cream sauce with mushrooms and onions.

strömming (STRUR-ming). *Swe.* Small Baltic herring.

stroop (strohp). *Dut.* Molasses; syrup.

struccoli (strook-KOH-lee). *Ita.* Rolls of sweet pastry wrapped around fruit and cream cheese.

Strudel (STROO-duhl). *Ger.* Flaky, paper-thin pastry dough filled with fruit filling, rolled, and baked.

struffoli (stroof-FOH-lee). *Ita.* Fried pastry pocket containing sliced onion.

stuet (stewt). *Nor.* Creamed.

stufato (stu-FAH-toa). *Ita.* Braised or stewed. Also brasato, stracotto.

stuffing (STUHF-eng). *USA.* A seasoned mixture, usually based on bread products such as crumbled cornbread or bread cubes, used to stuff foods such as meats, vegetables, eggs.

sturgeon (STUHR-juhn). *USA.* A large migratory fish that lives in the sea and goes up rivers to spawn; flesh is white, rich, firm, and tight in texture; used smoked and pickled, as well as fresh; sturgeon roe is a delicacy.

stuvad (STEW-vahd). *Swe.* Creamed.

stuvede (STOO-er-der). *Dan.* Creamed.

stuvet oksekød (STOO-ert). *Dan.* Beef stew.

su (soo). *Jap.* White rice vinegar, sweeter and milder than American vinegar.

suàn (swen). *Chi.* Garlic.

suan là tang (suan la tang). *Chi.* Hot-and-sour soup.

suan mei jiang (swen may jiang). *Chi.* Duck sauce; served with duck or goose; literally, plum sauce; made of plums, apricots, vinegar and sugar.

suan niúnai (suan niu-nai). *Chi.* Yogurt.

suave (SWAH-veh). *Mex.* Mild, subtle; as with seasonings, flavorings.

sub (suhb). *USA.* Hoagie.

submarine (SUHB-mah-reen). *USA.* Hoagie.

subric (soo-breek). *Fre.* A variety of croquette, without the egg wash and breadcrumbs; sautéed instead of fried.

succo (SOOC-co). *Ita.* Juice.

succotash (SUCK-uh-tahsh). *USA.* A dish made of corn and lima beans.

sucker (SUCK-ehr). *USA.* An abundant freshwater fish in America; important edible species are the fine-scale sucker, the redhorse sucker, and the larger buffalo; when taken from cold deep lakes or clear running streams, this fish has firm, sweet white meat.

suco (SOO-koh). *Por.* Juice.

suco de laranja (SOO-koh der lah-RAHN-jash). *Por.* Orange juice.

sucre (sewkr). *Fre.* Sugar.

sucre filé (sewkr fee-LAY). *Fre.* Spun sugar.

sudako (soo-DAH-ko). *Jap.* Octopus pickled in vinegar.

sudare (soo-dah-leh). *Jap.* The bamboo mat made for rolling sushi.

suédoise (sway-dwah). *Fre.* A cold sauce of mayonnaise flavored with apple puree and grated horseradish, a classic Swedish sauce.

suehn (suen). *Chi.* Bamboo shoots; fresh whole, cut shoots, or canned.

suet (SOO-eht). *USA.* The hard fat about the kidneys and loins in beef and mutton, used in making pastry, puddings, and tallow.

sugar (SCHOO-gahr). *USA.* A sweet crystalline substance, wholly or essentially sucrose, with color ranging from white to brown depending on purity; used as a sweetener and preservative of food; water soluble. See also Barbados sugar, beet sugar, berry sugar, brown sugar, carmelized sugar, castor sugar, confectioners' sugar, corn sugar, demerara sugar, dextrose, fructose, icing sugar, invert sugar, loaf sugar, lump sugar, powdered sugar, and raw sugar.

sugarcane (SCHOO-gahr-kahn). *USA.* A tall grass grown in warm climates from which sucrose is extracted to make sugar.

sugar crystallization (SCHOO-gahr krys-tah-lah-ZA-shun). *USA.* The different stages through which sugar passes during various candy-making processes: thread, soft ball, firm ball, hard ball, soft crack, hard crack, caramelized sugar.

sugar snap peas (SCHOO-gahr snahp pehs). *USA.* A variety of snap peas with edible pods; the whole pod may be cooked or eaten fresh.

sugo (SOO-goa). *Ita.* Sauce.

sugo de carne (SOO-goa day KAHR-neh). *Ita.* Gravy.

suiker (SIR-kur). *Dut.* Sugar.

suimono (soo-EE-moh-noh). *Jap.* Clear soup.

Suiza (soo-EE-sah). *Mex.* Swiss or Swiss-style.

suizenji nori (soo-ee-ZEN-jgee no-ree). *Jap.* A sashimi garnish for vinegared salads or clear soups.

sukiyaki (soo-kee-YAH-kee). *Jap.* A one-pot cooking method using thinly sliced beef and a variety of vegetables cooked in suet at the table.

sukker (SOOK-kerr). *Nor.* Sugar.

suklaa (SOOK-laa). *Fin.* Chocolate.

sultana (suhl-TAHN-nah). *USA.* A golden raisin, made from dried white, seedless grapes.

Sülz (ZEWL-tser). *Ger.* Aspic with meat, as head cheese.

summer pudding (SUM-ehr PUD-deling). *Bri.* Fresh raspberries and red currants stewed, sweetened, then sieved into a bread lined bowl, left to stand overnight, turned out, and served with cream.

summer squash (SUHM-mehr squash). *USA.* A pale bowl-shaped squash with a scalloped edge also known as scallop, Patty Pan or Cymling."

sun (suen). *Chi.* Bamboo shoots.

sunchoke (SUHN-chock). *USA.* A vegetable that looks like a potato with small knobs; thin, brown skin, white flesh; has nutty flavor when raw and slight artichoke flavor when cooked; best when cooked, but used raw in salads.

sunflower seeds (SUHN-flawr seeds). *USA.* Seeds of the sunflower plant; used roasted and eaten like nuts. Also seeds yield a light oil.

sunomono (SOO-no-mo-no). *Jap.* Vinegared foods.

suomalainen lammasmuhennos (soooa-mah-lahee-nehn LAHM-mahss-MOO-hayn-nohs). *Fin.* Finnish version of Irish stew; made with mutton, onions, potatoes, carrots, and turnips.

suomalaisleipä (SOO-wo-ma-lice-rooeys-LAY-pa). *Fin.* Yeast bread.

superfine sugar (SU-purr-fine SCHU-gur). *USA.* Sugar of very fine crystals; quickly dissolves in liquid.

Suppe (ZUP-per). *Ger.* Soup.

suppe (SOO-bber). *Dan.* Soup.

suppli (SOO-plee). *Ita.* Croquettes.

suprème de volaille (su-pre-meh day vo-lye). *Fre.* Breast of chicken in a luxurious sauce.

surf 'n' turf (suhrf n tuhrf). *USA.* Seafood and meat served on the same plate.

sur grädde (SUR GRAH-dea). *Swe.* Sour cream.

surimi (soo-REE-mee). *Jap.* Imitation crabmeat made from pollock and other fish, then colored to resemble crab legs.

surkål (SEWR-kawl). *Nor.* Sauerkraut.

surkål (SEWR-koal). *Swe.* Sauerkraut.

sursild (soor-seel). *Dan.* Sour herring.

surströmming (sewr-STRUR-ming). *Swe.* Fermented Baltic herring, a tradition in northern Sweden.

surume-ika (soo-roo-MAAH-ee-koht). *Jap.* A type of squid.

sushi (SZU-she). *Jap.* Zushi; seasoned cold rice with various other ingredients. See chirashi zushi, nigiri zushi, norimaki zushi.

susine (soo-ZEE-nee). *Ita.* Plums.

süsse (zewss). *Ger.* Sweet.

Süssespeisen (zewss-SHPIGH-zern). *Ger.* Sweet desserts. Also called Süssigkeiten.

Süssigkeiten (sue-see-KIT-tehrn). *Ger.* Sweet desserts. Also called Süssespeisen.

suzuki (soo-ZOO-kee). *Jap.* Sea bass.

svamp (svahmp). *Swe.* Mushrooms.

svarta vinbär (SVAHR-tah VEEN-baer). *Swe.* Black currant.

svartsoppa (SVAHRT-SOHP-pah). *Swe.* Black soup; a famous dish prepared from goose and pig's blood, spices, and other seasonings.

Sveciaost (SVAY-ssiah-oost). *Swe.* A semihard cheese with small holes; often spiced; most popular Swedish cheese.

svine (sveen). *Dan.* Pork.

svinekoteleter (SVEEN-koa-der-leh-ter). *Dan.* Pork chops.

svinemørbrad (SVEEN-murr-braa). *Dan.* Pork tenderloin.

svinesteg (SVEEN-stayg). *Dan.* Roast pork loin.

svinestek (SVEEN-stayk). *Nor.* Roast pork.

svisker (SVISS-kerr). *Nor.* Prunes.

swamp cabbage (swahmp KAH-bahg). *USA.* Palm cabbage.

sweat (sweht). *USA.* To cook in a little fat under a lid without browning.

Swedish meatballs (SWEE-dehsh MEET-bahlz). *USA.* A small meatball covered with a savory brown gravy.

sweetbreads (SWET-brehds). *USA.* Thymus gland of a young calf, sheep or pig; highly perishable.

sweet cicely (sweet SEHS-ee-lee). *USA.* An herb of the parsley family; anise-flavored leaves, stems, and seeds used in salads and boquet garnis; cicely.

sweet cream butter (sweet kreem BUHT-tehr). *USA.* Butter made from cows' cream with little or no salt; must contain 80% milkfat.

sweetened condensed milk (SWET-end kon-DENSD mehlk). *USA.* Milk with its water content reduced by one-half, and sugar added in ratio of 18 pounds to 100 pounds of milk; often confused with evaporated milk.

sweet majoram (sweet mah-JOHR-ruhm). *USA.* An herb of Mediterranean origins; of the mint family; warm, sweet fragrance and delicate oreganolike flavor; used in savory dishes; marjoram.

sweet milk (sweet mehlk). *USA.* Cows' milk.

sweet potato (sweet poh-TAH-toh). *USA.* A root vegetable with a reddish skin, sweetish taste, and texture like the regular potato; often confused with the yam.

sweet sop (sweet sohp). *USA.* The yellow-green fruit of a tropical American tree; has sweet yellow pulp.

sweet woodruff (sweet WUHD-rouf). *USA.* An herb of dark green starlike whorled leaves; used in cold punches and May Wine.

Swiss chard (swehss chard). *USA.* An ancient vegetable of the beet family, with white stalks and dark green leaves; other varieties are red and yellow.

Swiss cheese (swehss cheez). *USA* American-made Emmental.

Swiss meringue (swess mehr-RAHNG). *USA.* A glazing icing made of confectioners' sugar, egg white, and lemon juice; used for wedding cakes, special cakes, pastry writing; dries hard. Also called royal icing and royal glaze.

Swiss roll (swehss rohl). *Bri.* Jelly roll.

Swiss steak (swehss stehk). *USA.* Rump or round steak baked with tomatoes, onions, peppers, and seasoned with herbs and spices.

swordfish (SOARD-fesch). *USA.* A very large fish, found worldwide, with dense white meat; marketed as steaks or chunks; excellent for baking or broiling.

syboes (see-BOWS). *Sco.* Spring onions; young, tender green onions.

syllabub (SILL-ah-bub). *Bri.* A punch made with milk and cream, flavored with liqueurs and spices.

sylt (sewlt). *Swe.* Jam.

syltede rødbeder (SEWL-te-the ROHTH-beh-thor). *Dan.* Pickled beets.

syltetøj (SEWL-ter-toi). *Dan.* Jam.

syltlök (SEWLT-lurk). *Swe.* Pearl onion.

syr ('syr'). *Nor, Swe.* Milk that has been kept for months before eating.

syr (SI-roo). *Rus.* Cheese.

syrup (SEHR-up). *USA.* A thick, sticky sweet liquid made of sugar and any of various liquids, usually water, and flavoring; used on pancakes, waffles, ice cream.

T

taart (tahrt). *Dut.* Layer cake.

tabasco (tah-BAS-koh). *USA.* Very hot red pepper sauce.

tabbuli (tah-BUHL-lee). *Ara.* An Arabic salad made with burghul (crushed wheat), chopped tomatoes, onion, mint, parsley, lemon juice, olive oil, cinnamon, pepper; scoop with grape leaves, romaine, or lettuce. Also spelled tabouleh, tabbouleh.

table cream ('TA-buhl kreem). *USA.* Cream containing 18–30% milkfat. Also called coffee or light cream.

table d'hote (tah-bluh dot). *Fre.* General title for a meal of several courses at a fixed price.

table grapes (TA-buhl grapz). *USA.* Any of numerous varieties eaten fresh out of hand.

table salt (TA-buhl sawlt). *USA.* A finely ground free-flowing salt used in food preparation. Also known as cooking salt.

tacchino (tahk-KEE-no). *Ita.* Turkey.

taco (TAH-ko). *Mex.* A tortilla folded or wrapped around a filling, may be crisp or soft.

tadjin helou (TAH-jean hehl-LO). *Ara.* A very delicate stew made of beef and mutton, vegetables, dried prunes or raisins, and quinces, covered with pie pastry and baked in an oven.

tadka (TAHR-ka). *Ind.* Spice perfumed butter used for flavoring yogurt, dal, relishes, vegetables, some meats.

Tafelspitz (TAHF-fehl-spihtz). *Ger.* A kind of pot roast with top round of beef boiled and served with root vegetables, horseradish, and sauces.

taffy (TAHF-fee). *USA.* A soft, chewy candy made from sugar, molasses, butter, nuts, and flavorings. Also called saltwater taffy.

taffy (TOF-fe). *Bri.* Toffee; a brittle, crunchy candy made from sugar, butter, nuts, and flavorings.

tagliarini (tahl-yah-REE-nee). *Ita.* Very thin noodles, used in soups. Also tagliolini.

tagliatelle (tahl-yah-TEHL-la). *Ita.* A thin handmade pasta ⅜" wide; fettuccine, pappardelle.

tahari (TEH-ha-ree). *Ind.* Spicy rice and peas dish with turmeric and herbs.

tahina (tah-HEE-nah). *Ara.* Pureed chick-peas mixed with sesame paste.

tahini (tah-HEE-nee). *Ara.* Heavy sesame oil, almost a paste; made by crushing raw sesame seeds; not the type of oil used in Oriental cooking.

tahiyn (tah-HEEN). *Ara.* Flour.

tai tempura (TAH-ee TEHM-poo-rah). *Jap.* Fried fish cakes.

tako (TAH-koh). *Jap.* Octopus.

tako kushisashi (TOH-koh koo-SHEE-sah-shee). *Jap.* Broiled octopus on skewers.

takenoko (tah-KAY-no-ko). *Jap.* Bamboo shoots; fresh whole, cut shoots, canned shoots; mild, unpretentious taste, crunchy texture.

takuan (TAH-koo-ahn). *Jap.* A popular pickle made from daikon, the large white radish; often tinted yellow; fresh, canned, bottled.

tala (TEH-lah). *Ind.* Deep-fried.

tallarines (tahl-lah-REE-neez). *Spa.* Noodles.

Tallyrand (tahl-lee-rahnd). *Fre.* A garnish for sweetbreads and poultry consisting of macaroni mixed with butter and cheese, tossed with julienne truffle and diced foie gras.

talmouse (tahl-moos). *Fre.* Cheesecake.

tamaatim (ta-MAA-tim). *Ara.* Tomatoes.

tamago (tah-MAH-goh). *Jap.* Eggs; hanjuku (HAHN-joo-koo), soft-boiled; medamayaki (meh-DAH-mah-yah-kee), fried eggs; pōchi (POH-chee), poached; yude (yoo-DEH), hard-boiled.

tamal (tah-MAHL). *Mex.* Tamale.

tamale (tah-MAH-lee). *USA.* Highly seasoned meat filling rolled in cornmeal mush, wrapped in corn husks, and steamed. Also spelled tamal.

tamale pie (ta-NAH-lee pi). *USA.* A dish of cornmeal mush with a filling of chopped meats and hot chili sauce.

tamaras (TAH-mah-rahss). *Por.* Dates.

tamari (TAH-mah-ree). *Jap.* A dark, thick, dipping and basting sauce made from soybeans.

tamarind (TAHM-ah-rend). *Ind.* Brown pods of a tropical tree whose soft brown, sour pulp is used in Asia as a souring agent the way lemon juice is used; flavor is cross between apricots and dates with a tinge of lemon.

tamatar (ta-MAH-tehr). *Ind.* Tomato.

tamis (tah-mee). *Fre.* Tammy cloth; woolen canvas cloth used for straining soups and sauces.

tammy (TAHM-mee). *USA.* A fine gauze used for straining food. Also tammy cloth.

tampala (thahm-PAH-lah). *Ind.* Chinese spinach.

tandoori (tan-DOO-ree). *Ind.* Food marinated in yogurt with spices, then roasted at a high temperature.

tang (tang). *Chi.* Soup.

tángcù liji (tang-chu lee-jee). *Chi.* Sweet-sour boneless pork.

tangelo (TAHNG-eh-lo). *USA.* A hybrid citrus fruit; cross of a tangerine and grapefruit.

tangerine (tahn-jehr-reene). *USA.* A variety of mandarin orange with deep rose-orange skin and flesh.

tangmiàn (tang mien). *Chi.* Noodles in soup.

tanmen (TAHNN mahnn). *Jap.* A type of white instant soup noodle.

tansy (TAHN-zee). *Bri.* An herb with strong, bitter, aromatic flavor used to flavor puddings; now largely ignored.

tanuki soba (tah-NOO-kee SOH-bah). *Jap.* A type of brown buckwheat noodle.

taozi (tao-dzi). *Chi.* Peach.

tapas (TAH-pahs). *Spa.* Appetizers served in Spanish bars with cocktails, in great variety and profusion.

tapenade (tah-pah-nahd). *Fre.* A puree of anchovies, black olives, garlic, capers, with olive oil added to form a paste, tuna is sometimes added.

tapioca (tah-pee-O-kah). *USA.* Processed from the Brazilian cassava root, which is poisonous until heated during processing to release the hydrocyanic acid; popular use in sauces and fruit fillings that are to be frozen; does not become watery on reconstitution; makes clear sauces.

tapioca flour (tah-pee-O-kah flowr). *USA.* Made from finely ground tapioca; makes very clear glazes and sauces; same properties as tapioca.

taquitos (tah-KEE-tohs). *Mex.* Small tortillas with a small amount of filling, either rolled or folded, then fried until slightly crisp.

Taramasalata (TAHR-ma-sahl-LAHT-tah). *Ger.* Pink fish roe, bread, milk, olive oil, lemon juice, and garlic pureed, then served with crusty bread.

taratur (tahr-rah-TOR). *Ara.* Tahini sauce.

tari (TEH-fee). *Ind.* Gravy.

taro (TAH-roa). *USA.* A Tahitian plant grown throughout the tropics for its rootstock, which is high in starch and potatolike texture; its spinachlike leaves and asparaguslike stems are also eaten; an important staple in Polynesia, Central and South America, Africa, and Asia. Also known as dasheen.

tarragon (TAHR-ah-gahn). *USA.* An herb with a delicate aniselike flavor; essential in bouquet garni, in béarnaise sauce, and chicken à l'estragon; one of the fines herbs.

tart (tahrt). *USA.* Pie or pastry, sweet or savory; size varies from 2″ to full size pie.

tarta (TAHR-tah). *Spa.* Tart; small pie or pastry, sweet or savory. Also called tartaleta.

tårta (TOAR-tah). *Swe.* Layer cake.

tartar med aeg (TAH-tahr maydh ehg). *Dan.* A favorite smørrebrød: scraped raw beef, raw onions, and raw egg.

tartar sauce (TAR-tar saus). *USA.* See tartare.

tartare (tahr-tahr). *Fre.* A cold sauce made of mayonnaise, hard-boiled egg yolks, very finely chopped onions, capers, gherkins, served with fried fish or cold meats.

tarte (tahrt). *Fre.* Tart; tartlet; a small pie or pastry, sweet or savory. Also called tartelette, taurte.

tarte à l'oignon (tahrt ah l'yon-awng). *Fre.* Rich, creamy onion pie; served as an accompaniment to meats.

tarte des demoiselles Tatin (tart deh dehm-wah-zehl tah-teen). *Fre.* An apple tart baked upside down; devised by the Tatin sisters of Orléans, France; a layer of sugar is placed on the tart pan, the apples sliced covering the sugar, butter is put on top of the apples, then covered with crust and baked until the sugar caramelizes to a hard crust. It is turned out, upside down, on plate to serve.

tarte liègeoise (tahrt lee-zhwah). *Fre.* The famous Belgian dessert; a cross between the American fruit pie and an English trifle.

tartina (tahr-TEE-nah). *Ita.* Tart.

tartine (tar-teen). *Fre.* Slice of bread.

tartufi (tahr-TOO-fee). *Ita.* Truffle.

tarwebrood (TAHR-vuh-broht). *Dut.* Wheat bread.

Tascherln (TAHS-shuhr-rehn). *Ger.* Little pockets of dough, like ravioli, filled with savory fillings or jam; Austrian.

tatties (TAH-tees). *Sco.* Potatoes.

Taube (TAW-berr). *Ger.* Pigeon.

T-bone steak (T-bohn stayk). *USA.* A steak cut from the loin of beef with the bone resembling a T.

te (teh). *Mex.* Tea.

té (tai). *Ita.* Tea.

té (tay). *Spa.* Tea.

te (teh). *Dan, Nor.* Tea.

te (tay). *Swe.* Tea.

tebrød (TAY-brur). *Nor.* Tea cake.

Tee (tay). *Ger.* Tea.

teerl (TAY-ri). *Fin.* Black grouse.

teetä (TAY-tae). *Fin.* Tea.

Teewürst (TAY-voorst). *Ger.* Sausage of very finely ground pork tenderloin.

Teiggemüse (TIGHG-ger-mewser). *Ger.* Macaroni dishes.

tej patta (tayj PAH-tah). *Ind.* Bay leaf.

tekaka (TAY-kah-kah). *Swe.* Tea cake; crumpet.

tel (tayl). *Ind.* Oil.

temper (TEHM-pur). *USA.* To bring to a suitable state by mixing in or adding a liquid ingredient, then kneading to a uniform texture.

Temple orange (TEHM-puhl oranj). *USA.* A hybrid orange; the result of a tangerine and orange cross.

tempura (TEHM-poo-rah). *Jap.* Batter-fried foods.

tenderloin (TEHN-dehr-loyn). *USA.* The long, slender, tender muscle that runs through the loin of beef and ends at the ribs; is divided into filet mignon, chateaubriand, tournedos; the tenderest muscle of the carcass.

tentsuyu (TEHN-tsoo-yoo). *Jap.* Dipping sauce for tempura.

tepid (TEH-ped). *USA.* Lukewarm.

tequila (teh-KEE-yah). *Mex.* Distilled liquor made from agave in specific growing areas.

teri (tah-DREE). *Jap.* Glaze.

teriyaki (TEHR-re-yah-kee). *Jap.* Glaze-broiled; meat marinated in a sweet soy sauce mixture and grilled over charcoal so that a glaze is formed.

ternero (tehr-NEH-roh). *Spa.* Veal.

terrapin (TEHR-ah-pen). *USA.* An edible freshwater or tidal water turtle.

terrine (tay-reen). *Fre.* An earthenware pot similar to a casserole in which food is served and sometime prepared.

tetrazzini (teht-trahz-ZEE-nee). *Ita.* A rich pasta dish with a creamy cheese sauce and seafood or poultry.

tette melk (TEH-teh MELK). *Nor.* Milk in which tette leaves have been placed to preserve the milk and start a specially flavored culture.

thalj (talg). *Ara.* Ice.

thandai (than-DA-ee). *Ind.* Summer punch made with ground seeds, almonds, spices, sugar, and whole milk.

thé (tay). *Fre.* Tea.

thee (tay). *Dut.* Tea.

thee complet (tay kohm-PLAH). *Dut.* Tea served with food such as cookies, biscuits, or tarts.

thermidor (THERM-ee-dohr). *USA.* A method of preparing lobster using Mornay sauce as a base, but substituting mustard for the cheese. Add sieved tomalley, coral, and a little sherry, mix with chunked lobster tail meat, and stuff the lobster tail; sprinkle with grated Parmesan, and broil.

thick batter (thehk BAHT-tehr). *USA.* A batter that contains 2 parts flour to 1 part liquid, such as used for muffins and cakes. Also called a soft drop batter.

thick white sauce (thehk white saus). *USA.* A roux-liquid mixture that contains a fat-flour ratio of 3 tablespoons of each to 1 cup of liquid, such as used for puddings.

thicken (THEHK-en). *USA.* Give body to sauces, gravies, or soups by adding flour, cornstarch, or arrowroot.

thin batter (thehn BAHT-tehr). *USA.* A batter that contains 1 part flour to 1 part liquid, such as used for cream puffs, timbale cases, crepes, popovers, dip batters. Also known as pour batter.

thin white sauce (thehn white saus). *USA.* A roux-liquid mixture that contains a fat-flour ratio of 1 tablespoon of each to 1 cup liquid, such as used in soups or thin gravies.

thon (tawng). *Fre.* Tuna.

Thousand Island dressing (thou-sund EY-lund DREHS-seng). *USA.* A salad dressing with a Russian dressing base and chopped pickles, green peppers, cream, and seasonings added.

thousand-year-old eggs (THOU-sund-yeer-old-ehgs). *USA.* Pí dàn; Chinese duck eggs preserved in a clay casing made of ashes, lime, salt, and strong tea; rolled in rice husks, and buried for three months; the yolks turn greenish-brown, the whites turn black-purple. Also called hundred-year-old eggs.

thread (threhd). *USA.* The first stage of sugar crystallization: begins at 230°F, the syrup makes a two-inch coarse thread when dropped from a spoon.

Thunfisch (TOON-fish). *Ger.* Tuna fish.

thym (tang). *Fre.* Thyme.

thyme (time). *USA.* A pungent, aromatic herb used in seasoning and soups.

Tia Maria (TEE-ah Mah-REE-ah). *Spa.* A Jamaican coffee and spice flavored liqueur.

tidbid (TEED-beed). *Dan.* Light snack.

tien mien jiàng (ten meen GEE-ong). *Chi.* A thick, sweet, salty paste made from fermented red beans; used to flavor marinades and sauces and as a dipping sauce.

tiges (teezh). *Fre.* A type of Swiss sausage.

tikka (TIH-ka). *Ind.* Cutlet.

til (thel). *Ind.* Sesame seeds

tilefish (TILE-fisch). *USA.* A western Atlantic food fish, with unusually firm, but tender flesh, which is best compared to lobster meat or scallops.

Tilsit (TIHL-siht). *Ger.* A cooked cheese from raw cows' milk, with a thin yellow rind, straw-colored interior with holes, acidic taste, and sometimes flavored with caraway.

timbale (tim-bull). *Fre.* Thin, fried case for holding creamed mixtures; or unsweetened baked custard with meat, poultry, or vegetables.

timo (TEE-moa). *Ita.* Thyme.

tin (teen). *Ara.* Figs.

tinda (TIN-dah). *Ind.* A round gourd; a vegetable belonging to the cucumber family.

tippaleivät (TEEP-pah-leh-vat). *Fin.* May Day crullers; bird's nests; spiral shape, similar to pretzels.

tipsy pudding (tehp-see puhd-dehng). *Bri.* A dessert pudding of sponge cake soaked with liquor, covered with custard or whipped cream; similar to trifle.

Tirolen Eierspeise (tee-ROAL-ern IGH-err-shpigh-zer). *Ger.* Hard-boiled eggs, potatoes, anchovies in an Austrian casserole.

tiropita (tee-rop-PEE-tah). *Gre.* A cheese pie made with phyllo dough.

tisane (teh-ZAHN). *USA.* Herbal tea.

tlami (tah-AH-mee). *Ara.* Round, flat, soft-textured bread without pocket; used for mnaqish and as regular bread.

toad-in-the-hole (toad-en-thuh-hole) *Bri.* Sausage cooked in a batter.

toast (tost). *USA.* Browning the surface of a food by direct heat.

tocino (toa-THEE-noas). *Spa.* Bacon.

tocino de cielo (toa-THEE-noas day thee-AY-loa). *Spa.* A thick caramel custard dessert; not made with bacon.

toddy (TODD-de). *Bri.* A punch made of a mixture of whisky, sugar, and hot water.

toffee (TOFF-fe). *USA.* A hard, brittle, crunchy candy made with sugar and molasses, butter, nuts, flavorings; same as the British taffy.

tofu (TOA-foo). *Jap.* Fresh bean curd cake; white with a texture of well-baked custard, easily digestible; many types, each for a different use.

togan (TO-gahn). *Jap.* Winter melon; resembles a watermelon, but has white, firm flesh.

togarashi (to-GAHR-dah-shee). *Jap.* Red hot chili peppers; also, a seasoning that contains sesame seed, orange peel, and red hot chili peppers.

tokay grapes (to-KA grapz). *USA.* A purplish-red table grape with firm flesh, sweet taste, and with or without seeds.

Toll House cookie (tohl hahus KUHK-kee). *USA.* A cookie made with brown sugar, nuts, and chocolate chips in the batter; originated at the Toll House Inn in Massachusetts.

tomalley (toh-MAHL-lee). *USA.* The olive-green liver of the lobster; a delicacy.

tomat (toa-MAAD). *Dan.* Tomato.

tomate (to-maht). *Fre.* Tomato.

tomate (toh-MAH-tay). *Por.* Tomato.

Tomaten (tom-MAA-tern). *Ger.* Tomatoes.

tomaten (toh-MAH-tuh). *Dut.* Tomatoes.

tomater (too-MAH-tehr). *Swe.* Tomatoes.

tomates (toa-MAH-tayss). *Spa.* Tomatoes.

tomatillo (toh-mah-TEHL-loh). *Mex.* A green tomato, small and pungent (not an unripe tomato); used in salsa; also called tomato verde.

tomato (toh-MAY-toh). *USA.* The fruit of a plant cultivated for its usually large red or yellow fruit; used extensively in cooking, in salads, even in preserves; many varieties worldwide. See cherry tomatoes.

tomatsaft (toom-MAAT-sahft). *Nor.* Tomato juice.

tomatsoppa (too-MAT-SO-pah). *Swe.* Tomato soup.

tomber a glace (ton-bay au gla-say). *Fre.* To reduce a liquid until it has the appearance of a thick syrup.

Tomino (toh-MEE-noh). *Ita.* An excellent dessert cheese made of cows' milk with a delicate, fresh flavor, and a soft, smooth paste.

tonfisk (TOON-fisk). *Swe.* Tuna.

tong (tawng). *Dut.* Sole; a flatfish.

tongue (tuhngah). *USA.* The flesh of the beef tongue used as food.

tonija (tyoh-NEYN). *Dut.* Tuna.

tonkatsu (tong-KAHT-soo). *Jap.* Spicy, marinated pork, dipped in egg and breadcrumbs, then fried.

tonno (TOAN-noh). *Ita.* Tuna.

Topfen (TOHP-fehrn). *Ger.* An Austrian cows' skim milk cheese similar to cottage cheese; widely used in pastries. Also known as Quark.

top round (top rownd). *USA.* A cut from the inner part of a round of beef.

top sirloin (top SUHR-lown). *USA.* A cut from the top portion of the loin section of beef.

torkad frukt (TOR-kahd frewkt). *Swe.* Dried fruits.

tørkage (TURR-kaaer). *Dan.* Plain cake.

tordo (TOAR-do). *Ita.* Small thrush.

torigai (toh-REE-gah-ee). *Jap.* A cockle whose edible parts are tender and tasty; a mollusk of the clam family.

toriniku (toh-REE-NEE-koo). *Jap.* Chicken meat.

tororo konbu (toe-LOW-low KOHNG-boo). *Jap.* Konbu leaves that have been soaked in vinegar and shaved along the length of the leaf, then cut into thread form.

torpedo (tor-PEE-do). *USA.* Hoagie.

torrada (toh-RRAH-dah). *Por.* Toast.

tørret frugtsuppe (TURR-reht FREWKT-ssew-pper). *Nor.* Fruit soup made of dried fruits; served hot or cold.

torrfisk (TORR-feesk). *Swe, Nor, Dan.* Stockfish.

torrón (too-RON). *Ita.* A sweet nougat based on honey and almonds; may have figs or chocolate.

torsk (torshk). *Nor.* Cod.

torsk (toarsk). *Dan.* Cod.

torsk (torsk). *Swe.* Codfish.

torta (TOHR-tah). *Mex.* A cake; loaf.

torta (TOAR-tah). *Ita.* Tart, pie, or cake.

torta (TOR-tah). *Por.* A rolled and filled cake.

Törtchen (TUHR-chchn). *Ger.* Small tarts.

Torte (TOR-te). *Ger.* A rich cake made from eggs, nuts, and breadcrumbs; or meringue shaped like a cake.

tortellini (tor-te-LEEN-nee). *Ita.* Small rounds of egg pasta stuffed, folded, and wrapped with ends pinched together in a ring.

Torten (TOR-tern). *Ger.* A class of cakes, made of many eggs, ground nuts or dry bread crumbs, various and multiple fillings, covered with a rich frosting, and in numerous varieties.

tortiglione (tor-TEHG-lee-ohn). *Ita.* Almond cake.

tortilha de mariscos (tor-TEE-lya duh mah-REESH-koosh). *Por.* Omelet filled with chopped shellfish.

tortilla (tohr-TEE-yah). *Mex.* A thin, unleavened pancake of ground, dried maize, baked on a griddle.

tortilla (toar-TEE-lyah). *Spa.* Omelet.

tortilla de huevos (toar-TEE-lyah day WAY-bhoass). *Mex.* Omelet.

tortina (toar-TEE-nah). *Ita.* A tartlet.

tortino (toar-TEE-noa). *Ita.* A frittata that is cooked in an oven, therefore drier in the center than one cooked on a stove top.

tortoni (toar-TOHN-nee). *Ita.* Ice cream topped with chopped almonds or macaroons. Also biscuit tortoni.

tortue (tor-too). *Fre.* Turtle.

Toscanello (tohs-cah-NELL-loa). *Ita.* A ewes' milk cheese with a brownish yellow rind; pale, dense interior; mild, piquant taste.

toscatårta (TOH-ska-TOR-ta). *Swe.* An almond-topped cake.

toss (tohss). *USA.* To mix ingredients lightly without crushing.

tostada (tohs-TAH-dah). *Mex.* A crisp-fried tortilla that is served with guacamole, salsa, and assorted dips.

tostaditas (toh-tah-THEE-tahs). *Mex.* Totopas; little triangular pieces of crisp-fried tortillas.

tostato (to-STAA-toa). *Ita.* Toast.

totani (toa-TAH-nee). *Ita.* Small squids.

totopos (toh-TOH-pohs). *Mex.* Tostaditas; little triangular pieces of crisp-fried tortillas.

toucinho (toh-SEE-nyoh). *Por.* Smoked slab bacon.

toulouse, à la (too-looz). *Fre.* A garnish of white meats, mushrooms, truffles, in allemande sauce; a classic garnish.

tourin (too-rahng). *Fre.* Onion soup made with milk, cream, egg yolks; served with grated cheese.

tourné (toor-nay). *Fre.* A vegetable that is turned or shaped with a knife, as a mushroom cap.

tournedos (toor-ner-doaz). *Fre.* Slices of beef tenderloin, the most tender cut of beef.

Tournedos de Boeuf a la Oskar (toor-NAH-doaz day boof ah lah OHS-kahr). *USA.* Thick slices of sauteed beef tenderloin (or veal round steak) served with crabmeat and asparagus or artichoke hearts; topped with a rich creamy béarnaise sauce.

Tournedos Rossini (toor-ner-doaz roas-see-nee). *Fre.* Sauteed slices of beef filet on croutons or artichoke bottoms, topped with goose or duck liver slices, truffle slices, and Madeira wine sauce.

tourte (toor-teh). *Fre.* An open tart, or pie, usually round and savory; tart.

tourtelettes (toor-let). *Fre.* Small tartlets.

toute-épice (toot-ay-pees). *Fre.* Allspice.

tragacanth (TRAHG-ah-kahnth). *USA.* Vegetable gum used as an emulsifier and thickener in commercially made sauces, candies, ice cream. Also called gum.

Trappiste (trahp-pehst). *Fre.* A round, semihard cheese, with a soft rind and a dense smooth paste with small holes; made all over the world by Trappist monks. Port-Salut is the best known.

Trasch (trash). *Ger.* A Swiss liqueur made of pears and apples.

Traube (TROW-ber). *Ger.* Grapes.

travailler (tra-vye-yay). *Fre.* To beat or stir for blending or smoothing ingredients.

treacle (TRE-kehl). *Bri.* A very sweet, heavy syrup, golden or black, similar to molasses, used in making desserts such as puddings and tarts.

tree ear (tree eher). *USA.* Yún er; a Chinese fungus used in cooking for its interesting texture. Also called cloud ear.

trefoil (TREE-foyil). *USA.* Mitsuba; a member of a Japanese parsley family; flavor between sorrel and celery; attractive light green color; used to add flavor and color accent; a type of clover.

trenette (treh-NEHT-tay). *Ita.* A pasta similar to fettucine that is flat; the traditional pasta for pesto.

Trenton cracker (TREHN-tuhn KRAHK-ker). *USA.* A light, round, puffy cracker made of wheat flour; served with oyster stews.

trifle (TRI-ful). *Bri.* A layered dessert made of sponge cake soaked in fruit juice or liquor, covered with jam, custard, almonds, and whipped cream.

triglie (TREE-lyay). *Ita.* Red mullet.

trigo (TREE-goh). *Mex.* Wheat.

tripa (TREE-pah). *Por.* Tripe.

tripe (tryip). *USA.* The first and second stomachs of ruminants used as foodstuff.

tripe (TREEP-pay). *Ita.* Tripe.

tripes à la mode de Caen (treep-ah lah mod deo kahng). *Fre.* Tripe baked with calf's feet, vegetables, apple brandy or cider.

triple sec (TREP-pul sehk). *USA.* An orange-flavored, clear, colorless French liqueur. Also called Cointreau, Curaçao.

triticale flour (treht-ah-KALE-e flowr). *USA.* A nutritious sweet-tasting flour obtained from intergenetic hybridization by crossing durum wheat, hard red wheat, and rye; very high in protein and low in gluten; good bread flour when mixed with higher gluten flours.

trota (TRAW-tah). *Ita.* Trout.

trota salmonata (TRAW-tah sahl-moa-NAH-tay). *Ita.* Salmon trout.

trout (trout). *USA.* A highly prized game fish found mostly in freshwater; flesh is firm, succulent, and ranges in color from white to brilliant reds; very simple bone structure; many varieties worldwide.

trouvillaise (troo-vee-lay). *Fre.* A garnish of shrimp, mussels, mushroom caps in shrimp sauce.

trucha (TROO-chah). *Spa.* River trout.

trufa (TROO-fah). *Por.* Truffle.

Trüffel (TREWF-fehl). *Ger.* Truffle.

truffle (truff-uhl). *Fre.* A subterranean mushroomlike fungus used for garnishing and flavoring.

truite (trweet). *Fre.* Trout.

truite saumonée (tre-weet soa-mawng-ngay). *Fre.* Salmon trout.

truss (truhs). *Fre.* To secure with string or skewer, the wings and legs of any fowl, in order to hold its shape during cooking.

truta (TROO-tah). *Por.* Trout.

Truthahn (TROOT-haan). *Ger.* Tom turkey; gobbler.

Trut-henne (TROOT-he-neh). *Ger.* Turkey hen.

tsukemono (TSKEH-moh-noh). *Jap.* Pickles.

tubettini (too-beht-TEE-nee). *Ita.* Macaroni in shape of small tubes.

tuffaaha (tuf-FEHH). *Ara.* Apple.

tuile (tweel). *Fre.* A curved, crisp cookie made with crushed almonds; made curved by placing warm cookie on rolling pin.

tulipe (too-leep). *Fre.* A pastry shell made of a crisp cookie that is ruffled, while still warm, to make a cup to hold berries or ices.

tum (toom). *Ara.* Garlic.

tuna (TOO-nah). *USA.* A saltwater fish of varying size, from 300–400 pounds to 1000–1200 pounds, sought for its rich meat, which varies in color and oiliness depending on species; albacore is highest quality with its white meat; bonito has darkest meat and much sought-after by Japanese to dry for use in sashimi; used brined, canned, flaked, dried, fresh; an important worldwide food fish.

tuna (TOO-nah). *Mex.* Prickly pear.

tunge (TOONG-er). *Dan.* Tongue.

Tunke (TUHNG-keh). *Ger.* Gravy or sauce.

tunny (TOO-nee). *Bri.* Tuna.

turbinado sugar (tuhr-be-NAHD-o SHUH-gahr). *USA.* A partially refined, coarse-grained, beige-colored crystal containing the molasses portion of the sugar.

turbot (TUHR-boht). *USA.* A flatfish of the flounder family; found in both the Pacific and the Atlantic, but different; has delicate flavor and firm white meat. Also known as Steinbutte (German), Rombo chiodato (Italian), Piggvar (Scandinavian), Plat (Yugoslavia), Turbot (French).

turkey (TUHR-kee). *USA.* A game bird, as well as domesticated for commercial use; a truly original North American native; both toms and hens are used for food; traditionally roasted and served for Thanksgiving and Christmas meals.

turkey roll (TUHR-kee rohl). *USA.* Boned turkey meat, pressed in roll form; usually commercially prepared.

Turkish delight (TUHR-keesh de-LITE). *USA.* A Turkish confection of fruit paste, served with afternoon coffee; rahat loukoum.

turmeric (tehr-MEHR-rik). *USA.* A root spice of India, when dried yields a vivid yellow color used in curry powders and American mustard; may be substituted for saffron for color, but does not have flavor of saffron; basic spice in bread-and-butter pickles.

turn (tuhrn). *USA.* To shape fruit or vegetable with a paring knife.

turnip (TUHR-nehp). *USA.* A cultivated root vegetable of the mustard family; usually white with purplish top; its green leaves are also used as a vegetable.

turnip greens (TUHR-nehp grehns). *USA.* The tops of the cultivated root vegetable of the mustard family.

turnover (TUHRN-ov ehr). *USA.* Food encased in pastry and fried or baked.

turrón (toor-RON). *Spa.* A traditional Christmas chewy candy made of egg white, honey, and toasted almonds.

turtle (TURR-tuhl). *USA.* A marine reptile that lives both on land and in water; the female terrapin has the choicest of all turtle meat; the green meat from the top shell is considered best, meat taken from the bottom shell is white.

tutti-fruttl (TOO-ti FROO-ti). *USA.* Mixed fruits, chopped and preserved in brandy.

tvorog (TVO-rog). *Rus.* Cottage cheese.

twaalfuurtje (TWAHL-few-el-twae). *Dut.* Cold luncheon.

twelfth-night cake (TWELFTH-nite kake). *Bri.* Very rich spice cake made with candied fruits, dried fruits, almonds with almond paste filling and topping; a traditional cake.

Tybo (TEW-boh). *Dan.* A cooked cows' milk cheese, brick-shaped with large holes and yellow rind, straw-colored interior, mild, slightly acid taste.

tykmaelk (TEWK-mehlk). *Dan.* A junketlike dessert made from clabbered milk.

tyrolienne (tee-rohl-yehn). *Fre.* A garnish of fried onion rings and chopped tomatoes.

tyttebaer (TEWD-er-baer). *Dan.* Lingonberry.

tzimmes (TSEHM-mehs). *Jew.* A brisket casserole with carrots, dried fruits, syrup, and topped with dumplings and potatoes; traditional for Rosh Hashanah.

U

uccèlli (oot-CHEHL-lee). *Ita.* Birds.

uchepos (oo-CHEH-pohs). *Mex.* Special fresh corn tamales made in Michoacán, Mexico.

udo (OO-do). *Jap.* A stalk vegetable with a delicate aroma, a fennel flavor, and an appealing fresh crispness, used raw or barely cooked in salads.

udon (oo-dohn). *Jap.* Wide, flat rice noodles.

ugli fruit (OO-gli froot). *USA.* A Jamaican citrus fruit resembling a pear-shaped grapefruit, with lime-green to light orange skin, yellow-orange pulp; brightly acid-sweet with a zesty pungency.

ugnspannkaka (UNGNS-pan-KA-kah). *Swe.* Thick pancake baked in the oven.

ugnstekt (EWNGN-staykt). *Swe.* Baked or roasted.

uien (IR-uh). *Dut.* Onions.

uitsmijter (OUT-smi-ter). *Dut.* A substantial snack of bread piled with cold meats and topped with two fried eggs.

umé (oo-MEH). *Jap.* Plum.

umeboshi (oo-MEH boh-shee). *Jap.* Tiny red or green pickled plums; eaten at breakfast with rice and miso soup.

umeshu (oo-MEH-shoo). *Jap.* Plum wine.

umido (OO-mee-doa). *Ita.* Stew.

unagi (oo-NAH-gee). *Jap.* Eel.

Ungarische art (UHNG-gehr-ish ahrt). *Ger.* Hungarian style, usually meaning "with paprika."

unpolished rice (uhn-POHL-eeshed rics). *USA.* Rice grains that have had the bran layer and most of the germ removed; not to be confused with brown rice.

unsweetened chocolate (uhn-SWEET-end CHOK-o-laht). *USA.* A bitter-tasting chocolate used in baking; no sugar added.

uovo (WAW-vah). *Ita.* Egg; egg yolk is tuorlo d'uovo; egg white is bianco d'uovo; uovo affogato (WAW-vah ahf-foa-GAA-toa), poached egg; uovo al burro (WAW-vahahl BOOR-roa), fried egg; uovo molle (WAW-vah MOL-lay), soft-boiled egg; uovo piccante (WAW-vah pee-KAHN-teh), deviled egg; uovo sode (WAW-vah SO-doa), hard-boiled egg; uovo strapazzate (WAW-vah strah-pah-TSAA-tay), scrambled egg.

upside-down cake (UHP-side-dohwn kake). *USA.* A batter cake baked in a pan with the topping for the cake lining the bottom of the baking pan; when baked, cake is turned out upside down on a platter.

usli ghee (USE-lee khee). *Ind.* Indian clarified butter.

usu-kuchi shoya (oo-soo-KOO-chee SHOH-yoo). *Jap.* A light, clear, thin, salty soy sauce.

uunipuuro (OO-ni-poo-roa). *Fin.* Baked barley or rice porridge.

uunissa paistettu hauki (OO-nees-sah PYE-stet-too HOW-kee). *Fin.* Baked, stuffed pike.

uva (OO-bhahss). *Spa.* Grape.

uva passa (OO-vah PAHS-sah). *Ita.* Raisin. Also uva secca.

uvas (OO-vahss). *Por.* Grapes.

uva spina (OO-vah SPRR-nah). *Ita.* Gooseberries.

uzura no tamago (oo-ZOO-rah tah-MAH-goh). *Jap.* Quail eggs, speckled brown, 1 inch long, flavor of chicken eggs.

vaca (VAHC-ah). *Por.* Beef.

vaca cozida (VAHC-ah coo-ZEE-dah). *Por.* Boiled beef.

vaca guisada (VAHC-ah ghee-ZAH-doh). *Por.* Beef stew.

vacherin (vah-sher-rang). *Fre.* A dessert ring made of a flat coil of meringue with a piped edge to hold a filling of chantilly cream; the sides and open crown are decorated with large dots of meringue, then baked.

Vacherin Mont d'Or (vah-sher-reng mont dorr). *Fre.* A disc-shaped cows' whole-milk cheese of Switzerland with a soft, creamy, rich texture with small holes and delicate, buttery, sweet flavor.

vadelmat (VAH-dayl-maht). *Fin.* Raspberries.

våfflor (VOF-loor). *Swe.* Waffles.

vafler (VAHF-fehl). *Nor.* Waffles.

vaktel (VAHK-tayl). *Swe.* Quail.

Valencia orange (vah-LYNN-cee-ah oranj). *USA.* A sweet, thin-skinned, nearly seedless orange that produces an excellent juice.

valenciano (vahl-lyn-cee-AHN-noh). *Mex.* A chili pepper.

valencienne (vah-lehn-ceyeen). *Fre.* A garnish of rice pilaf with chopped sweet peppers in a tomato-flavored sauce.

välikyljys (vae-li-KEW-lyewss). *Fin.* Entrecôte of beef.

valkokaalisalaatti (VAHL-joa-KAA-li-SAH-laat-ti). *Fin.* Cabbage salad.

valnødkage (VAHL-nurd-kaer). *Dan.* Walnut cake.

valnødromkager (VAHL-nurd-ROHM-kaer). *Dan.* Walnut rum cookies.

vanaspati ghee (va-NAHS-pa-tee khee). *Ind.* Vegetable shortening.

vand (vahn). *Dan.* Water.

vandreuil (vahnd-rury). *Fre.* A popular fish found off the coast of Provence.

vaniglia (bigh-NEE-lyah). *Ita.* Vanilla.

vanilje (vah-NEEL-yer). *Nor.* Vanilla.

vaniljglass (va-NILY-GLAS). *Swe.* Vanilla ice cream.

vaniljsås (va-NEEL-SOHS). *Swe.* Custard.

vanilla (vah-NILL-lah). *USA.* The pod of a vine native to Mexico, picked immature, cured in a long process; used to flavor desserts, sugars, liqueurs.

vanille (vah-neey). *Fre.* Vanilla.

Vanille (vah-NIL-ler). *Ger.* Vanilla.

vanilleijs (vah-NIL-leh-ICS). *Dut.* Vanilla ice cream.

Vanille Rahmeis (vah-NIL-ler rahm-ighss). *Ger.* Vanilla ice cream.

vanillin (vah-NILL-lahn). *USA.* A synthetic vanilla, chemically created.

vann (vahn). *Nor.* Water.

vanukas (vah-NUSS-kohr). *Fin.* Pudding.

vapeur (vah-purr). *Fre.* Steam.

variety meat (vah-RI-eh-tee meet). *USA.* Internal organs, such as heart, liver, kidneys, sweetbreads, and offal.

varkenskarbonaden (VAR-kens-kar-boh-nah-den). *Dut.* Fried pork chops.

varkensvlees (VAHR-kuns-vlays). *Dut.* Pork.

varm choklad (varm shook-LAD). *Swe.* Hot Chocolate.

varmrätt (VAHRMT-reht). *Swe.* Hot dish.

vasikanlihaa (VAH-sik-kahn-LI-haa). *Fin.* Veal.

vasikanpaisti (VAH-sik-kahn-PAHI-sti). *Fin.* Roast veal.

Västerbottenost (VEHS-terr-bot-term-oost). *Swe.* A cows' milk cheese with a firm interior with small holes; a hard rind, covered with wax; pungent taste.

Västgötaost (VEH-shyur-tah-oost). *Swe.* A Swiss-type cheese.

vatten (VAH-tern). *Swe.* Water.

vattenglass (VA-tehn-GLAS). *Swe.* Sherbet.

vaxbönor (VAKS-boh-nor). *Swe.* Waxbeans.

veado, carne de (vay-AH-doo, KAHR-nay day). *Por.* Venison.

veal (veuhl). *USA.* Young beef, three to five months of age; when milk-fed, flesh is pale pink to white; when grass-fed, flesh is rosy pink.

Veal Cordon Bleu (veal KOR-dohn blu). *USA.* Paper-thin veal slices rolled around ham and Gruyère cheese, then breaded and sauteed until golden and crisp.

veal Orloff (veal ORR-lohf). *USA.* Saddle of veal or lamb prepared in the classic haute cuisine manner, with truffles, soubise, duxelles, covered with béchamel, and garnished with asparagus tips.

veal Oscar (veal OS-kahr). *USA.* Sautéed veal cutlets served with béarnaise, and garnished with asparagus tips and crab legs or crayfish tails.

veau (voa). *Fre.* Veal.

vegetable (VEGJ-tah-buhl). *USA.* A herbaceous plant, such as potato, cabbage bean, carrot, grown for an edible part, which is eaten with the principal part of a meal.

vegetable salt (VEGJ-tah-bul sawlt). *USA.* Pure salt, sodium chloride, with added vegetable extracts, such as celery, garlic.

veggies (VEHG-geez). *USA.* Vegetables.

vellutata (vel-loo-TAH-toa). *Ita.* A soup thickened with egg yolk.

velouté (ve-loo-tay). *Fre.* Velvet; a rich, white sauce made with a white stock, chicken or veal; similar to bechamel which is made with milk.

venison (VEN-eh-sun). *USA.* Deer meat.

vénitienne (veh-nee-cee-ehn). *Fre.* Fish fillets poached in white wine; served with a reduction sauce.

venkel (FEHN-kehl). *Dut.* Fennel.

venudo (veh-NOO-doh). *Mex.* Deer; venison.

verbena (ver-BEE-nah). *USA.* An herb with an exquisitely pungent, sweet lemony aroma; use in tea, add to wine punch, perk up frozen peas, refresh the flavor of icy-cold white wine. Also called the Scarlett O'Hara herb.

verde (BEHR-theh). *Mex.* Green.

verdura (vah-DOO-ray). *Ita.* Vegetable.

verjuice (VEHR-juic). *USA.* The juice of unripened grapes, used as sour flavoring in cooking.

vermicelli (ver-me-CHEL-lee). *Ita.* Very thin pasta, often used in soups and puddings.

Véronique (veh-rohn-neek). *Fre.* Garnished with white grapes.

vert-pré (vehr-preh). *Fre.* A garnish for grilled meats of straw potatoes, watercress, and butter.

very thick white sauce (VEH-ree thehk whit saus). *USA.* A roux-liquid mixture that contains a fat-flour ratio of 4 tablespoons of each to 1 cup liquid, such as blancmange.

verza (VEHR-dzah). *Ita.* Green cabbage.

vetchina (vee-chyee-NAH). *Rus.* Ham.

Vezzena (vez-ZEH-nah). *Ita.* A cows' partially skimmed milk hard cheese; used for grating or as a table cheese.

viande (vyahngd). *Fre.* Meat.

viande froides (vyahngd frwah). *Fre.* Cold meats.

Vichy water (VEE-shee WAH-tehr). *USA.* Water from the town of Vichy, France, thought to have curative qualities, especially for the liver.

vichyssoise (VEE-che-swoy). *USA.* Cream of potato and leek soup, garnished with chopped chives.

Victoria sauce (Vehk-torr-re-ah). *Fre.* A garnish for fish of lobster sauce with diced lobster and truffles.

Victoria, à la (Vehk-torr-re-ah). *Fre.* A garnish of small tomatoes stuffed with puree of mushrooms, quartered artichoke simmered in butter, and served with meat juices reduced with port or Madeira.

Viennoise (veen-wahs). *Fre.* "In the Viennese style"; coated with egg and breadcrumbs, fried; served with a classic garnish.

Vierfrucht Marmalade (feer-FRUKHT mahr-meh-LAA-der). *Ger.* "Four Fruit Jam"; made of cherries, currants, gooseberries, raspberries.

viili (VEE-lee). *Fin.* Clabbered milk, similar to yogurt.

viini (VEE-nee). *Fin.* Wine.

viinirypäle (VEE-nee-REW-pael). *Fin.* Grape.

viinimarjakiisseli (VEE-nee-MAHR-yah-KEES-say-li). *Fin.* Red currant sauce.

viipurin rinkilä (VEE-poo-rin reen-KEE-lah). *Fin.* A famous coffeecake ring.

vijgen (VAY-khuh). *Dut.* Figs.

Villalón (bee-lyah-LON). *Spa.* A ewes' milk cheese; cylindrical, white, sharp, and salty.

villeroi (vee-lo-wah). *Fre.* A sauce of velouté, truffle and ham essence, used to coat foodstuff before dipping in egg and breadcrumbs, then frying.

viltsuppe (vilt-SSEW-pper). *Nor.* Game or venison soup.

vinäger (vi-NAH-gehr). *Swe.* Vinegar.

vinagre (vee-NAH-greh). *Spa.* Vinegar.

vinagre (vee-NAH-gray). *Por.* Vinegar.

vinaigrette (vee-nay-groit). *Fre.* A mixture of oil and vinegar with herbs, salt, and pepper.

vinbär (VEEN-baer). *Swe.* Currant.

vindaloo (VEN-deh-loo). *Ind.* A dish highly seasoned with vinegar, garlic, curry, and rich meat; a hot and pungent curry.

vindruvor (VEEN-drew-voor). *Swe.* Grapes.

vine leaves (vine leevez). *USA.* Young Mediterranean grape leaves blanched and used to wrap savories.

vinegar (VEHN-eh-gur). *USA.* A sour liquid obtained by fermentation of certain liquids from fruits, usually, and used as a condiment or preservative. Types include white, cider, malt-based, wine, and herb.

vinsuppe (VEEN-ssew-pper). *Nor.* Wine soup.

violet (VI-oa-leht). *USA.* A crystallized flower used as a dessert garnish.

virgin olive oil (VEHR-gehn OYL-ehv oyl). *USA.* Oil from the second cold press of superior quality olives. See olive oil.

Virginia ham (vehr-GEHN-yah hahm). *USA.* Smithfield ham.

viroflay (vee-roh-fla). *Fre.* Indicates the use of spinach in the dish; usually spinach balls used as a garnish accompaniment.

vis (vis). *Dut.* Fish.

viskoekjes (fisch-KOOK-yus). *Dut.* Fish cakes.

vispgrädde (VISP-greh-der). *Swe.* Whipped cream.

vitela (vee-TEL). *Por.* Veal.

vitello (vee-TEHL-loa). *Ita.* Veal.

vitello tonnato (vee-TAHL-loa toan-NAA-toa). *Ita.* The classic dish of cold veal marinated in tuna sauce.

vitkålsoppa med kroppkakor (vit-KOAL-sop-pah mayd KROP-kah-kor). *Swe.* Cabbage soup with dumplings.

vitling (VIT-ling). *Swe.* Whiting, a fish.

vitlök (vit-lok). *Swe.* Garlic.

vitsås (VIT-soass). *Swe.* White sauce.

vitt bröd (vit brohd). *Swe.* White bread.

vla (vlah). *Dut.* Custard.

vlees (vlays). *Dut.* Meats.

voi (voa). *Fin.* Butter.

voileipäpöytä (VOY-LAY-pa-PUH-ew-tah). *Fin.* Cold table; an assortment of foods in the Scandinavian tradition. Same as smörgåsbord.

voileivät (VOY-LAY-voa). *Fin.* Sandwiches; voileivät lämpimät (VOY-LAY-voa lahm-pee-moa), hot sandwiches; voileivät kylmät (VOY-LAY-voa keel-moa), cold sandwiches.

vol-au-vent (vohl-o-vahn). *Fre.* Baked pastry filled with various sauced meat, fish, or poultry mixtures.

volaille (vo-lahy). *Fre.* Fowl, chicken, poultry.

volière, à la (vohl-yahr, ah lah). *Fre.* Game birds served decorated with their plumage.

vongola (VONG-goa-lay). *Ita.* Clam.

voorgerechten (VOR-her-rekten). *Dut.* Canapés; appetizers.

voorjaarssla (FOAH-yah-slah). *Dut.* Spring salad.

vorshmack (VOR-shmahk). *Fin.* A dish of ground mutton, beef, and salt herring cooked with garlic and onions.

Vorspeisen (FOAR-shpigh-zern). *Ger.* Hors d'oeuvre; first course.

vörtbröd (VURT-brewd). *Swe.* Maltbread.

vørterkake (VURR-ter-KAA-ker). *Nor.* Spice cake.

vørterøl (VURR-ter-url). *Nor.* A nonalcoholic beer.

vrucht (vrookh). *Dut.* Fruit.

Wachsbohnen (VAHKS-boa-nern). *Ger.* Yellow, or wax, beans.

Wachtel (VAHKH-terl). *Ger.* Quail.

Waffeln (VAH-fehln). *Ger.* Waffles

waffle (WAH-fuhl). *USA.* A crisp cake of a thin batter, baked between two special heated plates giving a honeycomb surface; eaten with sweet or savory toppings.

Wähen (VAY-en). *Ger.* Swiss open-faced tarts filled with fruit, vegetables or cheese; usually large.

wakame (WAH-kah-meh). *Jap.* A lobe-leafed seaweed, prized for its flavor and texture; available dried or fresh; used as salad ingredient and in soups; high in nutrition, no calories.

wakegi (wah-KAHY-ghee). *Jap.* Young, very mild green onions.

Waldorf salad (WAHL dorf SAH-lahd). *USA.* A salad of chopped apples, celery, and walnuts, mixed together with mayonnaise.

Waldmeister (VALT-mye-stehr). *Ger.* The herb woodruff.

walleye pike (WAHL-eye pik). *USA.* A freshwater fish of the perch family, with firm, white, fine-textured flesh; native of North American lakes.

Walnuss (VAL-noos). *Ger.* Walnut.

walnut (WALL-nuht). *USA.* The edible cream-white nut of a tree indigenous to Asia, Europe, and North America; eaten plain, pickled; in sweet or savory dishes; an oil is extracted from the nutmeats; a liqueur called brou is made from the husks. Varieties are black walnut, butternut, English walnut, hickory nut.

wan dòu (wan doh). *Chi.* Peas.

waraq (WAH-rah). *Ara.* Leaves used in mihshi; such as grape, swiss chard, and cabbage.

Warmbier (VERM-beer). *Ger.* Hot beer soup.

wasabi (wah-SAH-bee). *Jap.* Green horseradish; used to make a seasoning sauce; one of the strongest spices and unique to Japan; has a biting, fresh, cleansing taste; accompanies sushi and other raw fish dishes.

Washington (wahsh-eeng-tohn). *Fre.* A garnish of corn with cream sauce.

Wasser (VAH-sserr). *Ger.* Water.

wassil (WAH-suhll). *Bri.* A hot, spiced punch, usually served at Christmastime.

water chestnut (WAH-tehr CHESS-nuht). *USA.* The fruit of a long-stemmed water plant, whose starchy fruit has a crisp texture and delicate taste; used many ways.

water ice (WAH-tehr ics). *USA.* A frozen dessert of fruit puree or juice and flavoring; is smooth without addition of egg white; sherbet, granita, spuma.

watercress (WAH-tehr-crehss). *USA.* A peppery, slightly pungent plant with dime-sized dark green glossy leaves that grows in shallow streams; used as herb, in salads, and as garnish.

waterless cooking (WAH-tehr-lehss KOOK-eng). *USA.* Cooking slowly in a pot with a very tightly fitting lid, with about one tablespoon of water or liquid.

watermelon (WAH-tehr-mehl-luhn). *USA.* The large, oblong, roundish fruit of an African vine; has a hard green rind, plain or striped; pinkish-red or yellow pulp with black seeds.

wax beans (wahx behns). *USA.* A kidney bean whose pods turn creamy yellow when ready to use as snap beans.

weakfish (WEEK-fesch). *USA.* A fish of the drum family, often mistaken for trout; has lean, sweet, delicate flesh.

Weinkraut (VINE-krowt). *Ger.* Sauerkraut and apples simmered in white wine.

Weisse Bohnen (vighs BOA-nern). *Ger.* Butterbeans.

Weisse Rüben (vighs REW-bern). *Ger.* Turnips.

Weissbier (VIGHS-beer). *Ger.* White beer from Bavaria.

Weissbrot (VIGHS-broat). *Ger.* White bread.

Weisserübe (VIGHS-roo-be). *Ger.* Turnip.

Weissfisch (VIGHS-fiah). *Ger.* Whiting.

Weisskäse (VIGHS-kay-zeh). *Ger.* Cottage cheese.

Weissrüben (VIGHS-roo-behn). *Ger.* Parsnips.

Weisswurst (VIGHS-voorst). *Ger.* Delicate white sausage customarily eaten between midnight and midday in Munich; made of white pork and veal, flavored with wine and parsley.

Weizen (VYE-tsehn). *Ger.* Wheat.

well (wehl). *USA.* To make a well in flour is to make a hole in the middle of the mound to hold the liquid added.

Welsh cawl (wehlsh call). *Bri.* A Welsh dish similar to a New England boiled dinner, but with mutton; has potatoes, cabbage, meat, possibly carrots.

Welsh rabbit (Welsh RARE-beht). *Bri.* Melted cheese, usually mixed with milk, ale, or beer, and served over toast or crackers.

Wensleydale (WEHNS-slee-dale). *Bri.* A cow's milk cheese in both white and blue; the white is aged 3–4 weeks, flaky, moist, and mellow; the blue is aged 4-6 months, smooth, sweet, nutty, moderate veining.

wentclteefjes (VEN-tul-tayf-yus). *Dut.* French toast.

western (WEHS-tchrn). *USA.* A sandwich of white bread or toast, whose filling is an omelet made with chopped ham, green pepper, and onions.

Westfälischer Schinken (west-FAIL-ish-churl SHIN-kern). *Ger.* Ham made from acorn-fed pigs; lightly smoked, cured, uncooked, and served in paper thin slices with pumpernickel; rivals prosciutto, Bayonne, and Smithfield hams in quality.

Westminister (wehst-MEN-es-stuhr). *Bri.* Lymeswold cheese; the name used for export.

Westphalian ham (wehst-FAIL-ee-uhn hahm). *USA.* The famous German ham Westfälischer Schinken.

wheat (wheet). *USA.* A cereal grain used throughout the world in making flours; major U.S. varieties and forms are: **bran** (brahn), outer covering of the kernel, used to make cereals; **bulgur** (BUHL-gehr), ground whole kernel, called wheat pilaf; **cracked wheat** (krahkd wheet), crushed whole wheat kernels; **durum wheat flour** (DUH-rum wheet flowr), high in gluten, ground to make semolina for pasta; **hard red spring wheat flour** (hahrd rehd spreling wheet flowr), high in protein and gluten, excellent bread flour; **hard red winter wheat flour** (hahrd rehd WEHN-tehr wheet flowr), thinner kernel than hard red spring, flaky, moist, and good bread flour; **soft red winter wheat flour** (sawtt rehd WEHN-tehr wheet flowr), starchier than hard wheat, good pastry flour; **wheat-germ flour** (wheet-jehrm flowr), made by pulverizing wheat germ to the powder stage, toast slightly before using.

wheat germ (wheet jehrm). *USA.* The embryo of the wheat kernel, separated in milling process; rich in vitamins.

whelk (wellk). *USA.* A mollusk, distantly related to the conch and abalone; delicious meat.

whip (whehp). *USA.* Beat rapidly to incorporate air and expand the ingredients.

whip topping (whehp TOHP-eng). *USA.* A commercial product containing mostly vegetable oils that are used as a substitute for whipping cream.

whipped cream (whehpd kreem). *USA.* Cow's milk cream that has been beaten rapidly until it stands in stiff peaks.

whipping cream (WHEHP-eng kreem). *USA.* Cow's milk cream: two types— light, which has 30–36% milkfat, and heavy, which has 36–40% milkfat.

white asparagus (white ahs-SPAH-ah-guhs). *USA.* Similar to green asparagus, but stalks are white because they have not been exposed to sunlight during cultivation.

whitebait (WHITE-bate). *USA.* Very small herring and sprat fry; usually dipped in batter and deep-fried without being gutted.

white butter sauce (white buht-tuhr saus). *USA.* Beurre blanc.

white cake (white kahk). *USA.* Cake batter in which all ingredients are white and uses only the whites of eggs.

white chocolate (white CHO-ko-layt). *USA.* Tastes like chocolate, but is not a chocolate since it contains no cocoa; made of cocoa butter, milk solids, and sugar; used in confectionery.

whitefish (WHITE-fisch). *USA.* A small freshwater fish related to the salmon and trout; has delicate white meat, and is often smoked; its roe is used as a caviar substitute.

white meat (white meet). *USA.* White pork.

white mustard (white MUSS-sturd). *USA.* A European salad green, with small tender green leaves; used in salad or as a garnish.

white onion (white UN-yun). *USA.* Any of several varieties of globe onions with white flesh and translucent papery covering.

white pork (white pohrk). *USA.* The flesh of swine that are killed by complete bleeding; also called white meat.

white sapote (white sah-PO-tee). *USA.* A fruit that looks like a misshapen baseball with edible green skin that has a yellow blush when mature; flesh is white or yellow; texture is that of soft pear custard. Also called custard apple and cherimoya.

white sauce (white saus). *USA.* A sauce made from a white roux with milk; béchamel, velouté, also thin, medium, thick, and very thick white sauces.

white vinegar (white VEHN-eh-gahr). *USA.* Dilute distilled alcohol fermented to a 4% acetic acid count; used in cooking and pickling; maintains the color of the vegetable or fruit.

whiting (WHIT-eng). *USA.* A hake of the codfish family; most often referring to the silver hake.

whole milk (hole melk). *USA.* Cows' milk that contains at least 3.25% milkfat, and at least 8.25% protein, lactose and minerals; will form a cream line as the cream rises to the top; not homogenized.

whole-grain flour (hole-gran flowr). *USA.* Ground and pulverized cereal grains, such as wheat, oats, barley, or rye, using the entire, complete grains.

whole wheat flour (hole-whet flowr). *USA.* Ground and pulverized wheat grains, using the entire, complete grain.

whortleberry (HWEHRT-ehl-beh-ree). *Bri.* European blueberry.

Wiener Backhendl (VE-ner BAHK-heng-dehl). *Ger.* Chicken breaded and deep-fried, Vienna style.

Wiener Schnitzel (VE-ner Schnit-sel). *Ger.* Veal scallop dipped in flour, beaten egg, breadcrumbs, then fried in fat; served without a sauce; Wienerschnitzel.

wienerbrød (VEE-nerr-brurdh). *Dan.* "Vienna Bread," which the Danes call their own Danish pastry.

Wienerschnitzel (VEE-nehr-shnit-serl). *Ger.* Same as Wiener Schnitzel.

Wienerwurst (VEE-nehr-voorst). *Ger.* Frankfurter sausage.

wijn (vayn). *Dut.* Wine.

Wild (vilt). *Ger.* Game.

wild rice (wiyld rics). *USA.* Not a true rice; a grain native to North America; a distant cousin of common rice; high in protein and carbohydrate; parched, hulled and polished during milling.

Wildbrettpastete (VILT-bret-pah-stay-ter). *Ger.* Venison pie.

wilde eend (vilt aynt). *Dut.* Wild duck.

Wildgeflügel (vilt-geh-FLOO-gerl). *Ger.* Feathered game.

Windbeutel (VINT-boy-terl). *Ger.* Cream puff.

wine vinegar (wiyn VEHN-ee-gahr). *USA.* Sharp vinegars diluted with red or white wine; usually has a 5% acetic acid content.

wineberry (WIYN-beh-ree). *USA.* A small acid-tasting red raspberry of oriental origin.

winkle (WEN-kle). *Bri.* Periwinkle; a small, snaillike freshwater mollusk; roasted or boiled in shells. Known as bígaro (Spain), bigorneau (French), burríe (Portugal), tamakibi (Japan).

wintergreen (WEHN-tehr-green). *USA.* An evergreen native to North America whose deep green, round aromatic leaves are used as a flavoring.

winter melon (WEHN-tehr MEHL-un). *USA.* Usually smooth-skinned, striated, little or no netting; little or no aroma. Best known varieties are Casaba, Crenshaw, honeydew, Persian.

witlof (WIT-lof). *Dut.* Belgian endive; chicory; used braised, au gratin, in salads.

witte bonen (VIT-tuh BOH-nuh). *Dut.* White lima beans.

wohn yee (won-yee). *Chi.* A crinkly dried black fungus; same as Japanese kikurage.

won ton (wahn-tahn). *USA.* Hún tún; a Chinese noodle wrapper with a savory stuffing, folded in a small triangular shape, then fried for use as entree, or simmered in broth for soup. Also spelled wonton.

wong nga bok (wong yoh by). *Chi.* Celery cabbage; a solid, oblong head of wide, celerylike stalks ending in frilly, pale-green leaves; has a delicate celery-cabbage taste.

wood ear (wuhd eehur). *USA.* Yún er; an irregularly-shaped Chinese fungus used in Chinese cooking for its interesting texture. Also known as tree ear, cloud ear.

woodruff (WUHD-ruff). *USA.* An herb whose leaves are used dried or fresh to flavor teas, drinks and punches; its delicate flowers flavor May wine.

wop salad (wohp SAH-lahd). *USA.* A salad of lettuce with olives, anchovies, oregano, capers, garlic, and olive oil.

Worcestershire (WUS-tehr-sheer). *Bri.* An anchovy-base sauce to use on meats; usually bottled; similar to the Italian garum.

wormwood (WUHRM-wuhd). *USA.* An herb whose toxic leaves give absinthe its potency and anise its flavor; its delicate flowers give vermouth its taste.

worst (worst). *Dut.* Sausage.

worteles (VAWR-tuls). *Dut.* Carrots.

wu hsiang fun (oo SHEEONG fen). *Chi.* A five-spice seasoning; a variable mixture of star anise, fennel seeds, clove, cinnamon, and Sichuan peppercorns or licorice root; very spicy.

Wurst (voorst). *Ger.* Sausage.

Würstchen (VOORST-khern). *Ger.* Little sausage.

Würstelbraten (voorst-terl-BRAA-tern). *Ger.* Roast beef larded with frankfurters.

Würz (voorts) *Ger.* Seasoning; spice.

Würzfleisch (VOORTS-flighsh). *Ger.* A beef stew with sour cream sauce, served with dumplings or potatoes.

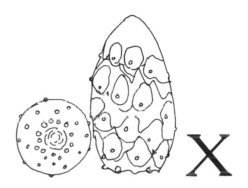

xarope (shah-ROU-puh). *Por.* Syrup.

xató (ZA-toh). *Spa.* A winter salad of endive, red chili peppers, garlic, almonds, oil, and vinegar.

xérèz (she-REHS). *Por.* Sherry.

xia (sia). *Chi.* Shrimp.

xiang cài (sian-tsai). *Chi.* Coriander.

xiangjiao (siang-jiao). *Chi.* Banana.

xiangsxu ya (siang-soo ya). *Chi.* Crispy duck.

xiangyóu (siang-yoh). *Chi.* Sesame oil.

xiao lóng bao (shiao loong bao). *Chi.* Small steamed buns.

xié (sieh). *Chi.* Crab.

xiè ròu dòufù (sieh row doh-foo). *Chi.* Fresh crabmeat mixed with soy paste.

xigua (ssi-gwah). *Chi.* Watermelon.

xihóngshì (ssi-hung-shi). *Chi.* Tomatoes.

Xihu cuì yú (ssi-hoo tsui yu). *Chi.* West Lake crispy fish.

xin xian de (sing sian de). *Chi.* Fresh.

xìngrén dòufù (sing-ren doh-foo). *Chi.* Almond gelatin.

xingzi (sing-dze). *Chi.* Apricot.

xiz jiao (sia jiao). *Chi.* Shrimp dumplings.

xoconostle (soh-koh-NOHS-tleh). *Mex.* Green prickly pear.

ya (yah). *Chi.* Duck.

yablochnyi (YAHB-lah-ku). *Rus.* Apple.

yakhni (YAHF-nee). *Ara.* Stew; refers to dishes made with potatoes as the main ingredient.

yakhni (YAHK-nee). *Ind.* Meat broth.

yaki hamaguri kushisashi (yah-KEE hah-MAH-goo-ree koo-shee-sah-SHEE). *Jap.* Baked white clams on skewers; a canned product.

yaki soba (yah-KEE soh-bah). *Jap.* A type of instant soup noodle.

yakimono (yah-KEE-moh-noh). *Jap.* Broiled foods.

yakitori (yah-KEE-toh-ree). *Jap.* Grilled chicken and vegetables on small skewers.

yam (yahm). *USA.* A root vegetable whose high starch content makes it a valuable food source throughout the world; has yellow or white flesh, brown skin, and is often mistakenly called sweet potato.

yama no imo (yah-MAH no EE-mo). *Jap.* Mountain yams; long, beige in color, hairy; mild, pleasant flavor.

yàn cài (yan tsai). *Chi.* Bird's nest; dried nests, either black or white, are soaked in water to restore their gelatinous texture and used to garnish soups at banquets and special occasions; very expensive.

yángrou (YANG-row). *Chi.* Mutton.

yao dòu (yao doh). *Chi.* Kidney beans.

yaoguo jiding (yao-guo jee-ding). *Chi.* Diced chicken garnished with cashew nuts.

yaourt (yah-oort). *Fre.* Yogurt.

yard-long-beans (yahrd-lohng-beens). *USA.* Bright Chinese green beans, about a foot long; flavor stronger than ordinary green beans. Also called long beans, dow ghok, asparagus beans, sassage.

yari-ika (yah-kee-ee-KAH). *Jap.* Grilled squid.

yarrow (YAH-row). *Bri.* Fine lacy leaves used as an herb or for tea.

yasai (yah-sah-ee). *Jap.* Vegetables.

yeast (yeest). *USA.* A microscopic fungus that induces fermentation, releasing carbon dioxide, important in making bread, cheese, beer, wine; a leavening agent; two types: compressed and active dry.

yellow cake (YEHL-oh kahk). *USA.* Cake made from batter in which egg yolks are used.

yellow eel (yehl-oh eel). *USA.* One name for ocean pout, a fish of the eelpout family whose flesh is sweet, white, and has few bones.

yemas de San Leandro (YEM-ah deh sahn lee-AHN-dro). *Spa.* Egg-yolk threads poured into hot syrup and twisted into sweets.

yemitas de mi bisabuela (yeh-MAH-tahs day mee bee-sah-BOH-lah). *Mex.* Egg yolks, sherry, and syrup formed into balls and rolled in cinnamon sugar.

yen wo (yehn woh). *Chi.* Yàn cài; birds' nest.

yerba maté (yehr-bah MAH-ta). *Spa.* Maté; an aromatic beverage made from the leaves and shoots of a South American holly rich in caffeine.

yezi (yeh-dze). *Chi.* Coconut.

ying-táo (ying-tao). *Chi.* Cherries.

yoghourt (YOGH-ourt). *Swe.* Yogurt.

yoghurt (YAH-hurt). *Dut.* Yogurt.

yoghurt (YOGH-oort). *Dan.* Yogurt.

yogur (YOA-goor). *Spa.* Yogurt.

yogurt (YOH-guhrt). *USA.* Ewes' or cows' milk fermented with lactic culture, turning it slightly acidic and custardlike.

yogurt (ee-OA-goort). *Ita.* Yogurt.

Yorkshire pudding (YORK-shur PUHD-deng). *Bri.* A popover batter mixture baked in drippings of the roast; traditional accompaniment for roast beef.

Yorkshire sauce (YORK-shur saus). *Bri.* Red currant jelly thinned with port wine and grated orange zest added.

youghurt (YOOG-ewt). *Nor.* Yogurt.

yóumèn sun (yoh-men sun). *Chi.* Braised bamboo shoots.

yóuyú (yoh-yu). *Chi.* Cuttlefish.

yú (yoo). *Chi.* Fish.

yuán báicài (yuan bai-tsai). *Chi.* Cabbage.

yucca root (YUK-kah root). *USA.* A root vegetable, shaped like an elongated sweet potato with pink to brown skin and white flesh; has a starchy taste; use peeled in soups, stews, or boiled and served like potatoes.

yú chì (yu tsi). *Chi.* Shark's fin; a delicacy, savored for its gelatinous texture.

yúchì tang (yu-tsi tan). *Chi.* Shark's fin soup.

yukka (yuhk-kah). *Tur.* Phyllo; leaf-thin sheets of dough, made from flour and water; used for sweet and savory dishes by layering with fillings. Also known as filo, brik, malsouka.

Yule log (yul lohg). *Bri.* Bûche de Noël; genoise or sponge cake decorated with buttercream to resemble a log.

yún er (yuhn ehr). *Chi.* Cloud ear; a fungus used for its interesting texture and colors. Also called tree ear, wood ear.

yúxiang ròusi (yu-siang row-sse). *Chi.* Shredded spicy-flavored pork.

yuzu (YOO-zoo). *Jap.* Citron; used almost entirely for its aromatic rind to flavor soups, simmered dishes, pickles, relishes, and sweet confections.

zabaglione (dzah-bah-LYOA-nay). *Ita.* A frothy dessert custard flavored with Marsala.

zafferone (dzahf-feh-RAA-noa). *Ita.* Saffron.

zaffran (ZAH-frohn). *Ind.* Saffron; same as kesar.

zafra (ZAHF-frah). *Ara.* Meat curds appearing when cooking meat in water.

zakuski (zah-KOOS-kee). *Rus.* Hors d'oeuvres, always accompanied by vodka.

zalm (zahlum). *Dut.* Salmon.

zampone (tsahm-POA-nay). *Ita.* A highly seasoned pork sausage encased in the skin of a pig's foot; served sliced.

zanahorias (thah-nah-OA-ryahss). *Spa.* Carrots.

zanjabiyl (zahn-jah-BEEL). *Ara.* Ginger.

zankha (ZAHN-kah). *Ara.* A special "meaty" smell or feel associated with uncooked meat.

zaozi (dzao-dze). *Chi.* Dates.

zapallo (zah-PAHL-loh). *Spa.* Calabaza.

zarda (ZAHR-dah). *Ind.* A sweet rice pilaf, with nuts, raisins, saffron, and spices.

zarzamora (thaht-thah-MOA-rahss). *Spa.* Blackberry.

zarzuela (thahr-THWAY-lah). *Spa.* A seafood stew, flavored with wine or liquor.

zactar (ZAHK-tahr). *Ara.* Plant found in the Middle East used as seasoning; also refers to a seasoning blended from zactar, thyme, majoram, simmaq, and salt.

zayt (zeyt). *Ara.* Oil.

zaytun (zey-TOON). *Ara.* Olives.

zayt zaytun (zeyt zey-TOON). *Ara.* Olive oil.

Zeeland oysters (ZEE-lahnd OYl-sturs). *USA.* Very fine oysters from Zeeland province of the Netherlands; sweet, succulent.

zeevis (ZAH-vees). *Dut.* Seafood.

zensai (ZEHN-sah-ee). *Jap.* Appetizers.

zenzai (ZEH-zah-ee). *Jap.* A chunky, sweet soup used as a pick-me-up and a dessert soup.

zènzero (DZEHN-dzeh-roa). *Ita.* Ginger.

zephire (za-feer). *Fre.* A small oval shaped forcemeat dumpling; a kind of quenelle, poached and served with a rich sauce.

zephyr (ZEH-fuhr). *USA.* A very light, airy, delicate cornmeal puff, served with salad or luncheon.

zeppole (tsee-POHL-lah). *Ita.* A kind of doughnut.

zest (zehst). *USA.* The outer rind of citrus fruit which is thinly pared off (without pith) for flavoring and garnishing.

zeste (zehst). *Fre.* The peel of citrus fruits which contains aromatic oil; used to flavor foods.

zhá (dzah). *Chi.* To deep-fry.

zhá gezi (dzah ge-dzi). *Chi.* Deep-fried pigeon.

zhá yú qíu (dzah yu chiu). *Chi.* Deep-fried fish squares, Sichuan style.

zhàcài tang (dza-tsai tang). *Chi.* Spicy vegetable soup.

zhangchá ua (dzong-cha ya). *Chi.* Duck smoked in camphor and tea.

zheng (dzeng). *Chi.* To steam.

zhi má yóu (dzai mah yoh). *Chi.* Chinese sesame oil; darker color, stronger taste than western sesame oil; used for seasoning.

zhi-má hú (dzi-ma hoo). *Chi.* Sesame cream.

zhoud (dzoh). *Chi.* Porridge.

zhou fàn (dzoh). *Chi.* Congee rice.

zhú (dzoo). *Chi.* Pork.

zhu jidàn (dzoo jee-dan). *Chi.* Boiled eggs.

zhú rou (dzhoo row). *Chi.* Pork meat.

zibd (ZIB-dah). *Ara.* Butter.

zibeth (zee-beht). *Fre.* A variety of chive from tropical Asia; seasons ragouts, salads, sauces.

Zigeuner Art (tsi-GOY-nehr art). *Ger.* "In the gypsy style."

Zigeunerspies (tsi-GOY-nehr-shpees). *Ger.* A kabob of meat cubes, peppers, and onions, grilled over open fire.

zik de venado (theek day bay-NAH-dhoa). *Mex.* Shredded cooked venison; served with onions, hot chili peppers, cilantro, and Seville oranges.

zimino (tsee-MEE-noa). *Ita.* Fish stew.

Zimt (tsimt). *Ger.* Cinnamon.

Zimtplätzchen (tsimt-PLETS-khehn). *Ger.* Cinnamon cakes.

zingara (zeen-gahr-rah). *Fre.* Gypsy style; a garnish of julienne of ham, tongue, mushrooms, truffles in demi-glace, with Madeira, tomato puree, and tarragon.

ziste (zeeest). *Fre.* The bitter white pith found in citrus fruits just under the peel.

ziti (TSEET-tee). *Ita.* Large tube pasta cut in pieces.

Zitrone (tsi-TROA-ner). *Ger.* Lemon.

Zitronenschaum (tsi-TROA-ner-showm). *Ger.* Lemon foam, a frothy Austrian dessert.

zosui (ZOO-swee). *Jap.* Rice gruel made from leftover, already cooked rice.

zoul (zowt). *Dut.* Salt.

zucca (TSOOK-kah). *Ita.* Squash; pumpkin.

zucchini (zoo-KEEN-nee). *Ita.* A slender green or green-striped summer squash about five inches long; known worldwide as marrow or marrow squash.

zucchero (TSOOK-kay-roa). *Ita.* Sugar.

zuccoto (tsook-KOHT-toa). *Ita.* A dessert of dome-shaped cake, sprinkled with liqueur, filled with whipped cream, chocolate, nuts.

Zucker (TSUK-kerr). *Ger.* Sugar.

Zuckererbsen (YSUK-kerr-ehr-psern). *Ger.* New green peas.

Zuckerrübe (TSUK-kerr-rewb). *Ger.* Sugar beet.

Zuckerwähe (TSUK-kerr-vaier). *Ger.* Swiss sugar tart.

Zuger Kirschtorte (TSUK-kerr KEERSH-tor-ter). *Ger.* A Swiss Kirsch-soaked cake frosted with pink sugar.

zumo (THOO-mo). *Spa.* Juice.

Zunge (TSUN-ger). *Ger.* Tongue.

Zungenwürst (TSUN-gerr-voorst). *Ger.* Tongue sausage.

zuppa (TSOOP-pah). *Ita.* A soup, usually vegetable, meat or fish, poured over fried or oven-toasted bread.

zuppe di pesce (TSOOP-pah dee PAY-shay). *Ita.* The generic name for fish soup.

zuppa Inglese (TSOOP-pah eeng-GLAY-say). *Ita.* A type of trifle; rum-soaked sponge cake layered with custard and cream.

zuppa rustica (TSOOP-pah roo-STEEK-kah). *Ita.* A hearty, peasant-style soup with potatoes, beans, and sausages.

zuurkool (ZEWR-kohl). *Dut.* Sauerkraut.

Zwetschgen (TSVEH-tsh-gern). *Ger.* Damson plums.

Zwetschkenknödel (TSVEH-tsh-kern-knur-derl). *Ger.* An Austrian plum dumpling dessert.

Zwieback (TSVEE-bahk). *Ger.* Toasted bread, crisp and slightly sweet.

Zwiebeln (TSVEE-berln). *Ger.* Onions.

Zwiebelgrün (TSVEE-berl-grewn). *Ger.* Scallion.

Zwiebelkuche (TSVEE-berl-koo-ker). *Ger.* Onion tart.

Zwischenrippenstück (TSVI-shehn-RIP-pern-shtayk). *Ger.* Rib steak.

zwitserse kaas (SWEHT-seh-zer KAI-zer). *Dut.* Swiss cheeses: Gruyère or Emmenthal.

zwitserse karbonade (SWEHT-seh-zer KAHR-bohn-ahde). *Dut.* Swiss steaks.

Wine Terms

acetic (ah-SEE-tick). All wines contain some acetic acid; any wine with an excessive amount will have a vinegary smell and can be called acetic.

acidity (ah-SIHD-eh-tee). Natural acidity provides a fresh, lively taste; excessive acidity makes the wine tart and sour.

aftertaste (AHF-tehr-tast). The taste that lingers in the mouth after the wine is swallowed. The longer a pleasant taste lingers, the finer the quality of the wine.

aggressive (ah-GREH-sehve). Applies to wines with high acidity, harsh tannins, or both.

amontillado (ah-mohn-teel-LAH-doh). A matured fino sherry, naturally dry; generally sweetened to be mellow in taste.

angelica wine (ahn-JEL-eh-kah wiyn). A sweet dessert wine produced in California.

angular (AHN-guu-lahr). Lacks roundness and depth.

apéritifs (ahp-ree-TEEFS). Drinks before a meal.

aroma (ah-ROA-mah). The smell of a relatively young wine before it has had time to develop its smell; in a mature wine it is called bouquet.

astringent (ah-STREHN-gent). Harsh and coarse to the taste because of the amount of tannin in the wine; a dry quality.

austere (aw-STEER). A hard, dry wine that lacks richness, needs aging.

balance (BAHL-lahnc). The harmonious concentration of fruit, level of tannins, and acidity creating symmetry; wines with good balance tend to age gracefully.

Balthazar (bahl-THAH-zahr). Extra-large champagne bottle that holds 16 regular bottles or 415 ounces.

Banyuls (ban-YULZ). Sweet dessert wines: reds, rosés and whites.

barnyard (BAHRN-yawrd). An unclean, farmyard, fecal aroma caused by unsanitary winemaking facilities or unclean barrels.

beeswing (BEEZ-wehng). A type of deposit sometimes found in port, so named because of the veined pattern it forms.

berrylike (BEH-ree-lik). Wines that have intense berry characteristics, such as suggests blackberry, mulberry, strawberry.

big (behg). A full-bodied wine that gives an intense feel on the palate.

blackcurrant (blahk-KERR-ent). The smell commonly associated with red Bordeaux wines; varies in intensity.

blanc (blawnk). White.

blended (BLEHN-dehd). The mixing of wines from different regions, or the addition of brandy or rectified alcohols as in fortified wines.

blush (bluhsh). A more savory wine than rosé with less color incorporated from grape skins.

body (BAH-dee). The weight and fullness of the wine as it crosses the palate.

Botrytis cinerea (boh-TREE-tes sin-eh-REE-ah). Noble rot, a fungus that attacks grapes, forming a mold that concentrates their flavor and sugar, producing sweet wines, high in alcohol and with a unique bouquet.

bottle-age (BOWT-tle-ajg). The length of time a wine is kept in a bottle, rather than in a cask.

bottle-sickness (BOWT-tle-SEHK-ness). Usually a temporary setback in the wine's flavor lasting for weeks or months after bottling, a result of the filtration and bottling.

bottle-stink (BOWT-tle-steenk). A bad smell that emanates from an old bottle upon opening; almost always dissipates instantly; not to be confused with corky.

bouquet (bo-KAY). The distinctive and characteristic fragrance or smell of a matured wine; technically different from aroma, which applies to a young wine.

brawny (BRAW-nee). A muscular, hefty, full-bodied wine; has plenty of flavor and weight; inelegant and unrefined.

breathing (BRETH-eng). What a wine does upon decanting it for a few hours.

breed (breed). Great distinction and polish in describing a wine impeccably made from very good vineyards.

briary (BRY-ah-ree). Aggressive, rather than spicy.

brilliant (BRYLL-yuant). A wine of clear color, not hazy or cloudy.

browning (BROWN-eng). When red wines age, their color changes from a ruby-purple through various color changes to ruby with a brown edge; they are then fully matured and not likely to improve.

brut (broot). Extremely dry; unsweetened; a term used to describe champagne.

butt (buht). A sherry or whisky cask holding approximately 491 litres or 519 quarts.

carafe (kah-RAHF). A stopperless container used to decant wine and serve it at table.

cask (kahsk). A wooden barrel used for storing wine and spirits.

caudalie (KAU-dur-lee). The length of time the aftertaste lingers in the mouth.

cedar (SEE-dahr). The smell of cedarwood, faint or overt, usually part of the bouquet of Bordeaux reds.

chablis (shah-BLEE). A pale, pale burgundy.

chambrer (SHAHM-bray). To bring wine to room temperature.

champagne (sham-PANE). A white, pale-pale amber, or pale pink sparkling wine; variously described as brut, extra-sec, sec, demi-sec.

chaptalization (shap-tally-zah-see-aw). The addition of sugar to grape must during fermentation to increase the alcoholic content.

character (KAHR-eck-tur). Indicates that a wine has a distinctive and individual stamp.

chateau (SHAH-toe). Refers to the wine-producing properties in Bordeaux.

chewy (CHEW-ee). Having a dense, viscous texture from a high glycerine content; wines of great vintages can often be chewy.

clairet (klair-ray). Specially vinified red Bordeaux wines, soon ready to drink, without much color or tannin; have a very slight alcoholic content; can be consumed as innocently as lemonade.

claret (KLAHR-eht). Red table wine of Bordeaux.

closed (klozd). Denotes that a wine is not showing its potential, which remains locked in because it is too young; aging up to a decade or so may be required.

complex (KOHM-plex). A term to describe a wine whose taste never gets boring and is interesting to drink; has a variety of subtle scents and flavors to holds one's interest in the wine.

cognac (KONE-yahk). French word for brandy.

concentrated (KOHN-sin-tra-ted). Denotes that the wine has depth and richness of fruit to give it appeal and interest; synonymous with depth.

corked (korkd). Flawed; wine has taken on the smell of a musty cork, resulting from an unclean or faulty cork; also referred to as corky.

coulant (koo-LANH). "Flowing"; easy-to-drink wines.

crémant (kreh-mawng). Indicates a degree of sparkle, between perlant and mousseaux.

crust (kruhst). A heavy deposit found in some bottles of vintage port.

deep (deep). A rich, full-bodied, mouth-filling wine; synonymous with concentrated.

delicate (DEHL-ee-kuht). A light, subtle, understated, shy wine; usually white wines.

demi (DEH-mee). Half.

demijohn (DEH-mee-john). A large bottle encased in wickerwork and holding at least a gallon.

demi-sec (DEHM-mee sehk). Relatively sweet; too sweet for most palates; a term to describe a champagne.

deposit (deh-POHS-eht). Fallout from chemical changes that give high-quality wines maturing in bottle greater character, complexity, and bouquet.

diffuse (deh-FUSZ). Unstructured and unfocused smell and taste; warm red wines often diffuse.

disgorge (dehs-GOHRJ). The champagne method of making sparkling wines; at one point the bottle has to be opened to remove a deposit of yeasty sediment.

domaine (doa-MAIN). Refers to the wine-producing properties in Burgundy.

dosage (DOE-sauge). Sweetening added to sparkling wine before the final corking.

double-magnum (DUH-bull-MAHG-num). A four-bottle bottle; holds three liters.

dry (dri). The opposite of sweet.

dumb (duhm). A dumb wine is a closed wine, but whereas a closed wine may only need time to reveal its richness and intensity, a dumb wine will never get better.

earthy (UHRTH-ee). A positive aroma of rich, clean soil, rather than woodsy or truffle scents.

elegant (ELL-ee-gahnt). Graceful, splendid, high-quality; unmistakable, but indefinable.

extra-sec (X-tra sehk). Slightly sweetened; a term describing a champagne.

extract (x-STRAHK). Soluble solids from the grape; contributes to the weight and fullness of the wine.

exuberant (x-ZOO-ber-rahnt). Gushy, nervous, vigorous.

fat (faht). A super sort of maturity; fat wines are quite rich with low acidity. If a wine is too fat, a flaw, then it is called flabby.

fermentation (fehr-mehn-TA-shun). The conversion of grape juice into wine through the process of converting sugar into alcohol by action of certain yeasts present in the juice.

feuillette (feh-YET). A chablis barrel.

fiasco (vee-ASK-ko). A chianti flask.

fine (fine). Denotes overall quality.

finesse (fee-NESS). Implies subtlety and distinction.

fining (FIN-eng). A method of clarifying wine by pouring a coagulant on top and letting it settle to the bottom.

finish (FEHN-esh). The final taste left after swallowing the wine.

fino (FEE-no). The finest sherry—delicate, dry, pale.

flabby (FLAHB-bee). A wine that is too fat, lacks structure, tastes heavy.

fleshy (FLEHSH-ee). Synonymous for chewy or meaty; has lots of body, alcohol, and extract, and has a high glycerine content.

fliers (FLY-ehrs). Specks of sediment.

floral (FLOW-ruhl). Having a flowery bouquet or aroma.

focused (FOH kussd). The scents, aromas, and flavors are precise and clearly delineated.

fortified (FOUR-tee-fied). Wine to which brandy or rectified alcohol has been added, sometimes halting fermentation before all the sugar is converted into alcohol.

forward (FOR-wahrd). A wine that fully reveals its charm and character.

fresh (frehsh). Cleanly made and lively.

frizzante (freh-SAHN-tee). Slightly sparkling, as opposed to spumante which is fully sparkling.

fruity (FROO-tee). Said of a wine that has the pleasant taste and aroma of fruit; a vague term.

full-bodied (fuhl-BOHD-ehd). Rich in extract, alcohol and glycerine; feels weighty and substantial in the mouth.

green (green). Made from underripe grapes; lacks richness and generosity; vegetal in character.

gris (greez). Pale, pinkish-red.

hard (hahrd). Abrasive, astringent with tannins, high acidity; a young vintage can be hard but should never be harsh.

harmony (HAHR-mo-nee). Balanced attributes; a highly desirable quality.

harsh (harsh). Too hard, a flaw in the wine.

herbaceous (hehr-BAY-shush). Has a distinctive herbal smell; usually thyme, basil, fennel, lavender, rosemary, or oregano.

hollow (HOHL-low). Shallow, dilute, lacks depth and concentration.

honeyed (HOHN-need). Has the taste and smell of honey.

hot (hoht). Too high in alcohol content, leaving a burning sensation in the back of the throat when swallowed; usually above 14.5% alcohol content.

hybrid (HIY-brehd). A cross between French and American vines; used for hardiness.

jammy (JAHM-mee). Has a great intensity of fruit from excellent ripeness; very concentrated; flavorful with superb extract.

Jeroboam (jeh-ruh-BOW-uhm). Large wine bottle with the capacity of four ordinary bottles, about 4/5 of a gallon.

kosher wine (KOA-shur wine). Wine for Jewish religious occasions made under the supervision of a rabbi, usually very sweet.

leafy (LEE-fee). Smells of leaves, rather than herbs; vegetal or green.

lean (leen). Slim, streamlined; lacks generosity and fatness; can still be pleasant and enjoyable.

lees (leez). The solid residue left in the cask after drawing off the wine.

legs (lehgs). The rivulets that run down the side of a wine glass after swirling, indicating, when pronounced, that the wine is rich in body and extract.

length (lenkth). Long; relates to a wine's finish. Its presence is sensed long after being swallowed, from thirty seconds to several minutes; a very desirable trait.

light (lite). Having a low degree of alcohol, or lacking body.

liquoreux (lee-quor-roh). A wine that is rich, sweet, and strong, as a Sauterne.

lively (LIV-lee). Fresh, exuberant; a young wine of good acidity; has a thirst-quenching personality.

long (lohng). Length; relates to a wine's finish; its presence is sensed long after being swallowed, from thirty seconds to several minutes; a very desirable trait.

lunel (loo-NEHL). A sweet dessert wine with a delicate bouquet.

lush (luhsh). Velvety, soft, richly fruity; concentrated and fat; never astringent or hard.

maderisé (ma-dare-ee-zay). Refers to the brown color and flat taste of a white wine that has been overexposed to air during production or maturation, giving an aroma and flavor reminiscent of Madeira wine.

marc (mahr). The pulpy mass of grape skins and pips that remain after the fermented grapes are pressed. Also refers to the brandy made from this pulpy mass.

massive (MAHS-sehv). High degree of ripeness and superb concentration; full-bodied and rich.

meaty (MEET-tee). Chewy, fleshy.

Methuselah (meh-THUS-eh-lah). A large champagne bottle whose capacity equals eight normal bottles.

moelleux (mweh-luh). Sweet, soft, rich.

monbazillac (maw-baz-zee-yak). A sweet, golden wine.

mousseux (moos-sur). Sparkling; not usually used for first-class wines.

mouth-filling (mowth-FIHL-eng). Big, rich, concentrated with fruity extract; high in alcohol and glycerine; chewy, fleshy, fat.

must (muhst). Unfermented grape juice or crushed grapes.

nature (NA-chur). Means that nothing has been added, in particular, sugar.

Nebuchadnezzar (nehb-uh-kahn-NEHZ-zahr). The largest of champagne bottles; holds the equivalent of 20 ordinary bottles.

nerveux (nehr-vo). Implies fineness with firmness and vitality, a term of praise.

noble rot (NO-bul roht). See *Botrytis cinerea.*

nose (noz). Smell, whether bouquet or aroma.

nouveau (neu-vo). The wine of the last harvest, during its first winter.

oaky (OAK-ee). A toasty, vanillin flavor and smell to the wine, imparted by new oak barrels.

off (owff). Not showing its true character; flawed, spoiled in some way.

oeil de perdrix (uhy der pehr-dree). "Eye of the partridge"; describes the pink color of certain rosé wines, some pink champagnes, and whites with a pinkish tinge.

oloroso (o-loh-ROH-soh). One of two basic types of Spanish sherry.

ordinaire (or-dee-nahr). Inexpensive, common; of unknown or unstated origin.

overripe (O-vehr ripe). From grapes left too long on the vine causing loss of acidity; produces heavy, imbalanced wines; not a desirable characteristic.

oxidized (OHX-eh-dizd). Excessively exposed to air during making or aging, causing loss of freshness; gives old, stale smell and taste.

palo cortado (PAHL-o kor TAH doh). A rare and excellent style of sherry; between fino and oloroso.

passito (pah-SEE-toh). An Italian sweet dessert wine; made from grapes that have had a short drying period after picking.

pelure d'oignon (peh-lewr on-yawng). "Onion skin," a description of the pale, orange-brown color of certain rosé wines and some old red wines.

peppery (PEHP-pehr-ree). Has aroma of black pepper and a pungent flavor.

perfumed (PEHR-fumd). Fragrant, aromatic; has strong perfume smell.

perlant (payr-yaw). Showing a little sparkle; less than crémant and much less than mousseux.

pétillant (pay-tee-yaw). Having a natural sparkle; less than a perlant wine.

plastering (PLAHS-tehr-eng). Boosting the acid content of a wine, usually sherry, by the addition of calcium sulphate.

plonk (plohnk). Slang for everyday wine.

plummy (PLUHM-mee). Smell and taste of ripe plums.

ponderous (POHN-dehr-us). Heavy and tiring to drink.

port (pohrt). A fortified wine, both red and white, produced in northern Portugal and matured in Vila Nova de Gaia.

pricked (priekd). The unpleasantly sharp quality caused by too much volatile acidity.

pruney (PROO-nee). Has character of prunes, is a flawed wine.

punt (puhnt). The hollow mound inside the bottom of certain wine bottles.

racking (RAHK-eng). Transferring fermented wine from one cask to another to separate it from its lees.

raisiny (RAY-sin-ee). A late-harvested wine with character of raisins; desirable in some ports and sherries, a major flaw in other wines.

rasteau (rass-toe). Sweet, amber, fortified wine; similar to a light, white Port.

ratafia (rah-TAH-fyah). Brandy mixed with sweet unfermented grape juice.

Rehoboam (rea-ah-BOH-um). A large champagne bottle holding the capacity of six normal bottles.

remuage (ray-mew-ahj). A technique for removing the deposit in champagne without removing the sparkle by shaking and progressively inclining the bottle until the sediment is on the cork, then removing the cork and extracting the deposit.

réserve (ray-serv). An uncontrolled term implying superior quality.

rice wine (rics wine). Wine made from the grain rice instead of grapes; called saké; technically a beer.

rich (rehch). High in extract, flavor, and intensity of the fruit.

riddling (REHD-leng). Same as remuage.

ripe (ripe). Grapes have reached the optimum level of maturity.

rosé (roa-ZAY). Pink wine made from black grapes pressed quickly to allow only the slightest tinge of color, varies from pale, pale pinks to deep, almost-red pinks.

rosso (roh-soh). Red.

rouge (rooug). Red.

round (rawnd). Fully matured, having lost youthful, astringent tannins; a very desirable character.

ruby (ROO-bee). Young red port, matured in wood.

Salmanazar (SAHL-mah-nah-zur). Third largest size of champagne bottle; holds 12 normal bottles.

sauterne (saw-TURN). A sweet, white wine of Bordeaux.

savory (SAY-vah-ree). Denotes a round, sweet, flavorful, and interesting wine.

sec (sehk). Dry or fermented out. In describing champagne, it means sweet; when describing other wines, it means dry or unsweetened.

sediment (SEHD-ee-mehnt). Solid matter deposited in the bottle during maturation, nearly always a good sign.

shallow (SHAHL-low). Weak, feeble, watery, lacking concentration.

sharp (shawrp). Bitter, unpleasant with hard, pointed edges.

silky (SIHL-kee). Velvety, lush; sometimes fat, but never hard or angular.

smoky (SMO-kee). Has a distinctive smoky characteristic, because of soil or barrels used to age the wine.

soft (sawft). Round, fruity, low acidity; absence of aggressive, hard tannins.

sparkling (SPAHR-kleng). Has undergone a secondary fermentation in vat or bottle and has become effervescent through the formation of bubbles of carbon dioxide gas.

spicy (SPI-cee). Aromas of pepper, cinnamon, and other well-known spices.

spritzer (SPEHT-zehr). White wine diluted with soda or mineral water.

spumante (spoo-MAHN-tee). Fully sparkling.

stale (stale). Dull, heavy wines that lack balancing acidity for freshness or are oxidized.

stalky (STAHL-kee). Synonymous with vegetal; green character.

still (stihl). Nonsparkling, as are the majority of table wines.

sulphur (SUHL-fuhr). When the flavor of sulphur is present in a wine, it is due to the careless use of this common disinfectant for wine, which is used to destroy harmful bacteria.

supple (SUHP-pul). Soft, lush, velvety, round and tasty; a highly desirable characteristic.

table wine (TA-bul wine). Any nonfortified wine.

tannin (TAHN-nehn). A substance of grape skins, stalks, and pips; gives the wine firmness, roughness when young; gradually falls away and dissipates with age; important in wine to be matured over a long period.

tart (tahrt). Sharp, acidic, lean, unripe; not pleasurable.

tartaric (tahr TAHR-eck). A naturally occurring acid in grapes and the main constituent of the acidity in wine.

tawny (TAHW-nee). Port aged in wood until it has acquired a warm, sandy color.

thick (thehk). Rich, ripe, concentrated, low in acidity.

thin (thehn). Shallow, watery, lacking in body; diluted; an undesirable characteristic.

tightly knit (TITE-lee neht). Wines that are tightly knit have good acidity levels, good tannin levels, and are well made. They have yet to open up and develop.

toasty (TOAS-tee). The smell of grilled toast; aged in barrels that are charred or toasted on the inside.

tobacco (toe-BACK-kah). Scent of fresh burning tobacco; a distinctive and wonderful smell in wine.

ullage (UHL-lahg). The amount that a container lacks of being full; the air space above the wine.

unctuous (UNK-choo-us). Rich, lush, intense with layers of concentrated, soft, velvety fruit, such as Sauternes.

varietal (vah-RI-ah-tuhl). Wine that is named after the grape variety from which it is made.

vegetal (VEHG-eh-tahl). Smell of stems from green, unripe grapes; undesirable characteristic; a major flaw.

velvety (VEHL-veht-tee). Lush, silky, rich, soft, smooth to taste; a desirable characteristic.

vin (vehn). Wine.

vin nouveau (vehn noo-voh). New wine, made to be drunk just after the vintage, such as Beaujolais.

vinho verde (veeh-no vehr-dee). A light, tangy wine of Portugal. Verde refers to its newness, not its color, which can be reds or whites.

vintage (VEHN-tahj). A vintage wine is one that bears the date of the vintage on the label.

viscous (VEHS-kos). Relatively concentrated, fat, almost thick with a density of fruit extract, plenty of glycerine and high alcohol content; if acidity is balanced, can be very flavorful and exciting; if lacks acidity, flabby and heavy.

volatile (VOHL-eh-tehl). Smells of vinegar caused by acetic bacteria; a serious flaw.

wood-aging (wuhd-AJ-eng). Maturation of wine in casks or barrels that permits minute amounts of air to interact with the components of the wine.

woody (WOOD-dee). Overly oaky.

yeast (yeest). Microorganisms that produce fermentation; occur naturally in grape skins, but special yeasts are also used.

Bibliography

Bordeaux: The Definitive Guide For The Wines Produced Since 1961, Robert M. Parker, Jr.; Simon and Schuster, New York.

Everyday Cooking With Jacques Pepin, Jacques Pepin; Harper and Row, New York.

Food For Fifty, 8th edition, West, Shugart, Wilson; Macmillan, New York

Food For Fifty, 7th edition, Shugart, Molt, and Wilson; Macmillan, New York.

How To Eat Better For Less Money, James Beard and Sam Aaron; Simon and Schuster, New York.

How To Enjoy Wine, Hugh Johnson; Simon and Schuster, New York.

Italy: The Beautiful Cookbook, Lorenza De Medici; The Knapp Press, Los Angeles.

Japanese Cooking: A Simple Art, Shizuo Tsuji; Kodansha International, Tokyo, New York, and San Francisco.

Knight's Foodservice Dictionary, John B. Knight; Van Nostrand Reinhold, New York.

Lebanese Cuisine, Madelain Farah, Portland, Oregon.

Mexican Cook Book; Sunset Books, Lane Publishing Co., Menlo Park, California.

Mrs. Beeton's English Cookery; Crown Publishers, New York.

Southern Herb Growing, Madalene Hill and Gwen Barclay; Shearer Publishing, Fredericksburg, Texas.

The Chef's Companion: A Concise Dictionary of Culinary Terms, Elizabeth Riely; Van Nostrand Reinhold, New York.

The Complete Seafood Book, James Wagenvoord and Woodman Harris; Macmillan, New York.

The Dictionary of American Food & Drink, John E. Mariani; Ticknor & Fields, New Haven and New York.

The Encyclopedia of Fish Cookery, A. J. McClane; Holt, Rinehart and Winston, New York.

The Good Housekeeping Cookbook, Harcourt, Brace & World, New York.

The Italian Cookbook, Staff Home Economists; Culinary Arts Institute, Chicago, Illinois.

The Only Texas Cookbook, Linda West Eckhardt; Texas Monthly Press, Austin, Texas.

The Prudhomme Family Cookbook, Paul Prudhomme; William Morrow and Company, New York.

The Vegetarian Epicure, Anna Thomas; Vintage Books/Random House, New York.

The Vegetarian Epicure Book 2, Anna Thomas; Alfred A Knopf, New York.

The Wine Handbook, Serena Sutcliffe; Simon and Schuster, New York.

Uncommon Fruits & Vegetables: A Commonsense Guide, Elizabeth Schneider; Harper & Row, New York.

Webster's Collegiate Dictionary.

World-of-the-East Vegetarian Cooking, Madhur Jaffrey; Alfred A Knopf, New York.

Refer to the many dictionaries and phrase books of Berlitz, Barron's, and Harrap's for help with pronunciations.